Metaphorical Conceptualizations

I0752094

Applications of Cognitive Linguistics

Editors
Gitte Kristiansen
Francisco J. Ruiz de Mendoza Ibáñez

Honorary editor
René Dirven

Volume 45

Metaphorical Conceptualizations

(Inter)Cultural Perspectives

Edited by
Ulrike Schröder
Milene Mendes de Oliveira
Adriana Maria Tenuta

DE GRUYTER
MOUTON

ISBN 978-3-11-135347-0
e-ISBN (PDF) 978-3-11-068830-6
e-ISBN (EPUB) 978-3-11-068835-1
ISSN 1861-4078

Library of Congress Control Number: 2021950451

Bibliographic information published by the Deutsche Nationalbibliothek
The Deutsche Nationalbibliothek lists this publication in the Deutsche Nationalbibliografie; detailed bibliographic data are available on the Internet at http://dnb.dnb.de.

© 2023 Walter de Gruyter GmbH, Berlin/Boston
This volume is text- and page-identical with the hardback published in 2022.
Typesetting: Integra Software Services Pvt. Ltd.
Printing and binding: CPI books GmbH, Leck

www.degruyter.com

Contents

Ulrike Schröder, Milene Mendes de Oliveira,
Adriana Maria Tenuta

Introduction

1 Metaphor and culture before conceptual metaphor theory

The development of conceptual metaphor theory in cognitive linguistics can be roughly divided into two essential periods: the first one being related to individualistic and universalistic matters, taking a more introspective approach, and the second one related to increasing research on embodiment *in situ*, language use, as well as its social and cultural context. However, research on the relationship of metaphor, language, and cognition was not first addressed in Lakoff and Johnsons *Metaphors we live by* ([1980] 2003), as often assumed. In fact, it can be traced back even to Aristotle and innumerable philosophical successors especially from the 17th century onwards.[1] Thus, if we take a close look beyond the limits of cognitive linguistics, we find that establishing a connection between metaphor, cognition, and culture has a long tradition and goes back at least to Johann Gottfried Herder. In his *Abhandlung über den Ursprung der Sprache*[2] ([1772] 2002), Herder discusses the gradual evolution of nature, mind, and language, taking the individual and not the world as the starting point for his epistemology. Therefore, according to Herder, it is no surprise that the 'wild languages' conceptualize the whole kingdom of nature as a kingdom of acting beings. This corresponds to a "sensuous main idea" (Herder [1772] 2002: 47–49) which is responsible for the personification of emotions such as anger (Herder [1772] 2002: 62). Following Herder, as the pioneer of the principle of linguistic relativity, Wilhelm von Humboldt ([1836] 1992) rejects the possibility of a language-free knowledge of reality still present in enlightenment and rationalism. Reality in itself is not accessible epistemologically, since it is always a perspectively and linguistically bound reality. As a consequence, it can only be perceived as the corresponding language suggests.

This paradigm of language as being conceptualized by a given cultural community coins American anthropological linguistics at the beginning of the 20th century.

1 For the history of cognitive metaphor research cf. Schröder (2012).
2 Treatise on the origin of the language.

Ulrike Schröder, Adriana Maria Tenuta, Federal University of Minas Gerais
Milene Mendes de Oliveira, University of Potsdam

https://doi.org/10.1515/9783110688306-001

Anthropological linguistics introduces an empirical turn by which metaphor comes into view as an essential constituent in the construction of worldviews. In his essay *Metaphorical expression in the language of the Kwakiutl Indians*, Boas ([1929] 1982) set out an ethnographic sketch of an everyday metaphor of the Kwakiutl naming instances such as "I *follow* the *road* made by my late ancestors" or "*walking along* on *flat*" thereby anticipating the PATH schema as defined by Lakoff and Johnson ([1980] 2003). Boas functionally arranged his list of expressions utilized metaphorically in everyday speech by the Kwakiutl speakers according to speech events in which they occur, and distinguishes between 'unhappy events', 'speeches', 'speaking of rival chiefs', 'marriage ceremonies', 'talking to children', and 'talking to intimate friends'. Certain metaphors are typical for certain speech events: for instance, when Kwakiutl speakers talk about other tribal leaders, they use metaphors related to animals, while talk in marriage ceremonies shows a high use of metaphors related to the concept of house etc. Whereas Boas' approach is still psychologically motivated, Sapir initiates a communicative and social turn by conceiving the world as an all along socially, emotionally, and culturally filtered reality, turning language into the essential guide for thinking: As the grammatical categories vary from one language to another, conceptual thinking is channeled differently (Sapir 1949: 159). Metaphor is of crucial importance in this process and Sapir already points to what Lakoff and Johnson ([1980] 2003: 10–13) will later call 'highlighting' and 'hiding':

> New cultural experiences frequently make it necessary to enlarge the resources of a language, but such enlargement is never an arbitrary addition to the materials and forms already present; it is merely a further application of principles already in use and in many cases little more than a metaphorical extension of old terms and meaning. [. . .] Language is at one and the same time helping and retarding us in our exploration of experience, and the details of these processes of help and hindrance are deposited in the subtler meanings of different cultures. (Sapir 1949: 10–11)

Yet the starting point of Benjamin Lee Whorf, Sapir's student, bears many parallels to conceptual metaphor theory as well as to cognitive grammar, especially his references to *gestalt* psychology, as one may check in *Grammatical categories* (Whorf [1939a] 1956) and *On psychology* (Whorf 1956). Whorf ([1939a] 1956) conceives the configurations that act in language as gestalt principles, since – for him – grammatical categories are also semantic categories. In his field studies on Hopi, he points to metaphorical concepts such as personifications (*objectifying*), synesthetic metaphors, as well as orientational metaphors typically used in the so-called *Standard Average European* (SAE), but by no means regarded as universal (Whorf [1941] 1956: 243–244). Additionally, Whorf ([1939b] 1956: 154–155) even points to gestural metaphors which, according to him, show more motion in speakers of SAE than in speakers of Hopi, what he associates with our more dynamic linguistic conceptualizations of reality. He also analyzes synesthetic metaphor and points to the bidirectionality of domains since we do not only map colors, shapes, textures, etc. onto sounds, tastes, emotions, and thoughts but also reversely:

> Our metaphorical system, by naming nonspatial experiences after spatial ones, imputes to sounds, smells, tastes, emotions, and thoughts qualities like the colors, luminosities, shapes, angles, textures, and motions of spatial experience. And to some extent the reverse transference occurs; for, after much talking about tones as high, low, sharp, dull, heavy, brilliant, slow, the talker finds it easy to think of some factors in spatial experience like factors of tone. Thus, we speak of 'tones' of color, a gray 'monotone', a 'loud' necktie, a 'taste' in dress: all spatial metaphor in reverse. (Whorf [1939b] 1956: 155–156)

Finally, Whorf anticipates Lakoff and Johnson's ([1980] 2003) TIME IS MONEY metaphor by showing that this metaphor exists in everyday 'fashions of speaking' in SAE languages, being evident in expressions such as *spend, save, lose,* or *buy time*, whereas Hopi does not conceive time as a countable unit (Whorf [1939b] 1956: 153–156).

2 Cognitive schemata and cultural models in anthropology in the eighties and nineties

According to Ibarretxe-Antuñano (2013: 318–319), the relationship between metaphor and culture has undergone three stages in cognitive linguistic research, namely, a so-called 'normalized' situation, a period of 'culture oblivion', and a 'culture renaissance'. The eighties and early nineties represent the first stage of this development, the late nineties and the turn of the millennium the second stage, and current research represents the third. It should be highlighted that, during the first stage, Lakoff and Johnson ([1980] 2003) still drew their attention to the cultural impact of metaphor, such as the Western influence on the conceptual metaphor TIME IS MONEY. Later, however, they showed an almost exclusive interest in philosophical, neurolinguistic, and universal matters (Lakoff & Johnson 1999). In the late eighties and nineties, cognitive anthropology gave birth to concepts such as 'instituted models', 'foundational schemas' (Shore 1996), 'culturally shared models' (Quinn 1991; Holland & Quinn 1987), and 'tropes' (Fernandez 1991). As a response to Lakoff and Johnson's *a priori* character of conceptual metaphor, Holland and Quinn (1987), for example, proposed the 'propositional model' of marriage as a journey that is embedded in the background of American culture. The authors do not see metaphors as engines of cultural models but rather the other way around: the models should be seen as creators of metaphors. In similar ways, many other anthropologically oriented studies deal with schemata beyond the mere linguistic level. Bradd Shore (1996) has shown how metaphorical conceptualizations can structure social-physical reality as well as our cultural practice and, vice versa, how metaphorical conceptualizations are abstracted from cultural practices. Thus, metaphors can be visually represented, e.g., in dance, painting, sculpture, gestures, posture, or spatial arrangements. An example is the fact that, in many societies, important people tend to sit more centrally and in a higher position than people who are less important (Kövecses 2005: 164). According to Shore (1996: 53), cultural communities frequently elaborate 'foundational schemas' that provide a source domain for "the creation of a family of related cultural models". Foley (1997: 236–237) shows how schemata of categorizations are intertwined and can lead to a metaphorical extension of such a system at the level of more abstract domains. He illustrates his point by referring to some Southeast Asian languages which are strongly stratified. The Burmese, for instance, have a grammatical classification system in combination with a schema that ranges from 'sacred' to 'profane', including the corresponding classification of the forms of address related to the personal category or object. For instance, the Burmese address elders, teachers, and strangers through the use of polite pronouns that are represented by feudal-era third person pronouns in lieu of first and second person pronouns. In such situations, one refers to oneself in the third person. In this perspective, in contrast to the occidental SCALE schema, with its 'upper' and 'lower' class, the universe is arranged in concentric circles, and Buddha is located at the center. Therefore, the crucial schema is represented by CENTER – PERIPHERY.

Thus, when Gibbs (1999) finally calls for *Taking metaphor out of our heads and putting it into the cultural world* at the end of the 20th century, this appeal must be read as addressed rather to the community of conceptual metaphor scholars since, beyond this universe, one can observe a productive continuum of studies related to the reciprocity of metaphor and culture.

3 The emergence of studies on conceptual metaphor and culture in the new millennium

At the beginning of the new millennium, several critical voices began to emerge, arguing for the inclusion of culture into studies of conceptual metaphor and metonymy. Enrique Bernardez (2005) launched some interdisciplinary considerations on the importance of culture in linguistic and typological descriptions as well as warnings against the tendency for scholars to lean on theoretical frameworks based solely on the English language. Moreover, the linguist argued that cognition should be viewed as not limited to the individual, in a solipsist fashion, but as including all human activity, which, at the same time, may have an impact on the very cognitive processes themselves.

One pioneering work within conceptual metaphor theory that seeks to systematize studies within and beyond the field of conceptual metaphor and culture, building up a theoretical framework by extending conceptual metaphor theory, is Kövecses' *Metaphor and culture* (2005). Kövecses maintains that our worldview is at large encapsulated in our conceptual system and that culture is constituted by frames or cultural models, which are indeed motivated by an embodied basis. However, concurrently, they are also embedded in a situational context, and culture is defined by concepts, ideas, values, principles, behaviors, and things that are specific to a particular language community (Kövecses 2005, 2017).

Therefore, one crucial point of departure for Kövecses' framework is Grady's (1997) distinction between corporally based 'primary metaphor' versus experientially based 'complex metaphor'. Grady asserts that "it may be appropriate to consider primary metaphorical patterns as something like templates, opposed to the more fleshed-out, blended conceptualizations that constitute metaphors *per se*. Primary metaphors are generic patterns, rather than concrete, vivid *instantiations*" (Grady 2005: 1608–1609). Now, according to Kövecses (2005: 68–69), while the primary metaphor is seen as having a nearly universal status, the complex metaphor may vary in different languages. The most famous example Kövecses gives is the primary metaphor THE ANGRY PERSON IS A PRESSURIZED CONTAINER, which can be found in languages such as English, Chinese, German, Japanese, Hungarian, Polish, Wolof, and Zulu. However, questions such as the way in which the container reacts, how the pressure arises, what type of substance can be found inside the container, what the consequences of an explosion are, whether the explosion will be something socially welcome or not, etc., can only be answered by means of the concrete, culture-specific metaphors that are intertwined with background models of the corresponding community.

Over the last ten years, Kövecses (2010, 2015, this volume) has combined culture- and discourse-oriented approaches in a context-sensitive grounding model of metaphorical creativity. As a consequence, the starting point is now the intersubjective context with its sphere of shared attention as well as the larger context that involves, in addition to the interlocutor, the circumstances under which an utterance is made: who interacts with whom, when and where, why the communication is taking place and what it is about. Those are the driving forces for the construction of meaning, which is now seen as a dynamic and creative process that interacts with the more or less conventional meaning of symbols based on an embodied experience (Kövecses

2015: x–xi). The contexts are frames that are nested in one another, such as the physical setting as the outermost frame that includes the social frame, which, on its turn, includes the cultural frame, and where, in the innermost frame, we find the speaker/conceptualizer, the hearer/conceptualizer, and the topic, as well as the flow of discourse, functioning as the immediate linguistic context, or cotext, in the sense of Langacker's (2008: 281) "current discourse space". Importantly, the cultural context frequently has nothing to do with the existence or the absence of a basic conceptual metaphor in a cultural group as compared to another but rather with questions related to the degree of conventionalization and elaboration of the vocabulary, different preferences concerning the salience of concepts, different 'experiential foci', different forms of framing the same concept, 'differential cognitive styles' as well as different preferences regarding metaphor or metonymy, which are reflected in the vocabulary (Kövecses 2015: 26–29).

4 Metaphorical conceptualizations in cultural linguistics

It is still in the nineties that Gary Palmer releases his groundbreaking work *Toward a theory of cultural linguistics* (1996). On the basis of the subsequently developed framework, cultural linguistics is established as a new research field, bringing together cognitive linguistics, anthropological linguistics, and ethnography of speaking. Palmer's book covers all fields of cognitive linguistics but focuses particularly on the idea of linguistic imagery: "The term invokes the anthropological tradition that culture is the accumulated knowledge of a community or society, including its stock of cognitive models, schemas, scenarios, and other forms of conventional imagery" (Palmer 1996: 290). Metaphor is essential for understanding linguistic imagery of cultural groups, especially Indigenous languages, as is shown in their metaphorical mappings. Palmer shows, for instance, that, in the Coeur d'Alene language, the tires of a car or truck are named "wrinkled feet" as a reference to the pattern on their tread. In a similar vein, according to Basso (1990: 15–24), the system for naming parts of motorized vehicles in the language of Western Apache of east-central Arizona is based on mapping the human body parts onto parts of the motor vehicles while preserving the body's cognitive topology (Palmer 1996: 224–225).

Later, Farzad Sharifian (2011, 2015, 2017) gives cultural linguistics an even more multidisciplinary direction by emphasizing that this new line of research also benefits from and contributes to areas of (applied) linguistics including world Englishes, intercultural communication, English as an international language, and cross-cultural pragmatics (Sharifian 2011: xv). One key concept Sharifian develops is 'distributed cognition', which he describes as

> the cultural knowledge that emerges from the interactions between members of a cultural group across time and space [. . .] cultural cognition is dynamic in that it is constantly being negotiated and renegotiated within and across the generations of the relevant cultural group, as well as in response to the contact that members of that group have with other languages and cultures. (Sharifian 2015: 476)

Frequently, studies in this field go beyond mere conceptual metaphor and its linguistic expressions. An example can be given by referring to large-scale metaphorical conceptualizations that underlie Aboriginal thinking, speaking, and acting when it comes to the interconnection between land, animals, and people. It is part of their interlocking cultural model to map conceptualizations of kinship onto the domain of land and, as a consequence, refer to part of their 'country' as 'grandfather' or 'mother' whereby the underlying metaphor can be described as LAND IS KIN, which emphasizes the relationship between person and place in the Aboriginal culture. According to this understanding, Sharifian (2011: 57) explains that members of this cultural group use expressions such as "grow up the country" meaning 'care for the country'. But this conceptualization goes far beyond its mere linguistic expression and has its roots in the concept of Aboriginal Dreamtime, during which ancestor beings are imagined as an amalgam of animal and human forms that traveled the land and created landforms and customs. In the end, they became transformed into features of the landscape in the shape of stones, trees, and, therefore, today, the land embodies the spirits of these ancestor beings as connected to people via kinship.

Also related to fundamental differences in the underlying cultural models, Yu (2015) points to Western and Chinese conceptualizations of person: While in Western cultures, PERSON is conceptualized as BODY + MIND, in Chinese culture, it is conceptualized as BODY + HEART, which concurrently reflects a more dualistic view of Western culture in contrast to a more holistic view in Chinese culture, which sees the heart as the center of both emotions and thought. That is to say, although a person consists of two parts, namely, the body and the heart (*xin*), these two are nevertheless not separate since the latter is an integral part of the former. Thus, the cultural conceptualizations of the heart give rise to metaphors that profile this internal body organ as a physical entity – the heart as container – as a part of the body – the heart as a ruler of the body –, and the locus of affective and cognitive activities, such as the heart as the house of all emotional and mental processes. Yu sees a connection between these preferential conceptualizations and ancient Chinese philosophy and medicine, in which the heart was conceptualized as the organ for thinking, feeling, will, reason, and intuition.

In a similar vein, Musolff (2017) goes beyond a mere linguistic analysis in his study on the conceptual metaphor NATION (STATE) IS A BODY in different languages. He shows this metaphor to be widely known in many cultures, nevertheless: Whereas British and American students, e.g., describe their occidental political system in terms of a body's health, anatomy, and metabolism, Chinese students tend to identify geographical places in China and to link them to parts of the human anatomy on the basis of functional correspondences between activities performed by parts of the body and politically significant characterizations of the locations. In contrast, the origins of this concept in Europe date back to the medieval Latin terms *corpus mysticum* and *corpus politicum*, which were translated into European vernacular languages in the sixteenth century. However, more subtle differences have also been detected between European languages: In English, the physical body of a prominent politician can be the ostensive target referent of the phrase *body politic*, whereas, in Germany, the term *Volkskörper* is negatively connoted since it is related to Nazi-reminiscent vocabulary. Yet in French, *corps politique* can be traced back to Rousseau's impact on revolutionary and republican thought.

5 New directions in research on metaphor, cognition, and cultural practice

Over the last twenty years, new directions have arisen in the field of metaphor, cognition, and culture that indicate upcoming tendencies. In this volume, we will focus on four lines of research, each looking at different aspects of the culture-cognition interface. Topics addressed by the authors are varied and include (a) cultural conceptualizations found in varieties of pluricentric languages such as English and Portuguese, (b) a dynamic view of culture which takes a cognitive-pragmatic perspective into account, and (c) the interplay between culture, language, and gesture, also in indigenous languages. It should be noted that these topics can converge and overlap in different ways. However, in the following we will discuss them more or less separately only for heuristic purposes.

A current tendency in studies of metaphor and culture addresses cultural aspects of word choice (more specifically of metaphorical expressions) in one language used in different geographical regions. Within this group, studies under the rubric of world Englishes (WE) are now prominent. However, Wolf and Polzenhagen (2006a) reminded us that, due to a strong focus on functional matters in pragmatics and intercultural studies over a long period of time, the important role of diverging conceptualizations in varieties of English had been neglected.

However, lately, scholars from the field of cultural linguistics as well as cognitive linguistics show more and more interest in those varieties and provide examples of cultural variation in metaphorical conceptualizations in WE as well as English as a Lingua Franca (ELF) (e.g., Sadeghpour and Sharifian (eds.), forthcoming). In another study, Wolf and Polzenhagen (2006b) compared Hong Kong English and German English, revealing the strong presence of the UNIVERSITY IS A FAMILY metaphor in Hong Kong English. When students were asked what they associate with this metaphor, they answered "obedience", in contrast to one of the studies' hypotheses that expected answers related to 'nurture' and 'care'. This reveals that it is not the metaphor itself that is unusual for participants of a Western culture but rather the lack of knowledge about the specific cultural inferences that are connected with it.

Another line of research that has gathered momentum in the last decade is one which brings together semantic and pragmatic aspects of metaphor use. Senkbeil (2020), for instance, looks at examples of idiomatic language in authentic discourse and shows that figurative meanings of idioms are closely connected to embodied or empractic knowledge. The author concludes that those idiomatic expressions are in general easily reconstructed in intercultural interactions and present no hindrance since they are transculturally shared or constructed *in situ*. Additionally, speakers are shown to employ metadiscursive cues to introduce their idioms. Mendes de Oliveira (2020) reports on a study on RESPECT in business communication based on the analysis of e-mails and interviews with Brazilian and German co-workers in an international company. One decisive result of this study showed that the recurrent image schema VERTICAL SPLITTING in the Brazilian interview excerpts was related to how participants acknowledge 'hierarchy' in their construals of 'face' in e-mail interactions in English as a lingua franca, whereas the image schema HORIZONTAL SPLITTING indicated how German participants construe 'face' as a transactional phenomenon in their e-mail exchanges.

It should be noted that the focus on *in situ* aspects of metaphor can be magnified when multimodality comes into play. In this respect, conceptual metaphor theory has profited from a comprehensive amount of work that draws attention to the gestural level of metaphor use in real interaction. One crucial contribution of these studies on metaphoric gesture is the finding that the so-called dead verbal metaphors may still be processed actively and be foregrounded and highlighted in gesture (Müller & Cienki 2009). Moreover, there is a growing number of studies showing how metaphoric gestures are related to cultural practice. These studies start from a more praxeological and phenomenological approach to embodiment by assuming that thinking, gesturing, signifying, and enacting habits are embodied by body-subjects in interaction with the world they inhabit as well as with other body-subjects their actions are coupled with. While the first generation of cognitive linguists has mainly adopted a more individual-psychological, meaning-as-conceptualization notion of linguistic meaning, this approach takes intersubjectivity and embodiment as ultimately fused together in structures of intercorporeality (Schröder & Streeck forthcoming; Cuffari & Streeck 2017).

A prominent example for the interconnectedness of metaphor, gesture, and cultural practice is the study on the Aymaras' mapping of the future onto the space behind and the past onto the space in front of the speaker (Núñez & Sweetser 2006; Reiter 2014). These mappings reflect their strong emphasis on visual perception as a source of knowledge since what is known – the past – is projected in front of ego and what is unknown – the future – in the back. In compliance with this conceptualization, speakers point to a more distant location in front of them when indicating an event that was further in the past and to a location nearer them to indicate an event that happened more recently. Moreover, by pointing in an upward angle to the front, they express that a referent event lies further in the past than events located by low pointing. In a similar vein, Yukatec Maya speakers employ a space-to-time metaphorical mapping in that they point towards the space at the speaker's feet when referring to 'now' or 'precise/specific' time and towards the space above the head of the speaker when referring to 'far/remote' time, either past or future. Furthermore, unfolding time is represented by a cyclical, rolling gesture (Brown 2014: 1211).

A more holistic view of the body is given by Geurt (2003), who conducts a study on the BALANCE schema in the Anlo Ewe culture and language in South Ghana. She points to the kinesthetic and proprioceptive schemas within the theory of *seselelame* ('feeling in the body, flesh, or skin') as a cultural model of this socio-cultural group. In Ewe, there is no distinction between emotion, sensation, perception, and cognition. Rather, Anlo epistemology and ontology depend upon the indigenous schema of *seselelame*. That means there is a sensibility in which the bodily feeling of balance is foregrounded as a source of vital information about the environment and the self. The BALANCE schema is needed to carry heavy loads on the head in everyday life, and someone's posture and gait are seen as indexes for a person's moral fortitude and psychological disposition. In addition to that, the BALANCE schema also participates in dancing rituals as well as in extra- and introverted modes of being across time. Such a schema can be understood as a 'foundational schema' in the abovementioned sense of Shore (1996) since it builds up the basic cultural model for a given community.

Another foundational schema is the guiding metaphor LIFE IS A SHOW, SPECTACLE, PLAY OR ENTERTAINMENT in the American culture, which is reflected not only in linguistic expressions Americans use in everyday life such as "You're *on*", "It's *showtime*", or "He *turned in a great performance*", as Kövecses (2005: 184–186) illustrates. Hall, Goldstein, and Ingram (2016) show how this metaphor is enacted in

Donald Trump's gestures by bodily quoting, transmodal stylizations, and metonymical reductions of others to laughable portrayals. In another study, Schröder (2017) reveals how the interconnected metaphor RAP IS A GAME / RAP IS COMPETITION is at the core of all four elements of Hip Hop – DJing, breakdance, graffiti, and rap – and incorporated in the whole gestural attitude of rappers, such as body posture, hand and facial gestures, gaze, object manipulation, movement as well as orientation in space.

6 Structure and chapters of the volume

This volume is a contribution to the current discussions on metaphorical conceptualizations and cultural variation. Most of the chapters comprise papers presented at the International Symposium on Linguistics, Cognition, and Culture (LCC), held in Belo Horizonte (Brazil) on 13–15 March 2019,[3] whose aim was to bring together contributions from researchers in the fields of cognitive and cultural linguistics who work on current issues related to metaphor from a(n) (inter) cultural perspective. The discussions in this volume are concerned with cognitive and cultural linguistics' theory regarding metaphorical conceptualization, the influence of culture on metaphor and metonymy, the impact of culture and cognition on metaphorical lexis, the interface of pragmatics and cognition when metaphor is studied *in situ*, that is, in real multimodal interaction, the application of insights into metaphorical conceptualizations to language teaching, and recent methods for revealing (inter)cultural metaphorical conceptualizations in corpus-based approaches as well as gesture studies. Therefore, the volume is organized into four sections, the first one dealing with theoretical and methodological issues, the second one being related to cultural metaphorical conceptualizations in specific cultural groups, the third one offering contributions from the perspective of cross-cultural metaphorical conceptualizations, and the last one introducing studies that point to the relevance of metaphorical conceptualizations in face-to-face intercultural communication.

The first section, **Theoretical and methodological reflections on metaphorical conceptualizations**, comprises two contributions. In chapter 1, **Zoltán Kövecses** explains his recent "extended conceptual metaphor theory", which deepens both our cognitive and situational understandings of conceptual metaphors in that it specifies different schematicity levels of metaphors and provides a description of types of context influencing the use of metaphor in discourse.

3 <http://www.letras.ufmg.br/simposiolcc/>

Within this framework, 'culture' can occupy different spaces. Kövecses explains that 'culture' can be equated with the notion of a 'conceptual system' and therefore represents a constantly evolving system characterizing a group of socially and historically situated individuals who make sense of their experiences in a more or less unified way. Alternatively, culture can be regarded as the situational context, which comprises ideas, values, artifacts and practices that characterize a linguistic community and are fairly active and salient in the minds of speakers employing particular cases of metaphorical conceptualizations. In chapter 2, **Frank Polzenhagen** proposes a critical reflection on the use of XXL-sized corpora in studies dealing with metaphor variation. By leaning on the analysis of the conceptualization THE NATION IS A FAMILY in American and West-African Englishes, he explains and illustrates several problems researchers can be confronted with by relying on results provided by different big-sized corpora in cross-varietal studies. While using meticulously selected examples of corpus searches, the author highlights the fact that such corpora differ substantially with respect to how they satisfy some important criteria in corpus linguistics, such as representativeness and reliability of search results. The chapter scrutinizes corpora that are widely used by world Englishes scholars, such as BNC, COCA, and GloWbE, but its insights can be easily generalized into cross-varietal corpus studies, serving thereby the readership of this volume interested in contrastive studies. Polzenhagen concludes his chapter by making a case for the use of small-scale corpora compiled for the specific purposes in a study.

The second section of this volume, **Cultural metaphorical conceptualizations**, includes three chapters that report on empirical studies concerning how metaphors are deployed in a certain culture or set of cultures. The first paper in this section, in chapter 3, presents **Vera da Silva Sinha** and **Heliana Mello**'s in-depth description of how the indigenous languages and cultures Huni Kuĩ, Awetý, and Kamaiurá in the Amazonian region conceptualize time. In these cultures, time is shown to be 'event-based' (Silva Sinha et al. 2012) and thus to be indexicalized by environmental 'happenings' related to, for instance, water level, the singing of birds and animals, or the position of the Moon, the Stars, and the Sun. The metaphorical expression of time as space, so popular in Indo-European languages, is not present. The authors also explain that event-based time intervals in the three investigated languages are included in temporal landmarks of lifestages, and life is considered an evolving learning process marked by different stages. These stages are not lexicalized as points or spatial positions on a timeline but as categories of social status. Another Amazonian language, Aguaruna, is the focus of chapter 4, which depicts an interdisciplinary study by the linguists **Ketty García-Ruiz** and **Jaime Huasco-Escalante**, and the biologist **Jhon Jairo López-Rojas** on resemblance metaphor (Ureña and Faber 2010) and metonymy.

In their analysis of compound nouns (binomials) of the ethnozoological lexicon of Aguaruna, the authors build on Berlin's (1992) fifth principle of ethnobiological nomenclature. This principle postulates that ethnobiological names often have metaphorical features that reveal a motivation for relating the name and the named referent. One of their findings is that most metaphorical mappings seem to be based on similarities of color or shape. Apart from these color and shape motivations (called prototypical image metaphors), the authors name other types of resemblance metaphor found in their corpus of binomials, such as behavior-based ones, as well as independent metonymies. In Chapter 5, **Patrick Kühmstedt** and **Hans-Georg Wolf** report on an investigation of metaphorical and cultural conceptualizations in a web-derived corpus of leading articles and letters to the editor in Guyanese (newspaper) English. This analysis aims to fill in the research gap on cultural conceptualizations in Caribbean Englishes and, at the same time, deepen the pool of research methods in cultural linguistics, which, to date, often takes a primarily ethnographic approach. Kühmstedt and Wolf's bottom-up approach consists of a cultural keyword analysis (Rayson 2008; Leech and Fallon 1992; Wierzbicka 1997), a keyword chain analysis (Peters 2017), and a semantic key domain analysis. Examples of conceptualizations found in the corpus are GUYANA IS A COMPANY, GUYANA IS AN OIL COMPANY, up to GUYANA IS A SUBSIDIARY OF EXXONMOBIL.

The third section of this edited volume, **Cross-cultural metaphorical conceptualizations,** takes a comparative approach in looking at conceptualizations in data from different languages. In Chapter 6, **Ulrike Schröder**, **Milene Mendes de Oliveira,** and **Thiago da Cunha Nascimento** explore the repercussion of an event at the Olympic Games in Brazil in 2016. The event in case is the booing action of the Brazilian crowd towards a French athlete at an Olympic stadium. Conceptualizations in reader comments in French, German, and English are contrasted with conceptualizations in Portuguese in the Brazilian media. The striking difference between the findings in Portuguese as compared to the ones in the other languages is that the cultural category SPORTS FANS is construed in a very idiosyncratic way in the Brazilian comments and is often combined with IN-GROUP and OUT-GROUP schemas as well the MONGREL COMPLEX cultural schema, the latter one as defined by Brazilian readers themselves. These findings are complemented by the subsequent analysis of a radio broadcast in which sports commentators recalled and reflected upon the incident. This analytical step highlights how cultural conceptualizations can be reflected upon, reinforced, and/or rejected in the here-an-now of interaction, and how they are interwoven with different speech styles (Spencer-Oatey 2008). In Chapter 7, **Augusto Soares da Silva** also turns his attention to the Portuguese language in an investigation of conceptualizations of ANGER in personal-experiential blogs. However, in this chapter, it is intralinguistic variation that is explored by looking at two varieties of this pluricentric language (Soares da Silva (ed.) 2014): European and Brazilian Portuguese. Since anger is claimed to be a universal emotion and to have a biological basis, a study that considers its linguistic expression in different cultures is especially interesting for a more thorough understanding of the interaction between language and culture. The study follows a sociocognitive framework and adopts a corpus-based and onomasiological profile-based methodology in investigating alternative metaphorical patterns related to the conceptualization of ANGER. The findings reveal that metaphorical expressions used in European Portuguese can be associated with conceptualizations that highlight an attempted regulation and an internalized expression of anger. By contrast, the expressions in Brazilian Portuguese unveil a more open and unrestrained manifestation of anger as an affirmation of the self. The author argues that these results are in line with previous research on Portuguese and Brazilian cultures which shows Brazil as more individualistic, indulgent, and emotionally expressive than Portugal. In Chapter 8, **Maíra Avelar, Lilian Ferrari,** and **Vera Pacheco** contrast literal and metaphorical verbo-gestural expressions of locative deixis in TV news and talk shows in Brazilian Portuguese and American English. Such a contrast is particularly intriguing given the fact that these two languages count on different configurations of locative deictic forms. While Brazilian Portuguese shows a fourfold system with the expressions "aqui" (nearer the speaker), "aí" (nearer the addressee), "ali" (near both the speaker and the addressee), and "lá" (distal from both the speaker and the addressee), American English relies on a twofold system with "here" (near the speaker) and "there" (either distal from both the speaker and the hearer or distal from the speaker, but near the addressee). Findings reveal that the most frequent gesture that goes along with the verbal expression of the deictic term is pointing. However, a preference for pointing with the index finger is identified in the Brazilian data and the salience of pointing with the open hand is identified in American English deictic occurrences. The prototypical function of gestures in the two groups was the referential one, with Brazilian speakers often making more references to narrative scenes being reenacted, and American English speakers making more references to people located in the immediate scene where interaction was taking place. In Chapter 9, **Karsten Senkbeil** and **Nicola Hoppe** address the recent discussions on the coronavirus and its associated disease, Covid-19, based on an analysis of news articles in the UK, the USA, and Germany. Each metaphorical expression is analyzed for its source domain, and this step is complemented by an examination of the communicative purpose of the metaphorical expression. Findings show that the metaphors CORONA PANDEMIC IS A WAR and SARS-COV-2 IS AN ENEMY dominated the political discourse in the UK and the USA in the spring of 2020, and also appeared consistently in the German public discourse. In the latter, however, SPORTS metaphors were also often used by German government officials in order to tone down some of the entailments of the WAR metaphor, even though, as the authors explain, WAR and SPORTS metaphors generally relate to the same event structure, as both emphasize agency, the combination of strategy and willpower, and the possibility of winning or losing. By exploring the intersection between cognitive linguistics and pragmatics, Senkbeil and Hoppe show that metaphors can help push political agendas while motivating the public to comply with public-health-oriented – yet often pretty unpopular – measures.

The last section of this volume, **Intercultural metaphorical conceptualizations,** contains two contributions that address *in situ* and multimodal use of metaphorical conceptualizations in interactions between cultures. In Chapter 10, **Adriana Fernandes Barbosa** examines the interplay of conceptualizations and gesture in a German as a foreign language class. After videotaping and transcribing both the verbal and the gestural levels of classroom exchanges, the researcher analyzes teacher-student interactions in explanations of particle and prefixed verbs provided by the instructor and negotiated with the learners. The findings of this study show that gestures used by the teacher in explaining prefixed verbs often portray image schemas and metaphorical mappings that evidence the online activation of certain cognitive structures. The author interprets the findings from her fine-grained analysis against the concept of 'embodiment' in cognitive linguistics. Moreover, she leans on Danesi's (2017) notion of 'conceptual fluency', which associates learning a second/foreign language with acquired conceptual – or, more specifically, metaphorical – competence in that language. In Chapter 11, **Ulrike Schröder** shows how verbal, corporal-gestural, and prosodic means are interwoven in intercultural talk-in-interaction. The author investigates *insitu* and *ad hoc* co-constructions of 'intercultures' and provides a detailed multimodal analysis of three sequences of face-to-face interactions. The analyses point to the fact that the pervasive metaphor CULTURE IS A CONTAINER is often activated and elaborated upon, via gestures, as part of the (self)reflexive experience of alterity involved in intercultural encounters. This chapter adds to the growing body of studies on multimodal aspects of metaphor use in real interaction and makes important considerations about the connection between cognitive linguistics and intercultural pragmatics.

The chapters in this volume make evident the variety of theoretical orientations, methods, as well as applications that can be associated with the study of metaphor and culture. With respect to theoretical foundations, the connection between cognition and culture, language in use, context, and multimodality can be identified. As for methods, two points are in order. First, the tendency to examine metaphorical conceptualizations in discourse, lexis, and interaction was evident in the chapters of this volume, which seems to set a definitive separation from studies that rely solely on introspection. Secondly, a variety of methods such as ethnography, gesture analysis, as well as corpus-based data collection and analysis stand out. These methods reflect the multiplicity of research questions that can be asked within the field. And last but not least, applications of metaphor studies that take a(n) (inter)cultural perspective are addressed for the fields of language teaching and intercultural communication. On a more general note, all the contributions in this volume should be acknowledged for enabling amplified (inter)cultural understanding.

References

Basso, Ellen B. 1990. *Western Apache language and culture: Essays in linguistic anthropology*. Tuscon: University of Arizona Press.

Berlin, Brent. 1992. Ethnobiological classification. Principles of categorization of plants and animals in traditional societies. Princeton: Princeton University Press.

Bernárdez, Enrique. 2005. Social cognition: variation, language, and culture in a cognitive linguistic typology. Cognitive linguistics. Internal dynamics and interdisciplinary interaction, 191–224. Berlin & New York: Mouton De Gruyter.

Boas, Franz. [1929] 1982. Metaphorical expression in the language of the Kwakiutl indians. In Franz Boas, *Race, language and culture*, 232–239. Toronto: Collier-Macmillan.

Brown, Penelope. 2014. Gestures in native Mexico and Central America: The Mayan cultures. In Cornelia Müller, Alan Cienki, Ellen Fricke, Silva H. Ladewig, David McNeill & Sedinha Teßendorf (eds.), *Body – language – communication. An international handbook on multimodality in human interaction. Volume 2*, 1206–1215. Berlin, Boston: De Gruyter Mouton.

Cuffari, Elena & Jürgen Streeck. 2017. Taking the world by hand: How (some) gestures mean In Christian Meyer, Jürgen Streeck & J. Scott Jordan (eds.), *Intercorporeality. Emerging socialities in interaction*, 173–201. New York: Oxford University Press, 2017.

Fernandez, James W. 1991. *Beyond metaphor: The theory of tropes in anthropology*. Stanford: Stanford University Press.

Geurts, Kathryn L. 2003. *Culture and the senses. Bodily ways of knowing in an African community*. Berkeley: University of California Press.

Gibbs, Raymond W. Jr. 1999. Taking metaphor out of our heads and putting it into the cultural world. In Raymond Gibbs & Gerard J. Steen (eds.), *Metaphor in cognitive linguistics*, 145–166. Amsterdam, Philadelphia: John Benjamins.

Grady, Joseph E. 1997. *Foundations of meaning: Primary metaphors and primary scenes*. Berkeley: Doctoral dissertation – Department of Linguistics, University of California at Berkeley.

Grady, Joseph E. 2005. Primary metaphors as inputs to conceptual integration. *Journal of Pragmatics* 37.1595–1614.

Hall, Kira, Donna M. Goldstein & Matthew Bruce Ingram. 2016. The hands of Donald Trump. *HAU: Journal of Ethnographic Theory* 6(2). 71–100.

Herder, Johann Gottfried. [1772] 2002. *Abhandlung über den Ursrpung der Sprache*. Edited by Hans-Dietrich Irmscher. Stuttgart: Reclam.

Holland, Dorothy & Naomi Quinn. 1987. *Cultural models in language and thought*. Cambridge: Cambridge University Press.

Humboldt, Wilhelm von. [1836] 1992. Über die Verschiedenheit des menschlichen Sprachbaues und ihren Einfluß auf die geistige Entwicklung des Menschengeschlechts. In Wilhelm von Humboldt, *Schriften zur Sprache*. Herausgegeben von Michael Böhler, 30–207. Stuttgart: Reclam.

Ibarretxe-Antuñano, Iraide. 2013. The relationship between conceptual metaphor and culture. *Intercultural Pragmatics,* 10 (2). 315–339.

Kövecses, Zoltán. 2005. *Metaphor in culture. Universality and variation*. Cambridge: Cambridge University Press.

Kövecses, Zoltan. 2010. A new look at metaphorical creativity in cognitive linguistics. *Cognitive Linguistics* 21(4). 663–697.

Kövecses, Zoltan. 2015. *Where metaphors come from. Reconsidering context in metaphor.* New York: Oxford University Press.

Kövecses, Zoltán. 2021. Extended conceptual metaphor theory: the cognition-context interface. In Ulrike Schröder, Milene Mendes de Oliveira & Adriana Maria Tenuta (eds.), *Metaphorical conceptualizations: (Inter)cultural perspectives*. Berlin, New York, forthcoming.

Lakoff, George & Mark Johnson. [1980] 2003. *Metaphors we live by*. Chicago: The University of Chicago Press.

Lakoff, George & Mark Johnson. 1999. *Philosophy in the flesh. The embodied mind and its challenge to western thought*. New York: Basic Books.

Langacker, Ronald W. 2008. *Cognitive grammar: A basic introduction*. Oxford & New York: Oxford University Press.

Leech, Geoffrey & Roger Fallon. 1992. Computer corpora: What do they tell us about culture? *ICAME Journal* 16, 29–50.

Mendes de Oliveira, Milene. 2020. Face and cultural conceptualizations in German-Brazilian business exchanges. *International Journal of Language and Culture* 7(1). Special Issue: Intercultural pragmatics and cultural linguistics. 63–83.

Müller, Cornelia & Alan Cienki A. 2009. Words, gestures, and beyond: Forms of multimodal metaphor in the use of spoken language. In Charles J. Forceville & Eduardo Urios-Aparisi (eds.), *Multimodal metaphor*, 297–328. Berlin, New York: Mouton de Gruyter.

Musolff, Andreas. 2017. Metaphor and cultural cognition. In Farzad Sharifian (ed.), *Advances In cultural linguistics*, 325–344. Singapore: Springer.

Núñez, Rafael E. & Eve Sweetser. 2006. With the future behind them: Convergent evidence from Aymara language and eesture in crosslinguistic comparison of spatial construals of time. *Cognitive Science* 30. 401–450.

Palmer, Gary B. 1996. *Toward a theory of cultural linguistics*. Austin: University of Texas Press.

Peters, Arne. 2017. FAIRIES, BANSHEES, and the CHURCH: Cultural conceptualisations in Irish English. *International Journal of Language and Culture* 4 (2). 127–148.

Quinn, Naomi. 1991. The cultural basis of metaphor. In James W. Fernandez (ed.), *Beyond metaphor: The theory of tropes in anthropology*, 56–93. Stanford: Stanford University Press.

Rayson, Paul. 2008. From key words to key semantic domains. *International Journal of Corpus Linguistics* 13 (4). 519–549.

Reiter, Sabine. 2014. Gestures in South American indigenous cultures. In Cornelia Müller, Alan Cienki, Ellen Fricke, Silva H. Ladewig, David McNeill & Sedinha Teßendorf (eds.), *Body – language – communication. An international handbook on multimodality in human interaction. Volume 2*, 1182–1193. Berlin, Boston: De Gruyter Mouton.

Sadeghpour, Marzieh & Farzad Sharifian (Eds.). 2021. *World Englishes and cultural linguistics*. Springer.

Sapir, Edward. 1949. *Culture, language and personality. Selected writings of Edward Sapir*. Berkeley, Los Angeles: University of California Press.

Schröder, Ulrike & Jürgen Streeck. *Jeitinho in words and gestures: Cultural concept, movement, and way of life* forthcoming.

Schröder Ulrike. 2017. Die kognitiv-pragmatische Dimension der kommunikativen Gattung Rap als battle. In Konstanze Marx & Simon Meier (eds.), Sprachliches Handeln und Kognition. *Theoretische Grundlagen und empirische Analysen*, 133–155. Berlin, Boston: De Gruyter.

Senkbeil, Karsten. 2020 Idioms in intercultural communication: A cognitive and pragmatic perspective. *International Journal of Language and Culture* 7(1). Special Issue: Intercultural pragmatics and cultural linguistics. 38–61.

Sharifian, Farzad. 2011. *Cultural conceptualisations and language*. Amsterdam, Philadelphia: John Benjamins.

Sharifian Farzad. 2015. Cultural linguistics. In Farzad Sharifian (ed.), *The Routledge handbook of language and culture*, 473–492. London, New York: Routledge.

Sharifian, Farzad (ed.). 2017. *Advances in cultural linguistics*. Singapore: Springer.

Shore, Bradd. 1996. *Culture in mind. Cognition, culture, and the problem of meaning*. Oxford: Oxford University Press.

Silva Sinha, Vera da, Chris Sinha, Wany Sampaio & Jörg Zinken. 2012. Event-based time intervals in an Amazonian culture. In Luna Filipović & Kasia Jaszczolt (eds.), *Space and time in languages and cultures II: language, culture, and cognition*, 15–35. Human Cognitive Processing Series 37. Amsterdam: John Benjamins.

Soares da Silva, Augusto (ed.). 2014. *Pluricentricity. Language variation and sociocognitive dimensions*. Berlin & New York: Mouton de Gruyter.

Spencer-Oatey, Helen. 2008. Face, (Im)politeness and rapport. In Helen Spencer-Oatey (ed.), *Culturally speaking: culture, communication and politeness theory*, 11–47. London: Continuum.

Whorf, Benjamin Lee. [1939a] 1956. Grammatical categories. In Benjamin Lee Whorf. *Language, thought and reality. Selected Writings of Benjamin Lee Whorf*. Edited by John B. Carroll, 87–101. Boston: Technology Press of M.I.T.

Whorf, Benjamin Lee. [1939b] 1956. The relation of habitual thought and behavior to language. In Benjamin Lee Whorf. *Language, thought and reality. Selected Writings of Benjamin Lee Whorf*. Edited by John B. Carroll, 134–159. Boston: Technology Press of M.I.T.

Whorf, Benjamin Lee. [1941] 1956. Language and logic. In: Whorf, Benjamin Lee. *Language, thought and reality. Selected Writings of Benjamin Lee Whorf*. Edited by John B. Carroll, 233–245. Boston: Technology Press of M.I.T.

Whorf, Benjamin Lee. [date unknown] 1956. On psychology. Whorf, Benjamin Lee. *Language, thought and reality. Selected Writings of Benjamin Lee Whorf*. Edited by John B. Carroll, 40–42. Boston: Technology Press of M.I.T.

Wierzbicka, Anna. 1997. *Understanding cultures through their key words: English, Russian, Polish, German, and Japanese*. New York & Oxford: Oxford University Press.

Wolf, Hans-Georg & Frank Polzenhagen. 2006a. Intercultural communication in English: a cognitive linguistic focus on neglected issues. LAUD Linguistic Agency 683. 1–26.

Wolf, Hans-Georg & Frank Polzenhagen. 2006b. Intercultural communication in English: Arguments for a cognitive approach to intercultural pragmatics. *Intercultural Pragmatics* 3(3). 285–321

Yu, Ning. 2015. Embodiment, culture, and language. In Farzad Sharifian (ed.), *The Routledge handbook of language and culture*, 227–239. Oxford; New York: Routledge.

Section I: **Theoretical and methodological reflections on metaphorical conceptualizations**

Zoltán Kövecses

Extended conceptual metaphor theory: the cognition-context interface

Abstract: My goal in the paper is to offer a new perspective on how conceptual metaphors (subsumed under "cognition" in the title) and culture (subsumed under "context" in the title) are related to one another. The view of conceptual metaphors that I employ here is a recent one called "extended conceptual metaphor theory" (Kövecses 2020). The new view is, in large part, based on two ideas: first, the notion that all conceptual metaphors exist on (roughly) four levels of schematicity and, second, that metaphors (including conceptual metaphors) are always used in the context of our available experiences at the time of their use. I dub this the "multilevel" and "contextual" view of conceptual metaphors, respectively. In other words, the question I am trying to answer is this: How can we fit together conceptual metaphor with the cultural context in which it is used?

Keywords: extended conceptual metaphor theory, cultural context, conceptual metaphor

1 Introduction

If we think of conceptual metaphors as sets of systematic relations (mappings) between two conceptual domains (or frames, or scenes) that are based on universal bodily experiences, it becomes very difficult to say how cognition interfaces with context at large, or, more specifically, how conceptual metaphors interface with cultural context. This is because, first, if conceptual metaphors reside in the head as a result of the effect of embodied cognition, it is hard to say what role context plays in the production of metaphors. In a way, when we use a metaphor, everything is already decided: we have stable mappings between the two domains, and there are metaphorical conventionalized linguistic expressions associated with those mappings. The production of metaphor is simply a process of selecting a linguistic metaphor that is attached to the mapping relevant to the situation at hand. Second, if conceptual metaphors are based on universal embodiment, the idea of universal meaning, or universal meaningfulness, preempts the possibility for contextual-cultural influence on metaphorical meaning making.

Zoltán Kövecses, Eötvös Loránd University

https://doi.org/10.1515/9783110688306-002

I believe we can get around these difficulties if we work with the new conception of conceptual metaphor I call "extended conceptual metaphor theory," or extended CMT, for short (Kövecses 2020). Two pillars of the new conception are that, first, it is a "multilevel" view of conceptual metaphor and that, second, it has a robust contextual component. What I do in the following sections is spell out some of the relevant details of this view and note, as we go along, how cognition and context, in general, and metaphor and cultural context, in particular, interact. I first describe the multilevel nature of conceptual metaphors, and then turn to its contextual component and how the multilevel and the contextual aspects are interlocked with each other in specific usage events.

2 The multilevel aspect of extended CMT

Following a long line of researchers (Rosch 1978; Lakoff 1987; Langacker 1987), in essence, this is what I suggest: Much of our knowledge about the world comes in large systems of concepts organized into hierarchies at various levels (superordinate level, basic level, subordinate level). The systems of concepts so connected are related by schematicity. This also applies to the "source domains" of conceptual metaphors that we can take to be large systems of concepts related to each other at several levels, or layers, of precision of specification (on the notion of "precision of specification"; Langacker 1987). The view entails that, given particular concepts, the various levels of schematicity form a continuous hierarchy; the various levels shade gradually into more or less schematic levels. My claim is that most (or, maybe, all) conceptual metaphors involve four different kinds of conceptual structure: image schema, domain, frame, and mental space. By "conceptual metaphor" I mean a subset of metaphors that are correlation-based, as opposed to resemblance-based ones (Grady 1999).

I propose that these conceptual structures can be regarded as occupying different levels in various schematicity hierarchies (Dancygier and Sweetser 2014). The four levels go from the most schematic to the least schematic, as represented in the diagram below:

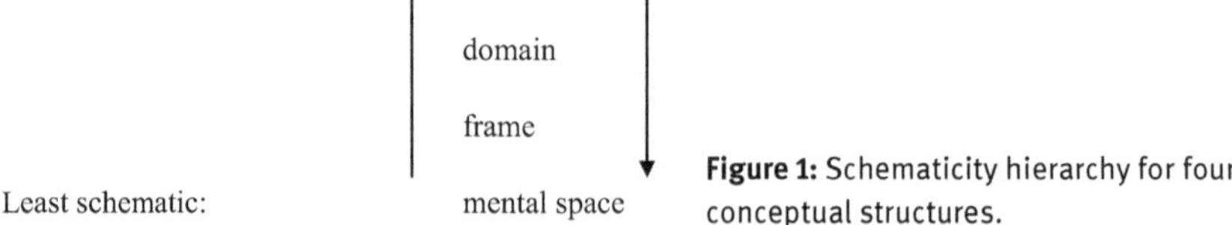

Figure 1: Schematicity hierarchy for four conceptual structures.

The upward arrow in the diagram indicates increasing schematicity, whereas the downward arrow indicates increasing specificity.

In brief, image schemas, domains, frames, and mental spaces are all used by conceptualizers / speakers for the purposes of lending organization and coherence to our experience. I take image schemas to be the most schematic and mental spaces the least schematic (i.e., the conceptually richest) cognitive structures that can have this organizing function. As we will see in the next section, they all can, and do, play a role in metaphorical conceptualization. In addition to these four levels, there is of course the level of communication, Level 5, where speakers and hearers use some symbols (linguistic or otherwise) that make manifest, or elaborate, the content of particular mental spaces. We can represent the relationship between the four levels in a schematicity hierarchy (SH) as follows:

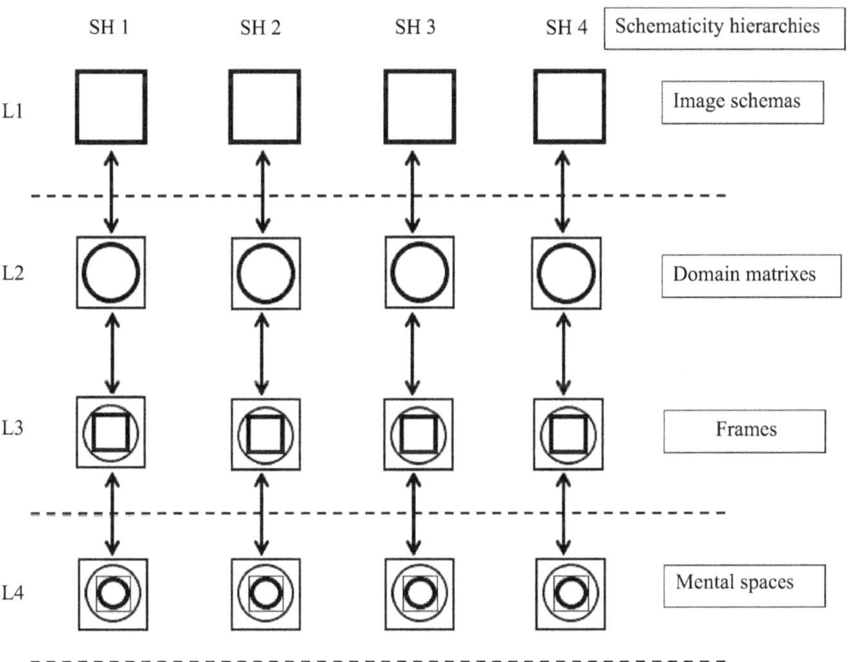

Figure 2: The schematicity hierarchy with three major distinctions between the levels.

The diagram represents the four levels of conceptual structures in four different schematic hierarchies (SH), one of which could be, for instance, the SH for BUILDING. The dotted line that separates IMAGE SCHEMAS and DOMAINS / FRAMES is intended to indicate that image schemas are analogue structures, whereas domains and frames are not. The bold dotted line between DOMAINS / FRAMES and MENTAL SPACES indicates that domains and frames are in long-term memory, whereas mental spaces are used in online processing in working memory, as noted by Fauconnier (1994). The dotted line between L4 and L5 separates the conceptual from the linguistic.

To take a simple example from Kövecses (2017), consider the following sentence: "John's life is without a foundation." It is clear that the sentence involves the LIFE IS A BUILDING conceptual metaphor, where we have the domain of BUILDING. But it also involves both more schematic and more specific metaphorical conceptual structures. It is based on the highly schematic image schema structure of OBJECT, on the one hand, and on the PHYSICAL SUPPORT frame (foundations support the walls) that structures the very specific mental space of JOHN'S HOUSE IS WITHOUT A FOUNDATION, on the other. Thus, the speaker of the sentence seems to simultaneously rely on four conceptual metaphors – instead of just one, which in the "standard" view would be at the domain level. These are:

Image schema level:
COMPLEX ABSTRACT SYSTEMS ARE COMPLEX PHYSICAL OBJECTS.
Domain level:
LIFE IS A BUILDING.
Frame level:
SOCIAL / PSYCHOLOGICAL STABILITY IS PHYSICAL SUPPORT: STABILITY IN ONE'S LIFE IS STRONG PHYSICAL SUPPORT IN THE STRUCTURE OF A HOUSE.
Mental space level:
THE LACK OF STABILITY IN JOHN'S LIFE IS THE ABSENCE OF A FOUNDATION UNDER JOHN'S HOUSE.
Utterance level:
"John's life is without a foundation."

Now let us see in somewhat more detail what characterizes these different conceptual structures (image schema, domain, frame, mental space), the conceptual metaphors that are based on them, and the issue of the degree to which the metaphors are embedded in context.

2.1 Image schema-level metaphors

Image schemas are essential conceptual structures that imbue experience with meaning (Johnson 1987; Lakoff 1987). Hampe (2005: 1–2) finds four features of image schemas especially characteristic. Image schemas are (1) directly meaningful preconceptual structures; (2) highly schematic gestalts; (3) continuous analogue patterns; and (4) internally structured, consisting of only a few parts. Because of their highly schematic nature, image schemas range over the entire conceptual system making a wide variety of concepts and experiences meaningful. For example, in the schematicity hierarchy above, the OBJECT image schema is present in the concept of BUILDING, that of PHYSICAL SUPPORT (OF THE WALLS), and that of LACK OF FOUNDATION IN JOHN'S HOUSE.

Many (if not all) conceptual metaphors involve image schemas. LIFE IS A JOURNEY is based on the SOURCE-PATH-GOAL schema, ANGER IS A HOT FLUID IN A CONTAINER on the TEMPERATURE (HOT/COLD) schema. Many primary metaphors involve image schemas, like the CONTAINER schema in STATES ARE CONTAINERS. As a result, the conceptual system, including abstract concepts, becomes embodied, that is, perception-based. This is precisely the property that enables them to make concepts, including metaphorical ones, meaningful.

On the whole, these and similar image schemas tend to be universal. The reason for this is that they are based on universal bodily experience (Johnson 1987; Kövecses 2005). Consequently, the conceptual metaphors that involve them also tend to be universal. If an image schema can be established in genetically unrelated languages, we can be reasonably certain that it is potentially universal or near-universal. What this means is that such image schemas are for the most part independent of context. They evolve in spite of the huge differences in the circumstances of human life. However, the issues of what particular use is made of them, which image schemas are particularly characteristic of a cultural context, and in what ways, may remain open to variation (Sinha and Lopez 2000).

2.2 Domain-level metaphors

According to Langacker (1987: 488), a "[d]omain [is] a coherent area of conceptualization relative to which semantic units may be characterized." Unlike image schemas, domains are not analogue, imagistic patterns of experience but propositional in nature in a highly schematic fashion. They are at a level immediately below image schemas. Image schemas make domains such as JOURNEY, BODY, and BUILDING (as concepts) meaningful. Domains have many more parts than image schemas, and are thus more information-rich.

Conceptual metaphors in CMT are usually described as relationships between *domains*. However, to think of conceptual metaphors as a set of mapping relations between two domains leads to a major problem: Source domains typically contain a lot more conceptual material than what is actually carried over to the target domain. If we think of all the concepts that are simultaneously presupposed by a given concept, that is, a domain matrix (Langacker 1987), it is clear that domains (in the sense of domain matrix) are highly inclusive knowledge structures. Not all concepts in a domain matrix are utilized in metaphorical conceptualization. The domain matrix for, say, BUILDING, represents our *entire* knowledge structure associated with this concept. But only select aspects of the domain matrix participate in the mappings between source and target concepts, and this is, as we will see, what leads us to the notion of frames in a schematicity hierarchy.

In CMT, we customarily distinguish concrete and abstract domains. Typical concrete domains that show up in metaphors include SPACE, PEOPLE, HUMAN BODY, ANIMAL, PLANT, TEMPERATURE, FOOD, NATURE, TOOL, BUILDING, TRAVEL, GAME, and so on. Typical abstract domains include TIME, MIND, EMOTION, MORALITY, MARRIAGE / RELATIONSHIP, SOCIETY, and others. Most of these domains (both concrete and abstract) may be universal (but not uniform), like PEOPLE, ANIMAL, FOOD, on the concrete side, and probably some conception of TIME, MIND, EMOTION, MORALITY, MARRIAGE, SOCIETY, on the abstract side. They have a much more complex structure than image schemas (e.g., they consist of many more elements). As a result, they are prone to a great deal more contextual-cultural shaping than image schemas (e.g., as regards the elements that make them up or how the elements are related to one another). They create the impression that, on the one hand, they tend to be (near-)universally spread across cultural contexts, but, on the other, they may be present in somewhat different shapes and sizes. This impression builds on observations that, for example, anthropologists, social psychologists, and linguists commonly make about the general presence of such conceptual metaphors as HUMANS ARE ANIMALS or TIME IS SPACE in languages of the world.

2.3 Frame-level metaphors

Frames (Fillmore 1982) are less schematic conceptual structures than domains. The difference between a domain and a frame can be captured by a difference in schematicity between the two: Frames elaborate particular aspects of a domain matrix; that is, particular higher level concepts within a domain. It can be suggested that frames involve more conceptually specific information than domains. For example, the BODY domain can be seen as being elaborated by several distinct frames, such as PERCEPTION, INGESTION, and EXERCISING (Sullivan 2013). These frames account for such metaphorical linguistic expressions as *I see what you mean* (PERCEPTION), *digest an idea* (INGESTION), and *a mental exercise* (EXERCISING) (Sullivan 2013). Together, such frame-level metaphors as UNDERSTANDING IS

SEEING make up what is known as the generic-level metaphor THE MIND IS THE BODY (Johnson 1987; Sweetser 1990). In general, the frames elaborating a domain consist of roles and relations between the roles, and the roles can be filled by particular values.

Those aspects of a domain that do participate in metaphorical mappings can be, and usually are, given in the form of *frames* – at a lower level of schematicity than that of domains. The frames elaborate the select aspects of domains. Thus, the source frames offer more specific information than domains, but they do not cover or exhaust all aspects of a source domain (matrix). We can illustrate this with our initial example LIFE IS A BUILDING. Out of the many aspects of the BUILDING domain, the one that gets elaborated by a frame is that of PHYSICAL SUPPORT (that captures the stability aspect of one's life). This has a variety of roles and relations, such as foundation, walls, support, and strength of structure. These are mapped onto a particular aspect of one's life.

Clearly, while domains can easily be near-universal (such as that of BUILDING), the frames that elaborate on aspects of a domain may not be. In the present example, SUPPORT works only for cultural contexts where buildings are built in a particular way: with foundations that support walls strongly enough for the whole structure to stand. In cultures where this is not the case, this frame-level metaphor would not work. Frames and frame-level metaphors, then, are not only less schematic than domains and domain-level metaphors, but they are also more sensitive to the influence of the cultural context in which they function.

2.4 Mental-space level metaphors

Mental spaces are the least schematic conceptual structures of the four discussed here (i.e., image schemas, domains, frames, and mental spaces). They are highly specific structures occurring in online processing in particular communicative situations. They contain the most specific information that derives from filling out generic roles with particular values (Fauconnier 1994).

Metaphors at the mental space level are elaborations of metaphors at higher levels (typically the level of frames). For instance, the mental space-level metaphor THE LACK OF STABILITY IN JOHN'S LIFE IS THE ABSENCE OF A FOUNDATION UNDER JOHN'S HOUSE derives from the frame-level metaphor SOCIAL / PSYCHOLOGICAL STABILITY (IN LIFE) IS PHYSICAL SUPPORT (OF A BUILDING). The mental space-level metaphor is more specific than the higher level ones (in a given schematicity hierarchy) because the roles and relations are filled by particular values (e.g., it is John's house, not a generic building). In addition, the mental space-level metaphor may make changes to the relevant frame; in this case, for example, it negates the existence of one of the elements of the frame. The processes of filling the roles and relations with specific values and making changes to the frame occur in a fully explicit context, that is, in natural discourse in a real communicative situation.

Given that mental spaces and mental space-level metaphors occur in real communicative situations, they are most susceptible to the influence of cultural context. Mental spaces borrow their structure from frames, but the generic structures from frames are further elaborated by specific information from context.

In summary, it makes sense to suggest that, given the schematicity hierarchy for conceptual metaphors, the influence of universal bodily experience is strongest in the case of image schema-level metaphors and weakest in the case of mental space-level metaphors. At the domain level, the influence is weaker than at the image schema level and with frames it is weaker than with domains. As regards the influence of cultural context, it is strongest in the case of mental space-level metaphors and weakest in the case of image schema-level metaphors. Frame-level metaphors display less contextual influence than mental space-level ones, but more than domain-level metaphors.

3 The contextual aspect of CMT

At this point the question arises: What do we mean by context? Among other things, a contextualist version of conceptual metaphor theory requires the characterization of the following issue: What are the most common contextual factors that play a role in the production and comprehension of metaphors?

3.1 Types of context and kinds of contextual factors

In my 2015 book *Where Metaphors Come From*, using examples from naturally occurring discourse, I presented a large amount of evidence that shows that the use of metaphors in discourse is influenced by a variety of contextual factors. These various contextual factors can be grouped into four large categories: situational context, discourse context, conceptual-cognitive context, and bodily context. Now let me briefly describe the various types of context and the more specific contextual factors that constitute them (for a detailed discussion and a large number of examples, see Kövecses 2015).

3.2 Situational context

The situational context comprises a variety of different contextual factors. Most commonly, this type of context can be thought of as including the physical environment, the social situation, and the cultural situation.

The *physical environment* can shape metaphorical meaning making. It includes the flora, the fauna, the landscape, the temperature, the weather, perceptual properties of the situation, and so on. For example, it is a common observation that American English metaphors relating to the physical environment are characteristically different from those of other English-speaking countries (Kövecses 2000). The small-scale, local environment, such as the visible events in or the perceptual properties of a situation, can also make its influence felt in shaping metaphors.

The *social situation* consists of social aspects of life that typically center around notions like gender, class, politeness, work, education, social organizations, social structure, and others. All of these can play a role in metaphorical conceptualization. For example, Kolodny (1975, 1984) shows that American men and women developed very different metaphorical images for what they conceived of as the "frontier" in America in the period before the 20th century. While the women commonly thought of the American frontier as a "garden to be cultivated," men conceptualized it as "virgin land to be taken" (for several additional examples on gender-related metaphors, see Kövecses 2005). Gender can of course also be thought of as part of culture, not only a social issue. In general, the distinctions in this section serve heuristic purposes only.

The *cultural situation* involves both the global context (the shared knowledge represented in the conceptual system) and the local context (the specific knowledge in a given communicative situation). An example of how the global context can affect metaphorical conceptualization is the way different concepts can produce differential metaphorical source domains in different cultures and languages, such as the metaphors for anger: ANGER IS HEAT (OF FLUID OR SOLID) in a large number of languages such as English and Hungarian, whereas in Chinese the metaphor can also involve GAS as its source domain – as a result of the influence of Yin and Yang theory (Yu 1998). The more immediate local context can play a similar role in the production of metaphors (Kövecses 2010, 2005, 2015).

3.3 Discourse context

The discourse context involves the surrounding discourse, knowledge about the main elements of discourse, the previous discourses on the same topic, and the dominant forms of discourse related to a particular subject matter.

The *surrounding discourse* is simply the linguistic context – often referred to as "cotext". Viewed from the perspective of the discourse's producer (the speaker), elements of the preceding discourse (either by the speaker / conceptualizer 1 or the hearer / conceptualizer 2) can influence the (unconscious) choice of metaphors, as is shown by an example taken from *The Times* by Kövecses (2010): "*which helped to tilt the balance – and Mr Hain – over the edge*". In this case, the contextually induced metaphor arises from the elliptical use of the verb *tilt* in the phrase *tilt Mr. Hain over the edge*. It is the presence of the word *tilt* in the immediate cotext that leads to the second use of the metaphor.

Conceptualizers often rely on their *knowledge concerning the main elements of a discourse*: the speaker, hearer, and the topic. For example, it is a common phenomenon in many newspaper articles that knowledge about the topic as a contextual factor leads to the creation of new metaphors (Kövecses 2010, 2015). An example of this involved David Beckham in an article in which the journalist remarked: "*Los Angeles Galaxy are sardines not sharks in the ocean of footy*" (Kövecses 2010). Here the relevant contextual knowledge includes that Beckham played for the Los Angeles Galaxy soccer team and that Los Angeles is located on the ocean with all kinds of fish in it.

The metaphors in one discourse can also derive from *previous discourses on the same topic*. This can take a variety of forms ranging from elaborating, extending, questioning, negating, reflecting on, ridiculing, to otherwise taking advantage of a metaphor previously introduced. For example, an MP in the British Parliament responded to the then Prime Minister Tony Blair who had said he did not have a reverse gear (i.e., he can only go forward) with the following statement: "but when you're on the edge of a cliff it is good to have a reverse gear" (example taken from Semino 2008). This was a humorous twist induced by the prior discourse on the PROGRESS IS MOTION FORWARD conceptual metaphor.

Certain forms of discourse can acquire *dominant status* in a community. When a dominant form of discourse related to a subject matter emerges, the metaphor used in or based on this discourse can become widespread both temporally (historically) and spatially (cross-culturally). For example, the discourse of Christianity commonly gives rise to the use of metaphors in the Christian world.

3.4 Conceptual-cognitive context

This type of context includes the metaphorical conceptual system at large, ideology, knowledge about past events, and the characteristic interests and concerns of a community or individual.

Concepts can stand in a metaphorical relationship with one another (e.g., LIFE IS A JOURNEY, ARGUMENT IS WAR) in long-term memory. Given such metaphorical relationships between concepts (such as between, say, ARGUMENT and WAR), their presence or absence in the *metaphorical conceptual system* may lead to the production and comprehension of particular metaphors. If the metaphorical connection between two domains does not exist in the user's conceptual system, he/she would not be able to come to use a particular metaphor. A metaphorical conceptual system can function as context in this sense. Given an intended metaphorical meaning (say, "supporting an argument"), we can search the conventional metaphorical conceptual system for the best choice of metaphor. This happens in cases where a conventionalized metaphorical meaning ("supporting an argument") is expressed via a conventional linguistic metaphor (such as *defend*), with a matching target element activating the relevant mapping in an existing conceptual metaphor (e.g., the meaning "supporting an argument" by means of the word *defend* in the ARGUMENT IS WAR conceptual metaphor as based on the mapping "defending one's physical position in war" corresponding to "supporting one's position in an argument"). The conventional metaphorical conceptual system is especially utilized this way when there are no other overriding contextual factors in the discourse situation that might influence the (unconscious) choice of a metaphor. In other words, it functions as the default case.

Ideology can also be a formative factor in how metaphors are used in discourse. One's ideological stance concerning major social and political issues may govern the choice of metaphors as work by, for instance, Goatly (2007) shows. A good example of how ideology might influence the choice of metaphors is George Lakoff's (1996) study of American politics, where, according to Lakoff, conservatives tend to use THE NATION IS A STRICT FATHER FAMILY metaphor, while liberals prefer THE NATION IS A NURTURANT PARENT FAMILY version of the generic metaphor THE NATION IS A FAMILY. For another example, we can mention the Marxist version of the SOCIETY IS A BUILDING metaphor with talk about "superstructure", and so on, or the Marxist idea of "class struggle". Goatly (2007) provides an important exploration into the metaphor-based ideology of capitalism.

Being aware of past events and states (i.e., items in short-term and long-term memory) shared by the conceptualizers may also lead to the emergence of specific metaphors in discourse. A special case of this involves a situation in which the speaker assumes that the hearer has a particular mental state. Such memories of events can belong to the life of a community or an individual. It has been often observed that the memory of historical events can lead to the production (and comprehension) of some metaphors (Deignan 2003; Kövecses 2005). Different historical contexts can create differential preferences for particular LIFE metaphors among Hungarians and Americans (Kövecses 2005). The particular events in a specific communicative situation preceding an act of metaphorical conceptualization may also produce similar effects.

People are commonly prompted to use particular metaphors (more precisely, metaphorical source domains) relative to their *interests and concerns* about the world (Kövecses 2005). Entire groups and individuals can be said to have certain characteristic interests or concerns that may affect the way they make meaning metaphorically. Since Americans are commonly regarded as dynamically-oriented, rather than passive, in their attitude to life, and, relatedly, are sports-loving in general, it is not surprising that they use a large number of sports metaphors. Similarly, if a person has some kind of professional interest, that person is likely to draw metaphors from his or her sphere of interest (for specific examples, see Kövecses 2005). In other words, the kinds of activities we engage in routinely affect the metaphors (the source domains) we use (Gelfand and McCusker 2001).

3.5 Bodily context

A particular state of the body can produce particular metaphorical conceptualizations in specific cases, such as a poet's or writer's illness. For example, I showed how Dickinson's choice of metaphors may have been influenced by her optical illness (Kövecses 2010, 2015). Such cases illustrate, more broadly, that people's bodily specificities influence which metaphors they tend to use. For instance, there is experimental evidence (Casasanto 2009) that left-handers prefer to use the MORAL IS LEFT, as opposed to the MORAL IS RIGHT, conceptual metaphor. Such metaphors contrast with the metaphors that evolve on the basis of universal properties of the human body (i.e., the correlation-based primary metaphors).

Given this kind of evidence and the many metaphorical examples that are based on local and temporary specificities of the human body (i.e., not on universal embodiment), one might take the body as a further form of the context. In this view, the body – especially those aspects of it that are activated in the ongoing communicative situation – can influence the choice of metaphors in natural discourse (Kövecses 2015a). The body is *not only* responsible for the production of hundreds of conceptual metaphors through the many correlations between subjective and sensorimotor experience (Grady 1997a, b; Lakoff and Johnson 1999), but it can also prime the use of particular metaphors in more immediate, local contexts, as further experimental evidence by, e.g, Gibbs (2006), Gibbs and Colston (2012), Boroditsky (2001) as well as Boroditsky and Ramscar (2002) indicates. In other words, the body can lead to the production of metaphors in discourse in the same way as the other contextual factors previously mentioned can. Given this, we can think of the body as an additional context type.

3.6 Local and global context

Within the varied set of contextual factors that were briefly introduced above, two general types of context can be distinguished: local and global. The *local context* involves the specific knowledge conceptualizers have about some aspect of the immediate communicative situation. Thus, the local context implies specific knowledge that attaches to the conceptualizers in a specific communicative situation. It corresponds, at least roughly, to Clark's (1996) "personal common ground". By contrast, the *global context* consists of the conceptualizers' general knowledge concerning their community's environment (physical, social, cultural). It involves knowledge shared by an entire community of conceptualizers. Thus, it is close to Clark's (1996) "communal common ground". The distinction between local and global context is mostly of theoretical nature. In many actual communicative situations, there is no sharp dividing line between the two general types of context.

4 The relationship between culture and context

From a cognitive anthropological perspective, the conceptual system can be equated with what we mean by *culture*. In perhaps the best-known formulation of this idea, Clifford Geertz wrote: "Man is an animal suspended in webs of significance he himself has spun. I take culture to be those webs, and the analysis of it to be therefore not an experimental science in search of law but an interpretative one in search of meaning" (Geertz 1973: 5). This view of culture-as-conceptual system also resonates in cognitive linguistics that adopts an encyclopedic view of meaning, in which our conceptualization of the world at large is encapsulated in our conceptual system, which, in turn, is shaped by the context at large.

I suggest that this way of thinking about the conceptual system enables us to view culture, in one sense, as (one kind of) context for metaphorical conceptualization. As I remarked earlier, the culture / conceptual-system-as-context may be the default case in the production of metaphors. The culture-as-conceptual system is a dynamic and constantly evolving system characterizing a group of people (a language community) who live in a social, historical, and physical environment making sense of their experiences in a more or less unified manner.[1] We can think

1 However, the metaphorical system of an individual may also be influenced by a person's unique, individual history (see, e.g., Kövecses 2005: 182–184).

of the conceptual system conceived of this way as one form of culture, which can function as context of a particular kind.

Culture can also be thought of as *situational context*. In this case, we can think of culture as defined by concepts, ideas, values, principles, behaviors, and things that are specific to a particular (language) community. These unique products of culture can also function as context for metaphorical conceptualization. The cultural factors that affect metaphorical conceptualization include the dominant values and characteristics of members of a group, the key ideas or concepts that govern their lives, the various subgroups/ subcultures that make up the group, the various products of culture such as artistic works, physical artifacts, TV shows and films, and a large number of other things. All of these cultural aspects of the setting can supply members of the group with a variety of metaphorical source domains (Kövecses 2005). In other words, I distinguish the general conceptual system as context from the set of specific ideas, values, practices, artifacts, etc. that characterize a linguistic community, and are thus fairly active and salient in their members' minds in particular cases of metaphorical conceptualization. I view this as the cultural aspect of the general situational context.

Given the classification of context types above, culture would be involved in two types of context: the situational and the conceptual-cognitive context. Aren't the other two types, discourse and bodily context, cultural then? Since we use our conceptual system to conceptualize everything – including, not only, the situational context, the various forms of conceptual-cognitive context, such as memory and concerns, but also the discourse context and the bodily context –, culture (as conceptual system) pervades all conceptualization. This is because the concepts (frames) constituting the conceptual system come with particular perspectives, elements of frames, emotions, evaluations, associations, etc. that are characteristic of communities of speakers. Thus, the concepts (frames) impose particular ways of seeing the world (i.e., the four, or more, types of context). In other words, when I speak about the discourse context or the bodily context, I do not mean that these types of context are culture-free. That is to say, one can think of culture most broadly as the conceptual system, which is inherent in and pervades anything we care to conceptualize. Nonetheless, as we know, there are less encompassing conceptions of culture, such as what I referred to as the situational context. In my view, the situational context, like the other types of context, consists of a global (less immediate) and a local (more immediate) aspect, as described above (for more discussion of the distinction, see Kövecses, 2015), and they both may fall under the influence of the general conceptual system, including its metaphorical part.

5 Conclusions

The idea that conceptual metaphors exist not on a single level of schematicity (such as that of domain) but consist of distinct but hierarchically related metaphors on four levels changes many things about the way we think about metaphor (Kövecses 2020). One of these issues, the one that I dealt with here, is the question of the nature of the interface between metaphorical cognition and (cultural) context. If we view conceptual metaphors as conceptual structures on a single level, it is next to impossible to capture the full complexity of the relationship; a metaphor will only be either a matter of embodied cognition or a matter of context-based (cultural) conceptualization. In the new view, a conceptual metaphor exists on four levels of schematicity and the constituent metaphors display conceptual structures with increasing and decreasing degrees of embodied cognition and contextual influence. A conceptual metaphor in natural usage is always a composite of both, the levels reflecting different degrees of them.

The other pillar of the new view is context. On the basis of a large amount of empirical evidence, I found that context affects metaphor use in such a way that contextual factors from the four context types (situational, discourse, bodily, and conceptual-cognitive) prime conceptualizers to choose conceptual and linguistic metaphors (Kövecses, 2015).

The bridge that connects context with higher-level metaphors (i.e., image schema-, domain-, and frame-level metaphors) in long-term memory is provided by mental space-level metaphors in working memory. It is the level of mental spaces that "absorbs" information from context and at the same time unites it with (schematically) higher-level metaphor structures. This way, it becomes possible to arrive at (at least) a tentative account of the interface between embodied metaphor cognition and (cultural) context.

References

Boroditsky, Lera & Michael Ramscar. 2002. The roles of body and mind in abstract thought. *Psychological Science* 13 (2). 185–189.

Boroditsky, Lera. 2001. Does language shape thought? Mandarin and English speakers' conception of time. *Cognitive Psychology* 43. 1–22.

Casasanto, Daniel. 2009. Embodiment of abstract concepts: Good and bad in right and left handers. *Journal of Experimental Psychology: General* 138 (3). 351–367.

Clark, Herbert. 1996. *Using language*. Cambridge: Cambridge University Press.

Dancygier, Barbara & Eve Sweetser. 2014. *Figurative language*. Cambridge: Cambridge University Press.

Deignan, Alice. 2003. Metaphorical expressions and culture: An indirect link. *Metaphor and Symbol* 18 (4). 255–271.
Fauconnier, Gilles. 1994. *Mental spaces*. New York: Cambridge University Press.
Fillmore, Charles. 1982. Frame semantics. *Linguistics in the morning calm*, ed. by The Linguistic Society of Korea, 111–137. Hanshin, Seoul.
Geertz, Clifford. 1973. *The interpretation of cultures*. New York: Basic Books.
Gelfand, Michele & Christopher McCusker. 2001. Culture, metaphor and negotiation. In Martin Gannon & Karen Newman (eds.), *Handbook of cross-cultural management*, 292–314. New York: Blackwell Publishers.
Gibbs, Raymond W. 2006. *Embodiment and cognitive science*. Cambridge & New York: Cambridge University Press.
Gibbs, Raymond W. & Herbert Colston. 2012. *Interpreting figurative meaning*. New York: Cambridge University Press.
Goatly, Andrew. 2007. *Washing the brain. Metaphor and hidden ideology*. Amsterdam: John Benjamins.
Grady, Joseph. 1997a. THEORIES ARE BUILDING revisited. *Cognitive Linguistics* 8. 267–290.
Grady, Joseph. 1997b. *Foundations of meaning: Primary metaphors and primary scenes*, Ph.D. Thesis, Department of Linguistics, University of California at Berkeley.
Grady, Joseph E. 1999. A typology of motivation for conceptual metaphor. In Raymond W. Gibbs & Gerard J. Steen (eds.), *Metaphor in cognitive linguistics*, 79–100. Amsterdam: John Benjamins.
Hampe, Beate. 2005. Image schemas in cognitive linguistics: Introduction. In Beate Hampe & Joseph Grady (eds.), *From perception to meaning. Image schemas in cognitive linguistics*, 1–12. Berlin: Mouton de Gruyter.
Johnson, Mark. 1987. *The body in the mind*. Chicago: The University of Chicago Press.
Kolodny, Annette. 1975. *The lay of the land: Metaphor as experience and history in American life and letters*. Chapel Hill: The University of North Carolina Press.
Kolodny, Annette. 1984. *The land before her: Fantasy and experience of the American frontiers, 1630–1860*. Chapel Hill: The University of North Carolina Press.
Kövecses, Zoltán. 2000. *American English. An introduction*. Peterborough, Canada: Broadview Press.
Kövecses, Zoltán. 2005. *Metaphor in culture. Universality and variation*. Cambridge & New York: Cambridge University Press.
Kövecses, Zoltán. 2010. A new look at metaphorical creativity in cognitive linguistics. *Cognitive Linguistics* 21 (4). 663–697.
Kövecses, Zoltán. 2015. *Where metaphors come from. Reconsidering context in metaphor*. Oxford & New York: Oxford University Press.
Kövecses, Zoltán. 2017. Levels of metaphor. *Cognitive Linguistics* 28 (2). 321–347.
Kövecses, Zoltán. 2020. *Extended conceptual metaphor theory*. Cambridge: Cambridge University Press.
Lakoff, George. 1987. *Women, fire, and dangerous things*. Chicago: The University of Chicago Press.
Lakoff, George. 1996. *Moral politics. How liberals and conservatives think*. Chicago: The University of Chicago Press.
Lakoff, George & Mark Johnson. 1980. *Metaphors we live by*. Chicago: The University of Chicago Press.
Lakoff, George & Mark Johnson. 1999. *Philosophy in the flesh*. New York: Basic Books.

Langacker, Ronald. 1987. *Foundations of cognitive grammar*. Stanford: Stanford University Press.
Rosch, Eleanor. 1978. Principles of categorization. In Eleanor Rosch and Barbara B. Lloyd, (eds.), *Cognition and Categorization*, 27–48. Hillsdale, NJ: Lawrence Erlbaum.
Semino, Elena. 2008. *Metaphor in discourse*. Cambridge: Cambridge University Press.
Sinha, Chris & Kristine Jensen de Lopez. 2000. Language, culture and the embodiment of spatial cognition. *Cognitive Linguistics* 11. 17–41.
Sweetser, Eve. 1990. *From etymology to pragmatics: Metaphorical and cultural aspects of semantic structure.* Cambridge: Cambridge University Press.
Yu, Ning. 1998. *The contemporary theory of metaphor: A perspective from Chinese.* Amsterdam: John Benjamins.

Frank Polzenhagen

Critical reflections on the use of corpora for cross-varietal metaphor research

Abstract: The present chapter critically reflects on the use of corpora for cross-varietal metaphor research. My immediate example is the conceptualization of COMMUNITY/NATION in terms of a FAMILY and, more specifically, its linguistic manifestations in American and West-African English, traceable in corpora of these varieties. However, my paper will be mainly concerned with methodological questions. In particular, issues of representativeness, manageability, comparability, and reliability of the available corpora will be foregrounded. I.e., rather than aiming at a detailed analysis of the COMMUNITY/NATION AS A FAMILY metaphor in itself, I will use this particular conceptualization primarily as a test case in order to point to some advantages and limits of various types of corpora.

Keywords: metaphor, corpora, American English, West-African English, conceptualization of community/nation

1 Introduction

For one of his landmark publications, Sinclair (2004) opted for the programmatic title *Trust the Text*, making a case for corpus-linguistic approaches. "Trust" in real life arises from "knowing" someone and from the "reliability" of this person. Hence, if Sinclair's metaphor is taken seriously, "to trust the text" implies (i) that the researcher undertakes a close analysis of the tokens obtained from corpora and (ii) that the reliability of the sources is checked and guaranteed. These aspects of trustworthiness are often difficult to meet with current XXL-sized corpora. Searches in, e.g., the BNC (British English, henceforth BrE) or COCA (American English, henceforth AmE) often yield a number of tokens that cannot be inspected individually anymore. In order to account for (i), we generally resort to sampling procedures. However, for most of the World Englishes no corpus equivalent in size to BNC/COCA is available, which makes comparison problematic. Corpora such as GloWbE add the concern with reliability. Culled from the Internet, its trustworthiness is rather limited. Websites come and go, the domain label of a site is no safe indicator of the country of origin of the contents, the date of online appearance

Frank Polzenhagen, University of Koblenz-Landau, Germany

https://doi.org/10.1515/9783110688306-003

is not conclusive as to the period of time the text was produced in, material from websites is copy-pasted to others in prolific number, etc. Those who use this corpus with due caution are well aware of these problems. In particular, the country labels assigned to the source texts are not reliable, which is highly detrimental to sound WE research. In order to obtain authentic and manageable data-sets from GloWbE, sampling needs to be followed by a careful check of each token as to its correct association with a particular variety. In sum, the researcher ends up in a time-consuming chain (if not circle) of sampling, checking, re-sampling and normalizing, without reaching a satisfying level of confidence. Much pain with limited gain.

In this light, much can be said in favor of another, lesser known, stance taken by Sinclair, i.e. that corpus "comparison uncovers differences almost regardless of size" (Sinclair 2001: xii). The 1-million-word corpora of the BROWN-family in particular have important advantages for WE research. They are compiled according to roughly the same principles, have about the same size, yield a manageable number of tokens, represent several text types (or genres), and make sure that the material stems from a specific time frame and a specific variety. A further option researchers have is to compile small-size corpora tailored for the specific needs of an investigation.

In the present paper, I wish to make a case for an approach that backs the decision in favor of a specific corpus as the basis of a study with a cross-check of the data in corpora of different types. I will mainly take the conceptualization THE NATION IS A FAMILY and its linguistic manifestations in AmE and West-African English (WAfrE) as an illustration. It was analyzed for the West-African setting by Wolf and Polzenhagen (e.g., 2009) and postulated by Lakoff (e.g., 2002 [1996]) to underlie dominant models of politics in the US. I will give substance to the above methodological considerations using data from COCA, GloWbE, BROWN-family corpora and a small corpus compiled for my specific purpose. My paper has the following structure: In section 2, I will give a brief introduction to the immediate subject of the paper, i.e. conceptualizations of the STATE/NATION. Section 3 starts with some general considerations on how metaphors can be identified and studied using corpus-linguistic means. I will then address three issues related to the use of large corpora: Corpus size and manageability (section 3.2), representativeness (section 3.3), and reliability (section 3.4). Section 4 presents data from a small-scale corpus of inaugural addresses delivered by US American and Nigerian presidents, respectively. Section 5 traces one specific fixed expression across the corpora. Some tentative conclusions are given in section 6.

A note may be in order on the corpora used in the present study. My data for AmE come from two standard corpora: FROWN and COCA. FROWN is a 1-million-word corpus from the so-called BROWN family of corpora, i.e. those modeled on the BROWN corpus of AmE compiled at Brown University (Rhode Island) in the 1960s. BROWN comprises 500 samples from texts from the year 1961. FROWN (compiled at the University of Freiburg) is a remake of this corpus for the early 1990s. COCA (Corpus of Contemporary American English) is a monitor corpus that has been updated on a yearly basis since 1990, and it has reached a size of more than 1 billion words. It also contains spoken texts; this component, however, was not considered for the present study, because other corpora used here do not contain spoken material. Thus, only the categories fiction, newspaper, magazine, and academic are considered, which yields a corpus of ca. 486.6 Mio words. The version of COCA I used was the one available on *www.english-corpora.org/coca/* in February 2020.[1] This website also provides a sample of COCA texts (COCA_sample, 1.7 Mio words),[2] which I used as an additional source.

My data for West African English come from three corpora: ICE-Nigeria (ICE-NIG), CEC and the Nigerian component of GloWbE (GloWbE_NIG). In terms of their design, ICE-Nigeria (representing Nigerian English, NigE) and CEC (representing Cameroonian English) belong to the extended family of BROWN corpora. ICE-Nigeria was compiled as part of the ICE project (International Corpus of English). It also contains spoken data; however, for the present study, only the written component was considered (ca. 400,000 words). The CEC (Corpus of English in Cameroon) was originally compiled as part of the ICE project by a team of Cameroonians (see Tiomajou 1995). Work on it stopped before completion, and the version used here is an unfinished one from this period and was also the basis for the analyses in Polzenhagen (2007) and Wolf and Polzenhagen (2009). It represents 11 genres and has ca. 900,000 words. Work on the corpus continued, and a revised version, under the label CCE, is available (Nkemleke 2008). GloWbE (Global Web-based English) contains 20 country-specific sub-corpora, the Nigerian component having more than 42 Mio words. All of the texts in GloWbE are taken from the web.

The composition of the small-scale corpus of inaugural addresses compiled for the present study is explained in section 4.

2 The conceptualization THE NATION AS A FAMILY

In the Western cultural context, there is a set of well-established metaphorizations of the STATE/NATION with a long history in philosophical, political, and public discourse. Prominent examples include the conceptualizations of the STATE/NATION as a SHIP (going back to Plato), as a MACHINE (e.g., within the so-called

1 The most recent version of COCA (March 2020) also contains texts from web-sources and movies.

2 I obtained the sample used in the present study on 23 November 2018, i.e. from an earlier version of COCA.

"machine paradigm" in the 17th and 18th century and used in many influential subsequent socio-political theories, e.g., by Max Weber), as a BUILDING (e.g., in the representation of feudal hierarchy), as an ORGANISM/PERSON (e.g., prototypically Hobbes' Leviathan), and, finally, as a FAMILY. There are several studies analyzing these metaphors from a cognitive-linguistic vantage point and tracing their development over time. The NATION AS AN ORGANISM/PERSON metaphor, for instances, has been thoroughly investigated by Andreas Musolff (e.g., 2010), THE STATE AS A MACHINE is the scope of Stollberg-Rilinger (1986). FAMILY metaphors in politics are studied in Lakoff (2002 [1996], 2006a, 2006b, 2008).

In addition to these metaphors with a general prominence across the Western context, we find metaphorizations that are more or less specific to particular countries or settings. Well-known examples are those proposed to characterize the US American nation, i.e. the traditional MELTING POT metaphor (e.g., John de Crevecoeur 1782 and Frederick Jackson Turner 1983 [1893]) and its numerous alternatives including SALAD BOWL, MOSAIC, PIZZA, ORCHESTRA. Since these metaphors have been hotly debated in American culture, there is a rich body of literature dealing with them. Classics include Kallen (1915) and Glazer and Moynihan (1963).

Furthermore, discourse brings forth a wealth of new metaphors, often with a very local application and short-lived, sometimes, however, with a broader presence. A recent cognitive-linguistic study of such metaphors is Vogelbacher (2019), in the specific context of the discourse on the Brexit.

The various metaphorizations differ quite significantly in the specific way they frame their target, i.e. the NATION/STATE. From a cognitive-linguistic vantage point, these differences can be spelled out in terms of the specific image-schematic structures and figure-ground constellations underlying the metaphors. Some of them are based on a hierarchical conception, along the vertical axis (UP/DOWN), e.g., the BUILDING metaphor, encoding social stratification. A prototypical example is the well-known representation of feudal society as a PYRAMID. Others are explicitly non-hierarchical, e.g., the NEIGHBORHOOD metaphor representing coexisting nations. Some highlight human agency, which is in turn hidden by others, e.g., the MACHINE metaphor. The FAMILY metaphor, specifically, is based on a hierarchical conception, views the NATION as a WHOLE consisting of PARTS with different functions, and brings into play primordial ties and mutual obligations as well as an emotional component.

However, these general metaphors can be spelled out quite differently, depending on the cultural model underlying their basic notions. This point is highlighted in Lakoff's (e.g., 2002 [1996]) analysis of FAMILY metaphors in US American politics. Lakoff distinguishes between a STRICT-FATHER and a NURTURANT-PARENT model of FAMILY, with distinct sets of priorities and moral values, which are mapped onto the concept of the NATION yielding, according to Lakoff, a conservative conception of society (STRICT-FATHER model) and progressive one (NURTURANT-PARENT model), respectively. I will return to Lakoff's account in section 4, from a cross-cultural perspective.

3 Issues of corpus-based metaphor research

3.1 Metaphor identification in corpora

Metaphor identification in corpora is still very much a manual procedure involving a close inspection of individual tokens. However, standard corpus-linguistic search options are a useful means of detecting at least a set of *potential* tokens of specific metaphors. Stefanowitsch's MPA (= Metaphorical Pattern Analysis; e.g., 2004, 2006), for instance, proposes to use a set of lexemes from the target domain as search items in order to identify potential metaphoric tokens. However, as the target domains are not always made explicit, a search along these lines will only produce a limited sub-set of potential tokens. In the sequence *he insulted her and she fumed*, for instance, there is no lexeme indicating ANGER other than *fume*, i.e., a source-domain item. In turn, a search restricted to potential source-domain items is limited, inter alia, in that it does not detect alternative metaphorizations of the target.

Metaphor studies using corpora thus often combine a source-domain and a target-domain approach. Then, their starting point is two lists of lexemes representing these domains. Ideally, these lists are encompassing (the more items they include, the better the coverage) and comprise the various word forms as well as relevant items from different word classes. Since the present paper is concerned primarily with methodological issues, I will, however, only use a minimal set of nominal items representing the source and target domains of the NATION AS A FAMILY metaphor under analysis. They are given in Table 1:

Table 1: Selected search items (source and target domain) for THE NATION IS A FAMILY.

Potential source domain items	*family*	Potential target domain items	*citizen*
	father		*nation*
	mother		*country*
	parent		*government*
	sister		*president*
	brother		*state*
	son		
	daughter		

It is evident that these are only *potential* source-domain or target-domain items for the metaphor pattern under analysis. This potentiality applies mainly to source-domain items: the majority of tokens produced by a search is likely to be literal, others might express metaphorizations of target domains other than the one investigated. However, potentiality may also apply to target domain items: for instance, *citizen* and *president* are also brand names, and such tokens do not refer to the domains under analysis. Given this potentiality, the raw list obtained from a corpus search has to be checked manually for the relevant metaphoric tokens. Several methods have been proposed for this purpose, the best-known being MIP (= Metaphor Identification Procedure) by the Pragglejaz Group (2007) and its elaboration MIPVU (proposed by a team from VU Amsterdam; e.g., Steen 2010). These methods have been used in many studies and thus can be said to serve as a standard of metaphor identification that ensures comparability in metaphor research.

3.2 Corpus size and manageability

An obvious argument in favor of large corpora is that they yield more tokens for analysis than small ones, i.e., they provide a broader empirical basis. This is less trivial than it may appear. While obtaining more tokens is desirable for many studies, in particular for items or structures with a relatively low frequency, it may well be a disadvantage for studies of high-frequency and moderate-frequency phenomena. The enormous number of tokens produced by XXL-size corpora in these cases easily exceeds what is manageable for a context-sensitive analysis. Table 2 shows the frequency data in the written component of COCA for the minimal list of lexical items proposed in section 3.1 to represent the source and target domains of NATION/STATE AS A FAMILY.[3] As stated in the introduction, the search was restricted to the written component of COCA in order to stay within the same medium as in later searches of other corpora, since the latter do not always contain sections with spoken language. Table 2 also presents the data for FROWN:

3 The search items in the list were not POS-tagged, i.e., the output does not only include sg. and pl. of the nominal forms but also some (though not all) forms of the zero-derived verbs, if applicable (e.g., *to father*, *to mother*, which are also relevant in the given context). A comprehensive search would need to consider further morphological forms of the verbs (e.g., participles) and other items obtained through word-formation processes, e.g., adjectives (*fatherly*, *motherly*, etc.). They were not included here since the search only serves the purpose of illustrating some issues rather than providing a comprehensive analysis. For the same reason, the data for the item *state* are not included (also see below).

Table 2: Absolute frequency of selected search items (source and target domain) for THE NATION IS A FAMILY in COCA_written (ca. 486.6 Mio words) and FROWN (1 Mio words).

	Type	Tokens COCA	Tokens FROWN
Potential source domain items	*family*	283,201	573
	father	177,119	448
	mother	208,243	479
	parent	141,760	225
	sister	60,473	143
	brother	76,423	195
	son	97,318	217
	daughter	69,715	153
Potential target domain items	*citizen*	42,558	108
	nation	99,720	331
	country	219,927	580
	government	202,787	527
	president	187,596	553
	total	**1,866,840**	**4,532**

Identifying the relevant metaphoric uses and classifying them requires a close inspection of each token and its context. The need for manual filtering is inarguably obvious: The vast majority of the tokens listed as "potential source domain items" in Table 1 are literal, others exemplify metaphoric uses other than those brought forth by NATION/STATE AS A FAMILY. For instance, among the 419 tokens of singular *father* in FROWN, about 60 are metaphoric. The vast majority of them, however, are used against the background of a religious model, *father* referring to God or a priest. There are 4 tokens that use *father* metaphorically for the originator of a particular notion or movement (1a-d):

(1) a. Tony Pastor, often called the *father* of American vaudeville
b. Lynden Pindling, the founding *father* of Bahamian independence
c. Wolfgang Pauli, '*father*' of the neutrino
d. Kant is, in a sense, Kierkegaard's intellectual '*father*'.
(FROWN)

Only 4 tokens of sg. *father* are instantiations of the conceptualization of the STATE/NATION as a FAMILY. (2) and (3) stem from the same source text and contain 3 of them; (4) refers to Native-American usage.

(2) Quayle makes much of the theme of the absent *father*; America under the Bush Administration looks like a house with an absent *father.* A man has no right to abandon the family for years and then show up one day and go upstairs and start spanking the kids. (FROWN)

(3) Children need love and discipline. They need mothers and fathers. A welfare check is not a husband. The state is not a *father.* (FROWN)

(4) Native Americans were often referred to as children protected by the 'Great White *Father*' in Washington. (FROWN)

The item *state* (excluded in Table 2) exemplifies yet another recurrent issue that calls for the individual inspection of the tokens. Verbal *to state*, which is not relevant in the present context, can be filtered out through a POS-tagged search restricted to nominal tokens. However, polysemy or homonymy require manual filtering. The following screenshot (Figure 1) illustrates this point for the case of the senses of *state*:

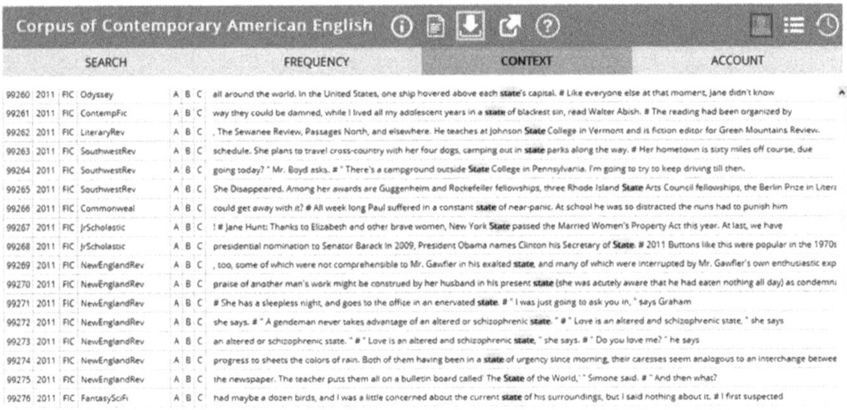

Figure 1: Screenshot of hits of nominal *state* in the COCA.

The need for a close inspection of all individual tokens gets us to the following hypothetical scenario for the COCA data in Table 2: Suppose that a manual filtering of the 1,866,840 tokens produced by the search can be performed at a rate of 10 per minute, such a (still very rough) preparation of the data set would take the devoted scholar about 390 working days, 8 hours each. This amounts to about 1.5 years of doing just that and is far beyond of what is reasonable. This is certainly not a problem restricted to metaphor research. The same type of context-sensitive manual inspection is required, for instance, in studies of morpho-syntactic structures.

Generally, this problem is circumvented by sampling procedures that cut the number of tokens down to a manageable size. For large corpora such as COCA and BNC, standard samples exist that can be used instead of the full data set (the so-called BNC-baby with 4 Mio words and a 1.7-Mio-word sample of COCA, also used in the present study). Sampling, however, somehow caricatures the original argument that large corpora yield a broader empirical basis. More importantly, sampling inevitably introduces a certain bias, potentially affecting the original representativeness of the data set, and it needs sophisticated techniques to keep this effect to a minimum.

Standard 1-million-word corpora of the BROWN family often provide an alternative to large corpora or samples based on them. The number of tokens obtained in FROWN for the exemplary list of source and target domain items, i.e., 4,532 (see Table 2), for instance, is both reasonably large and manageable for context-sensitive manual filtering. If the number of relevant tokens turns out to be too small, the search can be easily extended to bigger corpora. Furthermore, BROWN-type corpora have the advantage that they are mutually comparable, being modeled on roughly the same design principles. Even more importantly, they are carefully curated, a crucial issue highlighted in section 3.4.

3.3 Corpus size and representativeness

The second key argument made in favor of large corpora is their safer level of representativeness. As with corpus size, and closely related to it, this is not trivial. Certainly, low-frequency phenomena cannot be appropriately assessed and studied in small corpora; for them to reveal their profile, it needs a broad empirical basis. High-frequency and moderate-frequency phenomena, however, can often be traced in a reliable way with smaller corpora. Table 3 provides the frequency data for the minimal list of lexical items proposed earlier in three corpora: COCA (written component: 486.6 Mio words), the COCA_sample (1.7 Mio words), and FROWN (1 Mio words). The left columns show the absolute numbers, the right columns give the normalized frequency per 1 Mio words. As Table 3 shows, the aggregated normalized frequencies of the potential source items are consistent across these corpora. FROWN is richer with respect to the potential target domain items.

In the realm under investigation, the standard 1-million-word corpora also prove reliable and largely consistent with regard to variety-specific frequency patterns. Table 4 gives the normalized frequencies for the set of potential target domain items in corpora of AmE and WAfrE. They are significantly more frequent

Table 3: Frequency of selected search items (source and target domain) for THE NATION IS A FAMILY in COCA (written), COCA_sample and FROWN compared.

		absolute frequency			**normalized frequency (per 1 mw, rounded figures)**		
		COCA	**COCA sample**	**FROWN**	**COCA**	**COCA sample**	**FROWN**
Potential source domain items	*family*	283,201	932	573	582	548	573
	father	177,119	737	448	364	434	448
	mother	208,243	981	479	428	577	479
	parent	141,760	385	225	291	226	225
	sister	60,473	210	143	124	124	143
	brother	76,423	268	195	157	158	195
	son	97,318	339	217	200	199	217
	daughter	69,715	261	153	143	154	153
				total	**2,290**	**2,420**	**2,433**
Potential target domain items	*citizen*	42,558	124	108	87	73	108
	nation	99,720	350	331	205	206	331
	country	219,927	840	580	452	494	580
	government	202,787	670	527	417	394	527
	president	187,596	846	553	386	498	553
				total	**1,547**	**1,665**	**2,099**

in both corpora of WAfrE, ICE-Nigeria (written component, ca. 400,000 words), and CEC (ca. 900,000 words) for Cameroonian English.

Table 4: Normalized frequency of selected potential target domain items for THE NATION IS A FAMILY in AmE (COCA_written, FROWN) and WAfrE (ICE-NIG_written, and CEC) compared.

	American English		**West-African English**	
	COCA (per 1 mw)	**FROWN (per 1 mw)**	**ICE-NIG written (per 1 mw)**	**CEC (per 1 mw)**
citizen	87	108	135	263
nation	205	331	610	728
country	452	580	1,125	1,424
government	417	527	2,193	1,746
president	386	553	520	883
total	**1,547**	**2,099**	**4,583**	**5,044**

3.4 Corpus size and reliability

Standard corpora of the BROWN/ICE-family are carefully curated. In particular, the researcher can rely on the correct association of the source texts with the respective variety of English and a specific time frame. These standards of reliability, however, cannot be assumed to be met by large-size corpora culled from the internet, most notably GloWbE. Since more and more studies in WE use this corpus, and do so often quite uncritically, the question of its reliability is a growing and crucial concern.

GloWbE contains 20 country-specific sub-corpora, with a total of 1.9 billion words. The algorithms used in its compilation are outlined in Davies and Fuchs (2015a, b), in a special issue of *English World-Wide* devoted to the GloWbE shortly after its release. Reservations were expressed very early. Gerald Nelson, for instance, in the same special issue, raises, along with other problems, the issue of the correct association of a web-text with a particular variety of English. He concludes that "it may be that the sheer size of GloWbE will somehow statistically 'even out' these problems, [. . .]. I do hope that this will be the case, but in the meantime there are still many reasons to recommend the 'carefully-curated' approach to corpus building" (Nelson 2015: 39). Those who have worked with this corpus with due caution will agree with Nelson's skepticism. Davies and Fuchs (2015b: 46) acknowledge this problem in their response to Nelson's criticism:

> Of course, we never make the claim that the speakers are actually speakers of the dialect in question (it would be impossible to determine this for all 1.8 million web pages), but rather that the web page is simply from a web site in that country. Fortunately, however, we have provided researchers with the URLs for each of the 1.8 million web pages in the corpus, and links to the original web pages are given in the GloWbE interface as well. If there is a manageable number of web pages to work with [. . .], users may want to examine the original web pages, and see if they can identify the country of origin of the author/s.
>
> (Davies and Fuchs 2015b: 46)

To put it plainly, the responsibility lies with the individual researcher. Then, however, this should be clearly communicated. A statement to this effect is missing on the website of GloWbE. It is also far from clear how this issue should be dealt with in large-scale quantitative studies. While in qualitatively oriented studies a close inspection of the individual tokens has to be performed anyway, this is not generally done in quantitative ones. Such studies rather presuppose the reliability of the corpus, in particular with respect to the numbers that enter the statistics. In order to assess the extent of the problem, I will have a closer look at the Nigerian component of the corpus (GloWbE_NIG).

Results from a search in GloWbE_NIG for the item *nation*, i.e., one of the lexical items on our list, may serve as a starting point. This search yielded 14,441 tokens. Figure 2 is a screenshot of the first 30 hits.

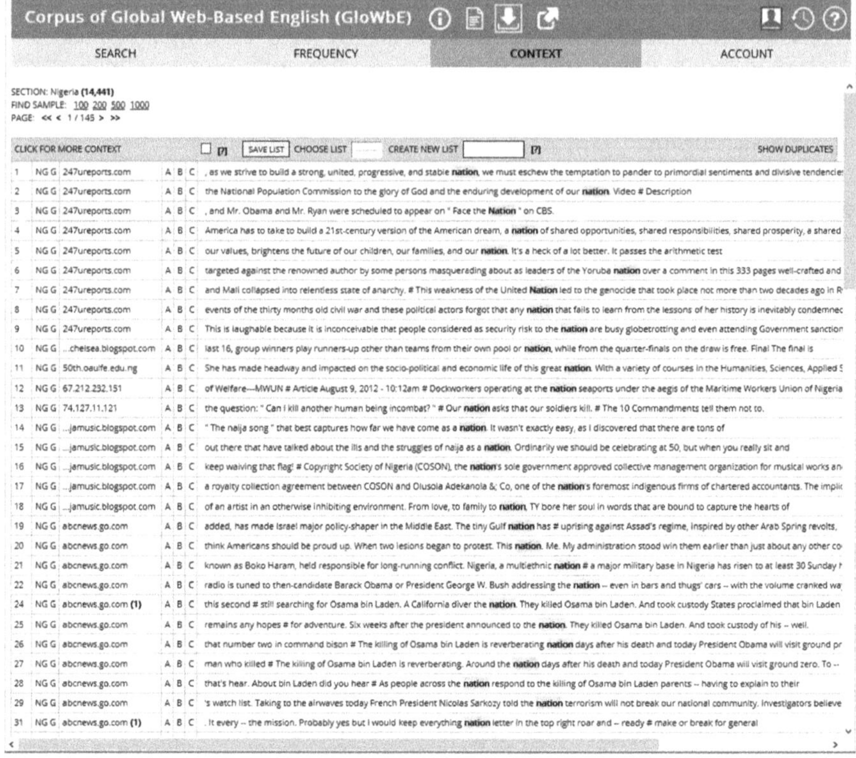

Figure 2: Screenshot of the first 30 hits for the search term *nation* in GloWbE_NIG.

A manual check of the source texts reveals that only 13 of these 30 tokens can be (more or less) safely said to stem from Nigerian speakers of English. 8 tokens are definitely not of Nigerian origin: 2 of them come from a speech by Bill Clinton, 1 from Mitt Romney, 4 from texts written by US-American journalists, 1 from a fan-blog of FC Chelsea. 2 tokens are flagged as duplicates. The remaining 7 tokens cannot be fully recovered anymore, due to broken links; however, they come from *abcnews.com* and are not likely to stem from Nigerians. The detailed breakdown is given in Table 5.

The reason why non-Nigerian texts feature in the Nigerian component of GloWbE appears to be quite straightforward: in the compilation of GloWbE, a google-based algorithm was used that associates a site with a specific country not

Table 5: Origin of the first 30 tokens of the search term *nation* in GloWbE_NIG.

token(s)	source	(likely) Nigerian	not Nigerian	duplicate	no longer traceable
1–2	speech by Goodluck Jonathan (Nigerian president)	2			
3	authors: Helen Cooper / Ashley Parker (US)		1		
4–5	speech by Bill Clinton		2		
6–9	author: Emmanuel Onwubiko	4			
10	UEFA announcement		1		
11	source: a Nigerian university	1			
12	report on a Nigerian trade union	1			
13	author: Candice Carter (Florida)		1		
14–18	Nigerian blog on music	5			
19	author: Matt McGarry (ABCnews)		1		
20	speech by Mitt Romney		1		
21	ABCnews report on Boko Haram				1
22	author: Christy Lemire (US)		1		
23				1	
24–28	ABCnews feed on Bin Laden				5
29	ABCnews report on Nicola Sarkozy				1
30				1	
	total	**13**	**8**	**2**	**7**

only on the basis of the respective country domain (e.g., .ng in the case of Nigeria). It also assigns country labels on the basis of questions such as "who links to that website [?]" and "who visits the website [?]" (see Davies and Fuchs 2015a: 4). It is not surprising, for example, that Nigerians "visit" or "link to" the various international standard outlets of daily news, e.g., *abcnews.com*. This, however, is not an indicator of a Nigerian origin of the authors of such source texts.

A look at the list of the 37,285 source texts of GloWbE_NIG (provided online with the corpus on *english-corpora.org*) quickly reveals that it is a far more systematic problem of the corpus, not restricted to texts from general news sites. Another domain that is particularly affected is sports, especially football (soccer). Source texts from this domain constitute a very substantial part of the entire corpus. This is, in itself, again not surprising, given the popularity of football in Nigeria. However, many of these source texts do not stem from Nigerian websites but are taken from popular international fan-blogs related to various top teams (e.g., FC Chelsea, FC Arsenal, AC Milan, FC Barcelona) and from general non-Nigerian news-websites related to football (e.g., *goal.com*, *laligatalk.com*, *theshedender.com*). The first 30 hits for the search term *nation* (Figure 2) provided an example thereof, with token 10 coming from a Chelsea fan-blog. In fact, when you take Chelsea-related websites as a case in point, the picture is as follows: About 1,200 source texts in the GloWbE_NIG come from various international Chelsea fan-blogs/websites (e.g., from *justchelsea.com*, *thechelseablog.org*, *chelseafc360.com*, *chelseadaft.org*, *bluechampions.com*, to name just a few); they alone represent well over 3% (!!!) of the source texts of GloWbE_NIG. The detailed breakdown is given in Table 6, considering only websites/blogs that contributed more than 10 source texts to GloWbE_NIG.

Table 6: Number of source texts in GloWbE_NIG coming from non-Nigerian Chelsea-related websites/blogs.

Chelsea website / fan blog	number of texts that entered GloWbE_NIG
justchelsea.com	92
thechelseablog.org	62
chelseafanzone.com	88
chelseafc360.com	126
chelseafcfansclub.com	45
chelseatickets.org	33
mychelseafc.com	18
chelsea-news.org	11
bluechampions.com	66
chelseadaft.org	201
weaintgotnohistory.com	454
total	**1,196**

In fact, when you search the entire GloWbE for tokens of *Chelsea*, you get the following result (Figure 3), showing its conspicuous presence in the Nigerian component (and, to a lesser degree, also in the Ghanaian sub-corpus):

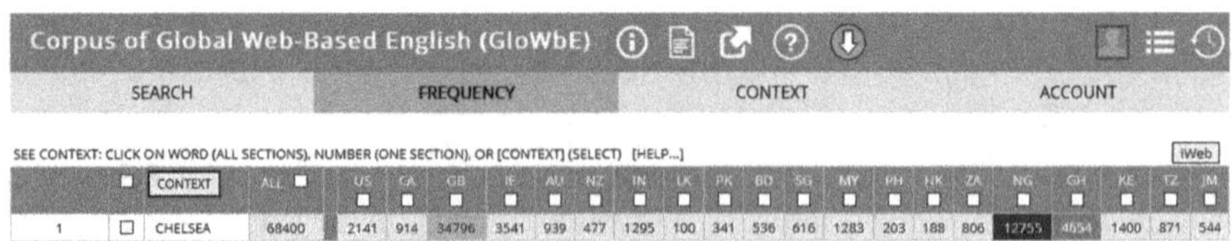

Figure 3: Tokens of *Chelsea* in GloWbE.

As to be expected, the problem extends to websites/blogs related to other British and non-British European top teams and to international sites on football in general. The following table gives the number of source texts in GloWbE_NIG that stem from such sites; the list is not exhaustive:

Table 7a: Number of source texts in GloWbE_NIG stemming from various non-Nigerian websites/blogs related to European football teams.

fan blogs/websites of selected British football teams	number of texts that entered GloWbE_NIG	fan blogs/websites of selected non- British football teams	number of texts that entered GloWbE_NIG
allarsenalnews.com	17	justbarcelonanews.com	26
arsenalblogger.com	19	barcacentral.com	32
myarsenalblog.com	25	barcafan-club.com	78
arsenalterritory.com	12	fcbarcelonaticketsonline.com	7
arsetalks.com	26	barcelonafans.org	7
welcometothegunnerstown.com	42	acmilan-online.com	87
goonermemoirs.com	59	valenciafootballclub.com	25
mufcdevils.com	11	justrealmadrid.com	27

Table 7b: Number of source texts in GloWbE_NIG stemming from various non-Nigerian websites/blogs related to football.

websites	number of texts that entered GloWbE_NIG	websites	number of texts that entered GloWbE_NIG
soccerfanbase.com	82	goal.com	255
soccerlimeyinamerica.com	42	todaysfootballnews.com	112
tribalfootball.com	187	breakingfootballnews.com	17
soccerroomtoday.com	63	footballgalleria.com	14
theshedender.com	141	latestfootballnews.net	28
john.futbal-fans.com	72	laligatalk.com	56
soccercaffe.com	30	footballlatestnews.com	11
footballmood.com	13	eyefootball.com	11

The problematic source texts from the domain of football listed in Tables 6 and 7a, b add up to ca. 7.5% of the total of source texts in GloWbE_NIG.

Given the popularity of football in Nigeria, it is not surprising that a considerable share of the internet activity of Nigerians is connected to that sport and that they frequently visit and link to the popular international fan blogs and news sites related to football in general and to specific teams in particular.[4] Nigerians, of course, also actively contribute to such sites and blogs, e.g., with texts they post as well as with comments. I.e., international football-fan blogs that are not Nigerian in the first place may contain some "Nigerian element".

In order to assess this potential Nigerian element, I had a closer look at the Chelsea blog *bluechampions.com*. It contributed 66 texts with a total of 258,169 words to the Nigerian component of GloWbE. This blog, which is no longer online,[5] was run by two Chelsea fans. The self-description of the first one, with the nickname *BlueChampion*, reads: "English is not his first language. Indian by birth and lives in Kuala Lumpur." The second one introduces himself as "Matt Clark. A 19 year old English student [. . .] at the University of Birmingham, England." 63 of the 66 texts taken from this blog were posted by Matt Clark or *BlueChampion*, only 3 are guest posts. Plainly, these texts represent British and Indian English, respectively, rather than Nigerian English. A Nigerian element in these source texts (if there is any) would thus be restricted to the comment section below the posts and would be very small. Indeed, below at least some of the posts, there are short comments by users with nicknames that suggest a West African origin.

A parallel situation can be assumed (and is present) in domains other than football, e.g., daily news (as illustrated above with the example of texts taken from *abcnews.com*), life style, religion, science and popular science, where general non-Nigerian websites appear frequently. In the domain of religion, for instance, one source text which contributed 27,855 words[6] to GloWbE_NIG is a mere reproduction of the entire *First Book of Mormon* (from *wjesus.org/nephiA.htm*), which is surely not a Nigerian text. The website wjesus.org is run by a speaker of Cantonese from Hong Kong and contributed 2 further source texts to GloWbE_NIG that are not of Nigerian origin either. 27 source texts stem from a website called *spaceship-earth.org*, authored by a white male (born in London, *www.spaceship-earth.org/Index.html*); it contributed 48,051 words to GloWbE_NIG and I could not find any Nigerian element. Many other problematic websites can be added.

---

4 Recall that "who visits" and "who links to" websites were criteria of the google-based algorithm used for the assignment of a particular country label to a site.

5 The relevant web-pages from *bluechampions.com* were recovered via archive.org and checked manually for authorship. The self-presentations of the bloggers come from a recovered version of bluechampions.com/bloggers/ from Oct. 13th, 2015. A video clip advertising the website is still online: www.youtube.com/watch?v=MbgqQSoCtBI (last access 27 July 2020).

6 This is noteworthy as the average length of the source texts in GloWbE_NIG is 1,143 words.

It is difficult to assess the full extent of the problematic cases in GloWbE_NIG and GloWbE in general. In any case, it cannot be taken for granted that we are still in the realm of what might be "somehow statistically 'even[ed] out'" by "the sheer size of GloWbE", to return to Nelson's criticism.[7] This has to be established individually for each study based on the corpus.

4 Small-scale specific-purpose corpora

4.1 A corpus of inaugural speeches

The present section makes a case for small-scale corpora compiled for the specific purpose of a study. Obvious advantages of such corpora include that (i) they are thematically adapted to the scope of the investigation, (ii) they hence contain far less tokens that are irrelevant to the study, and (iii) they are small enough to allow for a close reading of the contexts.

The standard objection made against them is that they are not representative. This is most certainly true, in a trivial sense. However, the underlying notion of 'representativeness' is worth considering: corpora such as COCA, BNC, BROWN-family type (including ICE) are "representative" in particular in that they are "big", in that they comprise different text types (in the case of BROWN-type corpora even according to the same design principles), and in that some of them comprise different modalities (written and spoken components). However, whether this type of "representativeness" is needed and useful depends on the specific object of investigation. If we wish to study, for example, the conceptualization of HOMOSEXUALITY, we do not really need a corpus with sections of texts from computer science and stock-market reports. Texts that are largely irrelevant given the scope of the investigation will blur the results of quantitative analyses. Furthermore, small-scale specific-purpose corpora may even be maximally "representative" in that they comprise the entire body of discourse in a

7 The impact of problematic source texts may be quite significant. I had a closer look at a recent large-scale study based on GloWbE on the present perfect across varieties of English (Fuchs 2016, summarized in Fuchs, van Rooy and Gut 2019). The problems come to the fore immediately when you have a look at the list of hits for individual verbs. Among the total of 723 tokens of *have got*, for instance, I counted more than 120 that come from the football-rated sites listed above, i.e., about 17%, leaving problematic cases from other domains aside. For lexical items with a strong affinity to the domain of sport, the problem is even bigger. Among the 584 tokens of *have won*, for instance, I found more than 200 of the kind described above, i.e., more than a third of the total, again leaving aside other issues. Unfortunately, Fuchs, van Rooy and Gut (2019) are mute on these problems with GloWbE.

given realm exhaustively, e.g., the texts of the successive constitutions of a country, or at least in a given time frame. It is this understanding of the notion of 'representativeness' that guides and licenses small-scale specific-purpose corpora.

Among the text types, or genres, that are particularly promising for an analysis of the metaphor system NATION AS A FAMILY are political speeches. In the following, I will have a closer look at one sub-genre of political speeches, i.e., presidential inaugural addresses. The rationale of this choice is straightforward: major functions of this genre are to re-unite the nation after a divisive election period, to provide a vision for the nation and to define the role of the elected president. Hence, appeal to generally accepted conceptualizations of the NATION in the respective cultural context can be expected to be prominent.

The following exemplary analysis is based on a small-scale corpus of inaugural addresses by American and Nigerian presidents, INAUG_US and INAUG_Nig respectively. INAUG_US comprises the inaugural speeches from Carter 1977 to Trump 2017 (see Table 8), with a total of ca. 22,000 words. All of them are the official transcripts provided on *www.americanrhetoric.com* (last access 27 July 2020).[8] INAUG_Nig is its Nigerian near equivalent (ca. 13,800 words);[9] not included, however, are the periods of military rule and the inaugural address by Shonekan, which I could not obtain. Its source texts are given in Table 8.

Table 8: Source texts of INAUG_US and INAUG_Nig.

INAUG_US	
Jimmy Carter, 1977–1981	Inaugural Address. January 20, 1977
Ronald Reagan, 1981–1989	Inaugural Address. January 20, 1981 Inaugural Address. January 21, 1985
George H. W. Bush, 1989–1993	Inaugural Address. January 20, 1989
William J. Clinton, 1993–2001	Inaugural Address. January 20, 1993 Inaugural Address. January 20, 1997
George W. Bush, 2001–2009	Inaugural Address. January 20, 2001 Inaugural Address. January 20, 2005

8 For analyses of the history and structure of the inaugural addresses of American presidents, see, e.g., Campbell and Jamieson (1990) and Austermühl (2014).

9 In order to obtain a corpus that is sufficiently big to be comparable to INAUG_US, I included two acceptance speeches (by Jonathan and Buhari) in INAUG_Nig in addition to their inaugural addresses. All of the sources of INAUG_Nig were last accessed 27 July 2020, Buhari's Acceptance Speech is no more available on the site indicated but can be accessed on vanguardngr.com/2015/04/buharis-acceptance-speech/.

Table 8 (continued)

INAUG_Nig	
Barack Obama, 2009–2017	Inaugural Address. January 20, 2009 Inaugural Address. January 21, 2013
Donald J. Trump, 2017–present	Inaugural Address. January 20, 2017
Shehu Shagari, 1979–1983	Inaugural Speech. October 1, 1979 maxsiollun.wordpress.com/great-speeches-in-nigerias-history/
military rule and a short presidency (Ernest Shonekan, 83 days)	no text from this period
Olusegun Obasanjo, 1999–2007	Inaugural Speech. May 29, 1999 maxsiollun.wordpress.com/great-speeches-in-nigerias-history/
Umaru Musa Yar'Adua, 2007–2010	Inaugural Speech. May 29, 2007 maxsiollun.wordpress.com/great-speeches-in-nigerias-history/
Goodluck Jonathan, 2010–2015	Inaugural Speech. May 5, 2010 sahelblog.wordpress.com/2010/05/07/nigeria-president-goodluck-jonathans-inaugural-speech/ Acceptance Speech. April 28, 2011 (Jonathan 2011a) vanguardngr.com/2011/04/president-jonathans-acceptance-speech/ Inaugural Speech. May 29, 2011 (Jonathan 2011b) visionafricamagazine.com/President_Goodluck_Jonathan%27s_Inaugural_Speech.html
Muhammadu Buhari, 2015–present	Acceptance Speech. April 1, 2015 (Buhari 2015a) cnbcafrica.com/news/special-report/2015/04/02/muhammadu-buhari-speech-nigeria/ Inaugural Speech. May 29, 2015 (Buhari 2015b) vanguardngr.com/2015/05/read-president-buhari-inaugural-speech/

The search in the corpus for the list of potential source and target domain items yielded the results given in Table 9. Not surprisingly, there is a much higher frequency of potential target-domain items in INAUG compared to the general corpora (Table 10), i.e., INAUG has a far greater density of relevant material due to its genre-specific thematic focus. The potential source-domain items, as a whole, have about the same frequency in both corpus components of INAUG, with 2045 per 1mw in INAUG_US and 1957 per 1mw in INAUG_Nig, although the frequency of individual items differs quite significantly (see Table 9).

Table 9: Frequency of selected search items (source and target domain) for THE NATION IS A FAMILY in INAUG_US and INAUG_Nig compared.

		Inaug_US (absolute frequency)	**Inaug_NIG** (absolute frequency)	**Inaug-US** (per 1 mw)	**Inaug-NIG** (per 1 mw)
Potential source domain items	*family*	18	8	818	580
	father	13	5	591	362
	mother	6	2	273	145
	parent	4	0	182	0
	sister	1	3	45	217
	brother	1	8	45	580
	son	1	1	45	72
	daughter	1	0	45	0
Potential target domain items	*citizen*	52	22	2,364	1,594
	nation	117	67	5,318	4,855
	country	47	50	2,136	3,623
	government	81	65	3,682	4,710
	president	37	46	1,682	3,333
	total	**379**	**277**	**17,227**	**20,072**

Table 10: Frequency of potential target-domain items for THE NATION IS A FAMILY in INAUG_US and INAUG_Nig compared to general corpora (COCA_written and ICE-NIG_written).

COCA per 1 mw	**ICE-NIG per 1 mw**	**IINAUG_US per 1 mw**	**INAUG_Nig per 1 mw**
1,547	4,310	15,182	18,116

In the following two sections, I will take a more detailed look at these items in order to see whether they are indeed used figuratively in the relevant sense. These two sections will also provide a more general analysis of how the domain of NATION/STATE is conceptualized in the inaugural addresses.

4.2 The conceptualization of NATION/STATE in INAUG_US

Of the 45 tokens of the potential source-domain items from the FAMILY domain, 32 are literal. *Father* is the only metaphorically productive kinship term in the data, with 10 figurative uses among the total of 13 tokens. 8 of these 10 tokens are instances of the fixed expression *founding fathers*, or refer to specific founders as *fathers*:

(5) a. George Washington, *father of our country* (Reagan 1981)
b. one of the greatest among the *Founding Fathers*, Dr. Joseph Warren (Reagan 1981)
c. Two of our *Founding Fathers*, a Boston lawyer named Adams and a Virginia planter named Jefferson (Reagan 1985)
d. Washington remains the *Father of our Country* (Bush 1989)
e. It is the honorable achievement of our *fathers*. (G.W. Bush 2005)
f. *Our Founding Fathers*, faced with perils that we can scarcely imagine, drafted a charter to assure the rule of law and the rights of man (Obama 2009)
g. At a moment when the outcome of our Revolution was most in doubt, the *Father of our Nation* ordered these words be read to the people (Obama 2009)
h. That's what will lend meaning to the creed our *Fathers* once declared. (Obama 2013)

The expression *founding fathers*, however, does not frame the NATION as a FAMILY. Instead, it is a procreation metaphor in which the nation is a metaphoric CHILD, i.e., a version of the NATION AS A PERSON metaphor. It is the same conceptualization that was famously used by Lincoln in his Gettysburg address:

> Four score and seven years ago our fathers brought forth on this continent a new nation, conceived in liberty, and dedicated to the proposition that all men are created equal.
> (Lincoln. *The Gettysburg Address*. 1863)

As a fixed expression, *founding fathers* emerged only at the end of the 19th century, and it gained currency from the 1920s onwards. Framing, e.g., George Washington as the *father of the country*, as it is done by Reagan (1981) and Bush (1989), is, from a modern perspective, also a procreation metaphor: Washington is presented as having brought forth the country. Historically, however, i.e., at the time of the US Independence movement, it is a metaphorization with a much broader background of interpretation: George Washington was viewed as an alternative FATHER, alternative to the English King George III, who liked to present himself as the father of his subjects. As shown by Schulz (1992), the Independence movement was, in this logic and respect, a metaphorical revolt against a father who mistreats his children. This is made very explicit in the following passage from Thomas Paine's *Common Sense*:

> But Britain is the parent country, say some. Then the more shame upon her conduct. Even brutes do not devour their young, nor savages make war upon their families; [. . .] I rejected the hardened, sullen tempered Pharaoh of England for ever; and disdain the wretch, that with the pretended title of FATHER OF HIS PEOPLE, can unfeelingly hear of their slaughter, and composedly sleep with their blood upon his soul. (Paine 1776)

In addition to instances of *founding fathers*, there is 1 token in INAUG_US of *father* referring to God:

(6) *Heavenly Father*, we bow our heads and thank You for Your love. (Bush 1989)

Again, this is primarily a procreation metaphor. However, the Christian notion of the 'family of man' certainly provides for the conceptualization of COMMUNITY (ranging from a community of believers to the entire human kind) in terms of a FAMILY.

1 token of *father* and the only figurative one of *mother* use these terms to refer to earlier generations:

(7) Now we must choose if the example of our *fathers and mothers* will inspire us or condemn us. (G.W. Bush 2001)

The remaining 2 figurative uses of kinship terms in INAUG_US are, in fact, the most interesting ones from the present perspective. They come in Obama's second inaugural speech and involve the only tokens of brother and sister in INAUG_US:

(8) Our journey is not complete until our gay *brothers and sisters* are treated like anyone else under the law -- for if we are truly created equal, then surely the love we commit to one another must be equal as well. (Obama 2013)

Here, the American nation is indeed framed as a FAMILY. However, it is important to notice that in Obama's speech, this passage comes immediately after a direct reference to Martin Luther King's *I have a dream* speech:[10] "to hear a preacher say that we cannot walk alone; to hear a 'King' proclaim that our individual freedom

---

10 An explicit reference to Martin Luther King is also made by Clinton in his 1997 inaugural speech.

is inextricably bound to the freedom of every soul on Earth" (Obama 2013). Obama thus extends the concern of the civil-rights movement to LGB rights. Martin Luther King's own use of *brother* and *sister* in his speech[11] is rooted in the Christian notion of the 'family of man' and the well-known usage of kinship terms in Black English, both being invoked by Obama.

In addition to the 13 figurative usages of kinship terms, there is one token that expresses an explicit analogy between nation and family in terms of a simile. It comes from Clinton's first inaugural address:

(9) We must provide for our Nation the way a *family* provides for its children. (Clinton 1993)

Here, too, the nation is the metaphoric CHILD. It is not a procreation metaphor; rather, it highlights the notion of 'nurturing' (also see below).

Generally, however, the relevant domains appear as distinct, albeit related, in the INAUG_US data: We find them catenated rather than metaphorically blended, as a chain 'self – family – community – nation', e.g., in the following examples:

(10) Let us all take more responsibility not only for ourselves and our *families* but for our communities and our country. (Clinton 1993)

(11) Each and every one of us, in our own way, must assume personal responsibility not only for ourselves and our *families* but for our neighbors and our Nation. (Clinton 1997)

In the use of kinship terms in INAUG_US, there is hence only scarce direct expression of a conceptualization of the NATION as a FAMILY. This is somehow difficult to match with Lakoff's (e.g., 2002 [1996]) influential account of the conceptual models underlying US-American political belief systems. According to Lakoff, conservative and progressive world views in the US reflect a metaphoric mapping of two distinct, competing, cultural models of the FAMILY: the STRICT-FATHER model for conservatives and the NURTURANT-PARENT model for progressives, respectively. These two models have quite different priorities, in particular the emphasis on strength in the STRICT-FATHER and on empathy in the NURTURANT-PARENT model. The strength of Lakoff's analysis is that it can account for the mutual

11 The relevant passage reads "I have a dream that one day, down in Alabama, with its vicious racists, with its governor having his lips dripping with the words of "interposition" and "nullification" – one day right there in Alabama little black boys and black girls will be able to join hands with little white boys and white girls as sisters and brothers" (King 1963, my emphasis).

misunderstanding that exists between the two camps: while both conservatives and progressives generally share the same well-known set of American cultural keywords and ideals (e.g., self-reliance, liberty), they derive them from the foci and the logic of their respective model, i.e., from different bases, and they do not mean the same things when they use the same terms. Furthermore, Lakoff's analysis can account for apparent incongruencies of stances taken by a specific camp, e.g., that conservatives generally advocate a pro-life attitude on the issue of abortion but support death penalty, while progressives, in turn, are pro-choice and reject death penalty, with both camps thus being "inconsistent" regarding their stance towards protecting or taking life. However, against the background of the specific priorities and foci of the underlying models, these stances *are* coherent.

In Lakoff's model, the NATION AS A FAMILY metaphor has to carry the load of providing the conceptual link between the relevant domains, cf.:

> I believe that the Nation As Family metaphor is what links the conservative and liberal worldviews to the family-based moralities [. . .]. I believe that this metaphor projects the Strict Father and Nurturant Parent moral systems onto politics to form the conservative and liberal political worldviews. (Lakoff 2002: 154)

Lakoff introduces this metaphor explicitly as an indisputable "fact":

> This is not a metaphor that I, as a cognitive scientist, like or dislike. It just is. That neural mapping exists just like gravity exists and species exist. I didn't create the metaphor. I'm just describing it. (Lakoff 2008: 88f.)

Given the assumed centrality of this metaphor at the conceptual level, one would expect that it is also central in the respective discourse domain, and thus traceable in terms of linguistic manifestations. As stated in section 4.1., inaugural addresses should be a particularly fertile ground for this metaphor system: they highlight traditional themes and values, have the function of providing common ground for the nation beyond political divisions and of presenting a vision of societal coherence. Furthermore, the INAUG_US corpus prominently represents both conservative and liberal worldviews. As seen above, however, NATION AS A FAMILY does only scarcely manifest in the data.[12] Instead, the speeches are dominated by two other metaphor systems, i.e., the general conceptualization of the NATION/STATE as an ORGANISM, in particular a PERSON, and as a UNITY OF PARTS.

12 The relevant metaphors were difficult to trace linguistically also in other studies. Cienki (2004, 2005), for instance, analyzed a corpus of TV debates between Al Gore and George W. Bush and found only few direct expressions of the metaphor sets in terms of which Lakoff spelled out the STRICT-FATHER and NURTURANT-PARENT models. At the level of entailments of these metaphors, Cienki's data also yielded a rather diffuse picture.

Expressions of the former abound in the speeches, including the following examples:

(12) Two centuries ago, *our Nation's birth* was a milestone in the long quest for freedom (Carter 1977)

(13) It is to make kinder *the face of the Nation* (G. Bush 1989)

(14) *a nation still mighty in its youth* and powerful in its purpose (Reagan 1985)

They often come in communion with HEALING and JOURNEY metaphors, e.g.

(15) I want to thank my predecessor for all he has done *to heal our land* (Carter 1977)

(16) And though *our Nation has sometimes halted* and sometimes delayed, we must follow no other course (G. W. Bush 2001)

The UNITY OF PARTS metaphor is exemplified by the following extract:

(17) These questions that judge us also unite us, because Americans of every party and background, Americans by choice and by birth are bound to one another in the cause of freedom. We have known divisions, which must be healed to move forward in great purposes, and I will strive in good faith to heal them. Yet those divisions do not define America. We felt the unity and fellowship of our Nation when freedom came under attack, and our response came like a single hand over a single heart. (G. W. Bush 2005)

4.3 The conceptualization of NATION/STATE in INAUG_Nig

In INAUG_US, roughly 30% of the kinship terms considered were instances of metaphoric usage, with *father* accounting for 10 of the 13 metaphoric tokens (see section 4.2). The situation is quite different in INAUG_Nig. There, 17 of the 27 kinship-term tokens are figurative (i.e., more than 60%). *Brother* stands out with 8 figurative tokens and no literal ones; however, *family* (a total of 8 tokens), *father* (a total of 5 tokens), and *sister* (a total of 3 tokens) also contribute 3 figurative instances each.

Among the figurative tokens of the kinship terms considered, there are 2 instances of *founding fathers* (Jonathan 2011b, Buhari 2015b) with reference to the founders of Nigeria. All the other 15 tokens are expressions of the conceptualization of various COMMUNITIES as FAMILIES, where COMMUNITY MEMBERS are BROTHERS and SISTERS and LEADERS/COMMUNITY ELDERS are FATHERS. Reference points range from local communities to Nigeria as a country and Africa as a whole. In (25), a political party is conceptualized as a FAMILY. The full data set is provided in (18) to (29); the relevant items are italicized:

(18) I salute all our traditional rulers, *fathers of our communities* and custodians of our cultural heritage. (Shagari 1979)

(19) To our larger *African family*, you have our commitment to the goal of African integration. (Yar'Adua 2007)

(20) I ask you, fellow citizens, to join me in rebuilding our *Nigerian family*, one that defines the success of one by the happiness of many. (Yar'Adua 2007)

(21) *My dear brothers and sisters*, it is with deep sense of loss and profound sorrow that I received the news of the passing on of His Excellency, President Umaru Musa Yar'Adua [. . .] (Jonathan 2010)

(22) *My brothers and sisters*, I call on all Nigerians to pray for the repose of the soul of our departed President. (Jonathan 2010)

(23) I have lost not just a boss but a good friend and *brother* (Jonathan 2010, with reference to Yar'Adua)

(24) I would like to specially acknowledge the presence in our midst today, of *Brother Heads of State* and Government, who have come to share this joyous moment with us. (Jonathan 2011b)

(25) To members of the *PDP family* and members of other political parties, who have demonstrated faith in our democratic enterprise, I salute you. (Jonathan 2011b)

(26) At this juncture, let me acknowledge and salute my friend and *brother*, Vice-President Namadi Sambo, and my dear wife, Patience, who has been a strong pillar of support. (Jonathan 2011b)

(27) *My brothers and sisters*, fellow citizens, we are all winners. (Jonathan 2011a)

(28) Our neighbours in the Sub-region and our *African brethren* should rest assured that Nigeria under our administration will be ready to play any leadership role that Africa expects of it. (Buhari 2015b)

(29) Finally *our brothers in the African Union and ECOWAS* have truly and clearly shown and demonstrate their commitment to our democratisation process. (Buhari 2015a)

The data are fully in line with the earlier comprehensive analysis of the African model of community in Polzenhagen (2007) and Wolf and Polzenhagen (2009). Triangulating findings from various realms and obtained through various methodologies, their comparative account shows that the conceptualization of societal units (community, country, etc.) in terms of families is not only far more frequent, salient, and productive in the (Sub-Saharan) African context than in the Western one, but that it is indeed the backbone of the cultural model of community in this setting, including the domain of politics.

5 *Brothers and sisters*: tracing a fixed expression

While the previous sections took the path from big to small corpora, the present one follows the inverse direction. It rests on the argument that findings from small corpora provide meaningful starting points for more extensive searches in larger data sets.

One of the observations from the analysis of INAUG_US and INAUG_Nig was the fairly prominent figurative usage of the expression *brothers and sisters* in the latter, encoding membership in a community. It has 3 tokens in this corpus, compared to 1 in the US data. A frequency search of this expression in the other corpora used in the present study yields the results in Table 11 (normalized frequencies). The table also provides the data for the items *brother* and *sister* in isolation.

Table 11: Normalized frequency (per 1mw) *sister, brother, brothers and sisters.*[13]

	AmE			WAfrE		
	COCA	COCA sample	FROWN	ICE-NIG written	CEC	GloWbE_ NIG
sister	124	124	143	113	183	121
brother	157	158	195	155	192	179
brothers and sisters	3.5	2.4	2	20	7.8	11.9

There is nothing particularly remarkable about the frequency profiles of *sister* and *brother* when the items are looked at in isolation. However, the fixed expression *brothers and sisters* is far more frequent in all the corpora of West African English. What is even more interesting for the present perspective, beyond mere frequency, is the distribution between literal and figurative usages.

ICE-NIG (written) produces 8 tokens of the expression. 6 of them are literal, referring to biological siblings. However, 5 of these 6 literal tokens stem from the same text, in which the narrator learns about having biological brothers and sisters. Both figurative usages of the expression in this corpus specify community membership.

(30) In as much as the government and oil/gas multinationals have their own faults, much of the problems confronting us today in the Niger Delta region, are caused by our own *brothers and sisters*.

(31) The NDDC has become highly politicized that it is regarded as a conduit pipe for siphoning public funds. It is on record that the top management staff of the NDDC who incidentally are from the Niger Delta region, had governorship ambition and thus rely on public funds to achieve these goals, deceiving our ignorant *brothers and sisters* that they have marching orders to address our developmental needs.

13 In the light of the criticism expressed in section 3, the data from GloWbE need to be taken with due caution. I went through the lists of websites from which the tokens stem. Among the first 1,000 hits for *brother* in the Nigerian component of GloWbE, I found only 23 tokens from problematic football-related source texts. The amount of problematic source texts from this realm is even smaller for *sister*. The list for the expression *brothers and sisters* is virtually unaffected by the above problem; I have checked all the 508 tokens manually. This is not surprising since these two kinship terms have no affinity to the domain of sports. However, their normalized frequency is counted on the basis of the total corpus size, which includes problematic source texts. The figures are hence not reliable; they can be expected to be higher. Furthermore, problematic source texts from other domains, e.g., in the present context, in particular 'religion', were not checked.

The CCE has a total of 7 tokens of this expression, all of them figurative. 5 of them are used against the background of the Christian notion of 'family of man' (i.e., the notion that all human beings are God's children and thus equal), 3 of them come in quotes from the Bible. The remaining 2 tokens express membership in a community in general:

(32) He stressed that his Government is not only interested in the Fund because GTZ initiated it but because it concerns the health development of *brothers and sisters in Cameroon.*

(33) From early in life children are introduced to adult kin as "other" fathers and mothers and to their children as *brothers and sisters.*

FROWN, by contrast, returns only 2 tokens, 1 of them literal, the other one figurative against the background of the notion 'family of man':

(34) Now is a time for blacks, whites, Asians, Hispanics, and others to respect diversity. No nation has ever done so. It can only work seeing that all folks under the sun are *brothers and sisters.*

COCA produces 1,740 tokens of *brothers and sisters*. In order to assess the share of literal and non-literal cases, I manually checked a random sample[14] of 1,000 hits, in which I counted 533 literal usages, i.e. 53%.[15]

Given that for a larger-scale comparative look at NigE there is, in terms of size, no alternative to GloWbE_NIG, I searched this corpus for tokens of *brothers and sisters*. This search yielded 508 hits. As stated above, the list is virtually unaffected by the problems with sports-related source texts discussed in section 3.4. I manually checked all of them and counted 54 literal usages, i.e., about 11%. Table 12 shows the results for COCA and GloWbE_NIG side by side. Hence, the expression *brothers and sisters* has a very distinct profile in NigE, compared to AmE, not only in terms of overall frequency but, in particular, with its high percentage of figurative tokens.

14 The online-interface on www.english-corpora.org/coca/ allows for automatic random sampling.
15 A parallel count in a random sample of 200 hits produced 110 literal cases, which confirms the results of the bigger sample.

Table 12: Normalized frequency (per 1mw) *brothers and sisters* and the distribution between literal and figurative usages in COCA (sample of 1,000 tokens) and GloWbE_NIG.

	COCA	GloWbE_NIG
brothers and sisters	3.5	11.9
literal usages	53%	11%
figurative usages	47%	89%

6 Conclusions

Corpus linguistics has proved to be an enormously fertile tool for the study of metaphor in and across varieties of English. In particular, it has contributed to a stronger empirical foundation and usage-based commitment of this research agenda, both complementing and challenging introspection-based approaches. Regular corpus work does not require sophisticated equipment and resources anymore, and the software needed for corpus analyses is readily available to every researcher who wishes to engage in corpus-based studies.[16] What is also available is a growing body of corpora covering varieties hitherto not or only poorly documented this way.

However, the corpora that are available differ quite significantly in terms of their design, size, and composition. The aim of the present paper was to reflect on this condition and in particular on what it needs to make sure that we can "trust the text", to use Sinclair's metaphor. Sinclair's TRUST metaphor inspires several crucial considerations that can help us determine which corpus, or corpora, we choose for a specific investigation. Criteria I highlighted in the present paper are representativeness, comparability, manageability and reliability. The different types of corpora differ with respect to how they satisfy these criteria; hence, the criteria should be carefully considered and weighed in communion prior to the actual analysis.

The present paper made a case for small-scale and standard 1 Mio word corpora. They are particularly suited for studies targeting metaphor in terms of their comparability and manageability. Metaphor-oriented studies usually operate with fairly extensive lists of lexis from both the source and the target domain, and

16 For a very useful overview of what is available in this realm, see Esimaje and Hunston (2019).

they require a close inspection of the individual tokens. Representativeness can be further ensured, if need be, in a follow-up study of larger corpora. A crucial advantage of these small-scale and BROWN-family corpora is their reliability, since they are carefully curated. The currently available large corpora such as GloWbE certainly are a major achievement; however, their reliability is still limited. Cleaner corpora of this size remain a desideratum.

References

Austermühl, Frank. 2014. *The Great American scaffold: Intertextuality and identity in American presidential discourse*. Amsterdam, Philadelphia: John Benjamins.

BNC = British National Corpus. www.english-corpora.org/bnc/

BROWN = BROWN Corpus of English. On ICAME collection of English language corpora, 2nd edition. CD-ROM. The HIT Centre. University of Bergen, Norway, 1999.

Campbell, Karlyn & Kathleen Jamieson. 1990. *Deeds done in words: Presidential rhetoric and the genres of governance*. Chicago: University of Chicago Press.

CEC = Corpus of English in Cameroon. Compiled as part of the International Corpus of English project. Unfinished version. Diskette.

Cienki, Alan. 2004. Bush's and Gore's language and gestures in the 2000 US presidential debates: A test case for two models of metaphors. *Journal of Language and Politics* 3. 409–440.

Cienki, Alan. 2005. Metaphor in the "Strict Father" and the "Nurturant Parent" cognitive models: Theoretical issues raised in an empirical study. *Cognitive Linguistics* 16 (2). 279–312.

COCA = Corpus of Contemporary American English. www.english-corpora.org/coca/

Davies, Mark & Robert Fuchs. 2015a. Expanding horizons in the study of World Englishes with the 1.9 billion word Global Web-based English Corpus (GloWbE). *English World-Wide* 36 (1). 1–28.

Davies, Mark & Robert Fuchs. 2015b. A reply. *English World-Wide* 36 (1). 45–47.

de Crevecoeur, John. 1782. *Letters from an American farmer*. London: Printed for T. Davies.

Esimaje, Alexandra U. & Susan Hunston. 2019. What is corpus linguistics? In Alexandra U. Esimaje, Ulrike Gut & Bassey E. Antia (eds.), *Corpus linguistics and African Englishes*, 7–35. Amsterdam, Philadelphia: John Benjamins.

FROWN = Freiburg BROWN Corpus of English. On ICAME collection of English language corpora, 2nd edition. CD-ROM. The HIT Centre. University of Bergen, Norway, 1999.

Fuchs, Robert. 2016. The frequency of the present perfect in varieties of English around the world. In Valentin Werner, Cristina Suárez-Gómez & Elena Seoane (eds.), *Re-assessing the present perfect in English: Corpus studies and beyond*, 223–258. Berlin: de Gruyter.

Fuchs, Robert, Bertus van Rooy & Ulrike Gut. 2019. Corpus-based research on English in Africa: A practical introduction. In Alexandra U. Esimaje, Ulrike Gut & Bassey E. Antia (eds.), *Corpus linguistics and African Englishes*, 37–70. Amsterdam, Philadelphia: John Benjamins.

Glazer, Nathan & Daniel P. Moynihan. 1963. *Beyond the melting pot.* Cambridge: M.I.T. Press and Harvard University Press.
GloWbE = Corpus of Global Web-based English. www.english-corpora.org/glowbe/
ICE-NIG = Nigerian component of the International Corpus of English sourceforge.net/projects/ice-nigeria/
Kallen, Horace. 1915. Democracy versus the melting pot. Part I: *Nation* 100 (2590). 190–194; Part II: *Nation* 100 (2591). 217–220.
King, Martin Luther. 1963. I have a dream. Speech delivered on 28 August 1963, at the Lincoln Memorial, Washington D.C. [https://www.americanrhetoric.com/speeches/mlkihaveadream.htm, last access 27 July 2020].
Lakoff, George. 2002 [1996]. *Moral politics.* 2nd ed. Chicago: University of Chicago Press.
Lakoff, George. 2006a. *Thinking points: Communicating our American values and vision.* New York: Farrar, Straus & Giroux.
Lakoff, George. 2006b. *Whose freedom? The battle over America's most important idea.* New York: Picador.
Lakoff, George. 2008. *The political mind: A cognitive scientist's guide to your brain and its politics.* New York: Penguin Books.
Musolff, Andreas. 2010. *Metaphor, nation and the Holocaust: The concept of the body politic.* London: Routledge.
Nelson, Gerald. 2015. Response to Davies and Fuchs. *English World-Wide* 36 (1). 38–40.
Nkemleke, Daniel. 2008. *Manual of information to accompany the Corpus of Cameroonian English.* Chemnitz: Chemnitz University of Technology (Department of English).
Paine, Thomas. 1776. *Common sense.* [www.gutenberg.net].
Polzenhagen, Frank. 2007. *Cultural conceptualisations in West African English: A cognitive-linguistic approach.* Berlin: Peter Lang.
Pragglejaz Group. 2007. MIP: A method for identifying metaphorically used words in discourse. *Metaphor and Symbol* 22 (1). 1–39.
Schulz, Dieter. 1992. Die amerikanische Revolution als Familienkrach. In: Dietrich Harth & Jan Assmann (eds.), *Revolution und Mythos*, 85–103. Frankfurt (Main): Fischer.
Sinclair, John. 2001. Preface. In Mohsen Ghadessy, Alex Henry & Robert L. Roseberry (eds.), *Small corpus studies and ELT: Theory and practice*, vii–xv. Amsterdam, Philadelphia: John Benjamins.
Sinclair, John. 2004. *Trust the text.* London, New York: Routledge.
Steen, Gerard et al. 2010. *A method for linguistic metaphor identification: From MIP to MIPVU.* Amsterdam, Philadelphia: John Benjamins.
Stefanowitsch, Anatol. 2004. HAPPINESS in English and German: A metaphorical-pattern analysis. In Michel Achard & Suzanne Kemmer (eds.), *Language, culture, and mind*, 134–149. Stanford: CSLI.
Stefanowitsch, Anatol. 2006. 'Words and their metaphors: A corpus-based approach'. In Anatol Stefanowitsch & Stefan T. Gries (eds.), *Corpus-based approaches to metaphor and metonymy*, 63–105. Berlin, New York: Mouton de Gruyter.
Stollberg-Rilinger, Barbara. 1986. *Der Staat als Maschine. Zur politischen Metaphysik des absoluten Fürstenstaats.* Berlin: Duncker & Humblot.
Tiomajou, David. 1995. The Cameroon English corpus project. In Ayo Bamgbose, Ayo Banjo & Andrew Thomas (eds.), *New Englishes: A West African perspective*, 349–366. Ibadan: Mosuro [Trenton (NJ), 1997: Africa World Press].

Turner, Frederick J. 1983 [1893]. The significance of the frontier in American history. In Ronald H. Carpenter (ed.), *The eloquence of Frederick Jackson Turner*, 193–218. San Marino: The Huntington Library.
Vogelbacher, Stefanie. 2019. *Scenario negotiation in online debates about the European Union: Analysing metaphor in communication*. Berlin: Peter Lang.
Wolf, Hans-Georg & Frank Polzenhagen. 2009. *World Englishes: A cognitive sociolinguistic approach*. Berlin, New York: Mouton de Gruyter.

Section II: Cultural metaphorical conceptualizations

Vera da Silva Sinha, Heliana Mello

Indexicalization and lexicalization of event-based time intervals in Huni Kuĩ, Awetý, and Kamaiurá

Abstract: This chapter explores the multiple ways in which human cultures and languages conceptualize time. We discuss the very notion of time from different perspectives as well as through the comparison of well-studied languages with lesser-known ones. Our focus is on concepts of time in three indigenous languages and cultures of Brazil: Huni Kuĩ, Awetý, and Kamaiurá. In these cultures, time is not organized and expressed metrically but is event-based. There are no lexical translation equivalents for 'time' in any of these languages and no names for days of the week, months of the year, year, or month. The data discussed are derived from a field-based anthropological linguistic study, demonstrating how event-based time intervals are indexed to temporal landmarks. The chapter focuses on time intervals in three domains: *life stages, times of day,* and *seasons.* The event-based time intervals are indexicalized by environmental happenings (water level, cool breeze, bird and animal songs), celestial bodies (sun, moon, and stars), and activities. The metaphorical-metonymical source domains for referring to past and future are cognitive and perceptual processes. For Awetý and Kamaiurá the past is not located behind the speaker but is *in their eyes*. The past consists of memories, which can be 'seen in the mind's eye', and so REMEMBERING IS SEEING. The future for Awetý and Kamaiurá is right in front of the speaker's eyes. For Huni Kuĩ, past events are located in the *heart,* and future events and plans are located in the *head* (mind). Therefore, in these cultures, past and future are conceptualized in terms not of spatial direction but by reference to embodied mental capacities: *memory, anticipation, intention,* and *imagination.*

Keywords: Time, event-based intervals, index, culture, language, Amazonian

1 Introduction

As Franssinetti et al. (2016: 1) have pointed out, "[t]ime is the most elusive dimension of everyday experiences". Despite the absolute impossibility of seeing or

Vera da Silva Sinha, Universidad de Las Palmas de Gran Canaria
Heliana Mello, Universidade Federal de Minas Gerais, CNPq

https://doi.org/10.1515/9783110688306-004

touching it, time can be sensed and represented in several different ways and on different scales. Drawing on naturalistic and experimental investigations, Benini (2017) argues that all living beings endowed with a nervous system, albeit basic, have a sense of time. Despite the different research fronts that have been explored to date, we still do not have a comprehensive mapping of all possible ways in which human beings conceptualize and represent time through linguistic means. Many well-studied languages, such as English, seem to have linear spatial metaphors at the core of temporal conceptualizations (Boroditsky 2000; Lakoff and Johnson 1999). Others, such as Spanish, take volume as a preferred source domain for metaphorical projection (Bylund and Athanasopoulos 2017). Our goal in this chapter is to contribute to knowledge and understanding of the multiple ways human cultures and languages have of conceptualizing and linguistically encoding time, through a discussion of the very notion of time from different perspectives, as well as through the comparison of well-studied languages with lesser-known languages.

Our focus is on concepts of time in three indigenous languages and cultures of Brazil: Huni Kuĩ, Awetý, and Kamaiurá. In a field-based anthropological linguistic study, the lexicalization and indexicalization[1] of time intervals by temporal landmarks in these languages were mapped out, focusing on three domains: *life stages, times of day,* and *seasons* (Silva Sinha 2019). The data collection used a combination of methods that varied from structured elicitation and comprehension tasks to open-ended questionnaires and interviews. Ethnographic information and observations of traditional time reckoning practices were gathered.

This chapter is organized as follows: we first briefly discuss the notion of time and its representation through linguistic means and we review the literature on *event-based time intervals*. After that, the methodology employed in the data collection is described. We then provide a discussion of event-based time in Huni Kuĩ, Awetý, and Kamaiurá. Finally, we conclude by summarizing our findings and exploring their possible generalization to other Amazonian languages.

2 Time across languages and cultures

Time is fundamental to human experience, cognition, and action (Klein 2008). However, the way it is perceived and encoded in language is highly variable and this variation seems to be partly dependent on culture. While some languages

1 Indexicalization: the temporal landmarks to which event-based time intervals are indexed; a *lexicalized* concept is one that is expressed by a regular and conventional word, phrase, or construction. (cf. Silva Sinha 2019)

have grammatical markings such as tense and aspect that signal temporal concepts, others lack these formal devices and rely on other means to convey such notions, such as a rich adverbial system. Languages such as Yukatec Maya and Mandarin lack grammatical tense, others such as Standard German lack grammatical aspect encoded in the verbal system. The calendric systems that speakers of the world's major languages rely on in their daily lives are unknown in many cultures, such as the Yélî Dnye, in Papua New Guinea (Levinson and Majid 2013) and the Maori in New Zealand (Meijl 1993). Thus, varied encodings for the notion of time have been documented in the languages of the world. Time is perceived in several ways: as fixed or continuous, static or flowing, as horizontally, vertically, leftwards or rightwards moving, besides moving from front to back (Fulga 2012: 29). Boroditsky et al. (2010), for example, mention that both English and Mandarin use horizontal/front-back special metaphors to talk about time; Mandarin speakers, however, also use vertical metaphors (*shàng* for 'up', *xià* for 'down'), employing a spatial metaphor related to the notion of "up" for earlier events, while "down" is used to refer to later ones. Frequency of use might motivate preferences in different languages. For instance, while English uses vertical metaphors (e.g., hand down knowledge) as well as Mandarin, they are not as frequent as horizontal ones (e.g., pass knowledge on), which are much more prevalent.

The study of lesser-described languages and their expression of time is a valuable enterprise, as it makes possible the appreciation of a multitude of conceptual structures that inform linguistic encoding. As will become apparent in section 3, Awetý, Kamaiurá, and Huni Kuĩ do not share the familiar view of time as contained amounts or lengths. The metaphorical expression of time as space, so popular in Indo-European languages, is not present. We thus invite our readers to delve into a universe that might be entirely new to them, in which time is conceptualized in terms of natural and social events themselves, making explicit an intrinsic connection between culture and language.

Although the term *event-based time* is recent, coined in relation to research on the Amazonian language Amondawa (Sinha et al. 2011; Silva Sinha et al. 2012), the phenomenon has been noted in several other anthropological and linguistic studies of non-Western societies. Huang (2016) investigated Bunun linguistic expressions of time in Isbukun, a dialect of Bunun (an Austronesian language spoken in the central and southern mountainous areas of Taiwan). As reported by Huang (2016), speakers of Bunun do not talk about time in terms of calendars and clocks; their time is "expressed in terms of daily chores and traditional rituals in the Bunun Community" (Huang 2016: 1). The Bunun do not have a word for time; neither do they have concepts of hour, minute or second.

The Bunun language has borrowed from Japanese the term *zikan*, which has the meaning of Japanese 'year' (official calendar from 1873),[2] and speakers employ this when it is required. However, traditionally they have used seasons to represent 'year', so the term *Hamisan* (winter) can also be used to express the notion of year. In this culture, there are only two seasons: *hamisan* (winter) and *talapal* (dry season). Furthermore, they also refer to *buan* (moon) to represent or 'count' the 12 months of the year. The moon has an important role for marking temporal events, so that festivals and rituals are planned in accordance with the lunar cycle. The words *hanian* and *dihanin* are used to designate 'day' and the *dihanin* refers both to 'day' and to 'sky', meaning 'day time', in opposition to 'night'. The author also notes that although the Bunun express 'calendrical units' such as 'month', it is "unusual to refer to a time point by its order in a year or a month" (Huang 2016: 6). The author concludes that the Bunun time concepts are derived from the event process and that "the starting of TIME coincides with the beginning of an activity and its ending with the activity's completion" (Huang 2016: 18). Time in this system is not a separate category but is fused with the event *per se*, as also reported for the Amondawa language (Sinha et al. 2011; Silva Sinha et al. 2012).

A similar system is reported by Bohannan (1953), who describes concepts of time among the Tiv community in Central Nigeria. The Tiv language does not have a word meaning 'time', and this notion is expressed by the use of terms referring to long and short 'duration'. For example, the word *cha* meaning 'far' "is used of space, of time and of kinship. However, such words are not dependent on time indication or reckoning for their primary meanings" (Bohannan 1953: 251). This language is reported to have three terms, *shighen, dzum, icin*, meaning 'occasion', all of which can be used nominally to refer to 'a time' or 'an occasion' and all of which can be used in the sense of 'at that time'. *Icin* can be counted; *shinghen* is used in the sense of 'now is the time', and *dzun* applies to longer intervals. These words can be used to indicate a temporal landmark for locating another event in time. The author states that when Tiv speakers place an event in time they "do so by referring it to a natural or social activity or condition using solar, lunar, seasonal, agricultural, meteorological or other events. Tiv ritual is not associated with a calendar, and for these reasons, ritual events are not usable as time indicators" (Bohannan 1953: 252). In these examples, the fusion of environmental happenings and activities to conceptualize event-based time intervals is evident.

There are several other cultures and languages that have been reported to use event-based time intervals. For example, in Tarifit (a Tamazight [formerly known

---

2 The traditional Japanese Calendar used before the introduction of the Gregorian Calendar in 1873 was lunisolar based on the seven-day week.

as Berber] language of North Africa) there is no word that designates the full cycle of day and night, and speakers use the Arabic loan word *yawm* to express this concept. “Day” is expressed by *swass* ‘daylight’ and night by *djirth* ‘absence of the light’. Human activity is governed in the first of these by the sun, and in the second by the constellations: “The parts of each entity are connected to certain events” (El-Arbaoui Jelouli 2013: 221).[3] The position and heat of the sun, meal times, light and dark, the breeze, and the length of shadows serve as *indexes* of temporal landmarks and time intervals. The author points out that, for these desert people, the day has more negative connotations than the night, because the light of the sun at *‘t’haa’* [noon] is dreaded, for the reasons that it hurts the body, and is an obstacle to all human activities (El-Arbaoui Jelouli 2013: 223). The fusion of event-based time and human value is clearly illustrated in this example.

More linguistically and geographically close to the languages that we describe below is the description (without using the term) of event-based time already provided by Baldus (1940), who describes concepts of time in a Tupian language of coastal Brazil. The Tupian people at this time used to have time intervals named after the *acajus* ‘cashew fruit’ and the stars *ceixu* ‘a constellation that appears in May’. These words were also used to name ‘year’. Baldus suggests that this was because the *caju* tree gives fruit only once a year. The Tupian people also indexed time intervals to other natural events: fruits ripening, fishes in the river, the level of the water, the heat of the sun, the rain and the sun, moon and constellations (Baldus 1940: 90–93). These same characteristics are found in the Awetý, Kamaiurá, and Huni Kuĩ cultures and languages described in this article.

3 Methodology

The Kamaiurá, Awetý, and Huni Kuĩ linguistic and cultural data described in this article were first detailed in Silva Sinha’s (2018) PhD Thesis. The methods used in the field research were elicitation, comprehension tasks, open-ended questionnaires and interviews, enhanced by information from ethnographic observations of traditional time reckoning practices.

This research looked at the interaction of language and culture in a variety of situations that could not be predicted. Therefore, it did not involve testing a specific linguistic feature in one particular situation with controlled variables, but it rather comprised an act of interpretation of multiple cultural and language fea-

3 The cited author does not specify which constellations, and in any case these do not correspond with those common to the European languages.

tures in different environments and situations, such as cooking, fishing, bathing in the river, walking in the field, harvesting cassava. There was a need for understanding cultural meanings, and this process required mediation and interaction between individuals and groups of people, and, sometimes, interaction between individuals and objects. We cannot understand another culture immediately in one conversation, or through a pre-designed interview or questionnaire, without the risk of misinterpretation.

The research also considered that the investigation of cultural concepts requires the unfolding of different layers of meanings. This scenario demands an understanding of the ways people construct explanations and thoughts about the world. All humans are social beings, and they interact with each other, mainly through language. People talk with each other to express and to share feelings, experiences and to communicate their ways of living in this world. The multiple methods employed were necessary to unravel how Kamaiurá, Awetý, and Huni Kuĩ people understand and conceptualize time.

The fieldwork was carried out with the collaboration of native speaker linguists and with the participation of members of each community. The engagement of the community and Collaborating Researchers was essential to the research methodology. The key roles of community members were designated as Collaborating Researcher, Research Consultant, and Research Facilitator. Research Consultants are all persons from the community who participated in the research by providing language and culture consultancy, conducted in data collection sessions. They actively participated in the entire process, providing data collected using all the different research instruments. The Research Facilitators are all persons from the community who participated actively in the project, helping as liaisons with other members of the community, with translation during informal conversations, clarifying cultural information and operating recording equipment.

The procedure to create engagement between the researchers and the community members followed a protocol that consisted of a formal conversation between the researcher, the Collaborating Researchers, and community leaders (chiefs and other authorities such as shamans). The community leaders were briefed about the project, its aims, and methods. The leaders of each community gave their public endorsement to the project and to our fieldwork visits. During this process, we had the opportunity to ask the community members for their support and permission. Informed consent for research participation was given verbally and collectively and was then registered in writing by the Collaborating Researchers.

The initial establishment of trust was mediated by the exchange of gifts. Gift exchange is a significant and highly appreciated cultural practice for these communities. In giving and receiving gifts, a bridge of communication is constructed, making it possible to establish a relationship of mutual respect, appreciation, trust, and friendship (Mauss 1966). The research team was aware of this practice and tried to fulfil specific requests from the community leaders, who were responsible for the further distribution of the gifts to community members.

An open-ended questionnaire that addressed the following topics was used: time adverbs, time interval terminology, and concepts (seasons, festivals, etc.), social activities during the day and night, cardinal points, names of celestial bodies, numbers, spatial metaphors for time. Interviews were carried out immediately following the administration of the questionnaire in order to clarify, supplement, and disambiguate the questionnaire data. The research also used structured language elicitation and comprehension tasks that consisted of drawings or photos on cards representing temporal sequences: the human life course, the divisions of the day, and the seasons and familiar crop life cycles. Consultants were asked to arrange the cards in accordance with their typical sequences, without instructions or cues being given about the configuration that they should follow; and to describe card arrangements. Ethnographic observation focused on traditional time reckoning practices specifically to understand cultural concepts of time, their linguistic expression, and the ways they are embedded in social life. Conversations about time concepts were observed. They either occurred spontaneously as part of everyday life, or emerged from structured discussions, sometimes in the context of the administration of the tasks, and sometimes in the context of demonstrations of time reckoning practices or engaging jointly in other activities such as crafting, fishing, food preparation, cooking, harvesting, and hoeing. All interactions were audio and video recorded. All the questionnaire data were transcribed in the native language, and then translated into Portuguese; the analysis was carried out in collaboration with the native speaker Collaborating Researchers. For more details, see Silva Sinha (2018: 101–131).

4 Event-based time intervals in three indigenous Brazilian cultures and languages

Awetý, Kamaiurá, and Huni Kuĩ people experience and define time through events that occur in nature, e.g., water level, sunlight, heat and position of the sun, and through activities in their social world, e.g., returning from the fields, wrestling competitions etc.. There are no lexical translation equivalents for 'time' in any of these languages and no names for days of the week, months of the year, or for year. These characteristics are also found in Amondawa (Sinha et al. 2011). In all these cultures, time is not organized and expressed metrically but is event-based (Silva Sinha et al. 2012). The event-based time intervals are indexicalized by environmental "happenings" (water level, cool breeze, bird and animal songs), celestial bodies (sun, moon, and stars), and activities. These happenings enable the people of these communities to define the time intervals that regulate their everyday life, their daily activities, and their cultural festivals. The event-based time interval is co-terminous with the event itself, in which the time interval is indexed to the event or activity that lends its name to the interval (e.g., "the sun is gone" [sunset]). In all these languages these indexes are related to environmental happenings and social activities (see Sinha et al. 2011, 2012; Silva Sinha 2018, 2019).

The lexicalization and the indexicalization of the event-based intervals and their temporal landmarks of life stages (lifespan) in these communities (Kamaiurá, Awetý, and Huni Kuĩ) are expressed and conceptualized in terms of social and biological indexes. In these cultures, people do not count their age in terms of years or months. These languages (like many other Amazonian languages) have very small number systems. In most cases, these consist of distinct terms for 'one' and 'two' with the combination of these words allowing for counting to 'three', 'four', 'five' or more, based on a compounding process, such as by juxtaposition, agglutination, or reduplication (Silva Sinha et al. 2017). Speakers of these languages consider life as being a process of learning, punctuated by different stages. Life stages for these communities should be thought of as categories of social status, not as points or spatial positions on a lifeline. For each life stage, there are certain kinds of knowledge and social responsibilities that are appropriate and necessary. The transitions between these stages can involve rites of passage and organized learning. However, the knowledge associated with one life stage category is not strictly demarcated from those of another. The knowledge of each stage can be acquired during previous stages. For example, if a young person has acquired 'adult' knowledge and responsibility (such as being a skilled fisherman or taking on household responsibilities, with a level of knowledge recognized by the entire community), he or she will be regarded and respected as a fully-grown person, at least as far as those activities are concerned. For these communities, the life stages are also characterized by physical and biological changes. For example, a girl will be considered a fully responsible person after she has gone through the rite of passage following her first menstrual period, in which she acquires the knowledge and skills of a woman in her community. Similarly, a boy, after the first manifestations of puberty, will undergo the rite of passage. Stages of life in these communities are not age-based. A very 'young' (in 'our' terms) girl who is married is considered an adult, but an older woman who has never married or had children will still be considered and treated as a youth, unless the biological signs of ageing are very evident. The difference from the age categories of 'western' societies is the focus on skills and abilities within life stages, rather than a point in a numbered timeline such as implied by the notion of 'teenage' in western culture.

An important feature to be noted about the conceptualization of time in Kamaiurá, Awetý, and Huni Kuĩ cultures and languages is that although many event-based time intervals and temporal landmarks are *indexed* by the spatial positions, shapes, and configurations of the sun, moon, and stars, these time expressions are not metaphors. The indexicalization of time intervals or landmarks seems to be metonymic (see García-Ruiz et al, this volume, sections 2.2.2 and 4.2), in the sense that an event-based interval or temporal landmark in all three languages can be defined by the spatial position, motion, or orientation of a heavenly body (or its emanation) in relation to a spatial landmark.

5 Indexicalization of time by 'happenings' and spatial landmarks

The position of the sun in the sky and the appearance of constellations indicate the period or time interval that is used to regulate social activities that people in the communities conventionally might do or can do. The position of the sun is a highly prominent temporal index, and the names of the parts of the day are in many cases based upon the sun's position and the presence or absence of light (Table 1).

Table 1: Parts of the day and night (some examples).

Language	Event-based intervals	Literal translation	Meaning	Index
Huni Kuĩ	*Bariã kapukea*	'sun-be turn-do'	'the beginning of the afternoon'	position of the sun
Awetý	*Kwat o'awajeju*	'sun lean/ beginning'	'the beginning of the afternoon'	position of the sun
Kamaiurá	*Kaaruk amue*	'forest-is [in shade]'	'in the afternoon'	the sunlight intensity and position of the sun

These event-based time intervals combine natural with social-conventional meanings, such that when the sun is in a certain position, people would habitually engage in certain activities, for example, the name of the interval used to refer to 'middle day' are *Bari manã nabi raka* 'sun half head lying' (*Huni Kui), Apyter-ype kwar-up* 'head over sun is' (Awety), and *Apyter uwaj* '[the sun] head half' (Awety). To refer to the intervals before the middle of the day and after early morning, they use the following expression: *bar kaya txakama* 'return from the field' (Huni Kuĩ),

Ko kytsaput aipok 'comeback from the field' (Awetý), and *Ko-pe-wara* '[back] from the field' (Kamaiurá). *Niwe raya ibu be ikaya* means 'working in the field time' (Huni Kuĩ). The word *niwe* means 'wind' and *be* means 'blow', so they refer to this time frame as 'a fresh time' to work in the fields since after that it becomes too hot to stay out in the open air. In this example, it is not only the natural environment happenings that index time but the activity 'back from the field time'. It was noticed that the *absence* of activities also index event-based intervals, e.g., *ypyp-ipawamue* 'later in the night' in Kamaiurá refers to the *ypy* 'beginning' of *-pipaw* 'silence', *-amue* 'when'. In the house at this time there is no noise, it is time to go to sleep (see Table 2). These are true time intervals, distinct from the actual activity, because the name of the interval does not imply that the activity is actually taking place. The temporal labels that refer to the position of the sun are not actually referring to exact points in time, but are also intervals (see also Silva Sinha 2019: 131).

Table 2: Parts of the day and night (some examples).

Languages	Event-based intervals	Literal translation	Meaning	Index
Kamaiurá	*Ypy pipawamue*	beginning-silence -when	'the silence begins later in the night, time to sleep'	the absence of activities
Awetý	Tatykym mokotu	moon-dark is	'is the night'	moonlight
Huni Kuĩ	*Bari mexu-aya*	sun dark-be	'there is no sunlight in the night'	the absence of the sunlight

Other indexical markers identified were the birdsong, monkey calls, the sound of the cicadas, the ripening of forest fruits, and the movement of animals. In Kamaiurá, for example, when a bird called *Yrywu'ajang* sings, it indicates that it is daybreak, and it is time to get up; the same is true for other birds, *Muruwiri* and *Ykyju*. However, it is important to note here that these indices vary from season to season. The moment when these birds, which never sing together, appear and sing, is dependent on the season. In Huni Kuĩ there is one species of monkey and several birdsongs that are also indices for daybreak. For example, when a *Hu* monkey calls, and the birds named *Hasin* and *Kebu* start singing, everybody in the village knows that daylight is coming. However, if the monkey *Hu* is singing at any other time, this indicates that the rain is coming. These animal behavioral indices are widespread, and they are also known by non-indigenous local people in the Amazonia region.

The seasonal intervals in Awetý, Kamaiurá, and Huni Kuĩ are named in categories for the dry and rainy seasons. These are usually translated into Portuguese, respectively, as summer and winter.[4] There are also names for subdivisions of these seasons. The indexical markers for seasonal time intervals in these cultures are also the sun, the intensity of the sunlight, the level of water in the rivers, the intensity of the rainfall, and the coolness of the air (breeze). The categorization of the seasonal event-based intervals by reference to the sun and the rain (and levels of water) is common to all these languages (see tables 3, 4, and 5).

For Huni Kuĩ, Awetý, and Kamaiurá, the sun has a central importance in both seasonal (Tables 3, 4 and 5) and the day and night intervals in these communities. The sun *Bariã* (Huni Kuĩ), *Kwaryp* (Awetý), *Kwarip* (Kamaiurá) is used to name the dry season, and its light and heat intensity indexes also the subdivision of the dry season as well as the part of the day. The absence of light at the end of the day indicates the end of the day and the beginning of the night. The moon is used to index parts of the night in Awetý, e.g., *taty-puku* 'later at night'. The moon is also employed for reckoning time. It can also index and reckon agricultural and hunting practices. Additionally, it can reckon and index women's periods and pregnancy. For these communities, the moon is a BEING represented in cosmology and mythology (Villas Boas and Villas Boas [1974] 2009; Seki 2010; Faleiros and Yawabane, 2015).

Table 3: Huni Kuĩ seasonal intervals.

a. *ui-yã* rain-is Raining	b. *ui-yã tae-i* rain-is beginning-PROG The beginning of raining	c. *ui beruKuĩ* rain fright The rain suddenly arrived
d. *ui napumã* rain strong The rain is strong	e. *ui-yã reske-aya* rain-is finished-is The raining is finished	
f. *Bari-ã* Sun-is Summer	g. *bari-ã tae-i* sun-is beginning-PROG The beginning of [summer]	h. *bari-ã beruKuĩ* sun-is fright The summer suddenly arrived
i. *bari-ã napumã* sun-is Strong The is [summer] is strong	l. *Bari-ã reske-aya* sun-is finished-is The [summer] finished	

4 The rainy season in tropical Northern Brazil more or less temporally coincides with the summer in temperate Southern Brazil, and the dry season in the North coincides with the Southern winter. The naming of the tropical dry season as "summer" and the rainy season as "winter", based upon weather patterns, is a feature of Brazilian Portuguese.

Table 4: Awetý seasonal intervals.

a. *Jo'yk-ype* breeze-density [cold breeze] winter	b. *O'-aju jo'yk* 3P.STAT breeze/water Is cold breeze	c. *Jo'yk mytet* Breeze half water Half way of cold breeze
d. *Y-watupe* water-full The [river] is full of water	e. *Jo'yk opap* breeze/water finished The [winter] finished	
f. *Kwarype* sun-inside Summer	g. *Kwa- za ju me* SUN-COLL STAT ASSERT Is [summer]	
h. *Kwaza tupyte-zan* sun- COLL is- TRANSL The [summer] is [strong]	i. *Kwa-za -tu opap* Sol – COLL NOM/action end The [summer] finished	

Table 5: Kamaiurá seasonal intervals.

a. *y-wp* water-density Rain seasons	b. *i-ro'ytsanga ypy* 2P/his-cold breeze beginning The cold breeze is beginning	c. *i-ro'ytsanga Mytet* 2P/his-cold breeze half Half [way] of the cold breeze	
d. *i-ro'ytsanga r-ahwa'apyt* 2P/his-cold breeze tip end The end of the tip of the cold breeze			
e. *Kwar-ip* sun -POSTP Summer	f. *kwara ypy* sun beginning the [summer] beginning	g. *Kwara mytet* sun half Half of the summer	h. *Kwa-rahwa'apyt* sun- tip end The end of the tip of the [summer]

Furthermore, to the water and sun indices, there are additional features that index some intervals in each of these three languages. In each case, these are related to the particular environmental conditions of the locality in which the community lives, and, in each language, specific events or happenings index the seasonal time intervals. For example, in Awetý and Kamaiurá seasonal terms, there is, in addition to the water-level index, a reference to the 'cool breeze' and the sensation of cold: *Jo'ykype* (Awetý) and *iro'ytsanga* (Kamaiurá) mean 'cool breeze', which is an index of the rainy season. In Huni Kuĩ, too, the rain, the level of the water, the sun and the intensity of heat and light are the basis of the seasonal indexicalization. However, there is also a reference to astonishment or surprise at the beginning of both rainy and dry seasons. The term *berukuĩ* literally means 'surprise, astonishment'; it does not make reference to activity but rather to the way people perceive the beginning of the fall of rain in the wet season and the heat of the sun in the dry season.

Some animal behaviors are used to indexically mark seasonal changes and associated activities. For example, in Kamaiurá, the onset of the sound of the cicada *Kuarai Jumi'ã* signifies the dry season when the river is drying up and there will be a lot of fish to catch. The event-based time gives us support to argue that the concepts of time are, in many cultures, directly linked with environmental happenings, celestial bodies (sun, moon, and stars), and social activities. Therefore, there are enough linguistic and cultural shreds of evidence confirming that event-based time concepts and this system are more widespread in traditional cultures than calendar and clock time concepts. The use of event-based time concepts can be claimed to exist in many cultures, but they are culture-specific, and occur in their ecological niches, having their own social structure and value system. It is important to highlight here that the totality of the indices based upon the environmental occurrences, social activities, and biological change in the body together make up the temporal fabric of life in Awetý, Kamaiurá, and Huni Kuĩ societies.

6 Time is not a line

Events do not occur on their own; they occur in the 'flow' of time or in a 'stream' of events. They are happenings that occur in relation to the time of utterance, in the past or future (Deictic time: D-time); or in relation to other happenings, in an event sequence (S-time). Both D-time and S-time are spatialized in many languages in terms of a timeline in which events are either "ahead" or "behind" the present moment (D-time); or ordered from earlier/before to later (S-time).

In these three languages, both D-time and S-time are expressed. For example, there are words for 'tomorrow' and 'yesterday'. Some event-based time intervals make up ordered, sequential systems (e.g., parts of the day, life stages). However, as we have emphasized, there is no representation of time in terms of a line in any of these languages. In all three languages and cultures, the past and future are not located behind (past) and in front (future) of the deictic origin 'now', as they can be in English. Nor is the past above and the future below the present, as sometimes occurs in Chinese (Boroditsky 2001; Fuhrman et at., 2011; Yu, 1998, 2012). Nor do we see the reverse pattern as in Aymara (Núñez and Sweetser 2006), in which the future is behind and the past in front; or in Vietnamese, in which time 'approaches' from the future, behind Ego, and continues 'forward' into the past (Sullivan and Bui 2016). Nor do the Huni Kuĩ, Awetý, and Kamaiurá speakers mentally travel in time, as it is claimed for Malagasy: "Malagasy moves backward into the future" (Dahl 1995). In fact, in the three languages, there is no 'mental time travel' metaphor of the Moving Ego. Events do not move on the timeline either, although they can "approach" the speaker and they can "pass" and "disappear". In fact, for Huni Kuĩ, Awety, and Kamaiurá, the past and future are not spatialized in relation to a time line, but are *psychological* concepts related to memory and anticipation of events. In Huni Kuĩ, past events are located in the *heart* and future events and plans are located in the *head* (which is thought of as the location of the mind and thinking). The source domain for conceptualizing past and future is not a spatial orientation (in front/behind, up/down, left/right), but it is the senses and their embodiment.

In Awetý and Kamaiurá, the PAST is located *in their eyes*. The past in this sense is linked with memories, and the memories can be *seen in the mind's eye*. This metaphor for the past can be compared with the English metaphorical usage of 'see' to mean 'understand', with the source domain VISION mapping to mental process through the conceptual metaphor UNDERSTANDING IS SEEING (Lakoff and Johnson 1980; Sweetser 1990). In Awetý and Kamaiurá, however, REMEMBERING IS SEEING. This has some similarity to what Dahl (1995: 199) reports for Malagasy, in which "The past . . . is seen 'in front of the eyes'."

For Awetý and Kamaiurá, by contrast, it is the FUTURE that is *in front of the eyes*. But this should not be understood as a 'reversal' of a time line, or different orientations of a time line. *In front of the eyes* should *not* be understood as meaning either 'future is ahead on a time line' (Awetý and Kamaiurá), or 'past is ahead on a timeline' (Malagasy). In fact, none of these languages have metaphors for past and future based on the model of time as 'passage', or the 'flow' of the 'river of time' (Smart 1949). The metaphor is different, and it has to do with memory and imagination.

In Huni Kuĩ, Awetý, and Kamaiurá, the future is marked in the language as a *possibility of completion*, or *desire for completion*, of an anticipated or intended event. The event is metaphorically located within sight, but not far away; it can be seen, it is not unknown. The visual field is the source domain to express future or desired events. The evidence gathered in this research suggested that in these cultures past and future are conceptualized not in terms of spatial direction but in terms of the embodiment of mental representational capacities: *memory, anticipation, intention,* and *imagination.*

7 Conclusion

Event-based time intervals exist in all cultures and languages, in contrast to metric time intervals (e.g., clock time and calendar time), which are not found in all cultures. Metric time is a cultural creation, which leads to the notion of 'Time as Such'. Event-based time intervals have been reported to exist in many other cultures all over the world; e.g., Bunun in Taiwan, the Malagasy people in Madagascar, the Tiv community in Central Nigeria, the Tarifit (known as Berber), the Amondawa, and other Tupian language-cultures in Brazil (see El-Arbaoui Jelouli 2013; Huang 2016; Sinha et al. 2011; Dahl 1995; Bohannan 1953; Baldus 1940). In English, event-based time is used in expressions like *let's meet at lunchtime* or *I will be around yours at teatime.*[5] In the city of Belém, in Northern Brazil, people traditionally make an appointment based on the rainfall, e.g., *vamos nos encontrar antes da chuva da tarde ou depois da chuva da tarde* ('let's meet up before the afternoon rain or after the afternoon rain').

The event-based time reported in this article is related to *seasons, times of day/night* and *life stages* in Huni Kuĩ, Awetý, and Kamaiurá cultures, as well as in the other cultures and languages that we have briefly discussed. The indexes used by speakers to refer to an event-based time interval are embedded in everyday life, in the communities' relationships with the environment, and in their cosmology. The sun, the moon, the stars, and natural and social happenings index the intervals of time. In all three languages, years are referred to as the dry season only, using the root meaning 'sun'. This indicates that the dry seasons are used as a basis to understand 'year'. The sun is central to the concept and to the naming of part of the day and the dry season in all three cultures. The same way, the moon and the absence of the sunlight are used to name the night intervals; the rain, on the other hand, is an intensity index for the rainy season.

All these cultures (Awetý, Huni Kuĩ, and Kamaiurá) have significant similarities in the ways in which they conceptualize event-based temporality. Their time intervals are indexicalized not only by environmental happenings, the movements of celestial bodies (sun, moon, stars) but also by the regularities of social life and habits.

The temporal concepts for these communities are not metric, not cyclical and not based upon a timeline. Traditionally, there are no references for weeks, months, and years; there is no term in the languages for 'time'. The same way, the life stages are not fixed to a point of a timeline (birthdays), and they are not a 'progression' on a timeline either; rather, life stages comprise a sequence of states of being. In this sense, we argued that life stages are *events* in the process of learning and acquiring skills, and therefore the stages are categories of social life and cannot be fixed points on a 'lifeline'. In contrast with 'Time as Such' and 'linear time', which relate to precisely measured (metric) time, in which punctual moments are located on a linear or cyclical timeline, event-based intervals

5 This is an attested expression in British English, in which 'yours' is used to refer to 'your house'.

cannot be precisely measured. In event-based time cultures, schedules cannot be exactly fixed. This is because the rhythm of everyday happenings brings the subjective necessity for people to experience and do things at or around the occurrence of the events that will trigger the activities. It is important to emphasize that 'time' is not the trigger of the event, but rather the event generates the relevant actions.

It is evident that the absence of metric time, of a concept of 'Time as Such', does not necessarily imply the absence of time. The cultural and linguistic repertoires of event-based time concepts described above used by these communities has illustrated this complex way to think and talk about 'time'. It is also important to emphasize again that metric time is a cultural invention, and the associated, resulting notion of 'Time as Such' is also a cultural invention. It is only our cultural familiarity with this notion that leads us to assume that it is common to all cultures. The assumption that linear time is predominant in all cultures can lead to misunderstanding of cultures that use exclusively event-based time concepts (Sinha and Gärdenfors, 2015).

Conceptually, speakers of the three languages locate past and future events in embodied cognitive and perceptual processes, rather than locating them along an oriented timeline. For Awetý and Kamaiurá, the past is *in their eyes*. Their past consists of memories, and memories can be 'seen' in 'the mind's eye'. Therefore, in Kamaiurá and Awetý, REMEMBERING IS SEEING. The future for Awetý and Kamaiurá is in front of the speaker's eyes but not far away; it is located in the immediate visual field. Past is not located behind the speaker for these cultures. As pointed out in section 6 above, it is likely that in these cultures past and future are conceptualized in terms not of spatial direction but of embodied mental capacities: *memory*, *anticipation*, *intention*, and *imagination*.

In the absence of metric time, of a concept of 'Time as Such', and of lexicalized concepts of past and future, Event-based time intervals give structure to a complex and traditional lifeworld. Overall, the evidence presented through this research shows that there are many similarities in the ways in which Awetý, Huni Kuĩ, and Kamaiurá conceptualize event-based time. These findings, together with other research on Amazonian languages referred to in this chapter, suggests that they all participate in a cultural areal conceptual complex encompassing Amazonian and many other South American linguistic families. However, there are many aspects of such cultural, linguistic, and cognitive systems that need further research in order to deepen the analysis of language, cognition, and culture.

References

Baldus, Herbet. 1940. O conceito do tempo entre os índios do Brasil [The concept of time among Brazilian Indians]. *Revista do Arquivo*, (LXXI). 87–94.

Benini, Arnaldo. 2017. *Neurobiologia del tempo*. Milano: Raffaello Cortina Editore.

Bohannan, Paul. 1953. Concepts of time among the Tiv of Nigeria. *Southwestern Journal of Anthropology* 9 (3). 251–262.

Boroditsky, Lera. 2000. Metaphoric structuring: understanding time through spatial metaphors. *Cognition*, 75 (1), 1–28.

Boroditsky, Lera. 2001. Does language shape thought? English and Mandarin speakers' conceptions of time. *Cognitive Psychology* 43, 1–22.

Boroditsky, Lera, Orly Fuhrman, & Kelly McKormick. 2010. Do English and Mandarin speakers think about time differently? *Cognition* 118. 123–129.

Bylund, Emanuel & Panos Athanasopoulos. 2017. The Whorfian time warp: representing duration through the language hourglass. *Journal of Experimental Psychology: General* 146. 911–916.

Casasanto, Daniel, Lera Boroditsky, Webb Phillps, Jesse Greene, Shima Goswami, Simon Bocanegra-Thiel, Ilia Santiago-Diaz, Olga Fotokopoulu, Ria Pita & David Gil. 2004. How deep are effects of language on thought? Time estimation in speakers of English, Indonesian, Greek, and Spanish. In Kenneth Forbus, Dedre Gentner & Terry Regier (eds.), *Proceedings of the 26th Annual Conference of the Cognitive Science Society*, 186–191. Mahwah, NJ: Lawrence Erlbaum Associates.

Dahl, Øyvind. 1995. When the future comes from behind: Malagasy and other time concepts and some consequences for communication. *International Journal of Intercultural Relations* 19 (2). 197–209.

El-Arbaoui Jellouli, Amar. 2013. *A cognitive approach to Berber-Tamazight sociocultural reality: the bioconceptual organization of 'Izri' poetics by Tarifit-speaking Riffian women* (PhD Thesis). Univesidad de Las Palmas de Gran Canaria, Las Palmas de Gran Canaria.

Faleiros, Álvaro and Leopardo Yawabane. 2014. *Assim se fez a lua* [So the Moon was made]. São Paulo: Publifolha, Brasil.

Frassinetti, Francesca, Marinella Cappelletti & Domenica Bueti. 2016. The neurobiology of time processing. *Neural Plasticity*, Article ID 1706373, Volume 2016.

Fuhrman, Orly, Kelly McCormick, Eva Chen, Heidi D. Jiang, Dingfuag Shu, Shuaimei Mao & Lera Boroditsky. 2011. How linguistic and cultural forces shape conceptions of time: English and Mandarin time in 3D. *Cognitive Science* 35. 1305–1328.

Fulga, Angelica. 2012. Language and the perception of space, motion and time. *Concordia Working Papers in Applied Linguistics* 3. 26–37.

Huang, Shuping. 2016. Time as space metaphor in Isbukun Bunun: a semantic analysis. *Oceanic Linguistics* 55 (1). 1–24.

Klein, Wolfgang. 2008. Time in language, language in time. *Language Learning* 58: Suppl. 1. 1–12.

Lakoff, George, & Mark Johnson. 1999. *Philosophy in the flesh: The embodied mind and its challenge to Western thought*. New York: Basic Books.

Levinson, Stephen C. & Asifa Majid. 2013. The island of time: Yélî Dnye, the language of Rossel Island. *Frontiers in Psychology* 4.

Mauss, Marcel. 1966. *The gift: Forms and functions of exchange in archaic societies*. London: Cohen & West Ltd.
Meijl, Toon van. 1993. Maori Meeting-Houses in and over time. In James J. Fox (ed.), *Inside Austronesian houses: Perspectives on domestic designs for living*, 201–225. Canberra: ANU Press.
Núñez, Rafael E. & Eve Sweetser. 2006. With the future behind them: Convergent evidences from Aymara language and gesture in the cross-linguistic comparison of spatial construals of time. *Cognitive Science* 30. 401–450.
Seki, Lucy. 2010. *Jene Ramŷjwena juru pytsaret: O que habitava a boca de nossos ancestrais*. [Jene Ramŷjwena juru pytsaret: What inhabited the mouths of our ancestors]. Rio de Janeiro: Museu do Índio-FUNAI.
Silva Sinha, Vera da, Chris Sinha, Wany Sampaio & Jörg Zinken. 2012. Event-based time intervals in an Amazonian culture. In Luna Filipović & Kasia Jaszczolt (eds.), *Space and time in languages and cultures II: language, culture, and cognition*, 15–35. Human Cognitive Processing Series 37. Amsterdam: John Benjamins.
Silva Sinha, Vera da, Wany Sampaio & Chris Sinha. 2017. The many ways to count the world: counting terms in indigenous languages and cultures of Rondônia, Brazil. *Brief Encounters* 1 (1). 1–18. http://briefencounters-journal.co.uk/BE/article/view/26/ (accessed 25 June 2020).
Silva Sinha, Vera da. 2018. *Linguistic and cultural conceptualisations of time in Huni Kuĩ, Awetý and Kamaiurá indigenous commuities of Brazil*. Norwich: University of East Anglia dissertation.
Silva Sinha, Vera da. 2019. Event-based time in three indigenous Amazonian and Xinguan cultures and languages. *Frontiers in Psychology* 10 (454). doi: 10.3389/fpsyg.2019.00454 (accessed 25 June 2020).
Sinha, Chris & Peter Gärdenfors. 2014. Time, space, and events in language and cognition: a comparative view. *Annals of the New York Academy of Sciences* 1326. 72–81.
Sinha, Chris, Vera da Silva Sinha, Jörg Zinken & Wany Sampaio. 2011. When time is not space: the social and linguistic construction of time intervals and temporal event relations in an Amazonian culture. *Language and Cognition* 3 (1). 137–169.
Smart, John Jamieson Carswell. 1949. The river of time. *Mind* 58 (232). 483–494.
Sullivan, Karen, & Linh Thuy Bui. 2016. With the future coming up behind them: Evidence that Time approaches from behind in Vietnamese. *Cognitive Linguistics* 27 (2). 205–233.
Sweetser, Eve. 1990. *From Etymology to Pragmatics: Metaphorical and cultural aspects of semantic structure*. Cambridge: Cambridge University Press.
Villas Boas, Orlando & Cláudio Villas Boas. [1974] 2009. *Xingu: The Indians, their myths* (Reprint edition). London: Souvenir Press.
Yu, Ning. 1998. *The contemporary theory of metaphor: A perspective from Chinese*. Amsterdam: John Benjamins Publishing Company.
Yu, Ning. 2012. The metaphorical orientation of time in Chinese. *Journal of Pragmatics* 44 (10). 1335–1354.

Ketty García-Ruiz, Jaime Huasco-Escalante,
Jhon Jairo López-Rojas

Resemblance metaphor and metonymy in the ethnozoological lexicon of the Amazonian language Aguaruna

Abstract: This chapter focuses on the analysis of resemblance metaphors and metonymies that operate in the ethnozoological lexicon of the Amazonian language Aguaruna. Our corpus is basically composed of binomials (noun-noun compounds) in which these semantic mechanisms are representative and useful for naming sub-generic species. In our analysis, we have mostly identified the mapping of prominent characteristics such as color and shape (metonymic bases) in resemblance metaphors. Many of our examples also reveal the preference for metonymies constituted by habitat data and the diet of the named entities, significant information for a hunting people like the Aguaruna. Finally, we see that, in the binomials analyzed, the source domains are not always other biological organisms (plants and animals), but can be elements of nature, cultural objects, and even mythological characters.

Keywords: ethnobiology, fauna, cognitive linguistics, metaphor, metonymy, Aguaruna, Jivaroan

> What is relevant here is that the semantic resources of language are productively employed in what might be called the metaphorical mapping of the ethnobiological landscape.
>
> —Berlin (1992: 259)

1 Introduction

Metaphors and metonymies are essential in our conceptualization of reality and in the understanding and the expression of our environment (Lakoff and Johnson 1980). Their effects can be seen in everyday language and in specialized areas such as the ethnobiological lexicon. Academic interest in exploring this nomenclature, directly or indirectly, by approaches that consider metaphoric and meto-

Ketty García-Ruiz, Pontificia Universidad Católica del Perú / Universidad Privada del Norte, Peru
Jaime Huasco-Escalante, Pontificia Universidad Católica del Perú, Peru
Jhon Jairo López-Rojas, Instituto Nacional de Innovación Agraria – INIA, Peru

https://doi.org/10.1515/9783110688306-005

nymic mechanisms, can be seen, for example, in the analysis of names of marine biology of Western languages (Ureña and Faber 2010; Ureña 2011; Tercedor, López, Márquez, and Faber 2012; Guasparri 2019). To a lesser extent, studies have also identified such mechanisms in Australian (Turpin 2013) and Amazonian languages (Valenzuela 1998; Zariquiey 2018).

This chapter builds on Berlin's[1] (1992) fifth principle of ethnobiological nomenclature. According to this principle, ethnobiological names usually have metaphorical features that reveal a motivation for relating the name to the named referent. In addition, for Berlin (1992), the names of animals and plants of sub-generic ranks, which usually include linguistically complex forms such as compound nouns (e.g., in English, *white oak*, *black oak*, and *red oak*), reflect this principle in the modifying constituent, where the shape, color, texture, smell, flavor, and other ecological characteristics of particular species are addressed. In this perspective, the aim of this chapter is to analyze metaphors and metonymies that operate in compound nouns (binomials) of the ethnozoological lexicon of the Amazonian language Aguaruna. In our analysis, in addition, we intend to reveal regularities in metaphorical and metonymic mappings as well as particular issues of the Aguaruna ethnozoological nomenclature system.

In theoretical terms, our analysis is framed by cognitive semantics as we consider that this approach allows us to understand, through the lexicon, how the speakers of Amazonian communities conceptualize their natural environment and, particularly, how they structure their deep ethnobiological knowledge, in which cognitive operations and cultural factors relevant to speakers (habits, beliefs, taboos, myths) come into play. Our study also includes an interdisciplinary perspective. This is reflected in our team, which is made up of both linguists and a biologist who works in the area under study. Considering the small number of publications of this nature related to Amazonian languages, we hope to encourage the development of similar studies with this paper.

In section 2, we show the relationship between ethnobiology and cognitive linguistics. We also review the classification of resemblance metaphors of Ureña and Faber (2010) and Ureña (2011). Next, we discuss the classification of metonymies as proposed by Radden and Kövecses (1999), Kövecses ([2002] 2010), and Evans (1997). Likewise, we present the linguistic nature of Aguaruna in broad terms and aspects related to the ethnobiological lexicon. In section 3, we present the methodology for data collection. In section 4, we analyze the metaphors and metonymies of the selected corpus, focusing on the regularities and particularities

1 Berlin (1992) proposes seven general principles of ethnobiological categorization (taxonomy) and five of nomenclature of plants and animals (lexical structure).

that emerge from the Aguaruna ethnozoological nomenclature. Finally, in section 5, we present the conclusion of our paper.

2 Theoretical framework

2.1 Ethnobiology and cognitive linguistics

In the late sixties and during the seventies of the last century, the so-called cognitive anthropologists strengthened fields of study that would become important for linguistics and psychology: perception and categorization. Berlin and Kay (1969), in their widely known work on the perception and categorization of color in traditional communities, proposed a universal approach to color based on basic categories (Boster 2005). Rosch, from a cognitive psychology viewpoint, also studied categorization and established that prototypical colors could be found in the chromatic complexity (Luque 2001).

The color studies showed that perception centered on focused colors, so that these colors were more likely to be named in various languages. Regarding this contribution from Berlin and Kay, Schmid states that "[t]heir research proved to be an important inspiration for cognitive linguists, because it indicated that there was a much closer and more direct tie between perception and naming than had previously been assumed" (Schmid 2007: 122). Certainly, categorization and perception, and their implications for the lexicon, are not only appreciated in the field of color research, but also in folk-biological taxonomies.

Berlin, Breedlove, and Raven (1973), as well as Berlin (1992), suggest precisely that societies basically organize the ethnobiological domain into five hierarchical ranks: (i) *unique beginner*, which considers the most inclusive categories, such as 'plant' and 'animal'; (ii) *life-form*, which includes subdivisions of the *unique beginner*, such as 'tree', 'mammal' or 'bird'; (iii) *generic*, which includes the largest number of biological entities that are derived from *life-forms*, such as 'oak', 'cow', or 'parrot'; (iv) *specific*, which specifies the *generic*, although it is less numerous; and (v) *varietal*, which specifies the previous rank, although its presence is quite small (see Figure 1). Among these, Berlin (1992) argues that the *generic* is the most psychologically prominent rank (therefore, it would be among the first that children learn) and the most numerous of all, since in folk taxonomies it can include around 500 taxa. Thus, the notion of a *generic taxa* in the naming and categorization of animal and plant domains is central. Along these lines, Schmid (2007) considers that the *generic level* is like a strip that divides biological reality and that it is helpful for speakers to name organisms at this level.

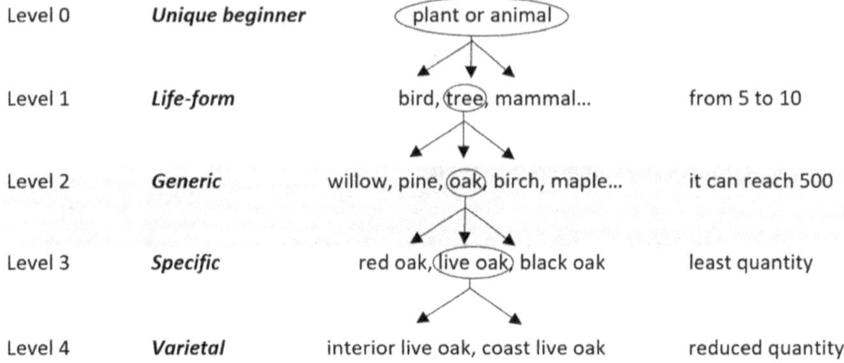

Figure 1: Ethnobiological ranks for the taxonomic organization (based on Berlin, Breedlove, and Raven 1973).

Berlin's notion of *generic level* is related to Rosch's concept of *basic level*. Essentially, *basic level* in taxonomies is an abstraction level that includes elements of easy cognitive recovery (*dog*), since they are quite clear mental images, as opposed to the subordinate (*poodle*) or superordinate (*animal*) items (Cuenca and Hilferty [1999] 2007). In this way, the basic level represents "a fundamental one for the organization of concepts underlying concrete nouns and it is one of the key concepts of cognitive linguistics" (Mihatsch 2016: 461–462).

At the linguistic level, Schmid (2007) points out that the terms at the *basic level* are usually morphologically simple, as at the *generic level* of folk taxonomies. In addition, he states that this level provides "the raw material for extensions of the lexicon by means of metaphor, metonymy, and word formation" (Schmid 2007: 124). In fact, in ethnobiological nomenclature, extensions of the lexicon operate with visibility at the sub-generic levels (*specific* and *varietal*), which is especially identified in compound words. For example, in their study of ethnobiological nomenclature in the Aguaruna language, Berlin and Berlin (1979) showed that both *generic* and *life-form* names are linguistically simple. By contrast, sub-generic level names have generally complex structures, such as binomials $[N\text{-}N]_N$, where the head noun indicates the category that includes the named species and the modifying noun defines the referent, thanks to the metaphorical and metonymic load it has. To that extent, and as we consider it in our work, ethnobiological binomials constitute fertile ground for studies in the field of cognitive semantics. Even though Berlin's proposal has been problematized (Boster 2005; Hunn and Brown 2011), many of the author's concepts remain relevant, such as, for example, the fifth of Berlin's nomenclature principle which specifies the semantic motivation revealed by ethnobiological names. Likewise important is the second principle, which states that "[n]ames for plants and animals commonly allude metaphorically to some typical morphological, behavioral, ecological, or qualitative characteristic feature of their referents" (Berlin 1992: 31). In our analysis of ethnozoological binomials, we consider these traits in metaphorical and metonymic transfers.

2.2 Resemblance metaphor and metonymy in the lexical analysis

2.2.1 Resemblance metaphor

The concept of metaphor is central to cognitive linguistics. With the studies presented by Lakoff and Johnson (1980) as well as Lakoff (1987), metaphor is conceived not as a mere poetic operation, but as part of the conceptualization process that human beings carry out. In broad terms, metaphor is seen as "understanding and experiencing one kind of thing in terms of another" (Lakoff and Johnson 1980: 5); that is, we understand a conceptual domain through another domain (Kövecses 2010: 4).

As part of the theoretical development of the conceptual metaphor theory, from the beginning there has been a concern to establish typologies. For example, Lakoff (1987) distinguishes *image metaphors* from *structural metaphors*, and Grady (1999) differentiates *resemblance metaphors* from *correlational metaphors*. According to Ureña and Faber (2010), to a greater or lesser extent, these classifications make a distinction between metaphors based on comparisons of physical or behavioral features (for example, *the computer mouse* or *Achilles is a lion*[2]) and metaphors based on more abstract and subjective correlations (such as LOVE IS A JOURNEY or A DISCUSSION IS WAR).

If we focus on the study of names of animal and plant organisms, several investigations have revealed the constant participation of metaphors based on physical or behavioral analogies (Guasparri 2007; Juliá 2009; Ureña 2011; Turpin 2013; Zariquiey 2018). Along these lines, it is pertinent to present the proposal by Ureña and Faber (2010) of *resemblance metaphors*, because it precisely includes these analogies. Basically, *resemblance metaphors* consider physical (shape, color, dimension) or behavioral (behavior, performance) characteristics as the basis of

2 The technological device is called a mouse because there is an analogy between the device and the physical appearance and movements of the rodent (Ungerer and Schmid [1996] 2006: 148). On the other hand, in *Achilles is a lion*, the brave behaviors of both Achilles and the lion are associated with how they face an opponent, and not with a comparison of the physical aspect (Grady 1997).

metaphorical projections from one domain to another. In this way, Ureña and Faber (2010) include in their proposal of *resemblance metaphor,* Lakoff's (1987) *image metaphor,* and Grady's (1999) *resemblance metaphor*. The criteria for both being part of a single category is due to the fact that mental images underlie both.

Although mental images are generally considered to be associated with the visual perception of physical attributes (such as color and shape), Ureña and Faber (2010) argue that it is possible that events or actions also evoke mental images (in this case, dynamic images). This means that mental images are formed not only through visual perception, but also through other channels of perception. Coinciding with this, for Ureña and Faber (2010), Lakoff's *image metaphor* and Grady's *resemblance metaphor* would be related to static mental images and to dynamic images, respectively.

Following the mental images criteria and the examples presented by Ureña and Faber (2010) in their study of marine biology, the following classification of *resemblance metaphors* is established: (i) *image metaphors*, based on static images, which prototypically consider color and shape traits; (ii) *behavioral based-metaphors*, which may have dynamic images or static images; and (iii) *metaphors with physical and behavioral motivations*, which constitute a transition between the first two (see Figure 2).

In the field of marine biology studied by Ureña (2011), there are prototypical examples for each group. A clear example of the first group, *image metaphor*, is *seahorse* (*Hippocampus*); named as such because the shape of the horse's head is projected towards the top of the named marine species. This is a metaphor based on visual perception (static image). According to Ureña (2011), these metaphors maintain a high level of iconicity between the source domain and the target domain. Likewise, these metaphors (which consider color and form) are seen as prototypical (Ureña and Faber 2010). Correspondingly, for our analysis, we chose to name as *non-prototypical image metaphors* those that take into account other features (texture, pattern, flavor, smell, sound). For the second group, *archer fish* (*Toxotidae*) is an example of a *behavior based-metaphor with dynamic image*, since it is not based on a correspondence of form or color (static image), but on the dynamic behavior performed by both the *archer* and the *fish*. In this case, actions are mapped: the archer throws an arrow towards a target as the fish throws drops of water at an insect close to the surface of the sea. Within this second group, Ureña and Faber (2010) state that it is possible to find *behavior based-metaphors with static image* such as in *hawk fish* (*Cirrhitidae*), in which the waiting position of the fish on the reefs is compared with the position of the hawk looking out for potential prey. As for the third group, they indicate that it is possible to find *metaphors with physical and behavioral motivations* such as in *boxer crab* (*Lybia tessellata*), where there is a similarity between the tweezers and the arms of the boxer as well as in the defense actions that both entities perform with their limbs.

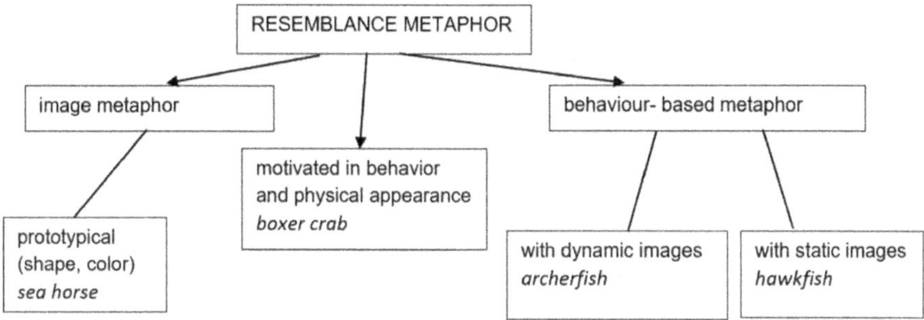

Figure 2: Classification of the resemblance metaphor based on Ureña and Faber (2010).

2.2.2 Metonymy

The revised *resemblance metaphors* do not operate in isolation, but are presented together with metonymies. As Kövecses (2013) suggests, in image metaphors it is a constant that there is a metonymic basis, given that a part of the entire entity is mapped to make the conceptual correlation with a part of another entity. This occurs when "the inevitably partial structure of the source, B, is used to conceptualize an equally inevitable part of the target, A, resulting in the metonymies 'A PART OF B FOR THE WHOLE OF B and A PART OF A FOR THE WHOLE OF A', given the general metaphor format A IS B" (Kövecses 2013: 75). Following this observation, several ethnozoological names involve metaphoric mechanisms that originate from metonyms or partial identifications of a whole.

Therefore, the definition and taxonomy of conceptual metonymy proposed by Radden and Kövecses (1999) and Kövecses (2010) is useful for our analysis due to their organization of a wide variety of metonymic relationships based on *idealized cognitive models* (ICMs). Precisely so, the definition of Radden and Kövecses (1999) of metonymy as "a cognitive process in which one conceptual entity, the vehicle, provides mental access to another conceptual entity, the target, within the same idealized cognitive model [ICM]" (Radden and Kövecses 1999: 21) helps to understand the ICMs as organizing domains of the world, since, as speakers, we understand 'reality' as parts of a whole (in a metonymic way).

Radden and Kövecses (1999) begin their organization of the various types of metonymies with two broad relational categories, *whole-part* and *part-part*. According to Littlemore (2015), Radden and Kövecses's proposal includes 6 ICMs within the *whole-part* category, and with them derives up to 21 types of metonymies (PART FOR WHOLE, ENDS FOR WHOLE SCALE, MATERIAL FOR OBJECT, etc.). Regarding the *part-part* relationship, the proposal includes 10 ICMs that allow them to activate up to 43 metonymies (THING PERCEIVED FOR PERCEPTION, EFFECT FOR CAUSE, PRODUCER FOR PRODUCT, etc.). Particularly, in our ethnozoological corpus, in addition to the names that contain metonymies that interact with *resemblance metaphors*, there is a considerable group of binomials in which metonymy operates independently in the modifier (Benczes 2006).

As a complement to the classification of Radden and Kövecses (1999), we consider the *sign metonymy* developed by Evans (1997). This metonymy is activated when "one biological entity signals the presence or availability of another" (Evans 1997: 136). We must consider that these metonymies are not limited to relating biological entities, but also include cultural elements (taboos and myths). Turpin (2013) presents examples of the Australian language Kaytetye in which she describes the presence of hazards through the songs of various species of birds. In addition to cultural factors, sign metonymies include associations of biological entities with meteorological occurrences. This is of special interest for our analysis because, in the Aguaruna lexicon, there are cases in which the presence of an ethnozoological species indicates the arrival of summer or the abundance of rainfall.

2.3 The Aguaruna language, its speakers, and its ethnobiological lexicon

Aguaruna is an Amazonian language spoken in the Peruvian regions of the Amazon, Cajamarca, Ucayali, Madre de Dios, and San Martín. Together with the Shuar, Wampis, Shiwiar, and Achuar, the Aguaruna is part of the Jivaroan languages spoken in Peru. According to the national census of 2017, in regions mentioned above there are 419 communities that house approximately 52,573 people who have Aguaruna as their first language (INEI 2018).

Historically, and after several migratory movements, many Aguaruna communities have occupied the upper basin of the Mayo River, known as the Alto Mayo region, located in the provinces of Rioja and Moyobamba, in the region of San Martín (Elliot 1998). According to Barreto (2009), these communities were strategically located near the Mayo River and its tributaries in order to take advantage of natural resources. Currently, there are 14 Aguaruna communities in this area (see Figure 3).

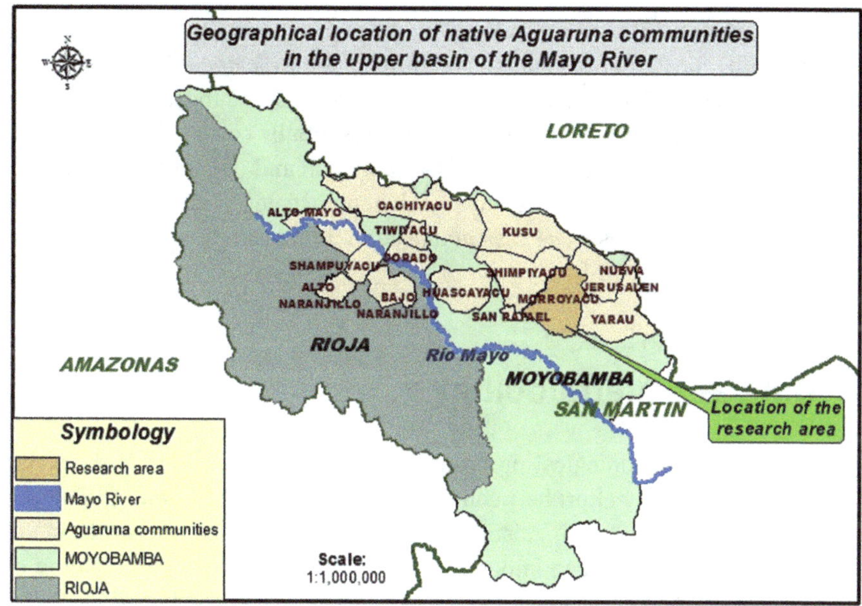

Figure 3: Location of the Morroyacu community. Source: Elaborated by the Environmental Engineer Raúl Reátegui-Ruiz.

The data we use in this chapter were collected and elicited in the community of Morroyacu (Moyobamba) in the months of January, July, and December 2019. This is a hamlet that has just over 30 homes, a kindergarten, and a primary school (both are bilingual). The population has a strong rooting towards their native language, as people of all ages speak it and, until now, children acquire Aguaruna as their first language. As for their daily activities, families cultivate agriculture, hunt, and fish for food. Morroyacu has a warm and moderately rainy climate with a temperature that varies from 16.4 to 28.4°C, which are appropriate environmental conditions for maintaining a varied flora and fauna.

Aguaruna is an agglutinative language of the nominative-accusative type with dominant SOV syntactic order (Corbera 1994). In relation to the class of words, it has open categories such as verbs, nouns, and adjectives, which are complemented by minor words, such as pronouns, determiners, adverbs, and interjections (Overall 2007). Phonologically, this language is characterized by its nasality, and at the morphosyntactic level, it presents case markers that are added to nominal categories.

In our study, we will analyze ethnobiological names. In Aguaruna, we can find names of animal and plant entities with the following profile: (i) simple nouns, which make up the majority and especially name generic levels of ethnobiological taxonomy, such as *punúk* 'crab' (*Cambaridae* spp.[3]); (ii) derivative nouns, which can be located at the sub-generic level, such as *jempé-kit* 'hummingbird with yellow beak' (*Trogonidae* spp.); (iii) noun-noun compounds, which have an important presence in the lexicon and which essentially cover sub-generic categories, such as *shuin katíp* 'type of rat' (*Akodon* sp.); and (iv) constructions with genitive, which are rare and also cover sub-generic categories, such as *iwanchí tugkuíji* 'type of stick insect' (*Phasmatidae* spp.). In this study, we focus only on the last two cases.

3 Data and methodology

Following the methodological proposal of Fleck (2007), this work is the result of an interdisciplinary effort between biology and linguistics. To that extent, the work team is composed of linguistic specialists and a biologist who works in the San Martín region. It is also important to recognize the active participation of members of the Morroyacu community in the interviews we conducted.

Within the framework of the ethnographic nature of our study, we can point out the following work sequence. First, we prepared a database of 151 entries with the help of Aguaruna-Spanish dictionaries (Minedu 1996; Aidesep 2011), technical documents on food (Creed-Kanashiro, Roche, Tuesta and Kuhnlein 2009), fauna (Dauphiné 2008; Patton, Berlin, and Berlin 1981), reports of fieldwork in Aguaruna communities (Brown 2014, Berlin and Berlin 1979), and texts of Aguaruna mythology (Chumap and García-Rendueles 1979). In other words, we elaborated what Fleck (2007) calls an "expected species checklist". Next, we made three trips to the Morroyacu community in the months of January, July, and December 2019. In each visit, we developed two group sessions and one personal interview with each collaborator. We usually worked with five adults (the men dedicated to hunting and the women to the care of the orchards) and one elderly male (a connoisseur of myths). In data elicitation, as proposed by Fleck (2007), we sought to compile ethnobiological names in the vernacular and to match these names to those in the initial list. Finally, we processed all the information and consolidated the final database of 92 entries.[4]

---

3 Throughout this paper, when we do not fully identify the species, we use the abbreviation sp. (singular form of species), and,- if it refers to multiple species of the same genus – spp. (plural form) after the generic name.

4 The final corpus can be seen at https://docs.google.com/spreadsheets/d/16fKicrnoHFkBOFC-Q1ZJAhKZiPX_cZQxCD9URzIuz6zg/edit?usp=sharing

In the formation of our database, we considered the noun-noun compounds that have the scheme $[N_{(MOD)}\ N_{(HEAD)}]_N$. We have chosen these binomials because their semantic motivation still maintains some transparency. In these binomials, the modifying name presents the metaphorical or metonymic load, while the head noun identifies the category that includes the referent named by the entire compound (in Aguaruna, this category usually refers, in taxonomic terms, to a *generic* rank or *life-form* rank). It should be noted that in our final database we have included two specific cases. Their specific nature lies in their complex structure (constructions with genitive) while their elements do not reveal the identity of the designated referent.

4 Resemblance metaphor and metonymy in the ethnozoological lexicon of the Aguaruna

In this section, following the classification of resemblance metaphors and the taxonomy of metonymies described above, we organize our analysis into three groups: (i) resemblance metaphors (*prototypic and non-prototypic image metaphor*, *behavior-based metaphor*, and *metaphor with physical and behavioral motivations*), (ii) independent metonymies, and (iii) specific cases.

4.1 Resemblance metaphors

In our corpus of 90 ethnozoological binomials, 72 present resemblance metaphors, which amounts to 80% of the total. Regarding the classification of resemblance metaphors (Ureña and Faber 2010), we note that there is primacy of the *image metaphor* with 67 cases; while there are only four *behavior-based metaphors* (with dynamic image) and one *metaphor with physical and behavioral motivations* (see Table 1).

Table 1: Distribution of resemblance metaphors in the analyzed corpus.

72 cases of resemblance metaphor				
image metaphor		with physical and behavioral motivations	behavior-based metaphor	
color, form (prototypical)	texture, pattern, flavor, sound (nonprototypical)		with dynamic images	with static images
52	15	1	4	0
93 %		1.4 %	5.6 %	0

Of the 67 binomials that present *image metaphors*, most are prototypical (52), that is, metaphorical mappings are based on the similarity of color or shape. There are also cases that we have called non-prototypical (15), which associate other features (dimension, texture, pattern, and even flavor). However, in many cases, it is natural that color is linked to shape, pattern, or texture. With regard to domains, in Aguaruna, the entities that serve as source domains are mostly animal and plant organisms, although there is a preference for naming animals in terms of other animals. To a lesser extent, we find comparisons with cultural objects (such as vessels and ornaments) and natural products (such as salt and stones).

4.1.1 Prototypical image metaphors

Initially, we focus on color. In (1) and (2), the preference of speakers to name two types of tarantula accurately makes them turn to widely known species of monkeys to perform metaphorical transfer. Of the species that serve as source domain, *yakúm* (*Alouatta seniculus*) and *wáshi* (*Ateles belzebuth*) speakers select the reddish and black colors, respectively, to identify tarantulas that have similar colors. In these metaphors, in addition, the identification of the hairs is important because these tarantulas are profusely hairy which bears resemblance to monkeys. Undoubtedly, speakers take advantage of the profound knowledge they have of monkeys in the designation of arachnids. These mammals are part of the Aguaruna diet and even their skin and teeth are used to make products (Creed-Kanashiro, Roche, Tuesta, and Kuhnlein 2009). On the other hand, the highlight of these binomials is that the modifying nouns identify species of monkeys and not a generic taxon or another grouped form. Then, the image metaphor operates in the binomial and manages to particularize the entity named by the head noun, that is, it allows the naming of sub-generic organisms (tarantula types):

(1) *yakúm tséje* 'reddish spider' (*Theraphosidae* spp.)
reddish howler monkey – spider

(2) *wáshi tséje* 'black spider, big and hairy' (*Theraphosidae* spp.)
black spider monkey – spider

As we have seen in the first cases, the colors of a known species are selected to overlap with another species. The same mechanism is observed in (3) and (4), in which the red color of the *jápa* 'deer' (*Mazama americana*) clearly defines the chromatic characteristics of two types of ants, *yutúi* and *tíship*. Our collaborators affirm that *jápa* is a red deer that stands out culturally because it appears in several Aguaruna myths. In these binomials, once more, image metaphors based on color underlie names that identify organisms of the sub-generic level:

(3) *jápa yutúi* 'reddish ant of painful sting' (*Paraponera clavata*)
red deer – ant

(4) *jápa tíship* 'reddish ant' (*Odontomachus bauri*)
red deer – ant

In the examples presented, image metaphors have a metonymic basis. Following Kövecses (2013), we assume that a part of a source entity (color, shape, pattern, texture, etc.) is selected by the entire entity to map it onto a similar part selected from another target entity. Thus, in (1), (2), (3), and (4), the PART OF A THING FOR THE WHOLE THING metonymy is activated, in which the color is the prominent part. With respect to the metonymic basis of color, Biggam (2012) has presented examples in which a fruit, for example *strawberry*, is identified by its chromatic characteristics, the color red, as seen in the names of horses in English, as it is the case of the 'strawberry roan' horse.

Plants are also considered in the lexical construction of ethnozoological names. The cases in which the *ipák* 'annatto' (*Bixa orellana*) and *súa* 'genip' (*Genipa american*) appear are especially relevant and regular, since both have great cultural importance for speakers. The seeds of the *ipák* vary from red to orange depending on the variety and the degree of maturity. That range of colors is the basis for identifying intensely red species such as an ant species in (5), a type of snake in (6), and a wasp in (7). In Figure 4, we show two cases:

(5) *ipák kámpa* 'red ant' (*Solenopsis invicta*)
annatto – ant

(6) *ipák dápi* 'medium red snake' (*Colubridae* sp.)
annatto – snake

(7) *ipák éte* 'red wasp' (*Vespidae* spp.)
annatto – wasp

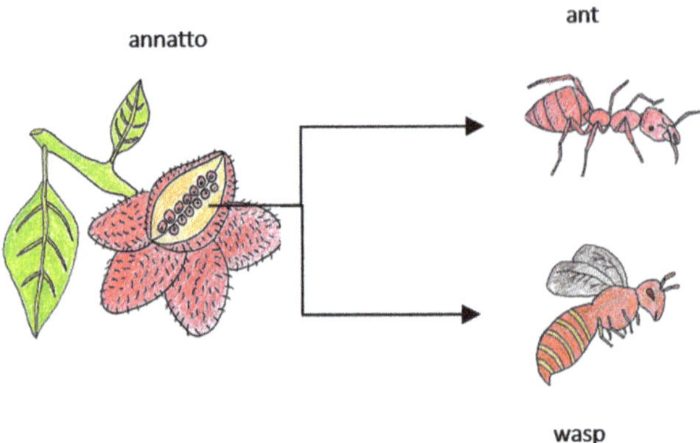

Figure 4: Metaphorical mapping of *ipák* 'annatto' onto two insects: a red ant and a red wasp. Drawing by Jaime Huasco.

On the other hand, the faint orange color of the *ipák* is also used to identify a species of hummingbird in (8) and a medium sized bird in (9). It should be noted that these types of birds have an orange color that is far from their most prototypical specimens; the prototypical hummingbird is green and blue and the latter is brown, hence the need to differentiate them lexically:

(8) *ipák jémpe* 'orange hummingbird' (*Trochilidae* spp.)
annatto – hummingbird

(9) *ipák chígki* 'orange baking bird' (*Furnarius leucopus*)
annatto – bird

It should be remembered that *ipák* is a plant that grows without difficulty and is used in several activities of notorious cultural importance in the community, such as painting ceramics, dyeing textiles, and painting the body in ceremonial activities. In addition, in Aguaruna mythology, *ipák* and her sister *súa* were originally women who, because of the loss of the husband they shared, decided to become plants that give people color. *Ipák* would provide warm colors, while *súa* would supply dark colors.

The seeds of *súa* (*Genipa americana*) are used to make natural hair dyes, to keep it silky and to cover gray hairs. As with her sister *ipák*, *súa* is a source of a color (deep dark) that stands out metonymically to establish similarity with black animal species. For example, a black owl in (10), a variety of dark ant in (11), and snakes covered in dark skin in (12) and (13). In fact, in the myths of Aguaruna, the animals that hugged *ipák* and *súa* had their skin dyed and changed their appearance forever. In Figure 5, we show two cases:

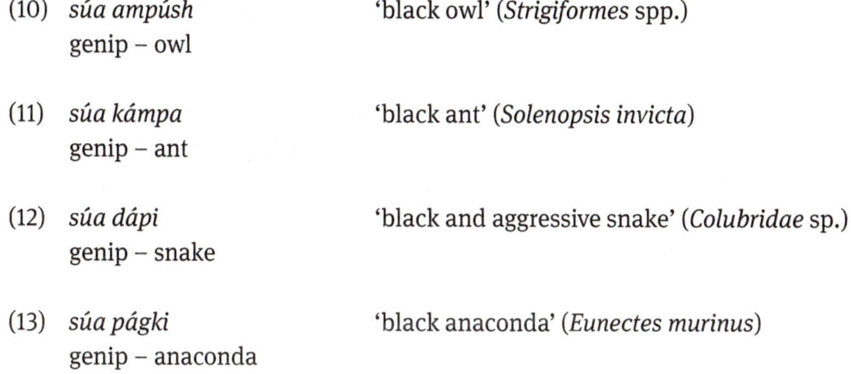

(10) *súa ampúsh* 'black owl' (*Strigiformes* spp.)
genip – owl

(11) *súa kámpa* 'black ant' (*Solenopsis invicta*)
genip – ant

(12) *súa dápi* 'black and aggressive snake' (*Colubridae* sp.)
genip – snake

(13) *súa págki* 'black anaconda' (*Eunectes murinus*)
genip – anaconda

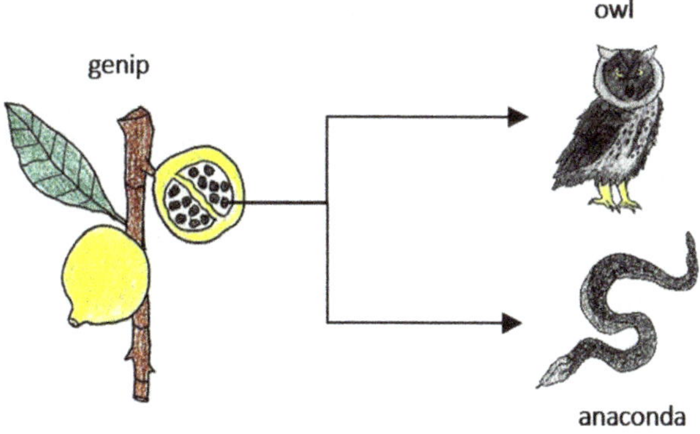

Figure 5: Metaphorical mapping of *súa* 'genip' onto two animals: a black owl and a black anaconda. Drawing by Jaime Huasco.

In addition to the examples presented, there is a significant number of cases in which a high variety of colors is considered salient elements that are metaphorically projected to entities of the animal world. Speakers take advantage of the intense green of the parrots, the white of the cotton, the luminosity of the firefly, the multicolor of the toucan and even the gray of the stones. That is, they use a wide color palette as a reflection of their thorough perception of the colors and tones that their surroundings offer.

After color, shape is highly regarded as the basis of image metaphors. In (14), the shape of a prototypical leaf is selected (in Aguaruna, there are approximately 17 words to name 17 varieties of leaves respectively) to establish the similarity with the wings of a lobster type. The resemblance is obvious, especially if we take into account the green color of the leaf and the type of lobster named. That is, there is a high iconic correspondence.

(14) *dúka mánchi* 'lobster with leaf-like wings' (*Scudderia* sp.)
leaf – lobster

In (15), the long, sinuous, and green stems of the climbing plants have metaphorical correspondence with long and green snakes, since they are similar. In (16), the elongated tubular shape and the dark brown color of the loose branches that rest on the banks of the rivers, and that are usually in a state of decomposition, are highlighted to map onto the shape and color of another type of snake. It should be noted that the named snakes hide precisely in places where the stems and branches described abound. Consequently, these metaphors also provide essential information for the conservation of life:

(15) *káap dápi* 'snake similar to vine' (*Philodryas argentea*)
vine – snake

(16) *wíchi – págki* 'rotten trunk-like anaconda' (*Eunectes murinus*)
rotten trunk – anaconda

Another group of names that represent interest for speakers are those that identify wasps.[5] In these cases, the recurring pattern is the designation of these insects based on the identification of their nests. In (17), the nest of a wasp species is identified by its similarity with the muzzle of the *kushi* 'coatis'. A similar mechanism is observed in (18), in which the comparison is projected from the ovoid shape of the human head to the oval shape of the nest of another type of wasp:

(17) *kúshi éte* 'type of wasp' (*Vespidae* spp.)
coatis – wasp

(18) *buúk éte* 'type of wasp' (*Vespidae* spp.)
head – wasp

We consider that, in (17) and (18), the nest is a metonymic vehicle used as access to the type of the designated wasp. It is possible that the nest has been selected as a metonymic vehicle because it is an element of easy perception, due to its volume and outstanding shape. In addition, we can highlight the pragmatic value

5 The wasps listed in this section were recognized in fieldwork as part of the family *Vespidae*. We maintain this label in the cases presented because we are still uncertain of the wasp's identification at the species level.

of appointing wasps by their nest, since in entomology it is affirmed that nests are peculiar for each species (García 1978). Basically, we understand the nest as a form of habitat, which is why we propose that the metonymy that serves as basis for metaphorical comparison would be HABITAT FOR INHABITANT. The same scheme is identified in (19), where the nest is compared with a clay vessel of an ovoid shape. In (20), the similarity is established with a basket made of dry braided leaves (in this case, the shape interacts with the pattern). Finally, in (21), the similarity of the nest with a container made of pumpkin is highlighted. In Figure 6, we show three cases:

(19) *piníg éte* 'type of wasp' (*Vespidae* spp.)
clay vessel – wasp

(20) *piták éte* 'type of wasp' (*Vespidae* spp.)
hanging basket – wasp

(21) *tsápa éte* 'type of wasp' (*Vespidae* spp.)
pumpkin bowl – wasp

In our initial database, there are up to 14 compound names for wasps. Although many of these names have lost semantic transparency, it is logical to assume that some follow the nest identification pattern. Regarding these names, it is possible to think that this pattern could be recurrent in other Amazonian languages. For example, Valenzuela (1998) has presented the shipibo name of *oxe bina* 'moon wasp' for a wasp whose nest is shaped like a moon.

4.1.2 Non-prototypical image metaphors

Another interesting group that we call non-prototypical image metaphors is related to the texture, pattern, dimension, and even flavor of the named species. According to Ureña (2011), the concepts respond to our interaction with the environment, within a process in which all our senses intervene: "[t]his means that [the concept] emerges because we receive information from different sensory-perceptual inputs" (Ureña 2011: 38). In the metaphors that we exemplify in this section, we evidence that the perception expands: in addition to the visual perception, flavor, and touch are considered.

In (22), the rough and bristly texture of the *nája* 'nettle' leaf resembles the lateral and spiny part of the body of the *pútu* 'armored catfish'. In fact, what has been compared is the sensation we experience with our hands when we manip-

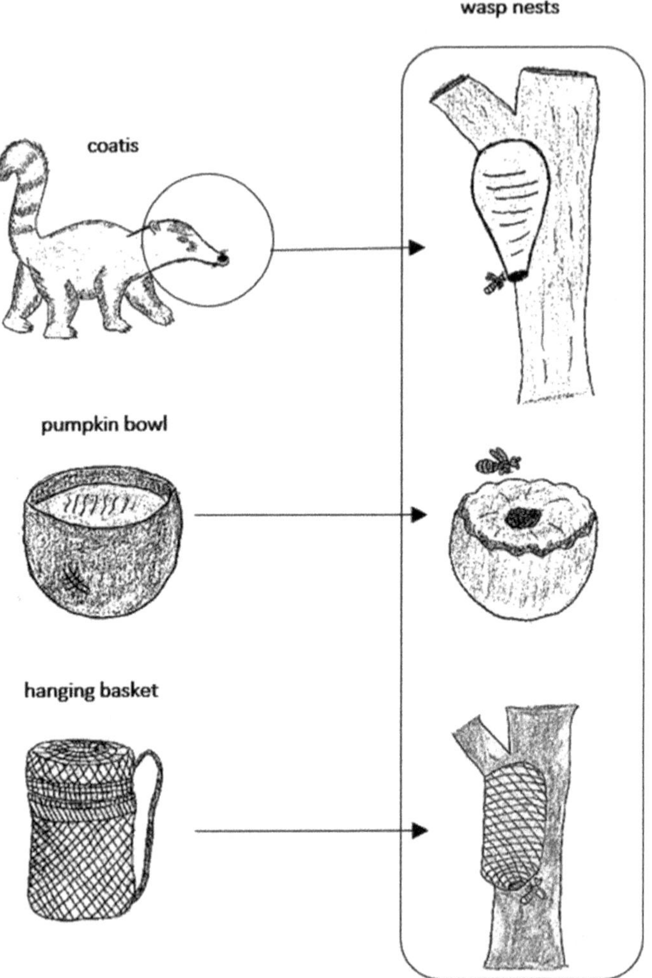

Figure 6: Metaphors based on the shape of the wasp's nest. Drawing by Jaime Huasco.

ulate both entities. On a perceptual level, nettle is a highly visible wild plant because it grows profusely in the surroundings of the community; in addition, it has medicinal relevance. Consequently, the use of this plant as part of the binomial allows the immediate identification of the variety of armored catfish that is named:

(22) *nája pútu* 'nettle-like armored catfish' (*Loricariidae* spp.)
nettle – armored catfish

With regard to pattern, visual perception focuses more on the details of the skin of mammals or snakes and the wings of insects. In (23), speakers mentioned that the skin of a type of sloth has scattered spots on the body, such as the spotted skin of the jaguar. In this case, the perception of the similarity of patterns in the skin of mammals serves to perform metaphorical transfer. In (24), speakers name a butterfly *ántach wámpishuk*, comparing its wings with the wings of an exemplary dragonfly. These wings are like transparent plastic sheets that have scattered lines on the surface. Even when the wings differ in shape, the speakers clearly recognize the similarity of the pattern; for this reason, the image metaphor in this binomial operates successfully:

(23) *yawá uyúsh* 'sloths with skin spots' (*Bradypus variegatus*)
jaguar – sloth

(24) *ántach wámpishuk* 'butterfly with transparent wings' (*Nymphalidae* spp.)
dragonfly – butterfly

A particular case is presented in (25) and (26). They are binomials that include the noun *wée* 'salt' to name and identify the salty taste of the categories they modify: in (25), a type of river snail and, in (26), a type of coatis, both with a peculiar salty taste. Regarding the participation of metonymy, we believe that the DEFINING PROPERTY FOR THE CATEGORY metonymy operates, since it evokes the characteristic flavor of the salt blocks, instead of shape or color. Then, it is the property of flavor that the speaker experiences when consuming salt that is projected metaphorically onto the domain of the designated species.

(25) *wée tsúntsu* 'big river snail' (*Pomacea* sp.)
salt – snail

(26) *wée kúshi* 'type of coatis' (*Nasua nasua*)
salt – coatis

As a corollary of the analysis of the prototypical image metaphors (color and shape traits) and the non-prototypical ones (texture, pattern, flavor), in general, we observe that, at the taxonomic level, binomials allow subcategorizing mostly *generic categories* and, to a lesser extent, *life-forms*. To sub-categorize, the head noun indicates the category (*generic* or *life-form*), while, through the modifying noun, a prominent part of a highly perceptible entity (usually plants or animals of the generic level) is selected to establish the metaphorical mapping. This metaphorical mechanism, then, functionally underlies the naming of entities that generally occupy *specific* and *varietal* levels.

4.1.3 Behavior-based metaphors (with dynamic image)

In our corpus, there are 4 binomial names of behavior based-metaphors. All these are based on dynamic images (in our data, we have not found behavior based-metaphors that have static images). The species named with these binomials are varied and the source domains involved include ethnozoological entities and a mythological being.

The metaphorical connection in (27) implies a detailed knowledge of the activity performed by peccaries (source) and a type of ant (target). The movement of peccary herds and their grouping around a leader is mapped onto the compact movement of advancing groups of ants led by a leader. Both entities have the objective of searching for food and defending against an opponent. Consequently, speakers understand the peccary and the ant based on their most visible activity, which is metonymically highlighted for use in the constitution of the metaphor:

(27) *páki katsáip* 'type of army ant' (*Eciton* sp.)
peccary – army ant

In (28), basically, the action of damage is metonymically highlighted both in an ant and in a type of armored catfish. Speakers have experienced the accurate attack of both and that is why the action of biting (of the ant – source) in the presence of a stranger is transferred to the action of stinging (of the armored catfish – target) in a risk situation:

(28) *yutúi kumpáu* 'type of armored catfish' (*Pimelodidae* spp.)
ant – armored catfish

Finally, in (29), the negative and sinister activity of *íwanch*, a diabolical being in Aguaruna mythology, serves to establish the metaphor with the perverse behavior of a species of deer. In the community of Morroyacu, several speakers represent *íwanch* as a hairy being who harasses people on roads. This description coincides with the stories collected by Brown (2014) in other communities of Alto Mayo. With regard to metaphor, this is activated because the deer (target domain) is described as an inedible animal, negatively connoted since it represents a danger to people, just like the *íwanch* (source domain). Some speakers even stated that the deer had the ability to hypnotize them to carry out its attack. Definitely, in this metaphor, there are restrictive cultural factors that delimit the conceptualization of the named referent. A similar situation is observed in (30), where aggressive behavior is again mapped:

(29) *íwanch jápa* 'deer that attacks man' (*Cervidae* sp.)
devil – deer

(30) *íwanch éte* 'wasp that attacks man' (*Vespidae* spp.)
devil – wasp

As we have seen, the recovery of deeper ecological and cultural knowledge is essential to clarify the semantic motivation involved in behavior-based metaphors (with dynamic images). In addition, although there are only four cases, the data shows that the entity that constitutes the source domain is not limited to the biological world, but also considers elements of the supernatural world, always as part of the process of sub-categorization of ethnozoological entities.

4.1.4 Metaphors with physical and behavioral motivations

In this section, behavioral traits and some "physical" similarity are shown to coexist. In (31), the dynamic image of an arrow traveling through the air at full speed (functional pattern of an object) is superimposed on the image of the hummingbird in rapid flight. In this case, although there is movement of the arrow and the bird, it is possible to think that the point of comparison is the line drawn by the two entities. That is, the speaker would compare an imaginary line produced by the movement. It is also likely that physical similarity is established between the arrow and the elongated peak of this type of hummingbird. In our corpus, there is only one case of this type of metaphor.

(31) *tséntsak jémpe* 'fast hummingbird' (*Trochilidae* spp.)
arrow – hummingbird

4.2 Independent metonymies

In line with what has been suggested by Kövecses (2013), we have seen that in resemblance metaphors, metonymy plays an essential role. In this section, the relevance of metonymy is maintained, however, it does not operate together with the metaphor, but independently through a modifying noun. As Benczes (2006) argues, the modifying element allows access to the target element within the same ICM; in addition, "the meaning of the compound is a combination of the second constituent, which also acts as the profile determinant, and the metonymical understanding of the first constituent" (Benczes 2006: 142). In our corpus, we have identified 18 such cases. It is interesting to see that almost all cases (16) refer to the knowledge of the habitat or of the diet of the named species.

In (32) and (33), as part of the Containment ICM, the HABITAT FOR INHABITANT metonymy is activated to identify some species. Kövecses (2010) has already argued that it is common to conceptualize places as containers for people. In Aguaruna, this metonymy not only implies a location, but also provides information for hunting, such as recognizing danger or building knowledge of a complex environment such as the Amazon forest. In (32), the meaning is related to location by identifying the space that a type of termite inhabits. In (33), a detailed location is evoked (a certain leaf) with the intention of staying protected from a dangerous insect, a type of wasp:

(32) *núgka kâbau* 'type of termite' (*Isoptera* spp.)
soil – termite

(33) *dúka éte* 'type of wasp' (*Vespidae* spp.)
leaf – wasp

For the following cases, considering the example of metonymy FOOD FOR CUSTOMER by Lakoff (1980), 'the ham sandwich is waiting for his check', we propose the metonymy FOOD FOR CONSUMER for cases in which the species is named by the food that it consumes, as in (34), (35), and (36).[6] Kövecses (2010: 184), with respect to Lakoff's example, states that the conceptual relationship between the food and the customer is undetermined. However, he adds that the relationship is 'clearly determined' within the restaurant. In the examples we present, the food-consumer relationship is determined because speakers are familiar with the diet of animals that surround them. Logically, their status as hunters has led them to consolidate this knowledge.

In this way, in (34), the fishing activity of Aguarunas has allowed them to identify a type of armored catfish through their peculiar consumption of rotten wood accumulated in superficial parts of the rivers. In (35), the information on the

6 These cases show a type of metonymy with some regularity in Aguaruna. However, as Bernárdez (2005, 2016) points out, it is convenient to continue investigating to determine if cases such as 'the ham sandwich is waiting for his check' or other similar ones are only isolated metonymic references or long-range metonymies which can lead to generalization.

fruit of a palm tree consumed by a type of peccary serves to increase the chances of the Aguaruna people of hunting it. Finally, in (36), they manage to identify a group of edible birds through what these consume: a leafy green fluff that covers the trunk of some trees. In the latter case, it should be noted that the head noun *shigki* (bird in general, of considerable size and hunted for consumption) is not a *generic* taxa, but of a *life-form* taxa (Berlin and Berlin 1979). Despite this and according to our collaborators, the binomial *juú chígki* can accurately identify a particular bird (medium size, and gray and brown plumage).

(34) *wíchi tsuútsun* 'type of fish' (unidentified)
rotten wood – fish

(35) *tuntúam páki* 'type of peccary' (*Pecari tajacu*)
palm fruit – peccary

(36) *juú chígki* 'medium gray and brown bird' (unidentified)
green bush trunk hair – bird

In Aguaruna, we can also find the so-called sign metonymies (Evans 1997: 136; Turpin 2013). In our corpus, there are cases in which biological entities are associated with weather changes and the presence of other species. For example, in (37), the presence of *páki* 'a type of peccary' is interpreted by speakers as an accurate sign of the arrival of summer, hence the binomial presents the noun modifier *esát* 'summer'. In (38), the song of the *pururi* 'a type of bird with onomatopoeic name' is a sign of high probability of the presence of the *páki* 'peccary', whose flesh is one of the favorite dishes in the community.

(37) *esát páki* 'type of peccary' (*Pecari tajacu*)
summer – peccary

(38) *páki pururi* 'type of bird' (unidentified)
peccary – bird

4.3 Specific cases of ethnozoological names

In addition to all the binomials reviewed, in our corpus, there are two specific constructions. Both ethnobiological names are constructions with genitive and differ semantically from the revised binomials in that their elements do not reveal the identity of the named referent. In (39), *yumí dukuji* 'mother of water' is the name of a larva that is temporarily concentrated on the banks of the rivers. Apparently, in this compound, a sign metonymy is activated, since the speakers affirm that, when they observe these larvae, they know there will be plenty of water (through rain). Considering the myths related to water, as well as possible threats to the stability of water in their territory, it is understandable that the Aguaruna people have lexicalized the expression *yumí dukují* to name a biological species that is an indicator of abundance of water. After all, this species is conceived as a mother who has a resource that, on the one hand, is sacred and, on the other, vital:

(39) *yumí duku-jí* 'water bug' (*Belostomatidae* sp.) (Lit.: mother of water)
water – mother.GEN

On the other hand, in (40), *iwanchí tugkuiji* 'devil's stick' is the name of an insect that has an elongated body and legs very similar to thin brown branches. In this sense, there is a metaphorical correspondence between the plant element *tugkui* ´stick´ and the insect, based on its similarity in shape, pattern, and color. Speakers state that, of all varieties, this is the most difficult to identify, due to their natural camouflage conditions:

(40) *iwanchí tugkuí-ji* 'type of stick insect' (*Apioscelis* spp.) (Lit.: Devil's Stick)
devil – stick.GEN

Regarding the presence of the *íwanch*,[7] this is explained by the diabolical being playing with appearances to deceive men (Chumap and García-Rendueles 1979). For speakers, that would be the reason why there are 'false' plants very similar to the original ones. For example, *iwanchí kukushji* 'devil's cocona', *iwanchí papaiji* 'devil's papaya', and *iwanchí munchiji* 'devil's passionfruit' are fruits harmful to human consumption, and they are more dangerous because they are extremely similar to their original versions: cocona, papaya and passionfruit.

So, *iwanchí tugkuíji* is an insect that can be deceiving because it looks like a thin branch. According to our collaborators, the damage caused by the insect is the confirmation of death. That is, if a person sees the insect, he/she would realize that he/she is dead. The *íwanch*, therefore, is a being that causes harm and for that purpose it uses the game of appearances.

7 We have already referred to this mythological being in binomial constructions in (29) and (30).

5 Conclusion

In this chapter, we have presented an analysis of resemblance metaphors and metonymies that operate in ethnozoological names of the Amazonian language Aguaruna, basically in binomials of the structure $[N_{(MOD)}\ N_{(HEAD)}]_N$. The lexical preference for this type of compounds to name animal and plant organisms has already been shown to stand out in Amazonian languages (Valenzuela 1998, Zariquiey 2018). In general, in these binomials, the modifying noun is the element that concentrates the metaphorical or metonymic load, while the head noun literally identifies a taxonomic category (*generic* or *life-form*) that includes the referent named by the entire compound.

First, following the proposal of Ureña and Faber (2010), we grouped resemblance metaphors into three classes: (i) *prototypical image metaphors* (color and shape) and what we have called *non-prototypical* ones (texture, pattern, flavor), (ii) *behavior based-metaphors* (with dynamic images), and (iii) *metaphors with physical and behavioral motivations*. The distribution shows that most resemblance metaphors select a static image of an entity (source domain) to metaphorically project it onto the named biological organism (target domain). Of the 72 binomials that have resemblance metaphors, 67 correspond to the image metaphor group. Of this group, most cases are prototypical, that is, they consider color and shape as a prominent feature. To a lesser extent, there are non-prototypical cases that consider texture, pattern, and flavor. However, there are cases where these features interact. That is, the perception of speakers jointly takes into account color and form, texture and color, or form and texture to name a particular species. This joint participation of color, shape, and texture traits is consistent with the visual metaphors that Turpin (2013) analyzes in the semantic extensions of plant and animal names in the Kaytetye language.

In this group of *image metaphors* (prototypical), the prevalence of color is not only linked to the perception of the environment (animals, plants, stones) but also to knowledge with a cultural and mythological basis. At this point, the regular presence of the *ipâk* 'annatto' and *súa* 'genip' plants is significant. The data show relatively systematic mapping of *ipâk* and *súa* to map colors (red and black, respectively) in various species. After color, shape is the most prominent image in metaphorical mappings. The data show an important regularity in the denomination of several types of wasp. Essentially, the speakers select the shape of the nests and establish the similarity with various elements (basket, plate, animal head, human head, etc.). In this case, the nest is a metonymic vehicle that allows us to access and identify the insect. It should be noted that the perception of the nest for naming a type of wasp was also recorded by Valenzuela (1998), who presents a case in the Amazonian language Shipibo. This gives rise to the need to verify whether the identification of wasps through their nests is a constant in Amazonian nomenclatures.

As for the group of *behavior-based metaphors*, we have only found four cases. In these occurrences, the behavior of animals and that of a mythological being (*íwanch*) have been mapped. This shows that the selection of elements of the source domain projecting onto the target domain is more complex and, in two cases, exceeds the sensory perception. This last feature is also seen in our specific cases, which are constructions with genitive (*yumí dukují* and *iwanchí tunkuíji*) that require deep cultural and mythological information for the recovery of their semantic motivation. On the other hand, it should be noted that we have only found one case of *metaphor with physical and behavioral motivations*.

In our analysis, we have also detected an important group of binomials (18 cases) in which the modifying noun presents the metonymic load; that is, it is an element that operates within an ICM (Benczes 2006). The interesting thing about these cases is the systematic presence of two types of metonymy: HABITAT FOR INHABITANT and FOOD FOR CONSUMER. This means that speakers have lexicalized information on the habitat and diet of ethnozoological organisms because it is essential for hunting, for being alert to possible dangers, or for organizing the copious knowledge of the Amazonian environment they have. Additionally, although to a lesser extent, we have found some sign metonymies linked to meteorological occurrences (summer and rainfall), important data for daily activities in the community.

Likewise, it is necessary to highlight two aspects that emerge from our analysis. The first is the predominance of the *generic* category as a head noun of the binomials, data that correspond to the findings of Berlin (1992). However, there is also a significant number of head nouns that name a *life-form* category. In both cases, these head nouns are modified by a noun that mostly names generic or specific levels, and which contains the metaphorical or metonymic charge. In this way, with the union of the head noun and the modifier, the speaker basically manages to subcategorize his/her ethnozoological reality. The second aspect to highlight is the recurrence of some significant references that are presented as head nouns. The most subcategorized references are *mánchi* 'lobster', *jémpe* 'hummingbird', *chígki* 'bird', *éte* 'wasp', and *dápi* 'snake'. These five names appear in 44 binomials, which evidences their high ethnozoological importance for the community. As for the modifying noun, the most relevant and productive ones are *jápa* 'deer', *ipák* 'annatto', *súa* 'genip', and *dúka* 'leaf'. These four expressions appear in 17 binomials, a number to consider.

In summary, our findings show the complex system of resemblance metaphors and metonymies that operate in the Aguaruna ethnozoological lexicon, in which the mapping of biological domains (animal and plant) and cultural references of the community come into play. In this sense, from the lexicon studied, our analysis contributes to the understanding of Aguaruna speakers' deep ethnozoological knowledge and, in turn, some of the conceptualization of their environment.

References

Asociación Interétnica de Desarrollo de la Selva Peruana (Aidesep). 2011. *Diccionario awajún-castellano*. Iquitos: Aidesep.

Barreto, Rocío. 2009. *Ocupación histórica del pueblo indígena awajún en las comunidades del Alto Mayo*. https://www.academia.edu/4678933/Ocupaci%C3%B3n_hist%C3%B3rica_del_pueblo_ind%C3%ADgena_Awaj%C3%BAn_en_las_comunidades_del_Alto_Mayo (accessed 10 July 2019)

Benczes, Réka. 2006. *Creative compounding in English: The semantics of metaphorical and metonymical noun-noun combinations*. Amsterdam & Philadelphia: John Benjamins.

Berlin, Brent. 1992. *Ethnobiological classification. Principles of categorization of plants and animals in traditional societies*. Princeton: Princeton University Press.

Berlin, Brent & Elois Ann Berlin. 1979. *Aspectos de la etnobiología aguaruna*. Berkeley: Universidad de California.

Berlin, Brent & Paul Kay. 1969. *Basic Color Terms: Their universality and evolution*. Berkeley: University of California Press.

Berlin, Brent, Dennis Breedlove & Peter Raven. 1973. General principles of classification and nomenclature in folk biology. *American Anthropologist* 75 (1). 214–242.

Bernárdez, Enrique. 2005. Social cognition: variation, language, and culture in a cognitive linguistic typology. In Francisco J. Ruiz de Mendoza and Sandra Peña Cervel (eds.), *Cognitive linguistics. Internal dynamics and interdisciplinary interaction*, 191–224. Berlin & New York: Mouton de Gruyter.

Bernárdez, Enrique. 2016. From butchers and surgeons to the linguistic method. In Manuela Romano & Maria Dolores Porto (eds.), *Exploring discourse strategies in social and cognitive interaction: Multimodal and cross-linguistic perspectives*, 21–38. Amsterdam & Philadelphia: John Benjamins.

Biggam, Carol. 2012. *The semantics of colour: A historical approach*. Cambridge: Cambridge University Press.

Boster, James. 2005. *Categories and cognitive anthropology*. In Henri Cohen & Claire Lefebvre (eds.), *Handbook of categorization in cognitive science*, 92–118. Amsterdam: Elsevier

Brown, Michael. 2014. Upriver: *The turbulent life and times of an Amazonian people*. Cambridge: Harvard University Press.

Creed-Kanashiro, Hilary, Marion Roche, Irma Tuesta & Harriet Kuhnlein. 2009. Traditional food system of an Awajun community in Peru. In Harriert Kuhnlein, Bill Erasmus & Dina Spigelski (eds), *Indigenous peoples' food systems: The many dimensions of culture, diversity and environment for nutrition and health*, 59–81. Roma: FAO.

Chumap, Aurelio & Manuel García-Rendueles. 1979. *"Duik múun. . ." Universo mítico de los aguarunas*. Lima: CAAAP.

Corbera Mori, Angel. 1994. *Fonologia e gramática do Aguaruna (Jívaro).* Campinas: Universidade Estadual de Campinas PhD thesis.
Cuenca, Maria & Joseph Hilferty. 2007. *Introducción a la lingüística cognitiva.* Barcelona: Ariel.
Dauphiné, Nico. 2008. *Bird ecology, conservation, and community responses to logging in the northern Peruvian Amazon.* Georgia: University of Georgia.
Elliot, Jorge. 1998. Los recursos forestales en las comunidades nativas aguarunas del Alto Mayo. *Tecnología y Sociedad: la revista del ITDG- Perú* 4. 18–21.
Evans, Nick. 1997. Sign metonymies and the problem of flora-fauna polysemy in Australian linguistics. In Darrell Tryon & Michael Walsh (eds.), *Boundary rider. Essays in honour of Geoffrey O'Grady*, 133–153. Canberra: Australian National University.
Fleck, David. 2007. Field linguistics meets biology: How to obtain scientific designations for plant and animal names. *Language Typology and Universals* 60 (1). 81–91.
García, Renán. 1978. Cuatro estudios sobre avispas sociales del Perú (hymenoptera: vespidae). *Revista Peruana de Entomología* 21 (1). 1–22.
Grady, Joseph. 1999. A typology of motivation for conceptual metaphor: Correlation vs. resemblance. In Raymond W. Gibbs, Jr. and Gerard J. Steen (eds.), *Metaphor in cognitive linguistics*, 79–100. Amsterdam & Philadelphia: John Benjamins.
Guasparri, Andrea. 2007. Etnobiologia e mondo antico: una prospettiva di ricerca. *Annali Online di Lettere – Ferrara Speciale* II (2). 69–90.
Guasparri, Andrea. 2019. Polysemy revisited. Metaphor and descriptiveness in folk animal naming. *Altorientalische Forschungen* 46 (1). 61–87.
Hunn, Eugene & Cecil Brown. 2011. Linguistic ethnobiology. In Eugene Anderson, Deborah Pearsall, Eugene Hunn & Nancy Turner (eds), *Ethnobiology*, 319–333. Nueva Jersey: Wiley-Blackwell.
Instituto Nacional de Estadística e Informática (INEI). 2018. *Perú, perfil sociodemocrático 2017.* Lima: INEI.
Julià, Carolina. 2009. El cuerpo humano en la creación y motivación de los nombres románicos de insectos. *Revue de Linguistique Romane* 73. 321–369.
Kövecses, Zoltán. 2010. *Metaphor: A practical introduction*, 2nd edn. Oxford: Oxford University Press.
Kövecses, Zoltán. 2013. The metaphor-metonymy relationship: Correlation metaphors are based on metonymy. *Metaphor and Symbol* 28 (2). 75–88.
Lakoff, George & Mark Johnson. 1980. *Metaphors we live by.* Chicago: University of Chicago Press.
Lakoff, George. 1987. *Women, fire and dangerous things.* Chicago: University of Chicago Press.
Littlemore, Jeannette. 2015. *Metonymy: Hidden shortcuts in language, thought and communication.* Cambridge: Cambridge University Press.
Luque, Juan. 2001. *Aspectos universales y particulares del léxico de las lenguas del mundo.* Granada: Método Ediciones.
Mihatsch, Wiltrud. 2016. Types of motivation in folk plant taxonomies. In Päivi Juvonen & Maria Koptjevskaja-Tamm (eds.), *The lexical typology of semantic shifts*, 457–492. Berlin & Boston: Mouton de Gruyter.
Ministerio de Educación del Perú (Minedu). 1996. *Diccionario aguaruna-castellano castellano-aguaruna.* Lima: ILV.
Overall, Simon. 2007. *A grammar of Aguaruna.* Melbourne: La Trobe University PhD thesis.
Patton, James, Brent Berlin & Elois Ann Berlin. 1981. Aboriginal perspectives of a mammal community in Amazonian Peru: Knowledge and utilization patterns among the Aguaruna

Jívaro. In Michael Mares & Hugh Genoways (eds.), *Mammalian biology in South America*, 111–128. Pittsburgh: University of Pittsburgh.

Radden, Günter & Zoltán Kövecses. 1999. Towards a theory of metonymy. In Klaus-Uwe Panther and Günter Radden (eds.), *Metonymy in language and thought*, 17–59. Amsterdam: John Benjamins.

Schmid, Hans-Jörg. 2007. Entrenchment, salience and basic levels. In Dirk Geeraerts & Hubert Cuyckens (eds.), *The Oxford handbook of cognitive linguistics*, 117–138. Oxford: Oxford University Press.

Tercedor, Maribel, Clara López, Carlos Márquez & Pamela Faber. 2012. Metaphor and metonymy in specialized language. In Pamela Faber (ed.), *A cognitive-linguistics view of terminology and specialized language*, 33–72. Berlin: Mouton de Gruyter.

Turpin, Myfany. 2013. Semantic extension in Kaytetye flora and fauna terms. *Australian Journal of Linguistics* 33 (4). 488–518.

Ungerer, Friedrich & Hans-Jörg Schmid. 2006 [1996]. *An introduction to cognitive linguistics*, 2nd edn. London: Pearson Longman.

Ureña, José M. & Pamela Faber. 2010. Reviewing imagery in resemblance and non-resemblance metaphor. *Cognitive Linguistics* 21 (1). 123–149.

Ureña, José M. 2011. *Metaphor in specialised language: An English-Spanish comparative study in marine biology*. Granada: University of Granada PhD thesis.

Valenzuela, Pilar. 1998. Luna-avispa y tigre-machaco: compuestos semánticos en la taxonomía shipiba. In Zarina Estrada, Max Figueroa, Gerardo López & Andrés Costa (eds.), *IV Encuentro Internacional de Lingüística del Noroeste*, vol. 2, 409–428. Sonora: UniSon.

Zariquiey, Roberto. 2018. *Etnobiología del pueblo Kakataibo. Una aproximación desde la documentación de lenguas*. Lima: PUCP.

Patrick Kühmstedt, Hans-Georg Wolf

Metaphorical and cultural conceptualizations in Guyanese newspaper English: novel insights and methodological approaches

Abstract: Many studies in cultural linguistics and cognitive sociolinguistics tend to employ a "top-down" procedure to identify cultural conceptualizations, i.e., they "determine conceptual metaphors first and only then look for linguistic evidence" (Krennmayr 2011). To this end, they are more often than not ethnographically informed by an emic and etic perspective as well as by intuition (see Sharifian 2011). While recognizing the value of those analyses, the present paper applies a corpus-assisted textual approach in order to explore – in a predominantly "bottom-up" fashion – culture- and variety-specific metaphorical and cultural conceptualizations in a Guyanese newspaper corpus. The corpus we compiled consists of a randomized selection of leading news articles and letters to the editor taken from the online versions of the country's two largest dailies, the *Guyana Chronicle* and the *Stabroek News*, which are published in (standardized) English. A British English subcorpus consisting of the same types of newspaper extracts from *The Guardian* provides a basis for comparison. The cultural metaphors and conceptualizations discussed are retrieved from a combination of corpus-linguistic methods that encompass a (cultural) keyword analysis (Scott 2001), an analysis of "cultural keyword chains" (Peters 2017), and a key semantic domain analysis conducted with the web-based corpus analysis software *Wmatrix4* (Rayson 2008). Thus, the following chapter represents one of the first studies on Guyanese (acrolectal) English in decades and hopes to enhance the understanding of the idiosyncratic interplay of language and cognition in the cultural context of Guyana.[1]

Keywords: cultural conceptualizations; Guyanese English; corpus linguistics; keyword chains; key semantic domains

1 We would like to thank the reviewers for their insightful comments and constructive feedback.

Patrick Kühmstedt, Hans-Georg Wolf, University of Potsdam, Germany

https://doi.org/10.1515/9783110688306-006

1 Introduction

Various varieties of English – more often than not, L2 varieties – have recently become subject to cultural-linguistic or cognitive-sociolinguistic analyses, mostly in an (ongoing) endeavor to unveil and systematize underlying cultural models and cultural conceptualizations in world Englishes. This has been the case for Australian Aboriginal English (e.g., Sharifian 2011, 2015), West African English(es) (e.g., Polzenhagen 2007; Wolf 2001; Wolf and Polzenhagen 2009), Hong Kong English (e.g., Latić and Wolf 2017; Polzenhagen and Wolf 2010; Wolf and Chan 2016), Indian English (e.g., Polzenhagen and Frey 2017), and Irish English (Peters 2017), to name just a few publications. The Caribbean, however, seems to be by and large *terra incognita* as far as cultural-linguistic or cognitive-sociolinguistic research is concerned. Apart from a book-length cognitive/anthropological-linguistic study on traveling conceptualizations in Jamaican (Patwa) by Hollington (2015), there are, to the best of our knowledge, no further in-depth accounts on cultural conceptualizations in Caribbean Englishes. The research gap is even more blatant when it comes to Guyanese (Standard) English, for which only very few (older) linguistics treaties exist in general (e.g., Edwards 1977). Hence, the present chapter intends to start filling this void by shedding some light on metaphorical and cultural conceptualizations in Guyanese (newspaper) English.[2]

A former British colony, the Co-operative Republic of Guyana (hereafter, shortly 'Guyana') is located at the north-eastern Atlantic coast of South America, between Venezuela, Brazil, and Suriname, and has a population of approximately 750,000 inhabitants. Though Guyanese Creole, or 'Creolese,' may be *de facto* the most-widely spoken language in the country, Guyana is nowadays the only state on the South American continent with English as the official language. For this reason, also the largest newspapers of the country, among them the state-owned *Guyana Chronicle* and the independent *Stabroek News* – which form the basis for this study – are published in (standardized) English.

A further, more specific objective of the present paper is to contribute to the methodological discourse in the fields of conceptual metaphor research and cultural linguistics/cognitive sociolinguistics. As can be noticed, a multitude of studies carried out within the theoretical paradigms of these disciplines prove to be "informed by both an emic and an etic [extra-linguistic] perspective"; and more often than not, these studies start off with an "ethnographic approach" (Sharifian 2011: 13), scrutinizing more or less cohesive corpora for certain *a priori* determined cultural categories. While the legitimacy of this "top-down" *modus*

2 See below for a distinction.

operandi (Krennmayr 2011) shall not be doubted, the question of a complementary – more textual, inductive – approach arises. In this sense, we aim to introduce a novel combination of corpus-linguistic methods for the identification of metaphorical and cultural conceptualizations (cf. also Polzenhagen, this volume). This primarily "bottom-up" methodological procedure, consisting of a cultural keyword analysis (Leech and Fallon 1992; Wierzbicka 1997), a 'chain' analysis of keywords (Peters 2017), and a key semantic domain analysis conducted with the web-based corpus analysis software *Wmatrix4* (Rayson 2018), shall be exemplarily applied to a corpus that includes leading articles and letters to the editors from the two above-mentioned Guyanese (English) newspapers. Relying in particular on this genre, the present explorative analysis seeks to evaluate the relevance and salience of certain conceptualizations in public Guyanese English (GuyE) discourse and, by doing so, lay the groundwork for further more in-depth research on metaphoricity and cultural conceptualizations in Caribbean Englishes and, above all, GuyE.

2 Theoretical framework

The theoretical concept of *cultural conceptualizations*, as applied in this study, is rooted in the linguistic paradigms of cognitive sociolinguistics and cultural linguistics, which are cognate strands of (cognitive) linguistics.[3] Both disciplines share the basic assumption that "language reflects and is shaped by cultural experience" (Polzenhagen and Wolf 2010: 284), though cognitive sociolinguistics tends to place social and cross-cultural linguistic variation at the center of investigation, whereas the exploration of "cultural conceptualisations" and "distributed cultural cognition" is foregrounded by Sharifian's (2011, 2015, 2017) cultural linguistics framework.

In the taxonomy of cultural linguistics, the notion *cultural conceptualization* serves as a "cover term" (Sharifian 2011: 3) for what Sharifian labels as 'cultural categories,' 'cultural schemas,' and 'cultural(-conceptual) metaphors,' all of which may be understood as concrete instantiations of cultural conceptualizations. As such, they represent the major analytical tools cultural linguistics deals with.

3 We take the conceptual frameworks of the two branches to be well-known and do not review their theoretical premises in detail (see, e.g., Wolf and Chan 2016: 249–250 for a comprehensive overview).

Cultural categories, as "the product of culture-specific categorizations" (Peters 2017: 131), may vary across different varieties of a global language such as English, which is usually reflected at a lexico-semantic level.[4] In particular, this variation may surface in the existence of certain culture/variety-specific signifiers and/or lexemes from the so-called 'common core' that carry different meanings, as is, for example, the case with the notion of the concept of *family* in Hong Kong English (cf., e.g., Latić and Wolf 2017; Geers 2018) or with expressions from the domain FAMILY/KINSHIP in Aboriginal English (cf., e.g., Sharifian 2006) as compared to (White) British or American English. 'Cultural schemas,' on the other hand, "extend the dimension of mere semantic categorisation" (Peters 2017: 131) in that they "capture beliefs, norms, rules, and expectations of behaviour as well as values relating to various aspects and components of experience" (Sharifian 2017: 7).

The third form of cultural conceptualizations is that of '(cultural-)conceptual metaphors,' which is based on the well-known Conceptual Metaphor Theory (CMT), first expounded by Lakoff and Johnson (1980; also see Kövecses, this volume). Thus, cultural linguistics and CMT provide a set of methodological tools that enable the analyst to access the specific beliefs and *weltanschauung* of a cultural group. It should be noted, however, that what from an etic perspective seems to be a cultural-conceptual metaphor may not necessarily be perceived as a conceptual 'mapping' from one domain onto another on the part of the speaker (Sharifian 2015: 524). In other words, from an emic perspective, no *cross*-domain mapping may take place. For this reason, we take a rather critical stance vis-à-vis the usage of the term 'metaphor' in this context, and prefer to replace it by the term 'cultural conceptualization' in order to avoid an overtly Western-centered cultural bias (see Wolf and Chan 2016: 266).

Hence, for the purpose of this paper, *metaphorical* conceptualizations are those conceptualizations where SOURCE and TARGET domain can be clearly distinguished; they can but need not necessarily be culture-specific. For *cultural* conceptualizations, on the other hand, it is often not easy to say – at least for 'cultural outsiders' – whether a given conceptualization involves one or two domains. Furthermore, cultural conceptualizations are cultural in the sense that they are culture-specific or restricted to a small number of cultures.

As the aforementioned manifestations of cultural conceptualizations are realized in actual language-in-use, the researcher can draw conclusions on "broader cultural cognitions associated with languages and language varieties" (Sharifian 2017: 5) by means of the analytical tools outlined above. Since cultural conceptual-

4 For intralinguistic cultural variation in Portuguese, see Soares da Silva (this volume).

izations and the collective cognition of a cultural group, in general, are constantly "negotiated and renegotiated across time and space" (Sharifian 2011: 8), it seems reasonable to expect a spectrum of within-group variation of certain cultural conceptualizations. Finally, although cultural cognitions are shared among all members of a cultural group, they are not evenly, but heterogeneously distributed. In other words, "all members of a speech community are linked to each other by a shared set of conceptualizations" (Peters 2017: 131), but not all members capture the same elements of this set of cultural conceptualizations in their individual cognitive systems (cf. Sharifian 2011: 5–8).

3 Data and methodology

3.1 Web-derived newspaper corpus

Given that to date, to the best of our knowledge, no corpus of GuyE is available, we chose to compile a corpus that makes use of the internet archives of national newspapers. Though there are a number of limitations of this particular genre with regard to a series of linguistic research questions, our rationale for the choice of newspapers as a data source is based on Mukherjee and Bernaisch (2015: 419), who state that

> newspapers may be considered 'cultural loudspeakers' with a nationwide range. They grant access to important local as well as international issues and events, provide interpretation schemata for – and relevant opinions on – these issues and events, and disseminate these interpretation schemata and opinions among millions of readers, thus possibly shaping their readers' world views and, on a larger scale, cultural connotations in the speech community.

In this sense, newspapers may well be regarded as both carriers and reflectors of a society's cultural cognition, since they usually tend to "address and potentially influence nation-wide audiences" (Mukherjee and Bernaisch 2015: 418–419) or well-defined local readerships. Hence, written press communication proves to be a useful and (relatively) easily accessible database that provides valuable insights into locally accepted norms and cultural conceptualizations. Note, however, that since newspaper corpora essentially embody sampled collections of very specific text categories, their representativeness – as that of virtually most other corpora – remains inherently limited in this respect (see Schilk, Bernaisch, and Mukherjee 2012: 147; and also McEnery, Xiao, and Tono 2006: 13–16).

Newspapers usually consist of diverse text categories[5] (e.g., news, editorials, comments, classified advertisements, obituaries, etc.), many of which have been subject to previous cultural-linguistic analyses (see, e.g., Peters 2018; Polzenhagen and Frey 2017; and Ranaweera 2018). Compiling our Guyanese (newspaper) English corpus, we basically followed the methodological approach applied by Hundt and Biewer (2007: 251–252). When building their SPEAC corpus (on Southern Pacific Englishes), they included front page leading articles as well as letters to the editor "[i]n order to cover more formal [journalistic] and more informal," casual writing styles. Especially the latter have been selected because they "represent [. . .] the least edited" parts of a newspaper and are "most typical of individual style" (Kachru 2003: 503). Thus, they allow a less 'filtered' view into the cognitions of (ordinary) language users than texts by professional reporters, though it has still to be taken into account that the (non-journalist) writers are presumably aware that their texts are being published, and correspondingly, may adhere to a more formal register in their writing.

In total, the GuyE newspaper corpus that forms the basis for our present study consists of a GuyE sub-section and a British English (BrE) reference sub-corpus. The former encompasses 192 newspaper articles and letters to the editor that were derived, in equal shares of 48 text items each, from the online platforms of the *Stabroek News* and the *Guyana Chronicle*, respectively.[6] These are two of Guyana's three largest daily newspapers with a nation-wide circulation (*The Statesman's Yearbook* 2019: 568), and possess easily accessible (and complete) internet archives. As, in addition, they are held to be quality newspapers – though it has to be mentioned that the *Guyana Chronicle* is a state-owned paper and has tended to report in favor of the ruling governments – rather than tabloids (such as, e.g., *Kaieteur News*) (Smock 2008: 88; Commonwealth Observer Group 2012: 18), they have been identified as suitably comparable to *The Guardian*, which was selected as the present-day BrE 'counterpart.' In particular, we normally downloaded two randomly selected text items each (or, more precisely, the whole webpages) published on the first and fifteenth day of every month in the year 2018 on the newspapers' websites. During this process, we paid particular attention to deriving

5 While newspaper-based corpus studies frequently employ the term 'text type' (cf., e.g., Schilk, Bernaisch, and Mukherjee 2012), we prefer the more neutral term 'text category' in order to avoid confusion with Biber's (1993: 244–245) notion of *text type* (see also Lee 2001).

6 At an earlier stage of this research project, Kühmstedt (2019) presented data at the *International Symposium on Linguistics, Cognition, and Culture* in Belo Horizonte, Brazil, that was retrieved from a smaller corpus comprising articles and letters to the editor merely from the *Stabroek News* (01/2018–12/2018). For the study presented here, this GuyE corpus was extended by adding newspaper extracts from the *Guyana Chronicle*.

only letters to the editor and news articles[7] whose author(s) could be identified by name (and whom we accordingly took to be native speakers of GuyE). By doing so, we intended to discard news reports (usually labeled on the newspapers' websites with "staff editor" as publisher) that had been wired to some extent by international press agencies, such as Reuters or DPA, or had even been copied from other newspapers (cf. Hoffmann, Hundt, and Mukherjee 2011: 268; Hundt and Biewer 2007: 252). For this reason, we sometimes had to deviate from the above-mentioned dates by one or two days, if necessary. Furthermore, we made sure that each author was only included once each month in order to increase the balance of our corpus. In this way, we obtained, in the end, a corpus comprising a total number of 205,702 words (see Table 1).

Table 1: Design of the GuyE newspaper corpus.

Variety	Newspaper	Section	Number of tokens
GuyE	*Stabroek News*	Leading articles	54,307
		Letters to the editor	26,658
	Guyana Chronicle	Leading articles	35,347
		Letters to the editor	32,255
BrE	*The Guardian*	Leading articles	30,585
		Letters to the editor	26,550

It is worth noting that the material for the BrE sub-corpus has largely been collected in exactly the same manner as for the GuyE one. However, since the letters to the editor in *The Guardian* turned out to be much shorter than the Guyanese equivalents, we decided not to download just two letters for each day, but the complete webpages with all relevant letters to the editor. Subsequently, we deleted those letters which were submitted by more than one person or by institutional representatives whose names were not given. Thus, we hoped to yield sub-corpora of similar sizes. Though the final distribution of tokens varies slightly, the different sizes should not pose too much of a problem, as all three newspaper sub-corpora consist of approximately 8,300 word types and the following analyses will generally be run, where necessary, on the basis of relative (normalized) frequencies.

7 We take those pieces as leading news articles that have been published in the sections '(Guyana) News' and 'UK News,' respectively.

3.2 Corpus-based identification of conceptualizations

The plethora of corpus-based analyses especially in the fields of cognitive sociolinguistics as well as metaphor research in general have testified to the relevance and manifold possibilities of corpus-linguistic approaches at the nexus of language, culture, and cognition, and have "put metaphor theory on a sounder empirical footing" (Semino 2008: 1999). Though their number has been increasing in the course of the past years, one of the main issues that remains is the retrieval of relevant data – *viz.* (cultural-)conceptual metaphors and metonymies – because conceptual mappings are apparently "not linked to particular linguistic forms" and there are, to date, hardly any annotated corpora that "corpus-based research on conceptual mappings [could] rely on"[8] (Stefanowitsch 2006: 1–2). Consequently, as a literature review attests, a broad spectrum of "strategies for extracting linguistic expressions manifesting conceptual mappings from non-annotated corpora" have been developed and employed in the framework of previous studies, some of which are summarized in Stefanowitsch (2006: 2–5):

(i) manual searching;
(ii) searching for source domain vocabulary;
(iii) searching for target domain vocabulary;
(iv) searching for sentences containing lexical items from both the source domain and the target domain;
(v) searching for metaphors based on 'markers of metaphor' (e.g., *metaphorically/figuratively speaking*).

This overview is by far not exhaustive, and all of these "automatic or semi-automatic" methodological approaches (Stefanowitsch 2006: 2) additionally require some form of manual annotation/extraction in order to determine if a potential lexical candidate is used in a literal or metaphorical sense.

Furthermore, Krennmayr (2011, 2013) distinguishes two basic major approaches, a "bottom-up" and a "top-down" mode of analysis, into which not only the techniques listed above can be classified but also more recently proposed corpus-linguistic *modi operandi* for the identification of cultural conceptualizations. According to her, top-down procedures (e.g., inquiries for source and target domain vocabulary, respectively) "determine conceptual metaphors first and only then look for linguistic evidence," whereas a textual bottom-up approach (e.g., manual search or exploring metaphors by means of 'markers of metaphors') is "interested in identifying linguis-

8 The largest – and, if not at all, only – available corpus annotated for metaphorical language use in English is the VU Amsterdam Metaphor Corpus Online (Steen et al. 2010).

tic – not conceptual – metaphor" (i.e., metaphorical expressions) first; conceptual metaphors that may underlie a text are "[o]nly at a later stage [. . .] formulated" on the basis of semantic allocation to possible conceptual domains (Krennmayr 2011: 193–194; cf. also Krennmayr 2011: 179–185, and 2013).

When it comes to research concerned in particular with cultural conceptualizations, it can be observed that the majority of studies conducted within the frame of this paradigm so far may actually be ascribed to Krennmayr's top-down approach. As stated above, much of the scholarly publishing in the fields of cultural linguistics and cognitive sociolinguistics employs an "ethnographic approach," and more often than not, papers appear to be based, to varying degrees, on a good bit of (well-informed) "intuition" (Sharifian 2011: 13). The present study recognizes the value of these approaches and intends by no means to replace them. In essence, however, we attempt here to approximate a rather 'bottom-up' investigation by "prompting the corpus itself to provide all lexis" (Güldenring 2016: 230) that might serve as a starting point for identifying relevant source and target domains, and to uncover prevalent cultural conceptualizations present in GuyE newspaper discourse. Since relying solely on such an approach would be insufficient, we have designed a mixed-methods approach, in the framework of which the principal bottom-up process is complemented by top-down analyses. Moreover, both quantitative as well as qualitative methods are employed with regard to the overall aim of extracting salient metaphorical and cultural conceptualizations from the collection of Guyanese newspaper excerpts at hand.[9]

3.2.1 Keyword analysis

In a first step, we carried out a cultural keyword analysis. The importance of keywords – that is, of words which occur significantly more frequently (in terms of relative frequencies) in one corpus than in a reference corpus (Scott 2001: 115) – was already highlighted by Leech and Fallon (1992). Along these lines, Polzenhagen and Wolf (2010: 294) attest the relevance of keywords from a cultural-linguistic perspective, too, given that "such frequency data may be readily interpreted in terms of Wierzbicka's notion of 'cultural keywords' [. . .], i.e. their 'statistical keyness' in the corpus reflects their 'cultural keyness'." For Wierzbicka (1997: 16), keywords take an important role, as she deems them to constitute "focal points around which entire cultural domains are organized," which is why we believe

9 Consequently, the approach introduced here could be referred to as corpus-driven. Since definitional demarcations to 'corpus-based' approaches are, however, not clear-cut, we will use both terms by and large synonymously here (for a discussion, see, e.g., Deignan 2005: 88–90).

they may be considered as potential indicators for culture-specific and culturally relevant source and target domains. Therefore, we conducted a keyword analysis, using the corpus analysis program *AntConc* (Anthony 2019).

3.2.2 Extended keyword chain analysis

The second step of our combination of methods leans on a novel (bottom-up) approach devised by Peters (2017), which he refers to as "extended 'cultural keyword chains.'" Using the keyword *fairy/fairies* as an example in the framework of his study on cultural conceptualizations in Irish English, he argues that each of the lemmata collocating with this keyword "has the potential to be a keyword in its own right" (Peters 2017: 139). Thus, Peters (2017: 143) was able to unveil, for example, "'banshee' > 'fairy' > 'fairy music' > 'music' > 'traditional music'" as cultural keywords of Irish English. Based on the keywords found by means of the previously described keyword analysis (see 3.2.1), Peters's procedure was then applied to our GuyE newspaper corpus.

3.2.3 Key semantic domain analysis

In addition to the previous two steps, which focused on keywords, we undertook a *key semantic domain analysis*, applying the web-based corpus-analysis software *Wmatrix4* (Rayson 2008). By means of the UCREL Semantic Annotation System (USAS), the semantic annotation component of this online tool automatically assigns each lemma of an uploaded corpus to a corresponding semantic field. The semantic tagset consists of 21 major semantic fields, which are further subdivided into 232 more fine-grained category labels. Furthermore, the semantic tagger works context-sensitively, so that not only multi-word units are recognized, but semantic discourse labels are also allocated on the basis of statistical probability in the case of conflicting semantic classification possibilities (Krennmayr 2011: 183). Given that "the semantic fields included in the tagset" – though not meant to represent source and target domains themselves – "can be broadly related to the domains of conceptual metaphor theory," the *Wmatrix4* interface for corpus analysis has been applied in conceptual-metaphor research before (Deignan and Semino 2010; see, e.g., Güldenring 2016, Krennmayr 2011), but, to our knowledge, not in cultural linguistics or cognitive sociolinguistics so far.

4 Results and discussion

4.1 Keywords

The 15 most frequent keywords in the GuyE newspaper sections in comparison to the corresponding British ones – as the result of the keyword analysis carried out by means of *AntConC* – are depicted in Table 2. Grammatical words, such as prepositions, pronouns, etc., have been omitted; the 'keyness,' as calculated by means of the default settings of the *AntConc* software, is established on the basis of the log-likelihood value, with a statistic threshold of $p < 0.05$, and ranges, for the below lexemes, from 409.93 through 45.84.

Table 2: Keywords (lemmatized) sorted by sections in comparison to the counterparts in *The Guardian*.

GuyE Letters + News	GuyE News	GuyE Letters to the editor
Guyana	Guyana	Guyana
president	president	editor
Guyanese	note	PPP
PPP[10]	be	Guyanese
ministry	Stabroek	president
persons	Guyanese	ministry
Stabroek	persons	regards
oil	ministry	faithfully
note	explain	sugar
sugar	oil	Jagdeo
Georgetown	GuySuCo	oil
minister	Williams	region
AFC	Georgetown	government
Jagdeo	state	Jagan
GuySuCo	sugar	minister

Given that we are dealing with newspaper extracts, the list of keywords discerned is, at a first glance, hardly surprising from a discourse-analytic perspective and does not seem to contain any lexical items that could be immediately identified as specific of Guyanese culture. Even so, in an effort to unveil potential culture- and variety-specific conceptualizations, we checked by hand the contexts of the

10 PPP refers to the *People's Progressive Party*, whose votership is predominantly of Indian descent.

above-mentioned keywords in the Guyanese data, and assessed whether the corresponding concordance lines included instances of metaphorical language. In doing so, we did not subscribe, however, to the wide-spread metaphor identification procedure (MIP) developed by the Pragglejaz Group (2007; cf. also Steen et al. 2010), but adhered to Cameron's (2010) discourse dynamics framework for metaphor. In contrast to Pragglejaz' approach, the latter method offers the advantage, as Mendes de Oliveira (2020: 69) points out, that it allows not only single words, but also "longer chunks of language to be classified as metaphorical."

As can be seen in Table 2, *Guyana* is (not surprisingly) the keyword with the highest keyness factor in both the news articles and letters to the editor. Hence, let us begin by analyzing some aspects of how linguistic metaphors containing *Guyana* and *Guyanese* are conceptualized. While doing so, we will largely discard, however, (general) personifications and orientational metaphors (see Lakoff and Johnson 1980) as well as metaphorical expressions in which the keyword in context collocates with a preposition. That is, conceptual mappings like THE COUNTRY FOR THE PEOPLE IN CHARGE (resulting from phrases such as *Guyana has to agree...*) or GUYANA/THE COUNTRY IS A CONTAINER (derived, e.g., from *they are required to remain in Guyana*) are not taken into account in our study because we do not regard them as specific to GuyE.

What is remarkable, first of all, is that *Guyana* is relatively frequently used (with more than a dozen instances out of 617 concordances in total, in which the keyword is used literally and metaphorically) in combination with lexical expressions from the ECONOMY domain, as the selection of representative examples (1)–(5) illustrates:

(1) *The remaining 25% – profit oil – is to be split evenly between Guyana and ExxonMobil.* (Stabroek_News_2018-12-16_MT)[11]

(2) *ExxonMobil will write off any decommissioning costs as expenses and that will lessen significantly future revenue for Guyana [...].* (Stabroek_Letter_2018-01-15_CSR)

(3) *Previously, I had proposed that our economic programme should essentially focus on making Guyana the Singapore of South America, the business hub in South America.* (Stabroek_Letter_2018-07-01_AT)

11 The structure of filenames of the corpus, from which the samples are taken, indicates, in the following order, the title of the newspaper, the section (news, letter to the editor), the date, and the initials of the author's name.

(4) *Maybe, Guyana's new parent company ExxonMobil Corporation will show the heart needed to save the sugar industry* [. . .]. (Stabroek_Letter_2018-01-15_NH)

(5) *Guyana's stake in such a large production will continuously build Guyana's capacity as a global leader in the industry.* (Stabroek_Letter_2018-01-15_CSR)

It can be clearly recognized that Guyana is associated, in the above extracts, with economic terms like *profit, revenue, costs, industry*, etc. and is envisaged as a "business hub" and "global leader in the industry." Hence, following Stefanowitsch's (2004) metaphorical-pattern analysis, one could formulate the conceptual mapping GUYANA IS A COMPANY. Moreover, since it can be observed that not only Guyana is conceptualized as an economic corporation, but other countries (Singapore) as well (see example (3)), one might even generalize the aforementioned formulation and come up with the conceptual metaphor COUNTRIES ARE COMPANIES. On the other hand, there are also examples in which the authors think about how one could *create more value from Guyana* (e.g., Stabroek_Letter_2018-07-01_AT). Consequently, it seems to be a small cognitive step to consider Guyana as a TRADABLE PRODUCT. The ambivalent relation that Guyana – on the one hand, as an alleged 'global player,' on the other as an 'object' that is dealt with – has especially vis-à-vis ExxonMobil,[12] seems to be reflected also in people's minds: GUYANA IS A COMPANY, as established above; simultaneously, however, sample (4) shows that ExxonMobil is perceived as *Guyana's new parent company*, expressing the conceptualization GUYANA IS A SUBSIDIARY OF EXXONMOBIL. This impression is further reinforced when looking at the following extract:

(6) *Also, writing on the cruel and unusual punishment of the sugar workers must take priority over the bungling of the Production Sharing Agreement between Exxon and the Government of Guyana, where the mouse has claimed to have had his way with the elephant.* (Stabroek_Letter_2018-01-15_NH)

By means of the conceptualization of A COMPANY IS AN ANIMAL, obviously grounded in the similarities in size and strength, the author of this letter to the editor expresses how he perceives the relationship between the South American country and the U.S. oil giant.

Apart from *Guyana* and *Guyanese*, *oil* and *sugar* constitute two further lexical items that occur as keywords in the leading news articles as well as letters to

---

12 ExxonMobil is an U.S. American corporation that has received the right to drill for oil off the shores of Guyana from 2020 onward.

the editor and whose 'keyness' seems to signal some socio-cultural relevance in Guyanese public discourse. As both a collocational analysis and a manual review reveal, *oil* – occurring 117 times in total – is amongst others associated, and partly forms nominal compound coinages, with terms such as *deal, commercial, profit, revenue(s), share, money,* etc., all of which coming from the ECONOMY domain. Hence, it appears reasonable to postulate the conceptualization OIL IS MONEY or, more precisely, that OIL STANDS FOR MONEY in a metonymical relationship (cf. Appel, Mason, and Watts 2015: 10); it is literally considered as an APOLITICAL ISSUE (see, e.g., Stabroek_Letter_2018-01-15_CSR) and seems to constitute, in this context, merely a COMMODITY.

Likewise, beyond the mere economic dimension, some social significance appears to be attributed to *oil*. At the time of the publication of the cited articles and letters to the editors, there were debates about plans to use a "part of the oil money as cash transfers to each Guyanese household" (Stabroek_Letter_2018-08-15_TO) or, at least, to the poorest ones, as the following examples illustrate.

(7) *Recent oil finds have created high expectations and hopes for the country [. . .].* (GuyChronicle_Letter_2018-07-01_AI)

(8) *[. . .] assume that utilisation of oil revenues would translate to development [. . .].* (GuyChronicle_Letter_2018-08-01_MDC)

(9) *[. . .] bauxite, gold, silver, manganese, rice, sugar, or oil can save us from impoverishment, underdevelopment, and international contempt.* (GuyChronicle_Letter_2018-08-01_MDC)

(10) *[. . .] he cited seven areas, all of which and more can be funded from the 95% of the oil revenue the government will have after giving the 5% in cash transfers to the poor and powerless.* (Stabroek_Letter_2018-08-15_TO)

Hence, as can be inferred from examples (7)–(10), Guyanese people seem to share the conviction that oil brings development, eradicates poverty, and benefits all citizens. These beliefs can be condensed in the conceptualization THE DISCOVERY OF OIL IS HOPE, or even OIL IS A SAVIOR.[13]

---

13 Further evidence for this conceptualization is provided, for example, by Hon. Trotman, Minister of Natural Resources, who, in an official speech, referred to the announcement that ExxonMobil agreed to produce oil in Guyana as "*the trumpet call that heralds the coming of 'first oil'* " (Co-operative Republic of Guyana 2016). However, even though this metaphor is clearly motivated by Christian mythology, we presume that the concept of a 'savior' is not exclusively a Christian

Finally, the keyword *sugar* occurs 113 times in total (metaphorically and literally used) and, thus, is almost as salient as *oil*. In 2018, the Guyanese sugar industry was affected by significant retrenchment measures; see the following excerpts:

(11) *One of their flogging horses was the sugar industry.* (Stabroek_Letter_2018-09-01_MAN)

(12) *[. . .] it is in full support of the move by the Special Purpose Unit (SPU) to secure a $30B syndicated bond to aid in revitalisation of the country's sugar industry.* (GuyChronicle_News_2018-04-01_SM)

(13) *The former president had told the nation that if the Skeldon project did not work, "well the sugar industry is dead."* (GuyChronicle_News_2018-02-01_ZH)

(14) *When the Trinidad sugar industry was in its death throes [. . .].* (Stabroek_Letter_2018-02-15)

The extracts show that the downsizing and successive closing of the sugar industry is notably conceptualized in terms of DEATH and DYING. This presupposes that the sugar industry/companies are conceptualized as LIVING BEINGS, as can be deduced, for instance, from samples (11) and (12). Hence, it can be supposed that, in the Guyanese collective cognition, THE SUGAR INDUSTRY IS A LIVING BEING THAT IS DEAD/GOING TO DIE.

4.2 Extended keyword chains

Examining the *AntConc* list of collocations with the keyword *Guyana* (with a mutual-information (MI) score ≥ 3), we discerned that the lemmata *nation*, *national*, and *nationality* co-occur quite frequently with the search term, altogether 17 times within a window span of five words to the left and right of the noun. For this reason, these items were taken to be the first potential candidates for the *extended keyword chain analysis* (see 3.2.2), which led us to further culture-specific conceptualizations. Just as in the previous step, we assessed whether these co-occurrences include instances of metaphorical language and cultural conceptualizations. We observed that *nation* is repeatedly used in combination with a

one, but exists in other religions as well. Therefore, SAVIOR is to be understood in a religiously connoted, yet universalist sense.

lexical register that is usually found in discourses revolving around architecture and design (as target domains), as for example in:

(15) *[...] a campaign free of hate, racial and all other forms of incitement is most desirable and essential to the efforts of building and sustaining a cohesive nation with a common destiny.* (Stabroek_Letter_2018-11-01_JOS)

(16) *The minister added that the purchase of a single plantation and its conversion into a village laid the foundation for establishment of a nation.* (GuyChronicle_News_2018-12-02_MO)

(17) *She has a proud record of being the matriarch of a family-owned business that has actively contributed to the academic moulding of the nation of Guyana for more than 50 years.* (GuyChronicle_News_2018-04-15_ST)

(18) *We must not glibly claim that we are bringing up the next generation, or that the children are the future of the nation, or that we mould the nation.* (Stabroek_Letter_2018-10-15_WBA)

Though the conceptualization THE NATION IS A BUILDING represents a well-established conventional metaphor (see, e.g., Kövecses 2010 [2002], and also Musolff 2000), the latter two examples make clear that the conceptualization of a static edifice does not go far enough. It seems that not only the internal structures (the 'walls,' so to speak) are open to modification, but that the very shape of the construct itself is malleable. Hence, we suggest the extended conceptualization GUYANA/THE NATION IS AN UNFINISHED CONSTRUCTION.

Departing from the 'extended' key root morpheme *nation**, one can realize that the collocates *sport* and, in particular, *cricket* play a notable role in Guyanese culture,[14] as the following examples indicate:

(19) *Cricket is our national sport; it is part of our shared heritage.* (GuyChronicle_Letter_2018-07-15_DH)

14 This presumption is substantiated by the *National Sport Policy* of the Co-operative Republic of Guyana (2019: 6), which states that "Guyana and cricket is synonomous [sic]."

(20) *[. . .] many would realise how simple it could be to have the city vibrant and full of life again with the great game of cricket in a well maintained historic venue. It was supposed to be an important part of our culture [. . .].* (GuyChronicle_Letter_2018-09-17_JC)

Therefore, we proceeded by focusing on these new keywords from the SPORTS domain. Manually checking the corresponding concordances, we found, on the one hand, that SPORTS may serve as a source domain to conceptualize principles of ECONOMY, which underscores the salience of sports in Guyanese culture:

(21) *In sports, when teams don't perform well, the owners sometimes fire the managers or coaches and even order benching and trading players for poor performance. Some team owners don't even wait until the end of the season. The same principles apply in the business sector [. . .].* (Stabroek_Letter_2018-12-15_EM)

On the other hand, there is a higher number of textual references (some of them presented below) that point to an intricate relationship between ethnicity – mainly in the form of racism – and sports:

(22) *Cricket is our national sport; it is part of our shared heritage. It is played by all ethnic groups in Guyana.*

(23) *Cricket in Guyana is better when it is a source of ethno-racial harmony [. . .].*

(24) *[. . .] racism has become part and parcel of the official management of cricket in Guyana.*

(all examples taken form GuyChronicle_Letter_2018-07-15_DH)

From the above examples, the conceptualization SPORTS IS ETHNICITY transpires.[15] Though the evidence for the existence of this conceptualization is provisionally based merely on one source of our corpus, the reference therein to the response by Anand Sanasie, member of the Guyana Cricket Board, indicates that the above-cited letter to the editor is part of a larger public discourse. In fact, as an additional online search has disclosed, there was a debate about "Dictatorship

15 Although it is actually used several times in the Guyanese newspaper sources, we deliberately intend to abstain from employing the term *"race"* here. The concept of "race" constitutes an artificial social construct without any scientific, i.e., biological foundation. Therefore, we wish not to reproduce it in modern-day (academic) discourse.

and Racism in Guyanese Cricket," initiated by columnist David Hinds (2018) with a same-titled article in the *Kaieteur News*. While the conceptualization SPORTS IS ETHNICITY is not necessarily shared by all members of the socio-cultural group in question, a close reading of the public echo to this issue and of various other sources found during this literature review has led to the assumption that this conceptualization does indeed have a larger collective-cognitive salience and is not merely idiosyncratic.[16]

Moreover, political and economic terminology, including *committee, management, monopolize, stakeholder,* etc., is employed in Guyanese sports contexts, as illustrated by example (25). This collocational correlation may be a cognitive-linguistic indication that ethnic contentions do actually not originate in sports, but in other spheres – politics, economy, etc. – and that these problems are projected onto sports.

(25) *I am contending that five or nine Indo-Guyanese men, elected by Indo-Guyanese clubs and stakeholders cannot effectively represent the interests of Afro-Guyanese stakeholders and players and other ethnic groups.* (GuyChronicle_Letter_2018-07-15_DH)

To prove this point, terms pertaining to the domain of ETHNICITY (*ethnic, ethnicity, race, racial, Afro-Guyanese, Indo-Guyanese, indigenous,* etc.) were concordanced and the contexts of the corresponding occurrences were discursively analyzed:

(26) *When you look at someone of African descent, you automatically look at the PNC, when you look at Indo Guyanese, you automatically think PPP.*[17] *When you look at the Indigenous person, you have no idea where they are going.* (Stabroek_News_2018-07-01_MLR)

(27) *On the idea behind the formation of a party seeking the Amerindian vote, Shuman, who made the announcement on his Facebook page, said, "We are very, very aware that the Indigenous vote is a swing vote. [. . .]"* (Stabroek_News_2018-07-01_MLR)

(28) *[. . .] leaders are often chosen by citizens based on their race, instead of on merit.* (GuyChronicle_Letter_2018-08-01_MDC)

---

16 See, for example, Ramzan (2016) resorting to this conceptualization: *football in my humble opinion is the number one sport in Guyana when it comes to people of ethnicity, when it comes to disadvantage folks [. . .].*

17 PNC is the abbreviation for the *People's National Congress* party, which is mainly supported by the Afro-Guyanese population.

(29) *[. . .] Cheddi Jagan should not be the presidential candidate, as Afro-Guyanese would revolt against an Indian leader [. . .].* (GuyChronicle_Letter_2018-09-01_HG)

(30) *Shouting at the top of their lungs, as PPP/C representatives have been doing on this issue just points Guyanese to the race-based way the PPP/C really thinks about the nation [. . .].* (GuyChronicle_Letter_2018-06-15_EH)

(31) *In their discussions, he said, they noted that ethnic politics has torn the country apart and done it a disservice.* (Stabroek_News_2018-07-01_MLR)

(32) *For them, it's all about race – the good lawyer even had the audacity to say openly that anyone who doesn't think voting is based on race in Guyana should be ignored.* (GuyChronicle_Letter_2018-06-15_EH)

Based on the above samples, in particular (26) and (27), we may recognize, on the one hand, that ethnicities and ethnic communities are defined in terms of politics, along the lines of political parties. Hence, the underlying conceptualization may be formulated as ETHNICITIES ARE POLITICAL PARTIES or, more generally, ETHNICITY IS POLITICS. On the other hand, the remaining examples illustrate that ethnic discourses that relate to politics can practically not be clearly distinguished from 'ethnicized' political discourses; they may be considered as manifestations of the conceptualization POLITICS IS ETHNICITY. So, overall, ETHNICITY and POLITICS are so closely entangled in Guyana that they seem to us (almost) isomorphic; that is to say, ETHNICITY IS POLITICS and POLITICS IS ETHNICITY appear to be interchangeable conceptualizations. Furthermore, taking the conceptualization SPORTS IS ETHNICITY into account (see above), what we find is a kind of 'blending' of SPORTS, POLITICS, and ETHNICITY. In other words, the data suggests that these domains are highly interwoven in the collective cognition of GuyE speakers.

To complete this section, let us briefly consider two additional aspects. Firstly, it was possible only due to the 'extended cultural keyword chain' technique that the metaphor A COMMUNITY/THE NATION IS A FAMILY – which has been attested in U.S. American English (Lakoff 2016 [1996]; see also Polzenhagen, this volume) as well as in Hong Kong English and Chinese English (Wolf 2008; Liu 2002) – could be verified for GuyE as well, as the following examples show:[18]

18 A COMMUNITY/THE NATION IS A FAMILY – or alternatively, COMMUNITY IS KINSHIP – is not an uncommon metaphor. COMMUNITY IS KINSHIP has been discussed extensively by Wolf and Polzenhagen (2009; see also Polzenhagen, this volume) for the African context, where, in many instances, it was found to be a cultural conceptualization rather than a metaphor. Unfortunately,

(33) *What manner of people are we, to see the suffocation of our Guyanese brothers and sisters in the sugar industry [. . .].* (Stabroek_Letter_2018-01-15_NH)

(34) *Let us also use this opportunity to strengthen the bonds of brotherhood and sisterhood and to make foremost the welfare of this land that is home to all of us; our Guyana.* (Stabroek_Letter_2018-11-01_JOS)

(35) *I am happy to join in this call for an end to discrimination, particularly, the institutionalised dehumanisation of LGBTIQ persons. I urge us to be proactive in their protection, and to resist the hate perpetuated against our brothers and sisters who on a daily basis face tremendous threats, and are denied of their basic human rights.* (Stabroek_News_2018-06-02_TP)

(36) *Ministers must see their own daughter in a next man's daughter, they must see the mothers, sisters, aunts as their own [. . .].* (GuyChronicle_Letter_2018-02-15_GC)

Secondly, when reviewing the collocations of the term *Guyana*, the verb *embark* (see example (37)) sparked our interest, so we proceeded by determining lexemes containing the root **embark** as new potential keywords, which occur 9 times in the GuyE subcorpus and not at all in the British part. Investigating their metaphoricity yielded, amongst others, the following results for metaphorical expressions:

(37) *But there is much more to be fixed before Guyana can confidently embark upon a renegotiation exercise.* (Stabroek_Letter_2018-02-01_TJ)

(38) *[. . .] thank you for your faith in me and embarking me upon this journey.* (GuyChronicle_News_2018-12-01_TR)

(39) *It confirms the fact that Guyana is about to embark on a path of premature deindustrialization [. . .].* (Stabroek_Letter_2018-10-15_MIA)

(40) *She explained to Stabroek News that as she was not sure of which career path she wished to embark on [. . .].* (Stabroek_News_2018-08-18_TP)

the data we used was not broad enough to draw any conclusion as to which aspects of the FAMILY model are prevalent in A COMMUNITY/THE NATION IS A FAMILY in GuyE: viz. "those grounded on the notions of 'birth,' 'creation,' 'causation,' 'lineage,' and 'inheritance,'" or rather "mappings from the nurture-and-care model" (Wolf and Polzenhagen 2009: 68), salient in African English.

(41) *Dr Jason Mars [. . .] has embarked on the establishment of a scholarship programme that would afford Computer Science Majors at the University of Guyana (UG) an opportunity to pursue PhD studies at the University of Michigan.* (Stabroek_News_2018-06-17_ML)

(42) *[. . .] though his government has not embarked on a multi-year negotiation with the GTU, it is something that is desirable.* (GuyChronicle_News_2018-09-01_SM)

(43) *His announcement comes at a time when the Guyana Teachers' Union (GTU) is threatening to up the ante over failed salary negotiations with the Education Ministry, which has already resulted in many teachers embarking on strike action [. . .].* (GuyChronicle_News_2018-09-01_SM)

As these examples show, the lemma *embark* is metaphorically used in the context of the well-established conventional conceptualization *X IS A JOURNEY*, where the metaphor vehicle *X* describes a somewhat challenging action that requires some commitment. Kövecses (2010; see also Kövecses, this volume), for instance, discusses this conceptual metaphor in some detail in relation with the target domains (*X*) LOVE, LIFE, and ARGUMENT. Interestingly, however, the semantics of the verb *embark* tends to point to a further specification of the source domain, which might correspondingly be formulated, especially with regard to GuyE, as A JOURNEY IS A BOAT RIDE. While the extent of the applicability and possible origins of this (provisional) conceptual metaphor, of course, remain to be explored, it might seem plausible to assume that it reflects the spatial perception and cognition of GuyE speakers: owing to Guyana's physical landscape, the country's infrastructure has hitherto relied, to a large proportion, on water transportation, especially in the interior, i.e., the hinterland beyond the municipalities located in the coastal strip; and also the very name *Guyana*, which is Amerindian for 'land of many waters,' points to the importance of the nearly 50 rivers in the country (cf. Seipp 2018; Connolly 2018: 18).

4.3 Key semantic domains

The fifteen most prominent key semantic domains in each text category of our Guyanese database – i.e., the (automatically tagged) semantic fields occurring with a significantly higher frequency in the GuyE newspaper subcorpus in comparison to the British *Guardian* one – are depicted in Table 3, following the order of their keyness (which, again, is expressed in terms of log-likelihood[19]).

Table 3: Key semantic fields sorted by sections in comparison to the counterparts in *The Guardian* (original UCREL labels are retained).[20]

GuyE Letters + News	GuyE News	GuyE Letters to the editor
GOVERNMENT	EDUCATION IN GENERAL	GOVERNMENT
UNMATCHED	UNMATCHED	GRAMMATICAL BIN
IN POWER	GENERAL ACTIONS/MAKING	IN POWER
GENERAL ACTIONS/MAKING	SMOKING AND NON-MEDICAL DRUGS	THE MEDIA
SMOKING AND NON-MEDICAL DRUGS	FARMING & HORTICULTURE	SUBSTANCES AND MATERIALS: LIQUID
SUBSTANCES AND MATERIALS: LIQUID	STRONG OBLIGATION OR NECESSITY	RESPECTED
GRAMMATICAL BIN	INDUSTRY	BUSINESS: GENERALLY
INDUSTRY	IN POWER	LAW AND ORDER
BUSINESS: GENERALLY	NO POWER	GENERAL ACTIONS/MAKING
NO POWER	GOVERNMENT	SMOKING AND NON-MEDICAL DRUGS
STRONG OBLIGATION OR NECESSITY	WORK AND EMPLOYMENT: GENERALLY	LIKE
MENTAL OBJECT: CONCEPTUAL OBJECT	BUSINESS: SELLING	MEASUREMENT: LENGTH & HEIGHT
FARMING & HORTICULTURE	EVALUATION: GOOD/BAD	BELONGING TO A GROUP
CHANGE	MEDICINES AND MEDICAL TREATMENT	EXPECTED
SPEECH: COMMUNICATIVE	SUBSTANCES AND MATERIALS: LIQUID	INDUSTRY

As can be seen, the key semantic field GOVERNMENT seems to be overly salient in the Guyanese part of our corpus. The mere occurrence of the semantic domain

19 The 'overuse' of all semantic fields mentioned in Table 3 is statistically significant, each having a log-likelihood value of 6.63 or above for a 99% significance ($p = 0.01$) (cf. also Deignan and Semino 2010: 173–176).

20 Some of the resulting categories (e.g., 'Pronouns,' 'Negative') have not been taken into account here, as they constitute grammatical rather than semantic domains.

GOVERNMENT is not surprising from a discourse-analytic perspective, since we are dealing with newspaper texts. Its significantly higher occurrence is, however, insofar remarkable as the same genre (*viz.* newspaper) holds for both GuyE and BrE; hence, GOVERNMENT-related expressions such as *government*, *president*, *constitution*, etc., to name but a few, seem to have – altogether – a higher presence and relevance in Guyanese (newspaper) English than in BrE newspaper discourse.[21]

In a subsequent step, the lemmata tagged as pertaining to one of the above-mentioned categories were again checked (manually) for their metaphorical-conceptual content; (key)words which have been discussed in the previous sections, however, have been discarded here. To demonstrate the value of this approach based on key semantic domains, the lemma *government*, which is provided by *Wmatrix4* as the expression with the highest frequency within in the semantic field of GOVERNMENT, shall serve as an example as to how some prevalent conceptualizations can be derived from its concordances.

Like many of the target domains considered previously, GOVERNMENT is conceptualized as a PERSON in GuyE. While general (i.e., neutral) personifications are not discussed here, some light shall be shed on three specific cases. Firstly, the following extracts indicate the conceptualization THE GOVERNMENT IS A MANAGER:

(44) *[. . .] Guyanese urgently need to start focusing on having a government that returns to the proven basic management by objectives principles [. . .].* (Stabroek_Letter_2018-12-15_EM)

(45) *While the government should not necessarily take on the management of those rights, it should be instrumental in the formation of such an agency or agencies [. . .].* (GuyChronicle_Letter_2018-07-01_AI)

This conceptualization makes sense in that the metonymical relationship of THE MANAGEMENT FOR THE COMPANY can be paralleled by the metonymy THE GOVERNMENT FOR THE COUNTRY. Thus, the result ties in with the finding THE COUNTRY IS A COMPANY, proposed in section 4.1. Moreover, the verbs and technical terms

21 In fact, some single – rather context-sensitive, culturally bound – BrE expressions (such as *council/councillor*, *lord(s)*, *prime minister*, etc.) occur more frequently in *The Guardian* than in the GuyE newspapers. Yet, in their totality, the occurrence of lexical items categorized under the semantic label GOVERNMENT is significantly higher in the Guyanese press. Thus, it may be inferred that the semantic/discourse field GOVERNMENT itself is more salient in the GuyE than the BrE part of our corpus.

related to the construction of buildings that collocate with *government* in the next examples seem to support the proposition that the conceptual perception THE GOVERNMENT IS AN ARCHITECT is wide-spread as well:

(46) *Government and Opposition must return to the drawing board and address the* concerns and fears of the people [. . .]. (GuyChronicle_Letter_2018-05-01_LL)

(47) *President Granger said Friday that several other government agencies are building capacity to be able to adequately and effectively deal with the upcoming oil-and-gas sector.* (GuyChronicle_News_2018-09-01_AG)

(48) *He also noted that government is looking to reshape and transform Guyana's image.* (Stabroek_News_2018-04-15_ZF)

Finally, it can be recognized that *government* is more often than not also used in contexts that expose a negative semantic prosody:

(49) *They further claim that the PPP Government stole 25% of the annual budget every year [. . .].* (Stabroek_Letter_2018-09-01_MAN)

(50) *[. . .] their accusations against the former PPP/C government of wholesale theft [. . .].* (GuyChronicle_Letter_2018-04-15_DG)

(51) *Whether it was the waste-to-energy plant or the lotto project to raise money for the city, it was swiftly shot down by the government.* (GuyChronicle_Letter_2018-12-15_MS)

(52) *The US$18 million signing bonus which the Government unlawfully refused to deposit in the Consolidated Fund [. . .].* (Stabroek_Letter_2018-09-01_MAN)

(53) *Time to stop voting for parties that then go on to do whatever they want, including facilitating government corruption and inept governance.* (Stabroek_Letter_2018-12-15_EM)

From the partly harsh choice of words and accusations (e.g., *stole*, *theft*), one might draw the conclusion that these samples represent linguistic manifestations of THE GOVERNMENT IS A CRIMINAL.

Departing in particular from the latter conceptual metaphor, it would elsewhere be possible to apply, in a recurrent process, an 'extended keyword chain' analysis (as presented in section 4.2) again. By doing so, one might corroborate the cultural conceptualization CORRUPTION IS A DISEASE, which can be found in some of the resulting instances (e.g., *corruption is one of the ills that has long plagued our country* (GuyChronicle_Letter_2018-06-01_TD)). Furthermore, it was by means of this combination of methods – key semantic domain and 'extended keyword chain' analyses – that we were able to identify the conceptualization DEMOCRACY IS A LIVING BEING, which is exemplified in the following concordances:

(54) *[. . .] lampooning of government is part of the lifeblood of democracy.* (Stabroek_Letter_2018-05-15_MJ)

(55) *The competitive races for office in the PNCR are healthy for democracy.* (Guy-Chronicle_Letter_2018-08-15_RB).

However, the 'semantic' category that prospectively may be of particular interest for cultural linguistics/cognitive sociolinguistics, and which has largely been neglected so far in research employing (whichever version of) the *Wmatrix* software, is the one labeled as *Z99: UNMATCHED*. This domain represents a kind of 'junk' section[22] subsuming all words and expressions that cannot be automatically identified by the USAS system as belonging to one of the other categories. The lexical resources of the semantic tagger feed on the dictionaries of the CLAWS POS tagger (Leech, Garside, and Bryant 1994), which, in turn, was originally designed to tag the British National Corpus. Furthermore, these resources have been "expanded by adding words which were collected from large text corpora" (Löfberg 2017: 74). Thus, it has to be acknowledged that the tagger is, to a certain extent, culturally biased, given that on the one hand, one of the major lexical sources is based on BrE and, on the other, no GuyE corpus exists yet, which the semantic tagger lexicon could have drawn from. For this very reason, however, the semantic tagger, and in particular the above-mentioned domain *Unmatched*, could actually serve as a source that allows not only for the identification of a range of loanwords in corpora (especially, in varieties other than British or U.S. American English), but also of culture-specific concepts that have undergone processes of nativization or contextualization (cf., e.g., Wolf 2001: 244–245).

As a result of the present key semantic domain analysis, the UNMATCHED category includes for GuyE, amongst others, names of places, persons, and parties

22 In their USAS guide, Archer, Wilson, and Rayson (2002: 36) even regard this semantic field as a subdivision of a domain they label as "Trash can."

(e.g., *PPP, AFC, Berbice, Granger, Jagdeo*), technical terms (such as *molasses, bauxite, Filaria*), transcriptions from interviewees' statements in Guyanese Creole (e.g., *seh, deh, fuh, juk, meh*) as well as typographical errors (like *theyre, wasnt,* etc.). Furthermore, one can find, in this 'semantic domain,' the following expressions (Table 4) which (*i*) are not part of the 'common core' of the English language; (*ii*) are not elucidated in any form (e.g., by translations in parentheses) in the Guyanese newspaper texts; and (*iii*) can be located, by means of a Google search, in other contexts and sources as well. As such, they are likely to represent 'nativized,' though not necessarily exclusive, idiosyncratic elements of the GuyE vocabulary.

Table 4: Culture-specific GuyE notions found in the GuyE Newspaper corpus.

GuyE expression	Explanation (source websites given in brackets)
banna	term for a (male) friend (https://www.urbandictionary.com/, http://wiwords.com/)
belly wuk	diarrhea or other form of upset stomach (http://wiwords.com/)
braddar	loud, obnoxious (https://islesman.wordpress.com/glossary-of-guyanese-terms-work-in-progress/)
Mash(ramani)	annual festival in commemoration of the foundation of the Republic of Guyana (source: https://en.wikipedia.org/)
obeah	form of sorcery (https://oed.com/)
plimpla	thorn (of a plant) (http://www.kaieteur.com/memorybank/, https://islesman.wordpress.com/glossary-of-guyanese-terms-work-in-progress/)
soca	Caribbean music style (https://oed.com/)
toshao	elected tribal leader of an Amerindian village or community (miscellaneous references)

The very existence of these lexical items as cultural categories – and especially in newspapers – may be regarded as linguistic evidence for the relevance of the correlating culture-specific domains such as (AMERINDIAN) COMMUNITY, SORCERY/WITCHCRAFT, and MUSIC in GuyE discourses. To provide but one example, a leading newspaper article entitled "Laurence Bakhsh: Working to promote an understanding of haemophilia" states:

(56) *Growing up Laurence Bakhsh and his brother Lloyd struggled to understand their condition and it was even more difficult for them to explain it to their peers many of whom taunted them and believed that someone had worked obeah on them.* (Stabroek_News_2018-04-01_OA)

This extract points to the fact that the cultural conceptualization A DISEASE IS A RESULT OF SORCERY (OBEAH), for instance, which also exists in similar forms in other varieties of English around the world, seems to constitute a widely distributed element in the collective cognition of GuyE speakers.

5 Conclusion

In the previous sections, we introduced a text-based, "bottom-up" (Krennmayr 2011) methodological procedure for the retrieval of conceptual metaphors and cultural conceptualizations. While the three methods employed can be applied separately, we hope to have demonstrated that they are even more beneficial when combined, owing to their interaction effects. First of all, a (statistical) cultural keyword analysis was carried out, following the pioneering work by Leech and Fallon (1992) and the cultural-linguistic considerations (in a broader sense) by Wierzbicka (1997). Taking the results from this analysis as a basis, we broadened the keyword analysis by applying Peters's (2017) method of analyzing "extended 'cultural keyword chains,'" which considers collocates of the previously identified keywords as new potential keywords. Finally, these two approaches were complemented by a key semantic domain analysis, using the online corpus analysis tool *Wmatrix4*, developed by Rayson (2008). The lemmata within those semantic fields that occurred, in their entirety, with a significantly higher frequency in the GuyE subcorpus than in the texts from the British *Guardian*, were again regarded as new potential keywords. Since many of the findings yielded especially by the last step of our mixed-methods approach turned out to be repetitive (as they had been discovered by means of the anterior steps already), they were not presented again in section 4.3; instead, we focused on a selection of newly-gained results. In doing so, particular emphasis was laid on the category labeled as 'Unmatched,' which hitherto had been largely disregarded in research employing the online tool *Wmatrix*.

The repetitiveness of results also shows that the approach described in this paper does not constitute a linear process. While the first and the second step can be considered as consecutive in that the 'extended keyword chain' analysis necessarily builds on the preceding keyword analysis, the third method, the key semantic domain analysis, could be applied 'independently.' Hence, the application of the latter corpus-analytical approach may be considered as one confirming the findings of the steps before, but definitely also represents a means to gain further insights. The order of the methods – all of which are not new in themselves, but have been combined in a novel way here – is, thus, somewhat flexible, though we would recommend the application of the *Wmatrix4* software as a final step because of the sheer mass of the resulting data sets.

Furthermore, the scope of the present study "in terms of which metaphorical data could be uncovered" was practically not limited to an *a priori* selection of possible cultural domains to be searched for (Güldenring 2016: 231). Yet, a complete automatization of the "bottom-up" (Krennmayr 2011) metaphor/conceptualization-identification process could not be achieved. It remains inevitable for the analyst, subsequent to each of the steps described above, to manually review every concordance line and assess the metaphorical or literal language use of the respective (statistical) keywords, in order to decide in each case whether or not they ultimately constitute *cultural* 'keyword candidates' or cultural metaphors/conceptualizations.

In the end, all of the culture-specific categories and cultural domains/conceptualizations that were identified in our GuyE newspaper corpus by means of this mixed-methods approach have the potential to constitute promising starting points for the further description and analysis of entire cultural models, i.e., complex reticular systems in which culture-specific "metaphoric, metonymic, as well as non-metaphoric conceptualisations in a socio-cultural group" are interrelated and linked to one another (Polzenhagen and Wolf 2007: 127). It must be mentioned, however, that especially a cultural-linguistic/cognitive-sociolinguistic analysis of key semantic domains on the basis of *Wmatrix4* is of course to be treated with caution, as words from the 'common core' of the English language are not recognized by the program as being potentially culture-specific (see the above example of *family* in section 2). Hence, it cannot be excluded that some cultural domains organized around entities from the 'common core' have not been detected here. In this sense, the application of the semantic-tagging function of the corpus analysis software *Wmatrix4* might possibly prove to be more fruitful with regard to the tenets of cultural linguistics/cognitive sociolinguistics at another stage of metaphorical/cultural conceptualization research in GuyE (or any other variety of English), for example, when source or target domains are already known.

References

Anthony, Laurence. 2019. AntConc (Version 3.5.8) [Computer Software]. Tokyo: Waseda University. https://www.laurenceanthony.net/software (accessed 1 March 2020).

Appel, Hannah, Arthur Mason & Michael Watts (eds.). 2015. *Subterranean estates: Life worlds of oil and gas*. Ithaca & London: Cornell University Press.

Archer, Dawn, Andrew Wilson & Paul Rayson. 2002. Introduction to the USAS category system. Benedict project report. http://ucrel.lancs.ac.uk/usas/usas_guide.pdf (accessed 1 March 2020).

Biber, Douglas. 1993. Representativeness in corpus design. *Literary and Linguistic Computing* 8 (4). 243–257.

Cameron, Lynne. 2010. The discourse dynamics framework for metaphor. In Lynne Cameron & Robert Maslen (eds.), *Metaphor analysis: Research practice in applied linguistics, Social sciences and the humanities*, 77–94. London & Oakville: Equinox.

Commonwealth Observer Group. 2012. *Guyana national and regional elections, 28 November 2011*. London: Commonwealth Secretariat. https://www.thecommonwealth-ilibrary.org/commonwealth/governance/guyana-national-and-regional-elections-28-november-2011_9781848591356-en (accessed 24 February 2020).

Connolly, Steve. 2018. *Journey back to Watooka: A story of Guyana*. Victoria: Friesen Press.

Co-operative Republic of Guyana, Department of Public Information. 2016. Minister Trotman's remarks: Seminar "Governance of the petroleum sector: Preparing for first oil." https://dpi.gov.gy/minister-trotmans-remarks-seminar-governance-of-the-petroleum-sector-preparing-for-first-oil/ (accessed 30 March 2020).

Co-operative Republic of Guyana, Department of Public Information. 2019. National Sports Policy (NSP). https://dpi.gov.gy/wp-content/uploads/2019/02/National-Sports-Policy-Guyana-Cabinet-January-2019.pdf (accessed 1 March 2020).

Deignan, Alice. 2005. *Metaphor and corpus linguistics*. Amsterdam & Philadelphia: John Benjamins.

Edwards, Walter F. 1977. Sociolinguistic models and phonological variation in Guyana. *Society for Caribbean Linguistics, Occasional Paper* 8.

Geers, Sarah. 2018. Conceptual metaphors of FAMILY in Hong Kong English. Paper presented at the 39th ICAME Conference, Tampere, Finland, 30 May–3 June.

Güldenring, Barbara. 2016. Metaphors in New English academic writing. In Christoph Schubert & Christina Sanchez-Stockhammer (eds.), *Variational text linguistics: Revisiting register in English*, 223–249. Berlin & Boston: Walter de Gruyter.

Haynes, Lillith M. 1997. One people, one nation, one destiny: Race, ethnicity and Guyanese sociolinguistic identity. In Edgar W. Schneider (ed.), *Englishes around the world. Volume 2: Caribbean, Africa, Asia, Australasia*, 25–39. Amsterdam & Philadelphia: John Benjamins.

Hinds, David. 2018. Dictatorship and racism in Guyanese cricket – Can we talk about this, Mr. Jagdeo? *Kaieteur News*, 8 July. https://www.kaieteurnewsonline.com/2018/07/08/dictatorship-and-racism-in-guyanese-cricket-can-we-talk-about-this-mr-jagdeo/ (accessed 1 March 2020).

Hoffmann, Sebastian, Marianne Hundt & Joybrato Mukherjee. 2011. Indian English – An emerging epicentre?: A pilot study on light verbs in web-derived corpora of South Asian Englishes. *Anglia* 129 (3–4). 258–280.

Hollington, Andrea. 2015. *Traveling conceptualizations: A cognitive and anthropological linguistic study of Jamaican*. Amsterdam & Philadelphia: John Benjamins.

Hundt, Marianne & Carolin Biewer. 2007. The dynamics of inner and outer circle varieties in the South Pacific and East Asia. In Marianne Hundt, Nadja Nesselhauf & Carolin Biewer (eds.), *Corpus linguistics and the web*, 249–269. Amsterdam & New York: Rodopi.

Kachru, Yamuna. 2003. On definite reference in world Englishes. *World Englishes* 22 (4). 497–510.

Kövecses, Zoltán. 2010 [2002]. *Metaphor: A practical introduction*, 2nd edn. Oxford & New York: Oxford University Press.

Krennmayr, Tina. 2011. *Metaphor in newspapers*. Utrecht: LOT.

Krennmayr, Tina. 2013. Top-down versus bottom-up approaches to the identification of metaphor in discourse. *Metaphorik.de* 24. 7–36. https://www.metaphorik.de/en/journal/24/top-down-versus-bottom-approaches-identification-metaphor-discourse.html (accessed 1 March 2020).

Kühmstedt, Patrick. 2019. Cultural conceptualizations in Guyanese English. Paper presented at the International Symposium on Linguistics, Cognition, and Culture/Simpósio Internacional de Linguística, Cognição e Cultura, Belo Horizonte, Brazil, 13–15 March.

Lakoff, George. 2016 [1996]. *Moral politics: How liberals and conservatives think*, 3rd ed. Chicago & London: University of Chicago Press.

Lakoff, George & Mark Johnson. 1980. *Metaphors we live by*. Chicago & London: University of Chicago Press.

Latić, Denisa & Hans-Georg Wolf. 2017. A corpus-based analysis of cultural conceptualizations from the domains of FAMILY and MONEY in Hong Kong English. *International Journal of Language and Culture* 4 (2). 197–214.

Lee, David Y.W. 2001. Genres, registers, text types, domains, and styles: Clarifying the concepts and navigating a path through the BNC jungle. *Language Learning & Technology* 5 (3). 37–72.

Leech, Geoffrey & Roger Fallon. 1992. Computer corpora: What do they tell us about culture? *ICAME Journal* 16. 29–50.

Leech, Geoffrey, Roger Garside & Michael Bryant. 1994. CLAWS4: The tagging of the British National corpus. In *Proceedings of the 15th International Conference on Computational Linguistics (COLING 94)*, Kyoto, Japan, vol. 1, 622–628.

Liu, Dilin. 2002. *Metaphor, culture, and worldview: The case of American English and the Chinese language*. Lanham, New York & Oxford: University Press of America.

Löfberg, Laura. 2017. *Creating large semantic lexical resources for the Finnish Language*. Lancaster: Lancaster University Ph.D. dissertation. https://doi.org/10.17635/lancaster/thesis/3 (accessed 1 March 2020).

McEnery, Tony, Richard Xiao & Yukio Tono. 2006. *Corpus-based language studies: An advanced resource book*. London & New York: Routledge.

Mendes de Oliveira, Milene. 2020. *Business negotiations in ELF from a cultural linguistic perspective*. Berlin & Boston: Walter de Gruyter.

Mukherjee, Joybrato & Tobias Bernaisch. 2015. Cultural keywords in context: A pilot study of linguistic acculturation in South Asian Englishes. In Peter Collins (ed.), *Grammatical change in English world-wide*, 411–435. Amsterdam & Philadelphia: John Benjamins.

Musolff, Andreas. 2000. Political imagery of Europe: A house without exit doors? *Journal of Multilingual and Multicultural Development* 21 (3). 216–229.

Peters, Arne. 2017. FAIRIES, BANSHEES, and the CHURCH: Cultural conceptualisations in Irish English. *International Journal of Language and Culture* 4 (2). 127–148.

Peters, Arne. 2018. 'Did you see what your ancestors gave you but your doctor failed to give you?': Cultural conceptualisations of ancestral communication in Black South African English. Paper presented at the 38th International LAUD Symposium/2nd Cultural Linguistics International Conference, Landau, Germany, 23–26 July.

Polzenhagen, Frank. 2007. *Cultural conceptualizations in West African English: A cognitive-linguistic approach*. Frankfurt/M. & Berlin: Peter Lang.

Polzenhagen, Frank & Sandra Frey. 2017. Are marriages made in heaven? A cultural-linguistic case study on Indian-English matrimonials. In Farzad Sharifian (ed.), *Advances in cultural linguistics*, 573–605. Singapore: Springer.

Polzenhagen, Frank & Hans-Georg Wolf. 2007. Culture-specific conceptualisations of corruption in African English: Linguistic analyses and pragmatic applications. In Farzad Sharifian & Gary B. Palmer (eds.), *Applied cultural linguistics: Implications for second language learning and intercultural communication*, 125–168. Amsterdam & Philadelphia: John Benjamins.

Polzenhagen, Frank & Hans-Georg Wolf. 2010. Investigating culture from a linguistic perspective: An exemplification with Hong Kong English. *Zeitschrift für Anglistik und Amerikanistik* 58 (3). 281–303.

Pragglejaz Group. 2007. MIP: A method for identifying metaphorically used words in discourse. *Metaphor and Symbol* 22 (1). 1–39.

Ramzan, Avenash. 2016. Guyana Beverage Inc renews partnership with Fruta Conquerors F.C. *News Room*, 12 November. https://newsroom.gy/2016/11/12/guyana-beverage-inc-renews-partnership-with-fruta-conquerors-f-c/ (accessed 1 March 2020).

Ranaweera, Mahishi. 2018. 'Nothing can we call our own but death': A diachronic analysis of Sri Lankan English morphological features and move structures of obituary notices in newspapers. Paper presented at the 39th ICAME Conference, Tampere, Finland, 30 May–3 June.

Rayson, Paul. 2008. From key words to key semantic domains. *International Journal of Corpus Linguistics* 13 (4). 519–549.

Schilk, Marco, Tobias Bernaisch & Joybrato Mukherjee. 2012. Mapping unity and diversity in South Asian English lexicogrammar: Verb-complementational preferences across varieties. In Marianne Hundt & Ulrike Gut (eds.), *Mapping unity and diversity world-wide: Corpus-based studies of New Englishes*, 137–165. Amsterdam & Philadelphia: John Benjamins.

Scott, Mike. 2001. Mapping key words to *problem* and *solution*. In: Mike Scott & Geoff Thompson (eds.), *Patterns of text: In honour of Michael Hoey*, 109–127. Amsterdam & Philadelphia: John Benjamins.

Seipp, Bettina. 2018. Länderkunde Guyana: Der Helikopter entführt in eine prähistorische Welt. *Die Welt*, 17 October. https://www.welt.de/reise/Fern/article182147166/Guyana-Der-Helikopter-entfuehrt-in-eine-praehistorische-Welt.html (accessed 1 March 2020).

Sharifian, Farzad. 2006. A cultural-conceptual approach and world Englishes: The case of Aboriginal English. *World Englishes* 25 (1). 11–22.

Sharifian, Farzad. 2011. *Cultural conceptualisations and language*. Amsterdam & Philadelphia: John Benjamins.

Sharifian, Farzad. 2015. Cultural linguistics and world Englishes. *World Englishes* 34 (4). 515–532.

Sharifian, Farzad. 2017. *Cultural linguistics: Cultural conceptualisations and language*. Amsterdam & Philadelphia: John Benjamins.

Smock, Kirk. 2008. *Guyana: The Bradt travel guide*. Guilford: Globe Pequot.

Steen, Gerard J., Aletta G. Dorst, J. Berenike Herrmann, Anna A. Kaal, Tina Krennmayr & Trijntje Pasma. 2010. *A Method for linguistic metaphor identification: From MIP to MIPVU*. Amsterdam & Philadelphia: John Benjamins.

Stefanowitsch, Anatol. 2004. HAPPINESS in English and German: A metaphorical-pattern analysis. In Michel Achard & Suzanner Kemmer (eds.), *Language, culture, and mind*, 137–149. Stanford: CSLI.

Stefanowitsch, Anatol. 2006. Corpus-based approaches to metaphor and metonymy. In Anatol Stefanowitsch & Stefan Th. Gries (eds.), *Corpus-based approaches to metaphor and metonymy*, 1–16. Berlin: Mouton de Gruyter.

The Statesman's Yearbook. 2019. London: Macmillan.
Wierzbicka, Anna. 1997. *Understanding cultures through their key words: English, Russian, Polish, German, and Japanese*. New York & Oxford: Oxford University Press.
Wolf, Hans-Georg. 2001. *English in Cameroon*. Berlin & New York: Mouton de Gruyter.
Wolf, Hans-Georg. 2008. A cognitive linguistic approach to the cultures of World Englishes: The emergence of a new model. In Gitte Kristiansen & René Dirven (eds.), *Cognitive sociolinguistics: Language variation, cultural models, social systems*, 353–385. Berlin: Mouton de Gruyter.
Wolf, Hans-Georg & Frank Polzenhagen. 2009. *World Englishes: A cognitive sociolinguistic approach*. Berlin & New York: Mouton de Gruyter.
Wolf, Hans-Georg & Thomas Chan. 2016. Understanding Asia by means of cognitive sociolinguistics and cultural linguistics – the example of GHOSTS in Hong Kong English. In Gerhard Leitner, Azirah Hashim & Hans-Georg Wolf (eds.), *Communicating with Asia: The future of English as a global language*, 249–266. Cambridge: Cambridge University Press.

Section III: **Cross-cultural metaphorical conceptualizations**

Ulrike Schröder, Milene Mendes de Oliveira, Thiago Nascimento

The 'Olympic Spirit' from a cross-cultural perspective: a cognitive-pragmatic analysis

Abstract: This article presents a cross-cultural investigation of reactions to the booing behavior of the Brazilian crowd against the French athlete Renaud Lavillenie during the 2016 Olympic Games in Brazil. We contrast the repercussion of the event in the public opinion in Brazil with those in Europe and in the USA and analyze metaphorical and other cultural conceptualizations as well as speech styles in comment sections of online news and in a Brazilian radio broadcast. Our findings show that the group-level conceptualizations by Brazilian fans differ from those by speakers in other countries. It is additionally revealed that online meaning construction in the radio broadcast unveils processes in which Brazilians either conform to the cultural conceptualizations identified in the comment sections or contest them from an outer observational point of view.

Keywords: cognitive linguistics; cultural linguistics; cultural conceptualizations; intercultural pragmatics; conversation analysis

1 Introduction

In the evening of August 15, 2016, the final of the men's pole vault took place as part of the Olympic Games in Rio de Janeiro. Thiago da Silva, a Brazilian athlete, won the gold medal, while the French athlete Renaud Lavillenie, previously considered favorite, won silver. The series of events leading up to this result started when Thiago da Silva, after three previous failures, passed at 5.98 meters. That pushed Lavillenie to 6.03 meters. The crowd started booing the French athlete

Acknowledgement: First of all, Ulrike Schröder would like to thank the sponsorship for the institutional partnership between the UFMG and the University of Potsdam by the *Research Group Linkage Programme*, due to the Alexander von Humboldt-Foundation, Germany. Additionally, Ulrike Schröder would also like to thank CAPES, the Coordination for the Improvement of Higher Education Personnel (Coordenação de Aperfeiçoamento de Pessoal de Nível Superior), for their fellowship *Capes-PrInt programme* which enabled her postdoctoral research year at the University of Texas in Austin, USA, and the University Duisburg-Essen, Germany.

Ulrike Schröder, Thiago Nascimento, Federal University of Minas Gerais
Milene Mendes de Oliveira, University of Potsdam

https://doi.org/10.1515/9783110688306-007

and he failed twice. Thiago da Silva cleared this height and set an Olympic record. Lavillenie gave a thumbs-down signal to the Brazilian crowd between his attempts and energetically criticized Brazilian fans' behavior after the event was over. He compared himself to the African American sprinter Jesse Owens, who participated in the Olympic Games in 1936 in Berlin, Germany.[1] He apologized for that comment at a press conference later. However, the Brazilian fans booed Lavillenie once again during the medal ceremony and by then the event had received quite a lot of attention from the press in different countries, where the practice of booing opponents had already come under criticism.

In this article, we explore the repercussion of the booing scene and its consequences for the public opinion in Brazil, in two European countries – Germany and Switzerland –, and in the USA.[2] First, we show the cultural conceptualizations found in the comment sections of online news items written in French, German, and American English. Afterwards, we proceed to show the cultural conceptualizations found in two Brazilian sources of media, namely, a radio program and readers' comments to online written articles. The analysis of cultural conceptualizations in the comment sections is complemented by an analysis of speech styles conveyed by Brazilians in a radio broadcast in which sports commentators recalled and reflected upon the incident. It is worth mentioning that our analysis is mostly based on Brazilian language and culture, which are contrasted with the abovementioned lingua-cultural units, due to the event in case having taken place in Brazil, the country that hosted the 2016 Olympic Games. Moreover, we wanted to look at how the booing behavior, typical of some Brazilian sports events, was interpreted by people from different cultural backgrounds. This contrastive perspective helps us shed light on the essence of intercultural encounters, i.e., the interaction – and questioning – of differing life-worlds.

In the upcoming section, we present the theoretical background for our study, which counts on tools and insights coming from cognitive and cultural linguistics, conversation analysis, interactional linguistics, and intercultural pragmatics. In a next step, we describe the empirical data our analysis is based on. We

1 Jesse Owens' participation in the Olympic Games was historical because he was an African American athlete playing in Germany, a country that was then being ruled by a Nazi political regime. However, contrary to Lavillenie's statement, Owens was not booed by the crowd, but emphatically celebrated.

2 We have chosen these languages and cultures to be analyzed here for the following reasons: We chose Brazilian Portuguese due to the place where the intercultural scandal happened; French for the athlete's nationality; and German and American English because of the scandal's resonance in the media of these countries. Additionally, these languages belong to the authors' language repertoires.

subsequently proceed to present the findings of the analysis of cultural conceptualizations in comments around the abovementioned event made by readers of online news reports in different countries and compare the findings with the Brazilian comments analyzed. In a second step, we choose interactional linguistics and intercultural pragmatics as the tools for the analysis of a radio broadcast about the event. This framework makes evident the use of different speech styles by Brazilian speakers and shows how different cultural conceptualizations are co-constructed in a concrete interactional encounter. Finally, we conclude the paper with a summary of our findings.

2 Theoretical framework

Traditionally, cognitive and cultural linguistics, on the one side, and conversation analysis as well as interactional linguistics, on the other side, are considered to represent two very different strands of linguistic research. Some would even consider those strands to be non-compatible. The former, cognitive and cultural linguistics, look primarily at the semantics of meaning making and therefore focus on more stable features of meaning. The latter, conversation analysis and interactional linguistics, look at online communication *in situ* with the aim to unveil the workings of verbal interactions, concentrating on the co-construction and negotiation of meaning.

However, recently, some authors working at the interface of cognition and interaction have started to recognize that the areas are actually not only compatible but complementary (Deppermann 2012; Kecskes 2015; Schröder 2015, 2017). The basic assumption by these authors is that the co-construction of meaning *in situ* has to be seen as an interplay of the basic values and assumptions coming from the interlocutors' speech communities *and* the online cognitive processes arising at the communicative situation itself.

Cultural linguistics (Palmer 1996; Sharifian 2011, 2017) is a field of studies that "explores the relationship between language, culture, and conceptualization" (Palmer and Sharifian 2007: 1). As stated by Palmer (1996), the field arose as a necessity for cognitive linguistics to include the study of culture in its framework. The main analytical tool of cultural linguistics revolves around the identification of 'cultural conceptualizations', which refer to products of cognitive processes that can be identified at a cultural level, such as conceptual metaphors and metonymies (Kövecses 2002, 2005), conceptual blends (Fauconnier and Turner 2002), as well as schemas, prototypes, and categories (Sharifian 2011, 2017). Cultural conceptualizations are shared in a cultural group through interaction and can be regarded as the group's 'repository of meaning', although they should be conceived as (a) heterogeneously distributed and (b) dynamic, since they are constantly negotiated and renegotiated (Sharifian 2011). As shown below, several cultural conceptualizations could be evidenced in the comments analyzed in this study.

Conceptual metaphor theory (Lakoff and Johnson [1980] 2003) has laid the foundations for the cognitive linguistic research on our bodily-anchored metaphorical talk about the world by revealing the cross-domain mapping of a set of correspondences, which is established between an already-known source domain and a still unformed target domain in our underlying conceptual system. For example, the sentence "that is a remarkably transparent argument" contains the metaphorical expression 'transparent', which unveils the conceptual metaphor UNDERSTANDING IS SEEING (Lakoff and Johnson 1980: 104). Later, Kövecses (2005) focuses on those metaphors understood at the same time as a linguistic, conceptual, neurological, embodied, social, and cultural phenomenon (Kövecses 2005: 293). In striving for an integration of universalistic and relativistic components, he takes up the distinction between 'primary metaphors' and 'complex metaphors' as introduced by Grady (1997) and transfers it to the question of universality and cultural relativity. In this connection, primary metaphors might be imagined as products of correlations of different dimensions of basic embodied experience, while congruent or complex metaphors give a vivid structure to these scaffolds like concrete scenes and images and vary from one culture to another. An example is the complex metaphor ANGER IS A HOT FLUID IN A CONTAINER, based on the primary metaphors INTENSITY IS SPEED, INTENSITY IS QUANTITY, and INTENSITY IS HEAT, and producing metaphorical expressions such as 'losing one's *cool*', or featuring anger *overcoming* – or *welling up* in – someone, or a person *flaring up* (Kövecses 2005: 27).

While metaphor establishes symmetrical correspondences between two domains, metonymy sets correspondences in an asymmetrical way "by conceptually *foregrounding* the source and by *backgrounding* the target" (Barelona 2002: 226). For example, as Barcelona (2002: 224/226) explains, in the utterance '*Marcel Proust* is tough to read', the subject noun phrase highlights the target subdomain PROUST'S LITERARY WORK, even though it is not primary if we consider that Proust was a person. The target subdomain is backgrounded, giving prominence to the whole domain matrix of PROUST, what results in a conceptualization that suggests seeing the literary work as an extension of Proust's personality. Here, cultural preferences, e.g., regarding frame constitution, also play a crucial role.

Categories show a relation between elements that can be described as *x is a kind of y*; *y* being the category and *x* being a member of it. For instance, the category BIRD has as its member the concept OSTRICH; thus, OSTRICH is a kind of BIRD. In schemas, by contrast, the relationships between elements can be thematic, spatial, or temporal. To illustrate, BILL and RESTAURANT are related schematically, since RESTAURANT may evoke the event schema of 'paying a bill' in a restaurant. In this example, the relationship between BILL and RESTAURANT is not only spatial but also clearly experiential (Sharifian 2011: 25). That is to say, cultural schemas are defined as "a sub-class of cognitive schemas that are abstracted from people's cultural, and therefore to some extent shared, experiences, as opposed to abstracted from an individual's idiosyncratic experiences" (Sharifian 2017). Very importantly, as Sharifian (2017) acknowledges, these afore-mentioned concepts, namely, conceptual metaphor and metonymy, categories and cultural schemas provide a basis for pragmatic meanings.

Conversation analysis (Sacks 1995) and interactional linguistics (Selting 1994; Couper-Kuhlen and Selting 2018) are areas of studies that focus primarily on the workings of language use in interaction. While conversation analysis (Sacks, Schegloff, and Jefferson 1974) introduced the basic terminology of the 'machinery' of talk-in-interaction (Sacks 1995: 169) such as the turn-taking system or repair, interactional linguistics was introduced in the nineties and builds on the groundwork of CA by incorporating the tenets of functional and anthropological linguistics and bringing into focus the question of prosody (Couper-Kuhlen and Selting 2001). An example of how cognitive and cultural linguistics, on the one hand, and conversation analysis and interactional linguistics, on the other hand, can be used as complementary tools is the study of membership categorization devices (MCDs), which was initiated as a topic of conversation analysis. Schegloff (2007a: 467) describes MCDs as collections of categories along with their rules of application. For instance, 'mommy' and 'baby' are understood to belong to the MCD 'family'. Other analytical tools associated with membership categorization are: a) 'category-bound activities,' which refer to actions usually linked with certain categories, as the gendered understanding that 'men (category) are reluctant to go to doctors (activity)'; and b) category-tied predicates, as in 'a mother (category) cares enormously for her baby (predicate)' (Stokoe 2012: 281). Such collections of categories, category-related actions, and predicates are not simply co-constructed *in situ* but have to be seen as linked to culturally entrenched conceptualizations, since they convey basic values and assumptions that reflect cultural aspects of a speaker's speech community. In this paper, we make the case that MCDs correspond to 'categories' in a cultural-linguistic perspective. Moreover, category-bound activities and category-tied predicates can be considered to be in schematic relations with members of certain categories. We consider the phenomena of categorization and schematization to be instantiated concurrently in language-in-use *and* as a product of cultural conceptualizations. This was shown to be the case in the analysis of comment sections below.

Finally, based on the assumptions of intercultural pragmatics (Kecskes 2014, 2015), reference will be made to Spencer-Oatey's (2008) rapport management framework since this approach offers a useful background for the analysis of cultural conceptualizations in situated language use. Spencer-Oatey introduces a holistic view on the way in which people manage harmony and disharmony in interaction and describes four types of 'rapport orientation' by which the polar separation between politeness and impoliteness is no longer maintained (Spencer-Oatey 2008: 31–33): (1) rapport enhancement orientation refers to the desire to strengthen or enhance harmonious relations between the interlocutors; (2) rapport maintenance orientation refers to the desire to maintain or protect harmonious relations between the interlocutors; (3) rapport neglect orientation refers to the lack of concern or interest in the quality of relations between the interlocutors; (4) rapport challenge orientation refers to the desire to challenge or impair harmonious relations between the interlocutors.

Schröder (2003, 2010, 2014a, 2014b) has shown in her work on different narrative perspectives applied by Germans and Brazilians in interviews about life concepts, as well as face strategies in intercultural encounters, how rapport can be intertwined with divergent speech styles: although complex, a tendency to rapport enhancement and maintenance orientation was revealed as being more present in the Brazilian participants' behavior as opposed to the German participants' communicative style that showed stronger rapport neglect or even rapport challenge orientation (Schröder 2014a, 2014b). When asked about influences in their past that contributed to the choice of their professional path or university course, German interviewees preferred to give a compressed answer from a more (self-)reflected point of view, whereas the Brazilian interviewees showed a tendency to switch back to the past and retell the story by 'zooming in' (Günthner 1999) to the original scenario. This frequently included more rhetoric means, a more poetic and appellative speech style, as well as more reenactments while the German interviewees were less involved and rather detached (cf. also Chafe 1982; Schröder 2003, 2010).

3 Empirical data

In the first part of the analysis, we were interested in looking at interpretations of the event by different audiences and investigating how they compare with interpretations in Brazil itself. Thus, we chose six online news reports. The criteria for our choices were (a) our degree of proficiency in the languages featured in the news and comments (French, English, German, and Portuguese), and (b) the availability of the news article online as well as open access to comments from readers. In the following paragraphs we describe the sources of media and also the analyzed reports.

News articles in the English language were extracted from *The Washington Post* and *The Huffington Post*. The former is a well-established broadsheet, and the latter has achieved considerable online reach in the past few years. Regarding the *Washington Post*'s news report, emphasis was given on Lavillenie's comparison and its negative consequences. It figures a tone of criticism towards the athlete for his approximation of two incomparable Olympic contexts (i.e. the 1936 Games and the 2016 Games). The *Huffington Post*'s news report focuses on the sharp reaction of the Brazilian crowd towards Lavillenie, especially during the medal ceremony.

The reports in the French language were extracted from *Le Monde* and *Francetv Sport* from France. The former due to its high circulation and reputation in France and the latter because it provides written versions of news and also because of its broad reporting on the Olympic Games 2016. *Le Monde*'s news report points to the fact that Lavillenie's bad comparison with Jesse Owens was due to his aggravation at that moment. Indeed, to report the facts, the news item makes use of the athlete's viewpoint, that is, it explores the pole vaulter's emotions for dealing with the booing. The *Francetv Sport*'s news article intends to use Brazil's perspective to report on the facts, portraying Lavillenie as arrogant but, at the same time, imputing to the Brazilian crowd its responsibilities for what Lavillenie has said.

In the German language, *Spiegel Online* from Germany and *NZZ* from Switzerland were chosen. The rather reflexive style report of the *NZZ* in comparison to *Spiegel Online* seemed to complement well the latter's descriptive style. The *Spiegel*'s article revolves around reporting on the event as well as on Lavillenie's apology for the comparison with Jesse Owens' participation in the Olympic Games. The *NZZ* is quite different in that it provides a meta-analysis of the crowd's reaction and attempts to explain why the Brazilian fans behaved the way they did.

Brazilian online news publishers chosen were *Folha*, a stable and traditional newspaper, and *Uol*, which mainly focuses on short articles. *Folha*'s news report criticizes the Brazilian crowd's behavior by describing later events in relation to the Brazilian crowd booing the French athlete: Lavillenie being comforted by Thiago Braz and the president of the International Olympics Committee after the medal ceremony as well as the impact of the booing event on Lavillenie's social network. *Uol*'s news report deals with Lavillenie's case by describing the French athlete's deeds after the booing: his apologies for his comparison and his expectations for a possible revenge should France host the Olympic Games in 2024.

In our analysis section, we have identified the comments with codes according to the online newspaper they were extracted from and their related country: FM

(France/*Le Monde*), FF (France/*Francetv Sport*), GS (Germany/*Spiegel*), SN (Switzerland/*NZZ*), USW (USA/ The Washington Post), USH (USA/The Huffington Post), BF (Brazil/*Folha*), and BU (Brazil/*Uol*).

After having organized the data, we proceeded to the identification and analysis of cultural conceptualizations. This conceptual analysis was connected with the CA concept of MCDs and its related analytical tools such as 'category-bound activities' and 'category-tied predicates'.

In a second step, an analysis of communicative styles and cultural conceptualizations conveyed by participants of the daily broadcasted Brazilian radio program *Jovem Pan* was carried out. The video features Bruno Prado, a commentator and journalist, Joseval Peixoto, a journalist and counselor, Marco Antônio Villa, a historian, and Thiago Uberreich, a reporter. They recall and reflect upon the incident involving Renauld Lavillenie. The eight-minute discussion was transcribed with the support of the EXMARaLDA software (Schmidt and Wörner 2009) following the conventions of GAT 2 (Selting et al. 2009). The aim of the analysis of this sequence from the Brazilian radio program *Jovem Pan* is to show how diverging views on the incident during the Olympics are aligned to some of the cultural conceptualizations displayed by readers in the comment sections and how these are displayed *in situ*.

4 Analysis

4.1 Cultural conceptualizations and categorizations in online articles' comments

In this section, we show our analysis of cultural conceptualizations in comments in reaction to online news articles written in English, French, and German. The analysis is complemented with insights from CA around the topic of categorization. After that, comments written by Brazilian readers are presented.

4.1.1 Readers' reactions in the international media

A look at the comments generated by the six news reports in the international media – in English, French, and German – allows us to unveil not only conceptual metaphors (Lakoff and Johnson [1980] 2003; Sharifian 2011) but also categories and schemas (Sharifian 2011: 24–29; Sharifian 2017). The results brought to light that categories are frequently used and mainly refer to national groups (i.e., 'the Brazilians', 'the French'), sport types (i.e., 'soccer', 'tennis', 'gymnastics'), and the group of fans associated with them. Moreover, some of the categories related to expected crowd behavior were perceived to be influenced by a specific SPORTSMANSHIP which could be described as a cultural schema. In the following, we present some excerpts in which readers relied on the process of categorization, and point to their different uses.

Categories often worked as a way to distinguish proper from improper behavior. As the following excerpts show, category-bound activities (Sacks 1972) are related to the category SPORTS FANS and could be found in nearly all comments, independent of their origin:

(1) GS7: *Unterstützung des eigenen Mannes ja, aber ungerechtfertigtes Ausbuhen des Gegners nein.*

(Supporting one's own team yes, but unjustifiable booing of the opponent no.)

(2) GS12: *Die eigenen Sportler anfeuern ist OK, Gegner ausbuhen und stören ein NOGO.*

(Cheering for your own athletes is OK, booing and disturbing opponents is a NO-GO.)

(3) USH6: *Supporting your team does not necessitate denigrating their competition.*

(4) FF1: *on a l'esprit sportif, on ne hue pas un athlète qui se concentre, même si ça fait parti de sa préparation mentale de passer outre.*

(We demonstrate sportsmanship, we don't boo an athlete who's concentrating, even if it is part of his preparation to overcome his opponent.)

(5) SN2: *Bedauernswert, das Fehlen an Fairness.*

(Pathetic, the lack of fairness.)

(6) USH7: *That's bad sportsmanship and the very worst of behavior in any condition.*

According to the SPORTSMANSHIP cultural schema, actions like booing and disturbing an adversary are presented as standing in opposition to the SPORTS FANS category. Interestingly, as we can see in the excerpts below, there is also a broader discussion around the Brazilian crowd's behavior related to the schema, which concurrently points to the metonymy SOCCER MATCHES STAND FOR THE OLYMPIC GAMES in the sense that the Brazilian crowd is frequently accused of treating the

Olympic Games the same as an ordinary soccer match. That includes the idea of soccer allowing for boos against the adversary:

(7) GS8: *Ist ja nicht das erste Mal, dass die Zuschauer bei diesen olympischen Spielen unangenehm auffallen und sich Benehmen (sic) wie beim Fussball.*

(It's not the first time that the spectators have attracted inappropriate attention at these Olympic Games and behave like in soccer.)

(8) USW6: *he [Lavillenie] got a boorish home crowd that thought they were at a World Cup match. (. . .) I'm sure he was shocked by the hostility (. . .).*

(9) USH23: *this sounds more like the behavior at a soccer match than an Olympics event.*

Also, recurring within the comments is the conceptualization of 'nationalism' schematically linked to the booing behavior of the Brazilian crowd, especially in comments written in German, but also in one written in French and one in English:

(10) GS12: *Das hat mit gesunder Rivalität nichts mehr zu tun, das ist blanker Nationalismus.*

(That has nothing to do with healthy rivalry, that is pure nationalism.)

(11) GS17: *Die eigenen Sportler anfeuern ist legitim aber einen Gast grundlos auspfeifen ist schäbig (hier eher nationalistisch).*

(To cheer for the own athlete is legitimate, but to boo a guest with no reason is sordid (here rather nationalist).)

(12) FM11: *On peut convenir que le public brésilien, fan de football, soit particulièrement Chauvin.*

(We may agree that the Brazilian crowd, soccer fans, are particularly *chauvinistic.)*

(13) USH13: *Patriots do not treat people from other countries like the Brazilians did. You can be proud of your country without putting anyone else down. They were rude.*

Nationalism is, according to this view, not related to the SPORTSMANSHIP schema. The conceptualization of nationalism is relevant because it contrasts radically with the MONGREL COMPLEX cultural schema identified in Brazilian comments that will be explained in the section below.

To sum up, in the international media, the category SPORTS FANS is often connected with the category-bound activity 'to support one's own team'. The way to support a team is influenced by a SPORTSMANSHIP cultural schema. In the category SOCCER FANS, on the contrary, a category-bound activity is 'to boo the adversary.' The Brazilian crowd – who were expected to belong to the SPORTS FANS category but ended up belonging to the SOCCER FANS category – is frequently described as nationalist by the international commentators (a category-tied predicate).

4.1.2 Readers' reactions in Brazil

In the following, we are going to point to the cultural conceptualizations that seem to mostly contrast from the other conceptualizations identified in the international media and presented above. We will briefly show how some Brazilians conceptualized the booing action of the crowd differently from commentators in the international media. After that, we will go on to argue for the existence of an IN- X OUT-GROUP cultural schema underlying the Brazilian comments. Below, we begin with excerpts in which commentators position themselves against the French athlete:

(14) BU12: *Arrogante! Não foi por causa das vaias que ele perdeu.*

(Arrogant! It was not because of the boos that he lost.)

(15) BU10: *As vaias não impedem de saltar.*

(The boos do not prevent him from jumping.)

(16) BF1: *Sempre tiveram vaias, tal como aplausos para Phelps e Bolt, por exemplo.*

(There have always been boos as well as applause for Phelps and Bolt, for example.)

Whereas the comments in French, English, and German outlined the booing to have no place in the category SPORTS FANS (related to the SPORTSMANSHIP cultural schema), it seems that, for some Brazilians, booing an opponent does seem to be a category-bound action linked with the conceptualization of SPORTS FANS.

The process of categorization also serves the purpose of separating in- and out-groups, which is characteristic of collectivist cultures (Triandis 1995; Pearson and Stephan 1998).[3] We consider these categories to be influenced by a more general IN- X OUT-GROUP cultural schema. In- and out-groups take different configurations in the data, though. In some cases, they represent national categories (e.g., the French X the Brazilians); in other cases, they refer to groupings of Brazilians (e.g., Brazilians on the stadium X other Brazilians). Both scenarios are shown below. The following excerpt shows how a reader categorizes Brazilians (we) and the Olympic Committee (they):

(17) BU10: . . .*infelizmente, é a primeira vez em mais de 100 anos que uma Olimpíada é disputada na América do Sul. Como eles querem que o povo se habitue a torcer educadamente se eles nunca nos deixaram participar?*

(Unfortunately, it is the first time in more than 100 years that an Olympics is played in South America. How do they want the people to get used to cheering politely if they never let us participate?)

The following excerpt points to different categories of Brazilians – viewers of the Games and athletes themselves:

(18) BF13: *Para aqueles que estão falando em falta de educação, não tiro toda a razão, mas é preciso que tenham em mente que aqueles que estão nos estádios assistindo aos jogos não são a massa pobre desse país, mas a parcela branca e "educada". Os pobres são aqueles que estão dentro das arenas dando um exemplo de respeito e humildade.*

(For those who are talking about lack of politeness, I do not completely disagree with them, but you have to keep in mind that those in the stadiums watching the games are not the poor mass of this country, but the white and "polite" part. The poor are those who are inside the arenas giving an example of respect and humbleness.)

The two categories of Brazilians, as described in the comment, are the wealthy audience of the Olympic Games and the athletes, many of latter coming from a

3 We are well aware of the weaknesses associated with etic frameworks that attempt to classify whole cultures as collectivist or individualist. However, we still consider this distinction to be useful in providing a first interpretation of certain communicative and conceptual patterns in studies that contrast two or more cultures (in this regard, see Bolten's dune model for describing cultures (Bolten 2014)).

poor social background. The reader explores the paradox of accusing a group of a lack of politeness who is usually associated with the display of politeness (via a category-tied predicate, according to which wealthy people are well-acquainted with 'refined behaviors'). Note, however, that disagreement is very mildly marked with "não tirar toda a razão" (lit. 'not to take out the whole reason'; rough gloss: 'not to completely disagree with someone'). This is a metaphorical expression that underlies the conceptual metaphor REASON IS A SUBSTANCE IN A CONTAINER. That is, REASON – a state in which one's reasoning is conceived of as adequate and correct – is metaphorically described as a SUBSTANCE IN A CONTAINER. To 'take out one's reason' is to deprive one of a state of self-assurance that results from the feeling of having made a correct judgment. This deliberate destitution could qualify as a major personal attack (or face-attack) on the interlocutor in the Brazilian culture. As can be noticed, the commentator attenuates (Holmes 1984) the disagreement (in 'not to take out *the whole* reason') in favor of a rapport-maintenance style (Spencer-Oatey 2008). This point will be further discussed in the analysis of speech styles below.

Sometimes, instead of two contrasting categories, just one is created, the one of the average Brazilian. In some cases, the commentators seem to regard themselves as an item out of the category. In that case, 3rd person verbs are used. However, there are also comments in which 3rd person and 1st person verbs are mixed and so does the position of the self (the commentator) in relation to the category (in or out of the category).

This mixing up of images of the self seems to be often intertwined with a conceptualization that is commonly referred to as the 'mongrel complex' (*complexo de viralata*),[4] which we will now call the MONGREL COMPLEX cultural schema. This schema refers to a feeling of inferiority displayed by many Brazilians when they compare themselves and their country to other nations, as we can see in the following comments:

(19) BF16: *O brasileiro nao tem nocao. Alias, o brasileiro em geral nao é referência para nada de bom.*

(Brazilians have no clue. By the way, Brazilians are no reference for anything good.)

4 Expression coined by the Brazilian playwright Nelson Rodrigues in the 1950s.

(20) BF9: *Os fatos mostram. Brasil: gigante pela própria natureza, porém, um anão diplomático,*[5] *anão olímpico e anão na educação.*

(The facts show. Brazil: giant by nature, however, a diplomatic dwarf, Olympic dwarf, and dwarf in politeness.)

In the second comment, size metaphors are used to mark contrast. First, an excerpt of the Brazilian anthem is used in which Brazil is depicted as a 'giant by nature'. Then, another size metaphor is used to refer to the MONGREL COMPLEX schema. The metaphor in case is TO SHOW A REPREHENSIBLE BEHAVIOR IS TO BE SMALL.

In the following comment, the category is not BRAZILIAN, but BRAZILIAN CROWD. In this case, the reader does not include him/herself in that category of Brazilian fans who behaved improperly.

(21) BF7: *Realmente, vexame, medalha de lata pra torcida, desde abertura, democracia começa com educação, vergonhoso, vaia mundial pra torcida brasileira.*

(Really, a shame, tin medal for the crowd, since the opening ceremony, democracy begins with education, shameful, worldwide boo to the Brazilian fans.)

In the excerpts above, readers seem to try to distance themselves from the category. Nevertheless, sometimes the boundaries are not so clear or are mixed, as shown in the next excerpts in which the readers criticize from an out-group perspective, but express a feeling (feeling ashamed) that is usually associated with in-group members:

(22) BF10: *No país do futebol o que esperar? Torcida vê salto com vara como se fosse um Fla-Flu. Senti vergonha pelo Brasil.*

(In the soccer country, what to expect? The crowd sees pole vaulting as if it were a Fla-Flu.[6] I felt ashamed for Brazil.)

---

5 This seems to be a reference to a statement given by an Israeli spokesperson in relation to a diplomatic disagreement between Brazil and Israel in 2014.

6 Fla stands for Flamengo and Flu stands for Fluminense; when these two football teams play against each other, rivalry is rather high.

(23) BF4: *"Uma vergonha o que os brasileiros fizeram. Demonstraram o nível de educação e cultura que temos. Falta muito ainda para sermos um País civilizado.*

(A shame what the Brazilians did. They have demonstrated the level of education and culture that we have. There is still a long way to go before we become a civilized country.)

In the latter excerpt, the reader mixes 3rd person verbs (*fizeram*; *demonstraram* – did; demonstrated) and 1st person plural (*temos; sermos* – we have; for us to be). The use of 1st person plural is widespread in the comments, which reinforces the existence of a strong orientation towards in-group:

(24) BU17*: Queremos ganhar sempre da maneira mais suja possível.*

(We always want to win in the filthiest way possible.)

(25) BF3: *Concordo que nos falta educação, mas acho que está havendo um certo exagero por parte do atleta.*

(I agree that we lack politeness, but I think there has been a certain exaggeration on the athlete's part.)

But there are also comments pointing to an opposite stance. One commentator refers explicitly to the MONGREL COMPLEX cultural schema when criticizing the negative comments made by other readers:

(26) BF14: *Complexo de vira-lata também cansa.*

(The mongrel complex makes me tired.)

The examples below show how Brazilians positively represent (at least for themselves) the national category BRAZILIANS from an 'in-group' perspective.[7] In the following example, 3rd person verb and 1st person pronoun are mixed again:

7 For a short description of how a national Brazilian identity was fostered in the beginning of the 20th century as well as how a nationalist narrative featured in the opening ceremony of the 2016 Olympic Games, see Malanski 2019.

(27) BF12: *. . . o brasileiro tem que mostrar nossa alegria, samba, mulatas, etc.*

(The Brazilian has to show our joy, samba, mulatas, etc.)

(28) BU20: *Sim: aqui é Brasil e somos assim mesmo: vibrantes, intensos e calorosos por demais.*

(Yes: here is Brazil and we are exactly like that: very vibrant, intense, and warm.)

(29) BF5: *Graças a Deus que impera aqui e no mundo é a lei do mais forte, aos fracos como o francês sobra o choro e a ressaca. . .*

(Thank God what is valid here and in the world is the law of the fittest, what is left to the weak like the Frenchman is crying and a hangover. . .)

In the latter excerpt, the out-group ('weak people,' with Lavillenie being part of this category) is also called upon. In general lines, this positive picture of the category BRAZILIANS created by Brazilians themselves – connected with a very strong demarcation of the out-group (in the latter example, the Frenchman Lavillenie and other 'weak people') – might be what commentators in international media have referred to as 'nationalism,' as presented above. In the following, we present some comments where direct speech is used toward out-group members, the non-Brazilian athlete(s):

(30) BU17: *Meu querido francês, o que rege aqui no Brasil é a lei de Gerson!*

(My dear Frenchman, what is valid here in Brazil is Gerson's law!)[8]

(31) BU18: *Chupa que é de uva!*

(Suck it because it has a grape flavor!)[9]

---

8 'Gerson's law is an expression used in Brazil that refers to the practice of trying to obtain advantages without caring about moral or ethical matters. Its origin dates back to 1976 when the footballer Gerson participated in a marketing campaign for cigarettes. In a TV commercial, the footballer says he likes to obtain advantages in everything he does, including buying cigarettes that are cheaper than others.

9 The phrase was used in a Brazilian song that became famous and is generally used for mocking adversaries.

(32) BU20: *E se vocês fossem tão educados e refinados assim sua intenção jamais seria de pagar com a mesma moeda da qual critica. Aceita que dói menos. Boa viagem de retorno a seu país.*

(And if you were so polite and sophisticated, your intention would never be to pay back on the same coin you criticize. Accept it, because it hurts less.[10] Have a nice return trip to your country.)

(33) BF11: *Byte [bye] gringo vocês e sua impafia (sic) colonizadora cansam.*

(Bye gringo, you and your colonizing arrogance are tiring.)

Another type of rather negative reference made towards the French pole vaulter refers to his crying, which is disapproved by some commentators. The examples below also demarcate very clearly the out-group area, strongly permeated by a negative emotional stance, which is reflected by the use of upper case and exclamation points standing for prosodic cues, as well as words representing the concept of 'crying', such as *chororo* and *mimimi*:

(34) BU5: *Agora o chororo é livre!!*

(Now crying is for free!!)

(35) BU7: *Portanto, caro francês, volta sim pra tua casa e chora por lá mesmo que é mais quentinho . . .. O CHORO É LIVRE !!!!! . . . VAI BRASIL !!!!!!!!!!!!*

(So, dear Frenchman, go back to your house and cry there because it is cozier. . .. CRYING IS FOR FREE!!!!! . . . GO BRAZIL!!!!!!!!!!!!)

(36) BU14: *mimimi. . ..choro de mal perdedor.*

(mimimi [imitation of a crying sound]. . . crying from a bad loser.)

To sum up, in the Brazilian comments a category SPORTS FANS arises in which two types of category-bound activities are acceptable: cheering and also booing. Cheering is, in its turn, a category-bound activity related to another category – the

---

10 Expression coined by a soap opera character in Brazilian TV in 2013. It refers to a suggestion given to a person who is in a difficult situation. It means 'if you accept that the difficult situation exists, you suffer less.' It is connected with an arrogant attitude from the person who utters the expression, as was the case whenever a certain character uttered it in the soap opera episodes.

IN-GROUP. Booing is targeted toward the OUT-GROUP. In the Brazilian comments, as was shown, this SPORTS FANS category is the default one. However, rejections of this schema are shown that relate to the MONGREL COMPLEX cultural schema. Moreover, it was noted that a negative action (a category-bound activity) from the perspective of the in-group members is linked with the OUT-GROUP, namely, crying.

Until now, we have focused on more stable processes of meaning construction, which count mostly on long-standing cultural conceptualizations. The following section is going to call attention to how the co-construction of meaning in interaction brings to the fore and discusses different cultural conceptualizations. The use of specific speech styles, which sets the tone for the discussions and reveals either alignment or non-alignment with the cultural conceptualizations identified in the previous section, is described in detail.

4.2 The use of different speech styles and cultural conceptualizations in a radio discussion

On August 16, one day after the incident, the participants of the daily broadcasted radio program *Jovem Pan* discussed the reactions to Lavillenie's statement.[11] In the following, we will focus on three participants: the commentator and journalist Bruno Prado, the journalist and counselor Joseval Peixoto, and the historian Marco Antônio Villa. What caught our attention in analytical terms were the different underlying speech styles accompanied by the positions represented by the three interactants. The speech styles are salient because they can be concurrently related to opposing cultural schemas: while Bruno Prado and Joseval Peixoto do not only defend the Brazilian crowd but also employ a speech style that can be related to the abovementioned IN-GROUP schema regarding the positive self-image, Marco Antônio Villa argues explicitly against the Brazilian crowd's behavior and also shows an opposing way of speaking.

Let's start with Bruno Prado, who is the first to introduce his opinion with regard to Lavillenie's reference to the Olympic Games in 1936:

Sequence 1: August 16th, 2016, Jovem Pan ((00:21-00:27))

01 BP: ´é:_´acho que ↑`um:_exagEro até do atlEta fran´CÊS,
I think it's an exaggeration even by the French athlete

02 ele `pOde <<l> ter ficado incomodAdo>´com as VAias;=né,
he could be upset about the booing right

11 The video can be accessed on YouTube: https://youtu.be/R1qrrluTJvA

03 <<h, creaky> MAS> faz parte °h h° do:: do jOgo;=né,
but that's part of the game isn't it

What especially attracts attention in this sequence are the high oscillations with respect to the intonation contours, pitch jumps, and, additionally, the accent density which generally all together point to an 'emphatic speech style' (Selting 1994). To a certain extent, these prosodic markers indicate a strong negative emotional stance similar to the comments we have seen in the previous section which referred to the concept of 'crying' attributed to the French behavior.

However, in the given context, its function might be additionally conceived as an attempt to attenuate the tension regarding the extreme attitude of the Frenchman. Hence, the prosodic cues serve to mitigate or downplay the situation (Caffi 2007; Holmes 1984). The high use of prosodic elements instead of lexical markers is typical for a Brazilian speech style even in situations of unease, as Schröder and Carneiro Mendes (2019) endorse. It concurrently reflects the wish to mitigate the whole situation, bringing out what Spencer-Oatey (2008) calls 'rapport maintenance orientation': the desire to maintain or protect harmonious relations between interlocutors.

When Joseval Peixoto takes the turn for the first time, he begins to defend the Brazilian crowd explicitly by stating a rhetorical question that displays a strong assertive force (Quirk et al. 1985):

Sequence 2: August 16th, 2016, Jovem Pan ((02:08-02:11))

01 AV: =<<all> o brasil vai ser legal quando ganha um
Brazil will be fine when it wins a
[prêmio nobel de mateMÁtica.>=né,]
nobel prize in mathematics right
02 JP: [(Oh professor) (-) quando tem gol]
oh professor when there's a goal
do sAntos o senhor fica em <<rall> si^!LÊN![cio;>]
by Santos do you stay quiet
03 AV: [não NÃO;]
no no

Similar to the first sequence, we can observe melodic intonational contours with accentuated rising falling pitch on the key word si^!LÊN!cio; (line 02); additionally, this climax is spoken with decreased tempo. However, in contrast to Bruno's speech style, the effect reached by Joseval's way of speaking can be more accurately described as rhetorical; it is by intention and not by coincidence that Joseval puts his words as carefully as he does. When he takes the next turn, he retells the story by recreating the scenario, setting up the whole atmosphere and the emotions which came into play:

Sequence 3: August 16th, 2016, Jovem Pan ((05:41-06:06))

01 JP: °hh (.) ele esteve nos estados unidos foi assim um GRANde do basquetebol_lá.
he was in the United States and there was a big basketball game

02 (---) chegou ´LÁ os cara também comendo pi´pÓca.=
he arrived there the guys were also having popcorn

03 =e_ele n nas das primEiras ´FILas;
and he was in one of the front rows

04 (---) começou jOgo o cara foi lá CESta;
the game started the guy scored

05 (--) ninGUÉM se manifestou.
nobody cheered

06 (-) foi pra outro lado CESta ali;
score on the other side

07 °h <<all, p> ele falou assim> se´rÁ que essa é uma preliminar eu entrei no estadio eRRA::do;=
he said like maybe it's an exhibition match and I'm in the wrong stadium

08 =<<acc> que que é ISso aí.>
what's this

09 <<cresc> o estádio veio abAixo quando o outro e!RRA!va.>
the stadium yelled when the other failed

10 ((smiles))

11 ((1.1))

12 fizeram manifesta´çÃo (--) ´!CON!tra o `!E!rro.
they cheered against the faults of the others

He retells the story to substantiate the credibility of his argument that this behavior is normal not only in Brazil but also in the USA. Such a 'retelling'-perspective – also described as 're-enactment' (Günthner 1999) – is typical for the Brazilian speech style as shown in the theoretical section (Schröder 2003, 2010). In our case, the story obtains an authentic flair through the scenic descriptions with emotional load (lines 02–06) and the use of direct speech (line 07). Moreover, the persuasive effects of the short, self-complacent, well set smile in line 10 along with the paraverbal elements, i.e., the well projected pauses in lines 02, 04, 05, 06, 11, and 12, display strong rhetoric force, next to the prosodic cues such as the lengthening of eRRA::do in line 07, and finally the exaggerated extra strong accents on e!RRA!va in line 09 and on !CON!tra and `!E!rro in line 12.

In contrast, Marco Antônio Villa, who for the first time takes his turn after Bruno's first statement, defends an opposite view maintaining that one cannot compare football to other individual Olympic disciplines:

Sequence 4: August 16th, 2016, Jovem Pan ((01:28-02:00))

01 AV: °h o sujeito precisa se concentrar por SA:lto tAl;
the guy needs to concentrate on jumping and all that
02 °h eu por exemplo se_eu me colocasse no papel DEle;
me for example if I was in his place
03 (.) °h eu teRIA dificuldade de-=
I would have difficulty to
04 =atÉ no silêncio eu <<all> não ia> me concentrar tudo mUndo inteiro me assisTI:Ndo tal.=
even with silence I couldn't concentrate with everyone watching me like that
05 BP: =o usain bo:lt pediu si[LÊNcio também,]
Usain Bolt also asked for silence
06 AV: [(.) é siLÊNcio] tAl,
it's silence and all that
07 °h agora a torcida no no na giNÁstica;
now the fans at at at the gymnastics
08 °h aplaudia !E!rro.
cheered for faults
09 (-) ah eu nunca vi esse neGÓ no ar;
ah I've never seen something like that on TV
10 <<acc, imitating the crowd> aplaudia erro ficava feliz <<all, slipping gesture> quando o cara escorregava;>=
applauded faults being happy when the guy slipped
11 =<<imitating the crowd, clapping hands, f> êh_êh_êh_Êh,>
hey hey hey hey
12 `PÔ (.) que_que_é ´Isso.=
pooh what what's that
13 =é <<f> bar↑!BÁ!rie.>
that's barbarism
14 BP: cê tem que saber [se comportar de acordo com o amBIENte.]
you have to know how to behave yourself according to your environment
15 AV: [(-) ´né (.) `é: (-) ˇÉ:, (-)]
right that's it that's it
16 nÃo é o coliSEU:.
it's not the coliseum
17 está achando que é o coliseu ro´MA::no ´tAl;
you think it's the Roman coliseum and all that

18 `en^tão ↑É sério ter um comportamento civilizAdo.`
so it's important to have a civilized behavior

19 `°h entÃo há (.) há há um nacionalismo BObo no brasIl;`
so there is is is a stupid kind of nationalism in Brazil

While Joseval Peixoto's stance shows high engagement and involvement,[12] Villa's stance can be more accurately described as oscillating between a 'zooming in' and 'reflecting' perspective, thereby displaying a much more detached style. This style can be seen when he retells what happened while simultaneously commenting on it at the prosodic level by putting an emphasis on `!E!rro` (line 08) through an extra strong accent as a verum focus (Höhle 1992), thereby reinforcing the impudence and incredibility of this act, as well as by imitating the crowd in an affective manner (line 11). Those prosodic hints can be conceived as implicit metacommunication (Bublitz and Hübler 2007; Unger 1990) which frame what is said as unbelievable, in the first case, and as sarcastic, in the second. On the other hand, the flow of the story is also interrupted explicitly by the insertion of metacommunicative comments on the situation itself, such as in line 09 and from line 13 on, when he starts with his summarizing, compressed analysis going beyond the immediate context of the Lavillenie incident: according to Villa, the incident can be conceptualized metaphorically (Lakoff and Johnson [1980] 2003) in terms of the historically entrenched scenario of a Roman coliseum.[13] Interestingly, it seems as if he anticipates this scenario metonymically by the gesture of clapping hands (Müller and Cienki 2009) together with the imitation of the cheering crowd (line 11) which he then first labels `bar↑!BÁ!rie` (*barbarism*) (line 13). In this way, we can observe what Mittelberg and Waugh (2009) call a 'two-step semiotic process': the metonymy of clapping hands accompanied by the yelling audience leads to the conventionalized metaphor of the coliseum.

Note that in line with our observations above, in opposition to Villa who tends to show either a 'rapport neglect orientation' or a 'rapport challenge orientation', as his communication interest is exclusively directed towards content or

12 In another sequence, he also uses the 'inclusive we' (Bühler [1934] 2011: 160) when responding to Antônio Villa: `ent´Ão o ouro tava na ˋnossa ˋMÃO;` ((02:49)) (so the gold was in our hands)

13 This metaphor also appears in one of the comments following the online news published by the NZZ. SN3: *war das nicht eigentlich auch schon bei den Römern im Kolosseum so?* (wasn't it already like that with the Romans in the coliseum?). As mentioned above, the article by the NZZ and the comments generated by it are those with the most instantiations of meta-analyses of this type.

'making his point', Bruno Prado changes his opinion in this sequence and adopts his stance toward Villa's point of view which again reveals his 'rapport enhancement' or 'maintenance orientation.'[14]

Villa continuously adopts an increasingly macro-analytical and educational stance, first prescinding from the concrete incident with Lavillenie, focusing on other athletes and other disciplines, then looking at other sport events, and finally approaching the topic of society itself. In the following sequence, he is talking about a soccer game between Brazil and Argentina:

Sequence 5: August 16th, 2016, Jovem Pan ((04:05-04:56))

01 AV: quando tUlio fez um gol com a mÃo numa copa aMÉ:rica;=°h
when Tulio scored a goal by hand at the Copa América

02 ele sal´DOU o gol o gol com a o c com a mÃo;
he scored the goal the goal by the b by hand

03 e diz que com argenTIna é melhor fazer um gol de forma irregulAr;
and said against Argentina an irregular goal is even better

04 ou seja <<f, with raised forefinger> !VE!ja a noção !É!tica que ele está dAndo> <<with two thumbs behind the shoulders> a uma criAnça por exemplo.>
just see which kind of ethical idea he is passing to a child for instance

05 porque o fute!BOL:!;
because soccer

06 a gente te (.) ele é ´!MAI:S! do que um esporte.=°h
we you it's more than a sport

07 <<acc> ele é uma leitura do braSIL.>=
it's a blueprint of Brazil

08 =o nelson rodrigues foi o priMEIro entender Isso.
Nelson Rodrigues was the first to see it this way

09 (-) né (.) ao usar o futebol para expliCAR o brasIl e tal.
right using soccer to explain Brazil and all that

10 então <<f> quando o locutor ba!BA!ca fAla que;
so when the stupid announcer says that

11 faZER um gol com_a mÃo (-) pode ser (.) tUdo bem.>
scoring a goal by hand can be okay

14 It is worth remembering that our aim in this article is not to focus on Spencer-Oatey's (2008) categories, but to show some tendencies of the interlocutors towards rapport management. Being so, the discussion clearly reveals Villa's interest in content over Prado's preference for harmonious relationships (in both respects: regarding the participants in the discussion, as well as to reestablish the relationship between 'Brazil' and potential 'observers').

12 e cOm argentina é melhor ´AIN:da.>=
and against Argentina it's even better

13 =<<f, pointing with the forefinger in front of him> ele é um iDIOta.
he's an idiot

14 ele é um iDIOta.=
he's an idiot

15 =porque ele tá> <<ff> estimu!LAN:!do °h que as pessoas ´viOlem por exemplo as !↑LEIS!;
because he's encouraging people to violate for example the law

16 <<acc, raised forefinger> no conjUnto da sociedade ele é um iDIOta.>
regarding the society as a whole he's an idiot

17 <<f, raised forefinger> e quE faz Isso estimUla a torcida i!`DIO!ta.>
and that's what encourages the idiot crowd

18 <<raised forefinger> que fAz o que ↑FEZ.>
it does what it did

19 entÃo °h a coisa (.) (tão) nós estamos aprende nós estamos vive é é um processo de CIvilização.
so the thing we learn we live it's it's a process of civilization

20 <<gesture of division with vertical hand> a civilização é muito LONge daqui.>
civilization is very far away from here

21 <<repeats the gesture of division> tem o at´LÂNtico.>
there's the Atlantic

22 (que_é) (.) <<moving both hands directed to each other>´e: entÃo deMO:ra para atravessar;>=
and it takes a long time to cross it

Again, Antônio Villa introduces an analogy based on a conventionalized and well-known metaphor at the reflexive macro-level: BRAZILIAN SOCIETY IS A SOCCER GAME (lines 05–07).[15] Furthermore, it is striking that he inserts a metacomment on the ubiquity of this metaphor (lines 08–09). Even more than in sequence (4), the lexical items Villa uses here to designate Brazil and the Brazilians show the explicitness of his speech style: while in sequence (4), he already called the attitude of the Brazilian crowd "barbarism" (*barbárie*) and said that Brazil preserves a "stupid kind of nationalism" (*nacionalismo bobo*), he now calls first only the announcer "stupid" (*locutor babaca*, line 10), then the announcer alongside the

15 Cf. for example Hardaway (1976); Liu and Farha (1996); Bergh (2011); Vierkant (2008).

crowd "idiots" (*idiota*, lines 13, 14, 16, 17). He puts an extra strong accent on those terms and holds that civilization has not arrived in Brazil yet (lines 19–22). At the prosodic and nonverbal level, this explicitness is underscored by loudness (lines 04, 10, 13, 15, 17), accent (lines 04, 05, 15, 17), and the raised forefinger (lines 04, 13, 15, 16, 17, 18); hints which frequently co-occur. By this content-oriented, nearly educational and directness displaying manner, Villa's speech style can be seen as opposed to the prototypical Brazilian speech style as revealed in Bruno Prado's and Joseval Peixoto's ways of speaking where rhetoric means, form, and the interpersonal level come to the fore, and things are said more indirectly, as other studies have already advocated (Meireles 2001; Carvalho and Trevisan 2003; Schröder 2003, 2014a, b; see theoretical section).

Hence, to sum up, in this section, we could observe on a micro-level an instructive interplay of what we have called in section 4.1.2 the IN- X OUT-GROUP cultural schema. While Bruno Prado and Joseval Peixoto strive to maintain rapport orientations aligned with expected behaviors in the in-group category, Villa detaches himself from in-group behavior and displays a rapport challenge orientation by his explicit and direct speech style.

5 Concluding remarks

In this article, we provided a cross-cultural analysis of reactions to an event that took place during the Olympic Games in Brazil in 2016. Our findings showed that the group-level conceptualizations of Olympic Games by Brazilian fans can differ substantially from group-level conceptualizations of speakers from other countries. More specifically, we have shown that the SPORTS FANS category is construed differently by Brazilian fans in comparison with other fans. Moreover, the IN- X OUT-GROUP and the MONGREL COMPLEX cultural schemas seem to constitute many of the Brazilian reactions to the event. We have also shown that instantiations of the IN- AND OUT-GROUP cultural schema can be negatively categorized by people from other cultural backgrounds as behaviors related to nationalism.

At the same time, we have shown that speech styles in online meaning construction can unveil processes in which Brazilians can either confirm the cultural conceptualizations identified in the comment sections, as Joseval Peixoto did in the radio broadcast, by reinforcing the appropriateness of the Brazilian crowd's reaction, or contest them from an outer observational point of view, as Antonio da Villa did.

The analysis has been predicated on two groups of theoretical and methodological frameworks: a cognitive and cultural linguistic perspective, as well as a conversation analytic and interactional linguistic perspective. The former has pointed to more or less stable meanings identified at the group-level of commentators' speech communities. The latter has shown that cultural conceptualizations are also co-constructed during online meaning negotiation and are interwoven with speech styles where also rapport management activities come into play and interlocutors show flexible stances, as Bruno Prado did. All in all, we have shown how both theoretical perspectives complement one another and provide a broader scope for cross-cultural analyses.

6 Appendix: Transcription conventions GAT 2

Short, adapted version of GAT 2 according to Selting et al. (2011).

[ ] [ ]	overlap and simultaneous talk
=	fast, immediate continuation with a new turn or segment (latching)
and_uh	cliticizations within units
hm_hm	bi-syllabic tokens
(.)	micro pause, up to 0.2 sec.
(-)	short pause of 0.2-0.5 sec.
(--)	intermediary pause of 0.5-0.8 sec.
(2.0)	measured pause of 2.0 sec.
:, ::, :::	lengthening (0.2-0.5 sec.; 0.5-0.8 sec.; 0.8-1.0 sec.)
((laughs))	non-verbal vocal actions and events
<<laughing> >	para-verbal and non-verbal action as accompanying speech with indication of scope
<<acc>	accelerando
(may i)	assumed wording
(i say/let's say)	possible alternatives
°hh hh°	in- and outbreaths
(xxx)	one unintelligible syllable
acCENT	focus accent
accEnt	secondary accent
ac!CENT!	extra strong accent
?	rising to high final pitch movement of intonation unit
,	rising to mid final pitch movement of intonation unit
-	level final pitch movement of intonation unit
;	falling to mid final pitch movement of intonation unit
.	falling to low final pitch movement of intonation unit
ˆSO	rising-falling accent pitch movement

```
ˇSO               falling-rising accent pitch movement
´SO               rising accent pitch movement
`SO               falling accent pitch movement
↑                 pitch upstep
↓                 pitch downstep
```

References

Anon, Jo. 2016. Lavillenie: En 1936, la Foule était contre Jesse Owens. On n'avait pas vu ça depuis. *Le Monde* August, 16. http://www.lemonde.fr/jeux-olympiques-rio- 2016/ article/2016 /08/16/jo-2016-lavillenie-en-1936-la-foule-etait-contre-jesse-owens-on -n-avait-pas-vu-ca-depuis_4983362_4910444.html. (accessed 02 February 2020).

Barcelona, Antonio. 2002. Clarifying and applying the notions of metaphor and metonymy within cognitive linguistics: An update. In René Dirven & Ralf Pörings (eds.), *Metaphor and metonymy in comparison and contrast*, 207–277. Berlin & New York: Mouton de Gruyter.

Bergh, Gunnar. 2011. Football is war: a case study of minute-by-minute football commentary. *Veredas* 15. 83–93.

Bolten, Jürgen. 2014. The dune model–or: How to describe cultures. *AFS Intercultural Link*, 5(2). 4–6.

Brühwiller, Tjerk. 2016. Sie pfeifen darauf. *NZZ* August, 16. http://www.nzz.ch/olympia2016/ brasilianische-zuschauer-sie-pfeifen-darauf-ld.111124 (accessed 02 February 2020).

Bublitz, Wolfram & Axel Hübler (eds). 2007. *Metapragmatics in use*. Amsterdam: John Benjamins.

Bühler, Karl. [1934] 2011. *Theory of language. The representational function of language*. Amsterdam & Philadelphia: John Benjamins.

Caffi, Claudia. 2007. *Mitigation*. Amsterdam: Elsevier.

Carvalho, Marília & Lino Trevisan. 2003. Relações interculturais entre trabalhadores brasileiros e alemães na VW-Audi de S. José dos Pinhais. *Revista Educação & Tecnologia* 7. 68–86.

Chafe, Wallace. 1982. Integration and involvement in speaking, writing, and oral literature. In Deborah Tannen (ed.), *Spoken and written language: Exploring orality and literacy*, 35–53. Norwood: Ablex.

Couper-Kuhlen, Elizabeth & Margret Selting. 2001. Introducing interactional linguistics. In Margret Selting & Elizabeth Couper-Kuhlen (eds.), *Studies in interacional linguistics*, 1–22. Amsterdam & Philadelphia: John Benjamins.

Couper-Kuhlen, Elizabeth & Margret Selting. 2018. *Interactional linguistics. Studying language in social interaction*. Cambridge, New York, Melbourne & New Dehli: Cambridge University Press.

Deppermann, Arnulf, 2012. How does 'cognition' matter to the analysis of talk-in-interaction? *Language Sciences* 34. 746–767.

Der Spiegel. Publikum pfeift – Lavillenie vergleicht mit 1936. *Der Spiegel* August, 16. http://www.spiegel.de/sport/sonst/olympia-2016-renaud-lavillenie-fuehlt-sich-wie-jesse-owens-a-1107863.html (accessed 02 February 2020).

Dicker, Ron. 2016. Pole vaulter cries on medal stand because Rio crowd keeps booing him. *The Huffington Post* August, 18. http://www.huffingtonpost.com/entry/rio-pole-vaulter-cries-medal-booing_us_57b57c9fe4b034dc7325b9fc (accessed 02 February 2020).

Fauconnier, Gilles & Mark Turner. 2002. *The way we think: Conceptual blending and the mind's hidden complexities*. New York: Basic Books.
Foley, William. 1997. Language and social position. In William Foley (ed.), *Anthropological linguistics: An introduction*, 192–214. Oxford: Blackwell.
Franceschini, Gustavo & Rodrigo Mattos. 2016. Prata, francês compara vaias no Rio às recebidas por Jesse Owens em 1936. *Uol* August, http://olimpiadas.uol.com.br/noticias/redacao/2016/08/16/derrotado-por-thiago-braz-frances-quer-revanche-na-mesma-moeda-em-paris.htm (accessed 02 February 2020).
Grady, Joseph E. 1997. *Foundations of meaning: Primary metaphors and primary scenes*. Berkeley: University of California at Berkeley PhD dissertation.
Günthner, Susanne. 1999. Thematisierung moralischer Normen in der interkulturellen Kommunikation. In Jörg Bergmann & Thomas Luckmann (eds.), *Kommunikative Konstruktion von Moral*, 325–351. Opladen: Westdeutscher Verlag.
Hardaway, Francine. 1976. Foul play: Sports metaphors as public doublespeak. *College English* 38 (1). 78–82.
Höhle, Tilman. 1992. Über Verum-Fokus im Deutschen. In Joachim Jacobs (ed.), *Informationsstruktur und Grammatik*, 112–141. Opladen: Westdeutscher Verlag.
Holmes, Janet. 1984. Modifying illocutionary force. *Journal of Pragmatics* 8. 345–365.
Kecskes, Istvan. 2014. *Intercultural pragmatics*. New York & Oxford: Oxford University Press.
Kecskes, Istvan. 2015. Language, culture, and context. In Farzad Sharifian (ed.), *The Routledge handbook of language and culture*, 113–128. New York & London: Routledge.
Kövecses, Zóltan. 2002. *Metaphor: an introduction*. Oxford & New York: Oxford University Press.
Kövecses, Zóltan. 2005. *Metaphor in culture: universality and variation*. Cambridge: Cambridge University Press.
Lakoff, George & Mark Johnson. [1980] 2003. *Metaphors we live by*. Chicago: The University of Chicago Press.
Liu, Dilin & Brian Farha. 1996. Three strikes and you're out. A study of the use of football and baseball jargon in present-day American English. *English Today* 12 (1). 36–40.
Malanski, Daniel. 2019. Cannibals, colorful birds, and exuberant nature: The representation of Brazilian nationalism and its tropical modernity in the 2016 Rio olympics. *Journal of Sport and Social Issues*. https://journals.sagepub.com/doi/abs/10.1177/0193723519889344 (accessed 02 February 2020).
Meireles, Selma. 2001. A negação sintática em diálogos do alemão e do português do Brasil. *Pandaemonium Germanicum* 5. 139–168.
Mittelberg, Irene & Linda Waugh. 2009. Metonymy first, metaphor second: A cognitive-semiotic approach to multimodal figures of thought in co-speech gesture. In Charles Forceville & Eduardo Urios-Aparisi (eds), *Multimodal metaphor*, 329–355. Berlin & New York: Mouton de Gruyter.
Müller, Cornelia & Alan Cienki. 2009. Words, gestures, and beyond: Forms of multimodal metaphor in the use of spoken language. In Charles Forceville & Eduardo Urios-Aparisi (eds), *Multimodal metaphor*, 297–328. Berlin & New York: Mouton de Gruyter.
Palmer, Gary. 1996. *Toward a theory of cultural linguistics*. Austin: University of Texas Press.
Palmer, Gary & Farzad Sharifian. 2007. Applied cultural linguistics: An emerging paradigm. In Farzad Sharifian & Gary Palmer (eds), *Applied cultural linguistics. Converging evidence in communication and language research* 7, 1–14. Amsterdam: John Benjamins.

Payne, Marissa. 2016. French olympian apologizes for comparing getting booed in Rio to Jesse Owens in Nazi Germany. *The Washington Post* August, 17. https://www.washingtonpost.com/news/early-lead/wp/2016/08/17/french-olympian apologizes-for-comparing-getting-booed-in-rio-to-jesse-owens-in-nazi-germany/?utm_term=. def0c02583d2 (accessed 02 February 2020).

Pearson, Virginia & Walter Stephan. 1998. Preferences for styles of negotiation: A comparison of Brazil and the US. *International Journal of Intercultural Relations* 22 (1). 67–83.

Quirk, Randolph, Sidney Greenbaum, Geoffrey Leech & Jan Svartvik. 1985. *A comprehensive grammar of the English language*. London: Longman.

Rizzo, Marcel. 2016. Ao lado de Bubka, Braz consola francês vaiado no pódio; Bach critica torcedores. *Folha* August, 16. http://www1.folha.uol.com.br/esporte/olimpiada-no-rio/2016/08/1803825-ao-lado-de-bubka-braz-consola-frances-vaiado-no-podio-bach-critica-torcedores.shtml (accessed 02 February 2020).

Sacks, Harvey. 1972. On the analyzability of stories by children. In John Gumperz & Dell Hymes (eds), *Directions in sociolinguistics: The ethnography of communication*, 325–345. New York: Holt, Rinehart and Winston.

Sacks, Harvey. 1995. *Lectures on conversation. Vol. 2*. Oxford: Basil Blackwell.

Sacks, Harvey, Emmanuel Schegloff, Emmanuel & Gail Jefferson. 1974. A simplest systematics for the organization of turn-taking for conversation. *Language* 50. 696–735.

Schegloff, Emmanuel. 2007a. A tutorial on membership categorization. *Journal of Pragmatics* 39 (3). 462–482.

Schegloff, Emmanuel. 2007b. Categories in action: Person-reference and membership categorization. *Discourse Studies* 9 (4). 433–461.

Schmidt, Thomas & Kai Wörner. 2009. EXMARaLDA – Creating, analysing and sharing spoken language corpora for pragmatic research. *Pragmatics* 19. 565–582.

Schröder, Ulrike. 2003. *Brasilianische und deutsche Wirklichkeiten. Eine vergleichende Fallstudie zu kommunikativ erzeugten Sinnwelten*. Wiesbaden: Deutscher Universitätsverlag.

Schröder, Ulrike. 2010. Speech styles and functions of speech from a cross-cultural perspective. *Journal of Pragmatics* 42. 466–476.

Schröder, Ulrike. 2014a. The interplay of (im)politeness, conflict styles, rapport management and metacommunication in Brazilian-German interaction. *Intercultural Pragmatics* 11 (1). 57–82.

Schröder, Ulrike. 2014b. Interkulturelle Kommunikation zwischen Deutschen und Brasilianern im Lichte von Strategien der (Un-)höflichkeit, divergierenden Konfliktstilen und Formen des Beziehungsmanagements. In Csaba Földes (ed.), *Interkulturalität unter dem Blickwinkel von Semantik und Pragmatik*, 207–224. Tübingen: Narr, Francke Attempto.

Schröder, Ulrike. 2015. The interplay of verbal, vocal, and visual cues in the co-construction of the experience of alterity in exchange students’ talk. *Journal of Pragmatics* 81. 21–35.

Schröder, Ulrike. 2017. A construção metafórica de palavras-chave para a descrição de experiências interculturais: um estudo a partir da análise da conversa multimodal. *Cadernos de Estudos Linguísticos* 59 (1). 111–133.

Schröder, Ulrike & Mariana Carneiro Mendes. 2019. Unterschiede im Gebrauch und in der Funktion prosodischer Merkmale im deutschen und brasilianischen Sprechen im Kontext des Transkribierens. In Thomas Johnen, Mônica Savedra & Ulrike Schröder (eds.), *Sprachgebrauch im Kontext – die deutsche Sprache im Kontakt, Vergleich und in Interaktion mit Brasilien*, 145–172. Stuttgart: ibidem.

Selting, Margret. 1994. Emphatic speech style – with special focus on the prosodic signalling of heightened emotive involvement in conversation. *Journal of Pragmatics* 22. 375–408.

Selting, Margret, Peter Auer, Dagmar Barth-Weingarten, Jörg Bergmann, Pia Bergmann, Karin Birkner, Elizabeth Couper-Kuhlen, Arnulf Deppermann, Peter Gilles, Susanne Günthner, Martin Hartung, Friederike Kern, Christine Mertzlufft, Christian Meyer, Miriam Morek, Frank Oberzaucher, Jörg Peters, Uta Quasthoff, Wilfried Schütte, Anja Stukenbrock & Susanne Uhmann. 2011. A system for transcribing talk-in-interaction: GAT 2; translated and adapted for English by Elizabeth Couper-Kuhlen and Dagmar Barth-Weingarten. *Gesprächsforschung –Online-Zeitschrift zur verbalen Interaktion* 12. 1–51. http://www.gespraechsforschung ozs.de/fileadmin/dateien/heft2011/px-gat2-englisch.pdf. (accessed 16 January 2015).

Sharifian, Farzad. 2011. *Cultural conceptualisations and language: Theoretical framework and applications*. Amsterdam: John Benjamins.

Sharifian, Farzad. 2017. Cultural linguistics. Amsterdam, Philadelphia: John Benjamins.

Spencer-Oatey, Helen. 2008. Face, (im)politeness and rapport. In Helen Spencer-Oatey (ed.), *Culturally speaking. Culture, communication and politeness theory*, 11–47. London: Continuum.

Stokoe, Elizabeth. 2012. Moving forward with membership categorization analysis: Methods for systematic analysis. *Discourse Studies* 14 (3). 277–303.

Tazé-Bernand, Thierry. 2016. Rio 2016 – L'affaire Lavillenie vue du Brésil: des Torts Partagés. *France Tv Sport* August, 17. http://www.francetvsport.fr/les-jeux-olympiques/rio-2016-l-affaire-lavillenie-des-torts-partages-vue-du-bresil-353867 (accessed 02 February 2020).

Triandis, Harry. 1995. *Individualism and collectivism*. Boulder: Westview Press.

Unger, Frank. 1990. Wie implizit kann Metakommunikation sein? *Zeitschrift für Phonetik, Sprachwissenschaft und Kommunikationsforschung* 43. 186–200.

Vierkant, Stephan. 2008. Metaphor and live radio football commentary. In Lavric, Eva, Gerhard Pisek, Andrew Skinner & Wolfgang Stadler (eds.), *The linguistics of football*, 121–132. Tübingen: Gunter Narr.

Augusto Soares da Silva

Metaphor, emotion, and intralinguistic cultural variation: metaphors of ANGER in European and Brazilian Portuguese

Abstract: Assuming that emotions are socially and culturally constructed, this article compares the metaphorical conceptualization of ANGER in European Portuguese (EP) and Brazilian Portuguese (BP). Individualistic versus collectivistic cultural influences determining the conceptual variation of ANGER in pluricentric Portuguese are examined. Adopting a sociocognitive view of language and developing a corpus-based and profile-based methodology, this study analyzes 610 examples of anger emotion as lexicalized in the nouns *raiva* "anger", *fúria* "fury", *ira* "anger/wrath", *cólera* "anger/wrath", and *irritação* "irritation" from a corpus of personal-experiential blogs. Cohering with insights from cross-cultural psychological research as well as with the findings of prior linguistic studies on anger, the study identifies the conceptual and cultural metaphorical profiles for ANGER in EP and BP national varieties. The qualitative and quantitative corpus-based analysis shows both the strong similarities as well as the subtle but relevant differences in the metaphorical conceptualization of anger in EP and BP. The two national varieties have the same metaphorical conceptual structuring of the anger emotion, but there are conceptual differences, and these differences are influenced by culture. EP appears to be more associated with the metaphorically construed attempted regulation and a more internalized expression of anger, which is in line with the more collectivistic and restrained culture of Portugal. In contrast, BP is more connected with the metaphorically unrestrained and open manifestation of anger as affirmation of the self. This correlation is in line with the more individualistic, indulgent, and emotionally expressive culture of Brazil. Accordingly, BP appears to be more akin to metaphorically construed high intensity of anger, while the somatization of anger is more fitting in EP.

Acknowledgements: This study has been carried out under the research project UIDB/00683/2020 (Center for Philosophical and Humanistic Studies), funded by the Portuguese Foundation for Science and Technology. I would like to thank two anonymous reviewers for their thorough and illuminating comments. Needless to say, the remaining errors are only mine.

Augusto Soares da Silva, Universidade Católica Portuguesa, Center for Philosophical and Humanistic Studies

https://doi.org/10.1515/9783110688306-008

Keywords: anger, emotions, conceptual metaphor, intralinguistic cultural variation, collectivism vs. individualism, corpus- and profile-based approach, Portuguese

1 Introduction

Anger is claimed to be one of the basic or universal emotions (e.g., Ekman 1992, 1999; Ortony and Turner 1990; Wierzbicka 1999), which is accurately recognized across cultures in terms of the facial expressions associated with it, and regularly lexicalized in the vast majority of languages of the world. The consistent and productive way in which we speak metaphorically (or otherwise figuratively) about emotions says a lot about the way we conceptualize the emotional experience, as stressed by conceptual metaphor theory since its very beginning (Lakoff and Johnson 1980; Lakoff and Kövecses 1987; Kövecses 1986, 1990). The alleged universality of the emotion category of anger and its regular and productive metaphorical (and metonymic) conceptualization account for the large number of studies on this subject both in psychology, particularly social psychology, and linguistics, especially cognitive linguistics (see Fontaine, Scherer, and Soriano 2013 and Soriano 2013 for an overview).

Like any other emotion, anger is by nature a *social* emotion (Glynn 2014) that is very sensitive to social variation and cultural influences. Therefore, anger varies across cultures, especially the specific ways in which anger is perceived, experienced, evaluated, (un)regulated, and manifested. Conceptual metaphor is not only constitutive of emotional experience, but it is also grounded in our individual, collective, and cultural experience, thus being fully contextualized, both socio-culturally situated, and discursively constructed. Some studies have shown that the emotion of anger and its metaphorical (and metonymic) conceptualization are profoundly associated with culture and that anger is experienced in different ways across societies and historical periods. For example, Geeraerts and Grondelaers (1995) and Gevaert (2005) have demonstrated the high influence of the medieval folk theory of the four humors, or fluids of the human body, and the four temperaments (yellow bile-choleric, black bile-melancholic, phlegm-phlegmatic, and blood-sanguine), which dominated medical thinking in Western Europe for several centuries, on the conceptualization of anger and other emotions, and Yu (1995) showed the importance of the folk emotion theory of five elements in Chinese medicine (wood, fire, earth, metal, and water). Cross-cultural emotion psychology suggests that in collectivistic cultures, as compared to individualistic cultures, anger is predominantly viewed as more negative and socially disruptive and is reported with a lower emotional intensity (e.g., Markus and Kitayama 1991; Matsumoto, Yoo, and Chung 2010). Performing a quantitative corpus-based analysis of ANGER metaphors in English, Spanish, and Russian, Ogarkova and Soriano (2014) showed both the similarities and particularly the differences in appraisal, expression, regulation, and the saliency of physiological aspects of anger in the three languages. However, these cross-cultural studies of anger, as well as the cross-cultural studies of emotions in general, have analyzed the differences between (very) dissimilar and geographically separated cultures and languages. Only a few studies have dealt with cultural differences in experiencing and communicating emotions within a single country or a single language (see Mortillaro et al. 2013; Soares da Silva 2020, on the emotion of pride).

The present study reinforces the idea that emotions have a biological basis but are socially and culturally constructed and explores this principle in the context of a *pluricentric* language (different national geographical centers within the same language – Soares da Silva 2014). I will analyze the cultural metaphorical conceptualizations of ANGER in the two national varieties of Portuguese, namely, European Portuguese (EP) and Brazilian Portuguese (BP). This study adopts a sociocognitive view of language as stressed by the second generation of cognitive sciences and cognitive linguistics, and the current trend of conceptual metaphor theory (extended from the Lakoff and Johnson's 1980 standard view), especially the usage-based and socioculturally contextualized approach to conceptual metaphor (e.g., Stefanowitsch and Gries 2006; Semino 2008; Steen 2011; Kövecses, this volume). It applies a corpus-based and onomasiological profile-based methodology, focusing on the alternative metaphorical patterns used to designate the ANGER emotion. The study combines a detailed qualitative analysis of the conceptual metaphors of ANGER found in the corpus with a quantitative analysis of corpus data. The classification of conceptual metaphors of ANGER is based on the typology of root metaphors of anger and their subtypes proposed by Soriano (2005) and Ogarkova and Soriano (2014). The data comprise 610 occurrences of five noun lexemes expressing anger in Portuguese, namely *raiva* "anger", *fúria* "fury", *ira* "anger/wrath", *cólera* "anger/wrath", and *irritação* "irritation" extracted from a corpus of blogs consisting of personal diaries about love, sex, family, friends, violence, etc.

I will first briefly review some evidence of the cultural variability of anger, focusing on underlying individualistic and collectivistic cultural influences. Subsequently, I will present the data and profile-based qualitative and quantitative methods for the identification, classification, and cultural comparison of the conceptual metaphors of ANGER in EP and BP varieties. Finally, I will carry out an analysis of the corpus data to determine whether and how the metaphorical conceptualization of ANGER differs between the two national varieties of Portuguese.

2 Cultural variability of ANGER

Some studies have shown that culture influences emotions in many different aspects (e.g., Mesquita, Frijda, and Scherer 1997; Russell 1991). One of the ways in which culture influences emotions has to do with the well-known opposition between individualism and collectivism. Hofstede's (1980, 2001) original work led to the mapping of world cultures based on individualism versus collectivism. Societies can be described in terms of how much they focus on individuals (individualism) rather than on society as a whole (collectivism), and this distinction reflects the extent to which identity is defined by personal choices and achievements (the *independent* self) or by the character of collective groups to which one is more or less permanently attached (the *interdependent* self). Although individualism and collectivism are both present in every society, there are societies in which individualism predominates and others where collectivism does; in the former, people perceive themselves as individual, autonomous entities with individualized goals and achievements; in the latter, people are not supposed to be independent from each other but should harmoniously fit into the societal organization of roles and duties.

Individualism versus collectivism and power distance, which captures the extent to which social inequality within a society is generally tolerated by its members (Hofstede 2001), are the main factors that potentially influence the variation of anger across cultures (see Ogarkova and Soriano 2014; Ogarkova, Soriano, and Gladkova 2016, for an overview). Cross-cultural emotion psychological research reveals remarkable differences with regard to the evaluation, regulation, and intensity of anger across cultures (e.g., Bender et al. 2012; Chon, Kim, and Ryoo 2000; Fernández et al. 2000; Fischer, Manstead, and Rodriguez Mosquera 1999; Matsumoto, Yoo, and Chung 2010). In collectivistic cultures, anger is predominantly viewed as more negative and socially disruptive and as an emotion that challenges social order and harmony, and thus, should be regulated and not externally manifested. In contrast, individualistic cultures see anger as a relatively more positive and more socially acceptable emotion, thus being more favorable towards its open and unrestrained manifestation. Moreover, the connection between anger and the body is emphasized in collectivistic cultures to a higher degree than in individualistic ones. As for power distance, in societies with high power distance (power comes before good and evil and inequality is normal; Hofstede 2001) such as Russia, Mexico, and China, experiencing or showing anger towards higher-status people is undesirable and even socially condemned. Cohering with this psychological evidence, Ogarkova and Soriano (2014) developed a corpus-based cognitively (conceptual metaphor theory) oriented linguistic study on the metaphorical conceptualization of ANGER in (British) English, Spanish, and

Russian, showing that metaphors emphasizing the negativity and enhanced regulation of anger are more salient in the more collectivistic Russian and Spanish societies than in the more individualistic English culture, and metaphors highlighting the somatic component of anger are more prominently represented in Russian than in English.

Hofstede's (2001) cross-cultural comparison model shows cultural differences between Portugal and Brazil.[1] With a score of 27 on the individualism (-collectivism) scale, Portugal is more collectivistic in relative terms than Brazil, which has a score of 38. According to Hofstede's model, the Portuguese collectivism manifests itself in a close long-term commitment to the member 'group', be that a family, extended family, or extended relationships. Furthermore, loyalty is paramount and overrides most other societal rules and regulations. Another relevant cultural dimension to the comparison between the two countries corresponds to what Hofstede (2001) refers to as *indulgence*, which is defined as the extent to which people try to control their desires and impulses, based on the way they were raised. Relatively weak control is called *indulgence*, and relatively strong control is called *restraint*. Portugal scores 33 on this dimension and therefore has a culture of restraint, whereas Brazil's relatively high score of 59 indicates that the country has an indulgent society. As for the cultural dimension of power distance, there are less differences between the two countries, with Brazil (69) exhibiting a slightly larger degree of power distance as compared to Portugal (63).

Seeking to present a synthetic panorama of Portuguese history and culture, Real (2017: 193–201) points out as fundamental traits of Portuguese culture collectivistic aspects such as the values of gregariousness and generosity, solidarity, and fellowship, the spirit of self-sacrifice, the culture of dialogue – in short, the search for the Other as a defining aspect of one's own identity. Another complementary attribute of the Portuguese people, according to Real (2017: 198–200), is their lyrical-sentimental or emotional character, well reflected in the long history of Portuguese literature. The expression of emotionality is more extroverted and more direct in Brazilians than in the Portuguese.

Studies by Brazilian sociologists, anthropologists, and historians, including the foundational historiographical works of Freyre (1933) and Holanda (1936) on Brazilian identity, and, more recently, Rezende and Coelho's (2010) study on the anthropology of emotions as well as the Almeida's (2007) sociological study on "the Brazilian's head", all highlight emotionality as a defining feature of Brazil-

1 The comparison between Portugal and Brazil with respect to individualism and to other dimensions of national culture (power distance, masculinity vs. femininity, uncertainty avoidance, long term vs. short term orientation, and indulgence) is available at https://www.hofstede-insights.com/country-comparison/brazil,portugal/

ian identity and culture. More specifically, Brazilian culture is characterized by a greater social acceptance of the display of emotions compared to other countries, i.e., Brazilians tend to express their emotions more easily and openly, in a more explicit and spontaneous way, in contrast to people from other societies and cultures.[2]

I have no knowledge about any empirical study that systematically compares the role that emotion plays in Brazilian and Portuguese societies. The linguistic studies by Schröder (2009, 2010), who analyzed cross-cultural differences in Brazilian and German communities found in interviews, show that Brazilian respondents made use of a more emotive, phatic, and expressive speech style, in contrast to the more referential and metalinguistic speech style in the German group (Schröder 2010). In addition, in interviews about love relationships, Brazilian responses contained more metaphors related to the passionate ideal of love, emphasizing the emotion itself and the present moment rather than the relationship and its future evolution, whereas in the German group, the preferential metaphorical conceptualizations focused on the relationship itself and were tied to a more rational, less emotion-centered ideal of romantic love (Schröder 2009). The results of Oliveira's (2020) recent cognitive and cultural-linguistic study on business negotiations in Brazilian and German speech communities based on interviews show that the Brazilian interviewees pursued a person-orientation strategy in the conceptualization of 'respect in business negotiations', whereas a task-orientation strategy stood out more conspicuously in the German set of responses. More specifically, the interpersonal exchange in business contexts has a more personal leaning (i.e., the private connection between business counterparts is foregrounded) in the Brazilian case and a more operative and task-related leaning in the German case (Oliveira 2020: 137). Additionally, in the conceptualization of 'conflict in business negotiations', Brazilian participants proved often to conceptualize conflict as something that triggers a set of personal emotions such as anger associated with GAME/FIGHT metaphors, whereas the salience of (task-oriented) RESOURCE metaphors was more clearly visible in the German group (Oliveira 2020: 137).

Based on these cultural differences between Portugal and Brazil, and the additional comparative studies on Brazilian tendency to a stronger emotional style and conceptualization in different life domains, we can formulate the hypothesis that there are small but significant differences in the metaphorical conceptual-

---

2 The history of Brazilian social thinking since Freyre (1933) and Holanda (1936) considers Brazilian emotionality as something not only characteristic of the national identity but also as an intrinsically ambivalent feature. It was viewed as being either a synonym of less civilized or, more recently, as a positive characteristic of Brazilian identity (Rezende and Coelho 2010).

ization and expression of the emotion of anger between these two national varieties of Portuguese. Specifically, in the relatively more collectivistic and restrictive culture of Portugal, negative evaluation, controlled expression, enhanced regulation, and somatization of anger would be more saliently profiled, while the unrestrained and overt manifestation of the emotion would be more prominently represented in the relatively more individualistic and indulgent culture of Brazil.

3 Methodology: a corpus-based analysis of the conceptual metaphors of ANGER

3.1 Data

The data for the present study were extracted from a 750,000-word corpus of blogs in EP and BP compiled from 2013–2015, especially designed for the study of emotions in both varieties, and comprise personal diaries about personal events, love, sex, family, friends, work, opinions about politics, football, religion, books, and movies. Despite this diversity of subjects, we selected blogs that were comparable, not only in terms of topics but also in terms of language register for both countries. We left out blogs with markedly literary or philosophical content and favored texts written in an informal register. Blogs are particularly apt for a study about emotions because emotions are frequently discussed at a personal experiential level on blogs, and the language is often narrative in structure (Glynn 2014).

We analyzed 610 occurrences of five noun lexemes expressing the emotion of anger in Portuguese, namely *raiva* "anger", *fúria* "fury", *ira* "anger/wrath", *cólera* "anger/wrath", and *irritação* "irritation". The lexemes *raiva* and *fúria* are the most frequent nouns for expressing the emotion of anger, and *raiva* works as a hyperonym of this emotion of anger. The *fúria*, *ira*, and *cólera* lexemes generally express a higher degree of angry agitation, while *irritação* generally expresses a less intense anger emotion. The lexemes *cólera* and *ira* are terms used in formal register. The terms *cólera* and *raiva* can also refer to infectious diseases caused by viruses (cholera and rabies, respectively). Table 1 presents the number of hits found for each anger noun in our corpus for the two national varieties of Portuguese.

The number of occurrences that have been analyzed is relatively low and does not constitute a big sample, which would have been more suitable for a cross-cultural study of this nature. However, as we will show later, the detailed annotation system developed for this study makes the use of a substantially bigger sample dif-

Table 1: Frequency of ANGER nouns in the corpus.

ANGER nouns	EP	BP
cólera	9	15
fúria	106	103
ira	20	28
irritação	29	23
raiva	138	139
Total	302	308

ficult. We only analyzed anger nouns and not adjectives such as *furioso* "furious", *irado* "angry", *irritado* "annoyed, angry", *zangado* "angry" or verbs such as *irritar-se* "become angry", because emotion nouns better summarize the emotion than do other parts of speech. Nouns such as *aborrecimento* "annoyance", *indignação* "indignation", or *frustração* "frustration" were not analyzed because they express more specific or different concepts than the anger concept.

3.2 Conceptual metaphors of ANGER and the profile-based approach

The present study adopts the onomasiological profile-based approach, focusing on the conceptual choices made by speakers of different regional, social, etc. backgrounds, between different lexical expressions for naming a given meaning/concept. It corresponds to the so-called *behavioral profile approach*, which combines multifactorial usage-feature analysis and statistical modeling to identify and quantify complex patterns in usage (e.g., Geeraerts, Grondelaers, and Bakema 1994; Gries 2003, 2010; Divjak 2010; Glynn and Fischer 2010). In our study, a profile or, more precisely, a *metaphorical profile* for a particular target concept such as the anger emotion is the set of alternative metaphorical patterns used to designate that target, together with their relative frequencies. The onomasiological perspective on metaphor involves, therefore, the selection of the preferred metaphorical sources for a given meaning/concept. Many previous studies on the cognitive/cultural model of emotions provide an onomasiological approach to metaphor and to lexical semantics in general, with an emphasis on how an emotion is expressed metaphorically in different cultural and historical contexts (e.g., Geeraerts and Grondelaers 1995; Gevaert 2005; Soriano 2005, 2013; Ogarkova and Soriano 2014).

The method for metaphor identification is based on Stefanowitsch's (2006) metaphorical pattern analysis. This method consists of searching for metaphorical expressions which contain words from their target domains, such as the five nouns expressing anger in Portuguese. The metaphorical expressions to which the target concepts and lexical items belong are identified as metaphorical patterns. On the basis of the metaphors they instantiate, groups of conceptual mappings are established. The identification of a *metaphorical pattern* is based on the syntactic/semantic frame in which the target lexeme occurs. For example, *fúria* "fury" was selected as one of the lexical items expressing the target concept of anger. A search for its occurrences in the corpus yielded the metaphorical expression *ataques de fúria* "fury attacks". This expression is then identified as the metaphorical pattern "NP attacks", in which other target lexemes or lexemes from the source domain can occur, such as *ataques de raiva* "anger attacks" or *ataques de armas* "weapon attacks". The pattern *ataques de fúria/raiva* is then considered to instantiate the metaphor ANGER IS A WEAPON.

For the metaphor classification, we followed the ANGER metaphors seminal classifications as proposed by Kövecses (1986) and Lakoff and Kövecses (1987), and, particularly, the revision of the original inventory proposed by Soriano (2005, 2013) and Ogarkova and Soriano (2014).

Metaphorical patterns of ANGER were manually extracted from the corpus and classified into conceptual metaphors. We searched for all the hits of the five aforementioned ANGER nouns (*cólera* "anger/wrath", *fúria* "fury", *ira* "anger/wrath", *irritação* "irritation", and *raiva* "anger") in the corpus, and then we eliminated the literal uses and isolated all the hits that constitute metaphorical patterns in the sense given above. Every metaphorical pattern was individually analyzed, taking into account the mapping established across the source and target domains, and was subsequently classified under a specific conceptual metaphor according to its source domain. The set of conceptual metaphors and their frequencies in the corpus for the ANGER concept as expressed by each of the five ANGER nouns constitutes the metaphorical profile of ANGER emotion.

The conceptual metaphor inventory is organized in two levels, as proposed by Soriano (2005) and Ogarkova and Soriano (2014). The higher level embraces 'root' metaphors (e.g., ANGER IS A PRESSURIZED FLUID IN THE BODY CONTAINER) heading a cluster of sub-metaphors. The sub-metaphors constitute the lower level of the inventory and comprise entailment (E) sub-metaphors (e.g., EXPLOSION in the root metaphor ANGER IS A PRESSURIZED FLUID IN THE BODY CONTAINER) and special case (S) sub-metaphors (e.g., THE EYES ARE A CONTAINER FOR ANGER with regard to its root metaphor THE BODY IS A CONTAINER FOR ANGER).

Table 2 summarizes 13 salient conceptual root metaphors of ANGER, their entailments (E) and special cases (S) identified by Soriano (2005, 2013) and Ogarkova and Soriano (2014) for different languages (namely Spanish, English, and

Russian), and also specific to the representation of ANGER in Portuguese.[3] Examples from our corpus will be discussed in Section 4.1.

Table 2: Root and subtype conceptual metaphors of ANGER (adapted from Ogarkova and Soriano 2014: 100–101).

Root conceptual metaphor ANGER IS A . . .	Subtype conceptual metaphor	Examples
PRESSURIZED FLUID IN THE BODY-CONTAINER	E HOT	*a ferver de raiva* "boiling with anger"
	E RISE	*raiva a crescer* "anger growing"
	E PRESSURE	*sufocar de raiva* "choke with rage"
	E COUNTERPRESSURE	*engolir a fúria* "swallow fury"
	E CONTENTION	*fúria contida* "contained fury"
	E COMING OUT	*descarregar a fúria* "discharge fury"
	E EXPLOSION	*explodir de raiva* "explode with anger"
FIRE		*atiçar a ira* "stoke the wrath"
ILLNESS		*não imune à fúria* "not immune to fury"
INSANITY	S BLINDNESS	*louco/cego de raiva* "crazy/blind with rage"
AGGRESSIVE ANIMAL	S EMOTER IS ANIMAL	*fúria de fera do mato* "wild beast fury"
OPPONENT IN A STRUGGLE	S CONTROLLER/SUPERIOR	*a fúria invadiu-me* "fury invaded me"
FORCE OF NATURE		*fúria de um vulcão* "fury of a volcano"
WEAPON		*alvo dos seus ataques de fúria* "target of his rage attacks"
FORCE	E ENERGY	*movido pela raiva* "driven by anger"
PHYSICAL ENTITY	E VISIBLE/HIDDEN OBJECT	*esconder a raiva* "hide anger"
	E POSSESSION	*perder a raiva* "lose anger"
	E MOVING OBJECT	*trazer raiva* "bring anger"
	S SOLID OBJECT	*barreira de raiva* "rage barrier"
	S SUBSTANCE	*raiva misturada com ódio* "anger mixed with hate"

3 The metaphors found in the corpus could be grouped differently. For example, more generic categories of source domains could be used, like animate vs. inanimate entities, concrete vs. abstract concepts. Some metaphors are more atomic (fire, force) and others more complex (pressurized fluid in the body container). Force of nature could be considered as a special case of force, just as fluid could be classified as a special case of physical entity, more directly of substance. The metaphorically conceptualized substance in the body container does not necessarily have to be a fluid, it can also be a gasiform substance. We prefer, however, to follow the classification of Ogarkova and Soriano (2014), which comprises an inventory organized into well-defined categories (root and subtype metaphors, and specific and generic metaphors), as well as the seminal classification of Kövecses (1986).

Table 2 (continued)

Root conceptual metaphor ANGER IS A . . .	**Subtype conceptual metaphor**	**Examples**
LIVING ORGANISM	S PLANT	*inflorescências de fúria* "inflorescences of fury"
	S ANIMAL	*urrar de raiva* "howl with rage"
	S HUMAN	*raiva justa* "just/righteous anger"
LOCATION	S CONTAINER	*passar o limite da raiva* "cross the boundary of anger"
THE BODY IS A CONTAINER FOR ANGER	S CHEST	*raiva no peito* "anger within the chest"
	S EYES	*olhar com fúria* "look at X with fury"
	S FACE	*fúria estampada na face* "fury stamped on the face"
	S HANDS	*mãos em fúria* "hands in fury"
	S HEAD/MIND	*mente em fúria* "raging mind"
	S VOICE	*grito de raiva* "cry of anger"
	S OTHER	*raiva sentida na pele* "anger felt in the skin"

The inventory comprises eight specific and five generic root conceptual metaphors of ANGER (Ogarkova and Soriano 2014: 100). *Specific* metaphors involve specific-imagery source domains invoking complex scenarios rich in detail and entailments, such as PRESSURIZED FLUID, FIRE, ILLNESS, INSANITY, AGGRESSIVE ANIMAL, OPPONENT IN A STRUGGLE, FORCE OF NATURE, and WEAPON. In the case of *generic* metaphors, the source domain is more generic than in the specific metaphors, and these source domains such as FORCE, PHYSICAL ENTITY, LIVING ORGANISM, and LOCATION can apply to almost any target domain. There are also conceptual metaphors in which the target domain is not the anger emotion per se, but some salient aspect of the emotion – such as the body of the emoter (THE BODY IS A CONTAINER FOR ANGER) –,[4] and conceptual metaphors less frequently instantiated or less conventionally referred to in literature such as ANGER IS A TOOL (*turn fury to use*), ANGER IS A MACHINE (*generate anger*), ANGER IS A BURDEN (*freighted with anger*), and ANGER IS AN IDEA (*understand X's anger*). Certain metaphors may occupy different places in this typology. For example, ANGER IS A HOT FLUID may be an entailment of the metaphor ANGER IS A PRESSURIZED FLUID IN THE BODY-CONTAINER, as shown in Table 2, but it can also be a root conceptual metaphor, as proposed by Ogarkova and Soriano (2014: 100). We relied on context to distinguish between the two possibilities. It is interesting to perceive the expressions (specific to Bra-

4 This is why BODY IS A CONTAINER FOR ANGER and ANGER IS A FLUID IN THE BODY-CONTAINER are not included within a broader CONTAINER category.

zilian Portuguese) *Não esquenta!, Fica frio!* (literally, "Don't get hot; stay cool!") as injunctions to keep calm or to control one's anger, which instantiate the HOT FLUID entailment. Conversely, an expression can instantiate more than one conceptual metaphor. For instance, *olhos inchados de raiva* "eyes swollen with anger" manifests both the THE BODY IS A CONTAINER FOR ANGER metaphor and the ANGER IS A PRESSURIZED FLUID IN THE BODY-CONTAINER metaphor. These cases, which occur frequently in the expressions that include the emoter's body parts, were analyzed as pertaining to the more comprehensive metaphor THE BODY IS A CONTAINER FOR ANGER. In a subsequent and complementary analysis of the productivity of the root metaphors of ANGER, these cases were added to the metaphor ANGER IS A PRESSURIZED FLUID.

Here are a few more observations regarding the identification and the classification of the metaphors of anger. First, we considered cases such as *ter raiva* "to feel anger", *estar/ficar com raiva* "to be angry/to become angry", *causar raiva* "to cause anger", *muita raiva* "a lot of anger", *(ai) que raiva!* "I'm so angry!" (lit. "such anger!") as non-metaphorical and literal. Indeed, although these uses can be metaphorical (instantiating the metaphors ANGER IS A PHYSICAL ENTITY, INTENSITY IS QUANTITY, THE BODY IS A CONTAINER FOR ANGER), they are strongly conventionalized and generalized expressions and, most importantly, do not contain any word that could trigger a metaphorical use (in contrast to *estar cheio de raiva* "to be full of/ filled with anger", *ter uma raiva enorme* "to have a great anger"). Moreover, we did not want to inflate the frequency of anger metaphors. Second, there are degrees of figurativity in the metaphorical expressions of anger and thus there is a continuum of conventionality/novelty (Kövecses 2010) of anger metaphors from more conventionalized or well-entrenched metaphors (such as *estar cheio de raiva* "to be full of/ filled with anger") to newer or creative ones (such as *ficar roxo/branco de raiva* "turning purple/white with anger" compared to *ficar vermelho de raiva* "turning red with anger", and *cuspir a raiva como uma cobra venenosa* "spitting out the anger like a poisonous snake"). Third, it is important to remember that the ANGER metaphors analyzed in this study are expressed by one of the five target nouns mentioned above, so some of the metaphors identified in Table 2 are instantiated in expressions that do not contain any of these targets, such as *cabeça quente* "hothead" instantiating the metaphors ANGER IS A HOT FLUID and THE BODY IS A CONTAINER FOR ANGER. Finally, the figurative conceptualization of anger as well as of emotions in general usually combines metaphor and metonymy (cf. the generic metonymy THE PHYSIOLOGICAL EFFECTS OF AN EMOTION STAND FOR THE EMOTION), as Kövecses has shown (1986), thus being an emblematic example of *metaphtonymy* (Goossens 1990), i.e., the interaction of metaphor and metonymy. In this study we focus on the metaphorical conceptualization of anger.

3.3 Quantitative analysis

The observational data extracted from the corpus identified in Section 3.1 and annotated through the detailed qualitative analysis of types and subtypes of conceptual metaphors of anger and of the semantic dimensions profiled by these metaphors presented in Sections 3.2 and 4.1–4.2 (see below) were submitted to quantitative analysis.

The absolute and the relative frequencies of the 16 types of conceptual metaphors of ANGER found in the corpus (13 types as in Table 2 plus 3 types; see Table 4 below), as well as those frequencies of the five semantic dimensions highlighted by clusters of conceptual metaphors, were calculated. As argued by Oster (2010), frequency of occurrence alone is not enough to describe the metaphorical expression of an emotion; it is also important to calculate the productivity of the conceptual metaphors found in the corpus.

The productivity index of a metaphor is defined in Oster (2010: 749) as the product of the number of patterns of this metaphor divided by the total number of metaphorical patterns, i.e., the relative frequency of this metaphor and the number of different linguistic expressions co-occurring with the anger concept that are a realization of this metaphor divided by the total number of different linguistic expressions. For example, there are three different linguistic expressions co-occurring with *raiva* "anger", *fúria* "fury", and *ira* "anger/wrath" in the corpus for the metaphor ANGER IS FIRE, namely the verb *atiçar* "to stoke" and the expressions *em incandescência* "ablazing, glowing", and *clarão de* "flashes of". Frequent conceptual metaphors can be more or less productive depending on the high or low number of different linguistic expressions in which these metaphors are instantiated. Productivity indexes were calculated for all conceptual metaphors of anger in the corpus of each national variety.

Chi-square (especially, the Yates chi-square, corrected for continuity) and Cramer's V tests were carried out on the absolute frequencies of the conceptual metaphors of ANGER found in the corpus in order to calculate the statistical significance and the strength of association between clusters of conceptual metaphors profiling semantic dimensions of anger emotion and European as well as Brazilian varieties of Portuguese.

4 Results

In the first two sub-sections, we will develop the qualitative analysis discussing examples of the conceptual metaphors of ANGER from our corpus presented in

Table 2 and identifying the semantic dimensions profiled by these metaphors. The quantitative analysis of the results of the profile-based qualitative analysis will be presented in the last three sub-sections.

4.1 Conceptual metaphors of ANGER

One of the most salient conceptualizations of anger in the folk model of emotions is the metaphor of a heated and pressurized FLUID inside the body container, as exemplified in (1)-(5). When the intensity of the emotion increases, the fluid heats up and can even boil (1), the fluid rises in the emoter (2) until there is no more space and it begins to exert pressure on the walls of the container. The emoter can resist the pressure, exerting a counterpressure or containing/refraining the emotion (3) and keeping the anger inside. Otherwise, he/she can lose control over the emotion, failing to stop the anger fluid from boiling over or exploding (4–5).

(1) *De cada vez que o meu sangue começa a borbulhar de irritação por alguma malfeitoria, mentira, distorção ou golpe baixo* [. . .] (Portugal, albergueespanhol.txt)

"Every time my blood starts to boil from irritation from some malfeasance, lie, distortion or low blow [. . .]"

(2) *Senti uma raiva a crescer dentro de mim, como nunca tinha sentido por ninguém.* (Portugal, andrusca95.txt)

"I felt an anger growing inside me like I had never felt for anyone."

(3) *apesar dos flavienses, e dos restantes portugueses, estarem animados de uma fúria contida, ela não vai permanecer assim indefinidamente* (Portugal, jmadureira.txt)

"although the Flavians and the rest of the Portuguese are animated by a contained fury, it will not remain so indefinitely"

(4) *Descarreguei meus sentimentos de raiva, dor e medo que represava desde criança, devido a uma educação preconceituosa!* (Brazil, amoscaqueperturbaoteusono.txt)

"I discharged my feelings of anger, pain, and fear that I had been repressing ever since I was a child, due to a prejudiced upbringing!"

(5) *Lorena vai rumo a São Cristóvão para procurar Juliano e ao chegar se dá conta de que ele voltou para os braços de Lucrécia. Cheia de raiva, ela tenta atropelá-los.* (Brazil, novelasebiografias.txt)

"Lorraine goes to St. Cristóvão to look for Juliano and when she arrives, she realizes that he has returned to the arms of Lucrécia. Full of anger, she tries to run them over."

Anger is also conceptualized as a FIRE inside a person that can be stirred up, be ablaze, and manifest itself in flashes in the emoter's eyes, as in examples (6) and (7). Still under the same cultural metonymic model of the physiological effects of anger that can also harm the emoter and those around him/her, anger can be conceptualized as an ILLNESS to which one is not immune (8). Most prominently, it can be construed as a psychological disorder that leads to irrational and violent behavior, especially as INSANITY, often expressed as loss of mind or blindness and in the form of attacks, typically of rage, as in (9) and (10). Irrationality and violence are also elaborated by the conceptualization of anger as an AGGRESSIVE ANIMAL inside the emoter, evoking the "beast inside" (Kövecses 1990: 62), the instinctual part of our nature that is neither dominated nor domesticated and overrides the purely rational and moral one. A special case sub-metaphor leads one to be conceptualized as a dangerous animal and to manifest all sorts of aggressive animal behavior, as exemplified in (11). The ideas of control and danger that the lack of control evokes are further elaborated by a very recurrent metaphor in which anger is personified as an OPPONENT IN A STRUGGLE that must be fought or controlled, as in example (12). If control is achieved, the fight is won; otherwise, the fight results in the defeat of the emoter. Also associated with the situation of no control or being out of control is the conceptualization of anger as a powerful NATURAL PHYSICAL FORCE that floods the emoter (*ondas de fúria* "waves of fury") and leads them to violent and dangerous behavior, which can also constitute a resolution (*fúria de um vulcão* "the wrath of a volcano") so that the emoter can face and overcome other forces, as in (13)-(14). This last case is elaborated by another quite frequent metaphor highlighting the high-power emotion in which anger is conceptualized as a WEAPON that the emoter uses efficiently against a target (15).

(6) *Sua pose arrogante atiça a ira do espectador* (Brazil, cineugenio.txt)

"His arrogant pose stokes the wrath of the spectator"

(7) *Ela sorriu diabolicamente para Derek, e este atirou-se a ela com uma raiva em incandescência.* (Portugal, andrusca95.txt)

"She smiled devilishly at Derek, and he threw himself at her with glowing rage."

(8) *Seguravam-no no cargo arames apenas – institucionalmente o Presidente, aliás não imune aos protestos e à temida fúria das gentes.* (Portugal, corta-fitas.txt)

"He was held in office only by wires – institutionally the President, incidentally not immune to protest and the feared fury of the people."

(9) *Orlando aproxima-se da mesa, faz pouco de Paulo, derruba vinho nele; Capitu, louca de raiva, crava um garfo na mão dele.* (Brazil, novelasebiografias.txt)

"Orlando approaches the table, makes fun of Paulo, pours wine on him; Capitu, crazy with rage, sticks a fork in his hand."

(10) *Viu nos olhos dele uma loucura que nunca tinha visto antes. Uma raiva incontrolável. Viu nos olhos do filho uma cegueira sem retorno.* (Portugal, falarsobretudoemaisalgumacoisa.txt)

"He saw in his eyes a madness he had never seen before. An uncontrollable rage. He saw in his son's eyes a blindness with no return."

(11) *Com isto a fúria dobrou de tamanho. E o delegado escumava pela boca feito fera do mato.* (Brazil, jornaldecaruaru.txt)

"With this the anger doubled in size. And the police chief, foaming at the mouth, was like a wild beast."

(12) *Apaixona-se por Carlos Daniel, onde enfrentará a fúria de Estephanie, a rivalidade com Leda e principalmente o ódio de Paola Bracho.* (Brazil, novelasebiografias.txt)

"She falls in love with Carlos Daniel, where she will face Estephanie's fury, a rivalry with Leda and especially the hatred of Paola Bracho."

(13) *Porquê matá-los a todos? Ele simplesmente sorriu e respondeu – Porque é divertido. Uma onda de fúria inundou-me. Mandei-lhe a poção e ele desvaneceu-se.* (Portugal, andrusca95.txt)

“Why kill them all? He just smiled and answered – Because it’s fun. A wave of fury flooded me. I threw the potion at him and he fainted.”

(14) *Você tem que ter a força de um leão e a fúria de um vulcão para vencer, ou você acaba cedendo a eles.* (Brazil, amoscaqueperturbaoteusono.txt)

“You have to have the strength of a lion and the fury of a volcano to win, or you end up giving in to them.”

(15) *Os alvos de seus ataques de fúria são qualquer pessoa que se atreva a contestar suas idéias mirabolantes e criticar sua maneira estapafúrdia de governar.* (Brazil, raimari9.txt)

“The target of his rage attacks is anyone who dares to challenge his nonsensical ideas and criticize his foolish way of governing.”

Finally, anger can be conceptualized based on more generic domains, as (i) FORCE and, by entailment, ENERGY, as in (16), (ii) PHYSICAL ENTITY and, by entailment, VISIBLE/HIDDEN OBJECT (17), POSSESSION (18), MOVING/MOVED OBJECT (19) or, by specification, SOLID OBJECT and SUBSTANCE (20), (iii) as LIVING ORGANISM, especially PLANT (21) and PERSON (22), (iv) as LOCATION and, by specification, CONTAINER (23). Not emotion as such, but a salient part of emotion can be the target of a metaphorical conceptualization, as is the case with BODY as container of anger and, by specification, any of its parts either visible (eyes, face, voice, etc.), as in (10)-(11), or internal (chest, head, veins, etc.), as in (1) (2).

(16) *percorre os EUA de lés a lés, movido por um sentimento de raiva e de vingança pelo que perdeu, o amor da sua vida.* (Portugal, corta-fitas.txt)

“He travels the U.S. from coast to coast, driven by a feeling of anger and revenge for what he has lost, the love of his life.”

(17) *e, na conversa, Lula não escondeu a irritação com as acusações feitas pelo operador do mensalão.* (Brazil, landisvalth.txt)

“and, during the conversation, Lula did not hide his irritation with the accusations made by the *mensalão*’s operator.”

(18) *Como é possível perder-te sem nunca te ter achado, minha raiva de ternura, meu ódio de conhecer-te* (Portugal, portodeabrigo.txt)

"How is it possible to lose you without ever having found you, my anger of tenderness, my hate to know you"

(19) *Enquanto dirigia, continuava mudando de raiva para aceitação e de volta pra raiva de novo.* (Brazil, colunadamorenarosa.txt)

"As he drove, he kept changing from anger to acceptance and back to anger again."

(20) *O fato daquela manhã se constituíra na gota d'água que fizera extravasar neles o veneno da raiva.* (Brazil, levibronze.txt)

"That morning's fact had been the drop of water ("the straw that broke the camel's back") that had caused the poison of anger to overflow in them."

(21) *Uma das muitas inflorescências de tal fúria é a história do "certificado energético"* (Portugal, irritado.txt)

"One of the many inflorescences of such fury is the story of the 'energy certificate'"

(22) *Então, e a liberdade de expressão? E a Constituição?, pergunta o PC, prenhe de justa fúria.* (Portugal, irritado.txt)

"What about freedom of speech? And the Constitution?, asks the PC [Communist Party], full of righteous fury."

(23) *Na sua fúria apenas residia o medo da perda.* (Portugal, milrazoes.txt)

"In his fury resided only the fear of loss."

4.2 Semantic dimensions in the conceptual metaphors of ANGER

As suggested by Kövecses (2000: 40–46) and other metaphor scholars (e.g., Soriano 2005, 2013; Ogarkova and Soriano 2014), conceptual metaphors of an emotion concept tend to form meaningful clusters highlighting affective semantic dimensions or foci. These semantic dimensions are focal characteristics of emotions profiled by metaphor, they are related to well-known constructs in emotion psychology like *valence* (akin to evaluation), *arousal* (related to intensity), *power*, or *regulation* (Fontaine, Scherer, and Soriano 2013), and they are indicators of cultural and linguistic differences. Among the semantic dimensions specifically relevant for ANGER are evaluation (typically, negativity), regulation, intensity, expression, and somatization (Ogarkova and Soriano 2014). Table 3 systematizes the conceptual metaphors of ANGER presented in Table 2 (above) that profile these five semantic dimensions. As can be seen in Table 3, the same conceptual metaphor can profile different semantic foci.

Table 3: Semantic dimensions profiled by conceptual metaphors.

Semantic focus		Conceptual metaphors
Negativity (harm/damage)		ANGER IS . . .
	to self	ILLNESS, INSANITY, AGGRESSIVE ANIMAL, OPPONENT, FORCE OF NATURE, FIRE, PRESSURE
	to others	WEAPON, AGGRESSIVE ANIMAL, FORCE OF NATURE
Regulation		ANGER IS . . .
	attempted/successful	FLUID-CONTENTION/COUNTERPRESSURE/HOT/PRESSURE/RISE, OPPONENT, ANIMAL
	unattempted/failed	FLUID-COMING OUT/EXPLOSION/HOT/RISE, ILLNESS, INSANITY, ANIMAL
Intensity		ANGER IS . . . FIRE, FLUID-HOT, FLUID-EXPLOSION, INSANITY, FORCE OF NATURE, AGGRESSIVE ANIMAL
Expression		. . . IS A CONTAINER FOR ANGER / ANGER IS . . .
	perceptible	EYES, FACE, VOICE, HANDS, MOUTH / FIRE, VISIBLE/HIDDEN OBJECT
	internalized	BODY, HEART, CHEST, HEAD
Somatization		BODY IS A CONTAINER FOR ANGER, ANGER IS A PRESSURIZED FLUID, ANGER IS ILLNESS

Emotions are naturally experienced and perceived as positive or negative. Anger is typically a negative emotion because it feels unpleasant, it is caused by something negative, leads to confrontation, and causes disruption to body functions and other negative effects for one's well-being. There are, however, some positive uses of anger in our corpus, such as *raiva justa* ("just/righteous anger"). As a specification of its *negativity*, anger is also harmful and damaging. The source domains in the metaphorical conceptualization of anger are intrinsically negative and harmful to both the self and others. The metaphorical source domains profiling negativity and harm/damage to the self include the characterizations of anger in terms of a physiological and psychological disorder (ILLNESS and INSANITY), as an aggressive ANIMAL causing physical damage to the emoter, as an enemy the emoter fights against (OPPONENT), as an uncontrollable FORCE OF NATURE causing damage to the emoter, as FIRE burning the emoter, and as a physically unpleasant sensation of swelling or PRESSURE on the body-container. Negativity and harm/damage to others are profiled by the metaphorical source domains of a tool aimed at harming another person, especially a WEAPON, of an AGGRESSIVE ANIMAL, and an uncontrollable FORCE OF NATURE potentially causing harm and damage to others.

Another semantic dimension elaborated by metaphors is the self-*regulation* one may exert on one's feelings and/or their manifestation and the intrinsic controllability of the emotion. The voluntary control exerted by the emoter over the anger emotion can be both successful or at least attempted and unsuccessful or unattempted. The metaphorical source domains profiling attempted/successful regulation include the characterization of anger as a pressurized, heated fluid kept inside the body container (CONTENTION, COUNTERPRESSURE, HOT, PRESSURE, RISE), as an enemy to fight in pursuit of self-control (OPPONENT), and as a controlled ANIMAL (e.g. *bridled fury*). The metaphors focalizing unsuccessful/unattempted regulation refer to anger as a FLUID that surges out of the emoter's body (COMING OUT) or makes it out in a violent way (EXPLOSION) or even uncontrollably rises and heats (RISE, HOT). They also refer to anger being an ILLNESS, INSANITY, and an uncontrolled ANIMAL (e.g. *wild fury*), or to the emoter displaying animal behavior (EMOTER IS AN ANIMAL).

Emotional intensity tends to be associated with high physiological arousal or excitation (Soriano 2013: 405), although there are intense emotions with no physiological excitation, as is the case of depression. Metaphorically profiled *intensity* in the conceptualization of anger is represented in terms of physiological heat, as in the metaphors ANGER IS FIRE and ANGER IS A HOT FLUID, ANGER IS AN EXPLODING HEATED FLUID, and in terms of physiological or psychological strong disruption, violence, and aggression, as in the metaphors ANGER IS INSANITY, ANGER IS A FORCE OF NATURE, and ANGER IS AN AGGRESSIVE ANIMAL. These metaphors stress the image of anger as an intense emotional experience with strong effects.

Several anger metaphors profile the perceptible versus internalized *expression* or manifestation of the emotion. The metaphors in one of the poles highlight perceptible manifestations of anger, typically its visibility as VISIBLE/HIDDEN OBJECT and FIRE or located in the EYES, the FACE, and other visible body parts or audibility located in the VOICE. The metaphors in the opposite pole profile an internalized expression of anger, as located inside the emoter or in internal body parts such as inside the BODY, HEART, CHEST, or HEAD.

Finally, metaphorically profiled *somatization* in the conceptualization of anger is captured by the generic metaphor THE BODY IS A CONTAINER FOR EMOTION and by the representation of anger as a PRESSURIZED FLUID in the body container and as ILLNESS.

4.3 Frequency and productivity differences in the conceptual metaphors of ANGER

Table 4 presents the number of hits found for each target anger noun in European Portuguese (EP) and Brazilian Portuguese (BP) sub-corpora, and how many of these hits constitute literal and metaphorical expressions.

Table 4: Literal and metaphorical uses of ANGER nouns in EP and BP sub-corpora.

ANGER nouns	EP			BP		
	hits	literal	metaphorical	hits	literal	metaphorical
cólera	9	0	9	15	0	15
fúria	106	8	98	103	7	96
ira	20	3	17	28	6	22
irritação	29	13	16	23	7	16
raiva	138	25	113	139	48	91
Total	302	49	253	308	68	240
%		16.23	83.77		22.08	77.92

The two national varieties of Portuguese show a clear preference for the figurative and metaphorical use (more precisely, metonymic and metaphoric, following the general trend of emotion concepts for metaphtonymy) of the five ANGER nouns, and the literal use of these terms is a little more frequent in BP than in EP. The most frequent ANGER nouns in the two national varieties are *raiva* "anger" and *fúria* "fury" and therefore are also the most used metaphorically. The formal terms *ira* "anger/wrath" and *cólera* "anger/wrath" are more frequent in BP, with no literal use of the emotion item *cólera* in our corpus, probably to distinguish it from the use of the same term with the meaning of infectious disease cholera. The low frequency of *irritação* "irritation", which is the less intense ANGER term, is also related to the fact that this emotion meaning is used more as an adjective (*irritado*) and as a verb (*irritar(-se)*) than as a noun.

Table 5 shows the absolute frequency (AF), the relative frequency (RF), the number of different linguistic expressions (NDE) co-occurring with the anger concept that are a realization of a certain metaphor, and the productivity index (PI) of all the conceptual metaphors of ANGER as expressed by the five target nouns found in our corpus.

Table 5: Frequency and productivity of conceptual metaphors of ANGER nouns in EP and BP sub-corpora.

Conceptual metaphors ANGER IS . . .	**EP**			**BP**		
	AF (RF)	**NDE**	**PI**	**AF (RF)**	**NDE**	**PI**
PRESSURIZED FLUID	62 (24.51)	36	600.15	54 (22.50)	39	566.13
HOT	5	3	4.03	0	0	0.00
RISE	8	6	12.91	5	3	4.03
PRESSURE	24	14	90.34	7	6	11.29
COUNTERPRESSURE	1	1	0.27	0	0	0.00
CONTENTION	6	3	4.84	9	6	14.52
COMING OUT	3	2	1.61	0	0	0.00
EXPLOSION	15	7	28.23	33	24	212.90
FIRE	4 (1.58)	3	3.23	2 (0.83)	1	0.54
ILLNESS	3 (1.19)	3	2.42	1 (0.42)	1	0.27
INSANITY	19 (7.51)	12	61.31	35 (14.58)	16	150.54
AGGRESSIVE ANIMAL	6 (2.37)	3	4.84	10 (4.17)	8	21.51
OPPONENT IN A STRUGGLE	14 (5.53)	12	45.17	24 (10.00)	14	90.32
FORCE OF NATURE	2 (0.79)	1	0.54	2 (0.83)	2	1.08
WEAPON	19 (7.51)	8	40.87	12 (5.00)	8	25.81
FORCE	10 (3.96)	8	21.51	5 (2.08)	5	6.72
PHYSICAL ENTITY	29 (11.46)	19	148.15	42 (17.50)	28	316.13
VISIBLE/HIDDEN OBJECT	3	2	1.61	14	7	26.34
POSSESSION	9	4	9.68	4	3	3.23
MOVED OBJECT	0	0	0.00	1	1	0.27
MOVING OBJECT	5	5	6.72	11	9	26.61
OBJECT	3	3	2.42	0	0	0.00
FOOD	1	1	0.27	2	1	0.54
INTENSITY IS SIZE	4	2	2.15	3	3	2.42
SUBSTANCE	3	1	0.81	5	2	2.69
POISON	1	1	0.27	1	1	0.27
INTENSITY IS QUANTITY	0	0	0.00	1	1	0.27
LIVING ORGANISM	12 (4.74)	7	22.59	7 (2.92)	7	13.17
PLANT	2	1	0.54	0	0	0.00
ANIMAL	0	0	0.00	0	0	0.00
HUMAN	10	6	16.13	7	7	13.17
LOCATION	3 (1.19)	2	1.61	0 (0.00)	0	0.00
DANGER/THREAT	1 (0.40)	1	0.27	2 (0.83)	2	1.08
DEVIL	3 (1.19)	1	0.81	0 (0.00)	0	0.00
IDEA	7 (2.77)	4	7.53	5 (2.08)	4	5.38

Table 5 (continued)

Conceptual metaphors	**EP**			**BP**		
ANGER IS . . .	**AF (RF)**	**NDE**	**PI**	**AF (RF)**	**NDE**	**PI**
THE BODY IS A CONTAINER FOR ANGER	59 (23.32)	27	428.33	39 (16.25)	20	209.68
CHEST	0	0	0.00	1	1	0.27
CRY	11	3	8.87	5	3	4.03
EYES	8	2	4.30	4	2	2.15
FACE	16	7	30.11	11	6	17.74
HANDS	2	1	0.54	1	1	0.27
HEAD/MIND	1	1	0.27	2	2	1.08
MOUTH	1	1	0.27	0	0	0.00
SKIN	1	1	0.27	0	0	0.00
SMELL	0	0	0.00	1	1	0.27
VOICE	19	11	56.20	14	4	15.05
Total	253	147		240	155	

The two national varieties of Portuguese converge in some fundamental aspects of the metaphorical conceptualization and expression of anger emotion. First, ANGER is metaphorically represented by predominantly the same root and generic conceptual metaphors and their subtypes (entailments and specifications) in both EP and BP sub-corpora. Cross-linguistically, the metaphorical conceptualization of ANGER in Portuguese is similar regarding the types and subtypes of conceptual metaphors to that of other different languages indicated in Table 2 above (cf. Section 3.2). Second, similarity has also been observed in the frequency and productivity of the conceptual metaphors found in the corpus. In fact, ANGER IS A PRESSURIZED FLUID IN THE BODY CONTAINER, ANGER IS A PHYSICAL ENTITY, and THE BODY IS A CONTAINER FOR ANGER are the most frequent and productive metaphors in both varieties, the latter being more frequent and productive in EP and the second one in BP. The less frequent and productive metaphors are also practically the same in the two varieties. They are those that have FORCE OF NATURE, DANGER/THREAT, ILLNESS, and FOOD as source domains. Moreover, two metaphors less conventionally referred to in the emotion metaphor literature were found in both varieties, namely ANGER IS A DEVIL, which can be classified as a special case of ANGER IS A CONTROLLER (which, in turn, is a special case of ANGER IS AN OPPONENT) or of ANGER IS A SUPERNATURAL FORCE, and ANGER IS A POISON, a special case of ANGER IS A SUBSTANCE. Finally, the two varieties also cohere, at some point, in the internal hierarchical organization of some salient metaphors and in the frequency of the five metaphorically represented ANGER nouns (cf. Table 4) as well as their metaphorical co-occurrence patterns.

Important differences between EP and BP were also observed in the metaphorical conceptualization of anger emotion. Two groups of differences were captured via corpus-based qualitative and quantitative analysis. The first one is more direct and superficial and concerns the distribution of the different conceptual metaphors. The second one is more indirect and fundamental and will be analyzed in the following sections.

Table 5 shows clear significant differences in the internal structure of the most salient conceptual metaphors and in the frequency and productivity of some root metaphors. As for the most salient conceptual metaphor in the corpus, EP shows a more elaborate internal structure than BP (more subtypes and more competition between them in EP), and, more importantly, PRESSURE is the most frequent and productive entailment of the PRESSURIZED FLUID metaphor in EP, whereas in BP the most frequent and productive entailment is EXPLOSION, which is the third most productive metaphor in the Brazilian corpus, even more productive than the BODY CONTAINER generic metaphor. The metaphorical representation of anger as a PHYSICAL ENTITY is not only more frequent and productive in BP than in EP, but also shows the high frequency and productivity of its two most perceptible entailments in BP, namely VISIBLE OBJECT and MOVING OBJECT. The physiological and generic metaphor BODY IS A CONTAINER FOR ANGER is more frequent and productive in EP than in BP, although both varieties show the same preference for VOICE-CRY and FACE body containers. Other differences between the two varieties in the distribution of the different metaphors involve the root metaphors ANGER IS INSANITY, ANGER IS AN AGGRESSIVE ANIMAL, and ANGER IS AN OPPONENT IN A STRUGGLE, which are much more frequent in BP than in EP.

4.4 Cultural differences in the metaphorically construed regulation and expression of ANGER

Let us compare the two national varieties of Portuguese regarding the metaphorically construed semantic dimensions or foci of anger emotion as identified in Table 3 above (cf. Section 4.2). Table 6 presents the distribution of the conceptual metaphors profiling the successful/attempted versus unsuccessful/unattempted regulation and the perceptible versus internalized manifestation of ANGER across the two national varieties as well as the frequencies of these two semantic dimensions and their four corresponding clusters of metaphors in our corpus.

Some clarifications regarding the clusters of metaphors are necessary before discussing the results. First, the two clusters of metaphors highlighting regulation of ANGER include not only the corresponding subtypes of the root metaphor ANGER IS A PRESSURIZED FLUID IN THE BODY CONTAINER, as mentioned in Table 2 above and discussed in Section 4.2, but comprise also the same subtypes encapsulated in the generic metaphor THE BODY IS A CONTAINER FOR ANGER. This means that this generic, primary metaphor has the same entailments as the FLUID root metaphor, as exemplified in (24)-(25). Example (24) from EP instantiates the emoter's successful regulation of the PRESSURE exerted by anger on the walls of the eyes container, whereas in (25) from BP the emoter loses control over the emotion, resulting the COMING OUT and even the EXPLOSION of the anger fluid on the emoter's hands.

(24) *Elisabeth olhou-o com raiva e, cautelosamente, retirou também a sua espada do cinto do vestido.* (Portugal, andrusca95.txt)

"Elisabeth looked at him angrily and cautiously removed her sword from her dress belt as well."

(25) *Quando to com raiva, ou sendo forçada a fazer algo que não quero meu rosto involuntariamente começa a formigar e minhas mãos ficam com o modo "socar"* (Brazil, likecockatoos.txt)

"When I'm angry, or being forced to do something I don't want to do, my face involuntarily starts to tingle, and my hands get into 'punch' mode"

Second, the HOT and RISE metaphorical entailments can both be used in contexts of the emoter's attempted and successful regulation of anger and in contexts of emoter's loss of control. The same applies to the AGGRESSIVE ANIMAL metaphor: although this metaphor typically highlights the emoter's failed regulation of anger, as all examples found in the corpus of BP show, it can also profile the emoter's attempted regulation, as in the example (26) from EP.

(26) *Até podia dizer que tenho pena dele, mas na verdade até parece bastante feliz, e assim ele ameniza a fúria da fera.* (Portugal, andrusca95.txt)

"I could say I feel sorry for him, but he actually seems quite happy, and that way he eases the fury of the beast."

Finally, the cluster of the metaphors highlighting the perceptible expression of anger comprises both the external body parts as containers of anger (the eyes, face, hands, mouth, skin, smell, voice), as shown in Table 3 above, and the coming out and explosion of the anger-fluid.

Table 6: Distribution of conceptual metaphors profiling regulation and expression of ANGER.

Semantic focus	Conceptual metaphors	EP	BP
Regulation	ANGER IS . . . / . . . IS A CONTAINER FOR ANGER		
attempted/ successful	FLUID/BODY-CONTENTION/COUNTERPRES./ HOT/PRESSURE/RISE; OPPONENT; ANIMAL	89 (35.18)	48 (20.00)
unattempted/ failed	FLUID-COMING OUT/EXPLOSION/HOT/RISE; ILLNESS; INSANITY; ANIMAL	71 (28.06)	114 (47.50)
Expression	. . . IS A CONTAINER FOR ANGER / ANGER IS . . .		
perceptible	CRY, EYES, FACE, HANDS, MOUTH, SKIN, SMELL, VOICE / FLUID-EXPLOSION/COMING OUT, FIRE, VISIBLE OBJECT, MOVING OBJECT	88 (34.78)	93 (38.75)
internalized	BODY, HEART, CHEST, HEAD	45 (17.79)	24 (10.00)

Metaphors emphasizing the successful or at least attempted regulation of ANGER are more saliently represented in EP (35.18%) than in BP (20%). In other words, the metaphorical understanding of anger as a fluid kept inside the emoter's body, as an enemy to fight in pursuit of self-control and as a controlled animal – in general terms, as an emotion that is (or needs to be) controlled and regulated – is more closely associated with EP than with BP. Conversely, metaphors highlighting the either unsuccessful or unattempted regulation of anger are much more prominently represented in BP (47.50%) than in EP (28.06%). The metaphorical conceptualization of ANGER as a fluid that comes out of the emoter's body or causes explosion, as illness and insanity, and as uncontrolled animal, that is, the metaphorically unrestrained manifestation of anger is, therefore, more closely associated with BP than with EP. The chi-square test, presented in Table 7, shows that the relationship between successful/attempted versus unsuccessful/unattempted regulation and the European versus Brazilian variety of Portuguese is statistically significant (p = <.0001).

Table 7: Association between regulation of anger and national varieties of Portuguese.

		EP	BP
Regulation	successful/attempted	89 (35.18%)	48 (20.00)
	unsuccessful/unattempted	71 (28.06%)	114 (47.50)

$\chi^2 = 21.2$, df=1, p = <.0001, *Cramer's V* = 0.2629

These results are in line with the collectivism/individualism differences between Portuguese and Brazilian cultures, as mentioned in Section 2. The relatively more individualistic Brazilian culture is more favorable towards the unrestrained and open manifestation of the intense emotional experience of anger as an affirmation of the self. In turn, the relatively more collectivistic Portuguese culture tends to repress the overt manifestation of intense negative emotion of anger in order to avoid or diminish interpersonal hostility and to ensure social order and harmony.

Metaphors highlighting the perceptible (typically, visible, audible) manifestation of anger are relatively more prominent in BP (38.75%) than in EP (34.78%) and, conversely, metaphors profiling a more internalized expression of anger are relatively more salient in EP (17.79%) than in BP (10%). This association is stronger if we take only all metaphorical patterns profiling the body container both in the metaphor ANGER IS A PRESSURIZED FLUID and in the metaphor THE BODY IS A CONTAINER FOR ANGER, which embrace the pole of overt manifestation, i.e., out of the body (COMING OUT, EXPLOSION) and the pole of covert (inside the body) expression (CONTENTION, COUNTERPRESSURE, HOT, PRESSURE, RISE): the overt pole is strongly prominent in BP, whereas the covert pole is clearly salient in EP (cf. Table 8, Expression 2). These two correlations are statistically significant, as shown in Table 8.

Table 8: Association between expression of anger and national varieties of Portuguese.

		EP	BP
Expression 1	perceptible	88 (34.78%)	93 (38.75%)
	internalized	45 (17.79%)	24 (10.00%)
Expression 2	out of the body	43 (17.00%)	66 (27.50%)
	inside the body	78 (30.83%)	27 (11.25%)

Expression 1: $\chi^2 = 4.88$, df=1, $p = 0.0272$, *Cramer's V* = 0.1487

Expression 2: $\chi^2 = 25.01$, df=1, $p = <.0001$, *Cramer's V* = 0.3513

Again, these results are consistent with the collectivism/individualism cultural differences between Portugal and Brazil. The relatively more collectivistic culture of Portugal represses the open expression of anger, as we have seen above, and coherently emphasizes anger as located inside the body container and the anger expressions related to containment, whereas the more individualistic culture of Brazil highlights the unrestrained and open manifestation of anger, especially the release of emotional fluid of the body containment.

4.5 Cultural differences in the metaphorically construed intensity and somatization of ANGER

Table 9 shows the distribution of the conceptual metaphors profiling the intensity and the somatic component of ANGER across the two national varieties as well as the frequencies of the two corresponding clusters of metaphors in our corpus.

Table 9: Distribution of conceptual metaphors profiling intensity and somatization of ANGER.

Semantic focus	Conceptual metaphors	EP	BP
Intensity	ANGER IS . . .		
	AGGRESSIVE ANIMAL, BODY-CRY, FIRE, FLUID-EXPLOSION, FLUID-HOT, FORCE OF NATURE, INSANITY	62 (24.51)	92 (38.33)
Somatization	ANGER IS . . . / . . . IS A CONTAINER FOR ANGER		
	A PRESSURIZED FLUID, ILLNESS, INSANITY-SOMATIC; BODY IS A CONTAINER	134 (52.96)	103 (42.92)

The BP variety appears to be more akin to metaphorically construed high intensity of anger (38.33%) than the EP variety (24.51%). This is consistent with the relatively more individualistic culture of Brazil as well as with other individualistic influences on anger emotional experience, such as the Brazilian preference for the unrestrained and open manifestation of anger, as seen above.

As for the somatization of anger, i.e., the physiological (rather than psychological) manifestation of the emotion, EP seems closer to the metaphorically profiling of the somatic component of anger (52.96%) than the BP variety (42.92%). It is important to note that the somatization of anger is also profiled by the metaphor ANGER IS INSANITY whenever it is expressed in somatic terms. Out of the 19 occurrences of the INSANITY metaphor found in the EP sub-corpus, 10 were used with somatic expressions, whereas only 9 somatically expressed examples out of 35 INSANITY metaphorical patterns were found in the BP sub-corpus. This EP preference for the somatic, physiological conceptualization of anger is coherent with the relatively more collectivistic culture of Portugal as well as with other collectivistic influences on anger experience, such as the Portuguese particular emphasis on the conscious control of the intense negative anger emotion and on its less expressive/outward manifestation.

The results from the chi-square test, presented in Table 10, confirm statistically the associations between BP and anger intensity and between EP and anger somatization.

Table 10: Association between intensity/somatization of anger and EP/BP varieties.

		EP	BP
Intensity	profiled intensity	62 (24.51%)	92 (38.33%)
	not profiled intensity	191 (75.49%)	148 (61.67%)
Somatization	profiled somatization	134 (52.96%)	103 (42.92%)
	not profiled somatization	119 (47.04%)	137 (57.08%)

Intensity $\chi^2 = 10.33$, df=1, $p = 0.0013$, *Cramer's V* = 0.1491
Somatization $\chi^2 = 4.59$, df=1, $p = 0.0322$, *Cramer's V* = 0.1005

Finally, the negativity (harm/damage) mentioned in Table 3 (see Section 4.2) as a culturally marked semantic dimension of anger shows a similar distribution across the two national varieties in our corpus, therefore, being not relevant to differentiate EP and BP, as shown in Table 11 and statistically in Table 12. This means that the expectation that metaphors emphasizing the negativity of anger would be more saliently represented in the relatively more collectivistic culture of Portugal is not confirmed.

Table 11: Distribution of conceptual metaphors profiling negativity of anger.

Semantic focus	Conceptual metaphors	EP	BP
Negativity (harm/damage)	ANGER IS . . .		
to self	AGGRESSIVE ANIMAL, FIRE, FORCE OF NATURE, FLUID-PRESSURE, ILLNESS, INSANITY, OPPONENT	68 (26.88)	66 (27.50)
to others	AGGRESSIVE ANIMAL, DANGER/THREAT, DEVIL, FORCE OF NATURE, POISON, WEAPON	28 (11.07)	26 (10.83)

Table 12: Association between negativity of anger and EP/BP varieties.

		EP	BP
Negativity (harm/damage)	N	96 (37.94%)	92 (38.33%)
	N_{total} -N	157 (62.06%)	148 (61.67%)

$\chi^2 = 0$, df=1, $p = 1$, *Cramer's V* = 0.0045

5 Conclusions

The present article has developed a corpus-based and profile-based analysis of the intralinguistic variation in the metaphorical conceptualization of ANGER in the two main national varieties of Portuguese. Developing a meticulous qualitative and quantitative analysis of 610 examples of anger emotion as lexicalized in the nouns *raiva* "anger", *fúria* "fury", *ira* "anger/wrath", *cólera* "anger/wrath", and *irritação* "irritation" from a corpus of personal-experiential blogs, the study has established the conceptual and cultural metaphorical *profiles* or sets of alternative metaphorical patterns for ANGER in EP and BP national varieties. The usage profiles emerged from clusters of specific imagery rich in entailments/specifications and more generic source domains mapping the emotion of anger and highlighting semantic dimensions of anger that are sensitive to cultural variation. These clusters of conceptual metaphors are consistent with insights from cross-cultural psychological research (e.g., Fontaine, Scherer, and Soriano 2013) as well as with the findings of prior linguistic studies on the sociocultural nature and on the cultural metaphorical conceptualization of the anger emotion (e.g., Geeraerts and Grondelaers 1995; Glynn 2014; and, particularly, Ogarkova and Soriano 2014 and Ogarkova, Soriano, and Gladkova 2016, whose typology of conceptual metaphors of anger was adopted here).

The qualitative and quantitative corpus-based analyses have shown both the strong similarities as well as the subtle but relevant differences in the metaphorical conceptualization of the emotion of anger in EP and BP. The two national varieties have the same metaphorical conceptual structuring of the emotion of anger, predominantly the same salient (frequent and productive) conceptual metaphors of anger, and the same internal hierarchical metaphorical organization. However, there are some conceptual differences, and these differences are influenced by culture. The differences in metaphorically conceptualizing anger in EP and BP varieties are intrinsically related to cultural collectivism versus individualism differences between Portuguese and Brazilian societies, especially the relatively more collectivistic and restrictive culture of Portugal and the relatively more individualistic and indulgent culture of Brazil.

The EP variety appears to be more associated with the metaphorically construed successful or at least attempted regulation of anger, particularly the metaphorical understanding of anger as a fluid that has to be kept inside the body, an enemy to fight in pursuit of self-control, or a controlled animal, i.e., as an emotion that has to be controlled and regulated. Furthermore, the EP variety appears to be more associated with a metaphorically more internalized expression of anger. These associations are in line with the more collectivistic and restrained culture of Portugal, which tends to regulate the socially disruptive emotion of anger and to repress the overt manifestation of this negative emotion in order to avoid or diminish interpersonal hostility and to ensure social order and harmony. In contrast, the BP variety is more connected with the metaphorically unattempted or failed regulation of anger, as a fluid that comes out of the body or causes explosion, as illness and insanity, or as an uncontrolled animal. It is also more connected with the externally perceptible, unrestrained, and open manifestation of anger as an affirmation of the self. This correlation is in line with the more individualistic, indulgent, and emotionally expressive culture of Brazil.

Accordingly, the BP variety appears to be more akin to the metaphorically construed high intensity of anger, which is consistent with the relatively more individualistic culture of Brazil. In turn, the somatization of anger is more fitting in EP, which is coherent with the relatively more collectivistic culture of Portugal as well as with other collectivistic influences on anger experience, such as its regulation and inward expression. However, the expectation that metaphors emphasizing the negativity of anger and its damage/disruption to the self and others would be more saliently represented in the more collectivistic culture of Portugal was not confirmed.

These results about the cultural variation in the metaphorical representation of anger nouns (*raiva, fúria, cólera, ira,* and *irritação*) in the EP and BP varieties provide empirical evidence about important theoretical principles and methodological orientations in the linguistic, psychological, and anthropological research of emotions. Theoretically, this study confirms the hypothesis that emotions, despite being grounded in bodily physiological experiences, are conditioned by culture, i.e., emotions have a biological basis, but are socially and culturally constructed. Most studies exploring the role of culture in the conceptualization of emotions have emphasized the comparison between different languages. This study highlights the role of culture in the conceptualization of emotions within the same language and in its pluricentric internal variation, in which the differences in cultural conceptualization are more subtle. Importantly, emotion concepts are not universal or physiologically grounded but are culturally specific, and this is true not only at a cross-linguistic level but also at an intralinguistic level. Thus, the exploration of the social and cultural nature of emotions must consider language-internal variation and sociolinguistic diversity. A second theoretical conclusion from this study about ANGER metaphors is the importance of understanding metaphor as not just a creative thought-structuring device, but also as socially and culturally situated, which implies a fully contextualized and variational perspective. Methodologically, the corpus-based and onomasiological profile-based approach to metaphor and emotions offers more realistic and falsifiable hypotheses and results for identifying, classifying, and interpreting conceptual metaphors and may adequately unravel the complex conceptual-cultural structure of emotion concepts.

References

Almeida, Alberto Carlos. 2007. *A cabeça do brasileiro*. São Paulo: Record.

Bender, Andrea, Hans Spada, Annelie Rothe-Wulf, Simone Traber & Karsten Rauss. 2012. Anger elicitation in Tonga and Germany: The impact of culture on cognitive determinants of emotions. *Frontiers in Psychology: Cultural Psychology* 5. 1–20.

Chon, Kyum Koo, Ki-Hong Kim & J. B. Ryoo. 2000. Experience and expression of anger in Korea and America. *Korean Journal of Rehabilitation Psychology* 7 (1). 61–75.

Divjak, Dagmar. 2010. *Structuring the lexicon: A clustered model for near-synonymy*. Berlin & New York: Mouton de Gruyter.

Ekman, Paul. 1992. An argument for basic emotions. *Cognition & Emotion* 6. 169–200.

Ekman, Paul. 1999. Basic emotions. In Tim Dalgleish & Mick Power (eds.), *A handbook of cognition and emotion*, 45–60. Sussex: John Wiley & Sons.

Fernández, Itziar, Pilar Carrera, Flor Sánchez, Darío Páez & Luis Candia. 2000. Differences between cultures in emotional verbal and non-verbal reactions. *Psicothema*, suppl. 12. 83–92.

Fischer, Agneta, Antony S. R. Manstead & Patricia M. Rodriguez Mosquera. 1999. The role of honour-related vs. individualistic vales in conceptualizing pride, shame, and anger: Spanish and Dutch cultural prototypes. *Cognition & Emotion* 13 (2). 149–179.

Fontaine, Johnny J. R., Klaus R. Scherer & Cristina Soriano (eds.). 2013. *Components of emotional meaning. A sourcebook*. Oxford: Oxford University Press.

Freyre, Gilberto. 1933. *Casa-Grande & Senzala*. Rio de Janeiro: Editora Record.

Geeraerts, Dirk, Stef Grondelaers & Peter Bakema. 1994. *The structure of lexical variation. Meaning, naming, and context*. Berlin & New York: Mouton de Gruyter.

Geeraerts, Dirk & Stefan Grondelaers. 1995. Looking back at anger: Cultural traditions and metaphorical patterns. In John Taylor & Robert E. MacLaury (eds.), *Language and the construal of the world*, 153–180. Berlin & New York: Mouton de Gruyter.

Gevaert, Caroline. 2005. The anger is heat question: Detecting cultural influence on the conceptualisation of anger through diachronic corpus analysis. In Nicole Delbecque, Johan van der Auwera & Dirk Geeraerts (eds.), *Perspectives on variation. Sociolinguistic, historical, comparative*, 195–208. Berlin & New York: Mouton de Gruyter.

Glynn, Dylan. 2014. The social nature of ANGER. Multivariate corpus evidence for context effects upon conceptual structure. In Peter Blumenthal, Iva Novakova & Dirk Siepmann (eds.), *Les émotions dans le discours. Emotions in discourse*, 69–82. Frankfurt: Peter Lang.

Glynn, Dylan & Kerstin Fischer (eds.). 2010. *Quantitative methods in cognitive semantics: Corpus-driven approaches*. Berlin & New York: Mouton de Gruyter.

Goossens, Louis. 1990. Metaphtonymy. The interaction of metaphor and metonymy in expressions for linguistic action. *Cognitive Linguistics* 1 (3). 323–340.

Gries, Stephan T. 2003. *Multifactorial analysis in corpus linguistics: A study of particle placement*. London: Continuum Press.

Gries, Stephan T. 2010. Behavioral profiles. A fine-grained and quantitative approach in corpus-based lexical semantics. *The Mental Lexicon* 5. 323–346.

Hofstede, Geert. 1980. *Culture's consequences: International differences in work-related values*. Beverly Hills, CA: Sage.

Hofstede, Geert. 2001. *Culture's consequences: Comparing values, behaviors, institutions, and organizations across nations*. Thousand Oaks, CA: Sage.

Hollanda, Sérgio Buarque de. 1936. *Raízes do Brasil*. Rio de Janeiro: Editora José Olympio.
Kövecses, Zoltán. 1986. *Metaphors of anger, pride, and love. A lexical approach to the structure of concepts*. Amsterdam & Philadelphia: John Benjamins.
Kövecses, Zoltán. 1990. *Emotion concepts*. Berlin & New York: Springer.
Kövecses, Zoltán. 2000. *Metaphor and emotion*. New York & Cambridge: Cambridge University Press.
Kövecses, Zoltán. 2010. *Metaphor. A practical introduction*. Second edition. New York & Oxford: Oxford University Press.
Lakoff, George & Mark Johnson. 1980. *Metaphors we live by*. Chicago: The University of Chicago Press.
Lakoff, George & Zoltán Kövecses. 1987. The cognitive model of anger inherent in American English. In Dorothy Holland & Noam Quinn (eds.), *Cultural models in language and thought*, 195–221. Cambridge: Cambridge University Press.
Markus, Hazel R. & Shinobu Kitayama. 1991. Culture and the self: Implications for cognition, emotion and motivation. *Psychological Review* 98. 224–253.
Matsumoto, David, Seung Hee Yoo & Joanne Chung. 2010. The expression of anger across cultures. In Michael Potegal, Gerhard Stemmler & Charles Spielberger (eds.), *International handbook of anger: Constituent and concomitant biological, psychological, and social processes*, 125–138. New York: Springer.
Mendes de Oliveira, Milene. 2020. *Business negotiations in ELF from a cultural linguistic perspective*. Berlin & Boston: Mouton de Gruyter.
Mesquita, Batja, Nico H. Frijda & Klaus R. Scherer. 1997. Culture and emotion. In John W. Berry, Pierre R. Dasen & T. S. Saraswathi (eds.), *Handbook of cross-cultural psychology. Volume 2: Basic processes and human development*, 255–297. Needham Heights, MA: Allyn & Bacon.
Mortillaro, Marcello, Pio E. Ricci-Bitti, Guglielmo Bellelli & Dario Galati. 2013. Pride is not created equal: Variations between Northern and Southern Italy. In Johnny J. R. Fontaine, Klaus R. Scherer & Cristina Soriano (eds.), *Components of emotional meaning. A sourcebook*, 366–376. Oxford: Oxford University Press.
Ogarkova, Anna & Cristina Soriano. 2014. Variation within universals: The 'metaphorical profile' approach and ANGER concepts in English, Russian and Spanish. In Andreas Musolff, Fiona MacArthur & Giulio Pagani (eds.), *Metaphor in intercultural communication*, 93–116. London: Continuum.
Ogarkova, Anna, Cristina Soriano & Anna Gladkova. 2016. Methodological triangulation in the study of emotion. The case of 'anger' in three language groups. *Review of Cognitive Linguistics* 14 (1). 73–101.
Ortony, Andrew & Terence Turner. 1990. What's basic about basic emotions? *Psychological Review* 97. 315–331.
Oster, Ulrike. 2010. Using corpus methodology for semantic and pragmatic analyses: What can corpora tell us about the linguistic expression of emotions? *Cognitive Linguistics* 21 (4). 727–763.
Real, Miguel. 2017. *Traços fundamentais da cultura portuguesa*. Lisboa: Planeta.
Rezende, Claudia Barcellos & Maria Cláudia Coelho. 2010. *Antropologia das emoções*. Rio de Janeiro: Editora Fundação Getúlio Vargas.
Russel, James A. 1991. Culture and the categorization of emotions. *Psychological Bulletin* 110. 426–450.

Schröder, Ulrike. 2009. Preferential metaphorical conceptualizations in everyday discourse about love in the Brazilian and German speech communities. *Metaphor and Symbol* 24. 105–120.
Schröder, Ulrike. 2010. Speech styles and functions of speech from a cross-cultural perspective. *Journal of Pragmatics* 42 (2). 466–476.
Semino, Elena. 2008. *Metaphor in discourse*. Cambridge: Cambridge University Press.
Soares da Silva, Augusto (ed.). 2014. *Pluricentricity. Language variation and sociocognitive dimensions*. Berlin & New York: Mouton de Gruyter.
Soares da Silva, Augusto. 2020. Exploring the cultural conceptualization of emotions across national language varieties: A multifactorial profile-based account of PRIDE in European and Brazilian Portuguese. *Review of Cognitive Linguistics* 18 (1). 42–74.
Soriano, Cristina. 2005. *The conceptualization of anger in English and Spanish: A cognitive approach*. Doctoral dissertation. University of Murcia, Murcia, Spain.
Soriano, Cristina. 2013. Conceptual metaphor theory and the GRID paradigm in the study of anger in English and Spanish. In Johnny J. R. Fontaine, Klaus R. Scherer & Cristina Soriano (eds.), *Components of emotional meaning. A sourcebook*, 410–424. Oxford: Oxford University Press.
Steen, Gerard J. 2011. The contemporary theory of metaphor – Now new and improved! *Review of Cognitive Linguistics* 9 (1). 26–64.
Stefanowitsch, Anatol. 2006. Corpus-based approaches to metaphor and metonymy. In Anatol Stefanowitsch & Stephan T. Gries (eds.), *Corpus-based approaches to metaphor and metonymy*, 1–16. Berlin & New York: Mouton de Gruyter.
Stefanowitsch, Anatol & Stefan T. Gries. 2006. *Corpus-based approaches to metaphor and metonymy*. Berlin & New York: Mouton de Gruyter.
Wierzbicka, Anna. 1999. *Emotions across languages and cultures: Diversity and universals*. Cambridge: Cambridge University Press.
Yu, Ning. 1995. Metaphorical expressions of anger and happiness in English and Chinese. *Metaphor and Symbolic Activity* 10 (2). 59–92.

Maíra Avelar, Lilian Ferrari, Vera Pacheco

Prototypical and metaphorical uses for locative deixis in Brazilian Portuguese and American English: a verbo-gestural data analysis

Abstract: This paper aims at investigating how deictic expressions can be analyzed cross-culturally by taking two unrelated languages into account: Brazilian Portuguese and American English. We focus on which prevalent manual gestures can be associated to locative deictic referents in Brazilian Portuguese and American English. We base our theoretical remarks on propositions made in cognitive linguistics, articulating classic concepts, such as Idealized Cognitive Models – ICM, and more recent formulations, such as the Metaphoricity Principle. In our methodological procedures, the parameters of the Linguistic Annotation System for Gestures (LASG) are described, regarding both gestural forms and functions. For the comparative analysis, 40 videos were selected, retrieved from American and Brazilian TV news and late-night talk shows, stored at the Distributed Little Red Hen Lab. More specifically, we describe how manual gestures operate along with speech to point to referents both present in the immediate interactional scene and projected in a non-immediate scene narrated by the speaker. Results showed that verbo-gestural deictic compounds can be organized as radial categories with prototypical central members, which include referential uses, and peripheral ones, which include pragmatic and discursive uses directly correlated to the degree of metaphoricity activation of each member. In sum, the comparison between Brazilian Portuguese and American English datasets indicates cognitive resemblance between both languages, even though some cultural differences on the performance of correlated gestural forms could be identified.

Keywords: Deixis, idealized cognitive models, metaphoricity. gesture studies

Maíra Avelar, Vera Pacheco, Universidade Estadual do Sudoeste da Bahia
Lilian Ferrari, Universidade Federal do Rio de Janeiro

https://doi.org/10.1515/9783110688306-009

1 Introduction

The influence that language and culture exert on each other is one of the main areas of debate in linguistic studies. The idea of "linguistic universals" in the Chomskyan tradition clearly treats these two dimensions as distinct categories. On the other hand, functionalist paradigms have always taken cultural issues into account, in one way or another. In particular, cognitive linguistics has witnessed an increasing interest in the relationship between language and culture. It acknowledges the assumption that language that has developed within a community is intimately related to that community's culture (Janda 2007).

One important area that reflects the embedding of cultural concepts in language is the use of deictic expressions. Traditionally, deictic elements have been classified in terms of separated and seemingly unrelated categories, such as person (e.g., *I*, *you*, etc.), time (e.g., *today*, *now*, etc.), place (e.g., *here*, *there*, etc.), discourse (e.g., *in the next paragraph*, etc.), and social parameters such as the distinction between formal and informal terms of address (Levinson 1983: 68–94). However, experiential and cognitive approaches to deixis have shown that some generalizations are missed out if only reference to the speech event is taken into account. As Marmaridou (2000) puts it, deictic categories are prototypical structures (Rosch 1973, 1978) that are organized by reference to culturally motivated knowledge structures related to speech events (Lakoff 1987). For example, while reference to the hearer is expressed by "you" in English, French speakers have to choose between two forms – "tu" and "vous" – according to cultural values related to social distance/proximity.

In line with experiential and cognitive approaches, this paper aims at investigating how deictic expressions can be analyzed cross-culturally by taking two unrelated languages into account: Brazilian Portuguese and American English. Our main research question focuses on which prevalent manual gestures can be associated with locative deictic referents in Brazilian Portuguese and American English. More specifically, we describe how manual gestures operate along with speech, to point out to referents both present in the immediate interactional scene and projected in a non-immediate scene narrated by the speaker. We also aim at investigating how locative deictic uses can be interrelated in terms of prototypicality and metaphoricity in both languages by using verbo-gestural data.

We based our theoretical remarks and our methodological procedures on propositions made in cognitive linguistics, articulating classic concepts, such as Idealized Cognitive Model – ICM (Lakoff 1987), and more recent formulations, such as the Metaphoricity Principle (Müller 2008).

The paper is organized as follows: in the second section, we present the inter-relation between metaphoricity, prototypicality, and deixis from a cognitive-linguistic view. In the third section, we describe the methodology, presenting firstly our research question and hypotheses, as well as our data sample regarding both languages. After that, the parameters of the Linguistic Annotation System for Gestures (LASG) are described, regarding both gestural forms and functions. For the comparative analysis of the verbo-gestural locative deictic compounds, which is presented in section 4, we selected 40 videos retrieved from American and Brazilian TV news and late-night talk shows, stored at the *Distributed Little Red Hen Lab*, co-directed by Francis Steen and Mark Turner.

Results from our data-driven illustrations showed that verbo-gestural deictic compounds can be organized as radial categories with prototypical central members and peripheral ones, which include pragmatic and discursive uses directly correlated to the degree of metaphoricity activation of each member. The comparison between Brazilian Portuguese and American English datasets indicates cognitive resemblance between both languages, even though the deictic spatial relations are linguistically established in different ways.

2 On metaphoricity, prototypicality, and deixis: some remarks from cognitive linguistics

Based on a systematic and discursive view of metaphors, Müller (2008) proposes that metaphors should be analyzed when used. In that sense, metaphoricity can be activated in online interactive processes, functioning as a powerful multimodal resource to construct meaningful utterances, allowing the speakers to establish mutual understanding through the process of creating, elaborating, and establishing metaphoric meaning. According to Müller (2008), verbo-gestural metaphors are in general outcomes of an underlying metaphoric conceptualization. The study of gesture in discursive and interactive sequences also demonstrates the dynamic nature of metaphoricity, as gestures can work as a foregrounding mechanism that directs the interlocutor's attention to some portions of the speech. At the same time, metaphoricity is, in principle, modality-independent, as it can be expressed not only through speech-gesture integration, but also monomodally, i.e., exclusively by gesture or exclusively by verbal means.

Considering Müller's (2008) proposition on metaphoricity as a general cognitive principle, Cienki (2008) proposes three parameters when identifying and analyzing conceptual metaphors and metaphorical expressions in use: (i) the degree of conventionality of a conceptual metaphor in a given culture (from conventional to novel); (ii) the degree of conventionality of a metaphorical expression in a given culture (from conventional to novel), and (iii) the degree to which a metaphorical expression is highlighted in a given instance of use (making it cognitively more salient). Considering that the parameters of identification and analysis of conceptual metaphors and metaphorical expressions are gradient, the potential for activation of metaphoricity is scalar. In that way, "the underlying conceptual metaphors can be more or less frozen or defrosted, or more or less asleep or awake (depending on the metaphor one wants to use for metaphoricity itself)" (Cienki 2008: 10).[1]

Also considering a gradient level of categorization, and in line with philosophical and psychological models of categorization based on family resemblances (Wittgeinstein 1958) and prototypes (Rosch 1973, 1978), Lakoff (1987) proposes that gradience arises from the degree to which cognitive structures that represent knowledge organization (ICMs) fit our assumptions about the world ('perfectly', 'very well', 'somewhat well', 'badly', etc.). According to the author (1987: 379), "the center, or prototype, of the category is predictable. And while the noncentral members are not predictable from the central member, they are 'motivated' by it, in the sense that they bear family resemblances to it". Based on Lewandowska-Tomaszczyk (2007), the main properties of radial category structures in the sense of Lakoff can be summed up as follows: (i) subcategories can be seen as bearing family resemblance to one another; (ii) the noncentral subcategories are motivated by the central member, but the correlation among them is neither predictable nor arbitrary; (iii) structuring principles (i.e., propositional, metaphorical, metonymic, and image-schematic) need to be considered as links, or even as cognitive motivations, between the central and noncentral category members.

As for deictic structure, Marmaridou (2000) specifically proposes that the ICM of Deixis involves the linguistic act of pointing to an entity, performed by an authorized speaker (the deictic center), and directed to an unfocused addressee. In multimodal contexts, deictic expressions are usually associated with pointing gestures, since these are the 'non-linguistic actions' that build up a referential inter-relation between the utterance and its spatial-temporal circumstances of occurrence (Avelar and Ferrari 2017). Specifically regarding the act of pointing, Kendon (2004: 200) states that "[p]ointing gestures are regarded as indicating an object, a location or a direction, which is discovered by projecting a straight line from the farthest point of the body part that has been extended outward, into the space that extends beyond the speaker". As remarked by Ferrari (2014), if a

1 *Frozen* or *asleep* are both terms used in literature to indicate a low potential for activation of metaphoricity; inversely, the terms *defrosted* or *asleep* indicate a high level of activation of metaphoricity.

particular linguistic item fits this ICM perfectly well, it is a prototypical member of the deictic category. To illustrate prototypical deictic meanings, the author proposes the following illustration (Ferrari 2014: 105):

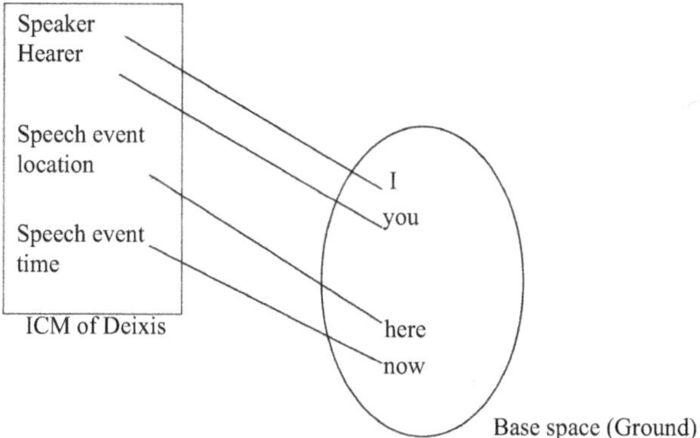

Figure 1: Prototypical deictic meanings.
Source: Ferrari (2004: 105)

As Figure 1 shows, the Idealized Cognitive Model of Deixis includes the main elements of the speech event: speaker, hearer, location, and time. These roles are normally mapped onto prototypical uses of *I*, *you*, *here*, and *now*, respectively. So, if someone arrives at someone else's home and says "I am here now", the utterance aligns with the ICM of Deixis, since "I" refers to the current speaker, "here" refers to the addressee's home, and "now" refers to the moment in which the utterance is produced. However, if the speaker is on a bank line and says to someone next to her "You must have patience to wait in line", the use of "you" differs more from the ICM of Deixis, since it doesn't only refer to the addressee, but also includes the speaker and other people who are in line. Moreover, metaphorical uses conserve traces of the prototypical locative, related to SPACE (the source-domain), but are used to demarcate abstract ideas, objects, or entities, and can also perform discursive and pragmatic functions. In this sense, metaphorical uses can be considered even more peripheral to the ICM of Deixis.

As mentioned above, cognitive processes are taken to reflect embodied cognition, as argued by Lakoff (1987, 1990) and Johnson (1999, 2007). For instance, it is thus the architecture of our visual system that determines our categorization of colors as focal (e.g., red, blue, etc.) and non-focal (e.g., reddish, light blue, etc.). It is also our bodily experience in space that allows us to conceptualize abstract concepts, such as time, as movement in space, for example. Therefore, cognitive processes such as prototypical categorization and metaphorical mappings demonstrate the fact that our body not only experiences the world around us, but also structures our cognition.

In the following section, we present our research question and hypotheses, which address prototypicality, metaphoricity, and locative deictics, which proved to be important in the analysis of Brazilian Portuguese and contrast Brazilian Portuguese and American English multimodal data.

3 Methodology

3.1 Research question and hypotheses

For structuring spatial relations, Brazilian Portuguese has four basic deictic forms acknowledged by speakers – "aqui" (nearer the speaker), "aí" (nearer the addressee), "ali" (near both the speaker and the addressee), and "lá" (distal to both the speaker and the addressee) –, whereas American English (as well as other varieties of the English language) has a two-way distinction, linguistically expressed by "here" (near the speaker) and "there" (either distal to both the speaker and the hearer or distal to the speaker but near the addressee)[2].

As previous studies based on Brazilian Portuguese data have shown (Avelar and Pinheiro 2017; Avelar and Pinheiro, in press), spatial deictics have prototypical uses as locatives and less prototypical uses that function as metaphorical extensions of the central meaning. Prototypical uses can be illustrated below:

Ele teve uma audiência **aqui** no Fórum Criminal *[He had a hearing **here** at the Criminal Court]*

Closed-hand Extended Thumb (THUMB)

Figure 2: Prototypical deictic use.
Source: Jornal da Record

2 It should be noted that there is no direct correspondence between Brazilian Portuguese locative deictics and English ones. In fact, while "aqui" is usually translatable by "here", "aí", "ali" and "lá" are translatable by "there", depending on the context.

As can be noticed in the example (Figure 2), the reporter points to a specific place, the Criminal Court, right behind her, as can be visualized on the building's name sign, "Fórum Criminal" (Criminal Court). As stated by Kendon (2004: 208), pointing with the thumb, called 'thumb gesture', is used when the speaker locates an object behind him/her. In less prototypical uses, Brazilian Portuguese multimodal data shows that intermediate deictic uses, which lie between prototypical locative uses and clearly metaphorical ones, may function as discursive markers due to the conceptualization of discourse as a form of motion through space (Avelar and Ferrari 2017). These intermediate uses can be illustrated in the following example (Avelar and Ferrari 2017: 84):

É lá na família que o ser humano aprende respeito. [*It's there in the family that the human being learns respect*]

Palm-down Bended Index Finger (Pointing down)

Figure 3: Pointing-down gesture performed with "there".
Source: Retrieved from Avelar and Ferrari (2017: 84)

As discussed by the authors (2017), although this sample could be considered contradictory at first glance, as the gesture spatially indicates "here" (index finger pointing to the ground, near the speaker) and the speech explicitly uses "there", this contradiction is only apparent; the gesture performs a metaphoric discursive function of emphasis. Given that discourse is conceptualized as motion through space, the discourse topic ("family") is metaphorically represented as the actual location along this ongoing movement.

In order to investigate if these correlations between speech and gesture can also be found in other samples of verbo-gestural locative deictic compounds, as well as in cross-linguistic data analysis, our research question is:

Which prevalent manual gestures accompany locative deictic referents in both Brazilian Portuguese and English?

Given the assumption that cognition is embodied (Johnson 1987) and that gesture depictions can embody lexical and grammatical categories (Janda 2007), this research question leads to the following hypotheses:

1. Pointing gestures are the most frequent gestures that go along with the uttered locative deictic in both languages.
2. The referential function (in gestures) is the most common one.[3]
3. The nearer the verbo-gestural locative is to the deictic center, the less metaphoricity can be activated in the investigated online interactions, and vice versa.

According to Kendon's (2004) definition of gesture as "a movement of visible effort", it is commonly hand gestures which are focused in gestural analysis. In that sense, our two hypotheses are linked to this type of gestures and, more specifically, to the forms and functions of each gesture stroke, i.e., the obligatory phase of the gestural excursion, in which it is possible to identify the gestural iconic expression.

To test our hypotheses, we collected 40 videos (ten examples of each deictic gesture) from Brazilian Portuguese TV News as well as 20 videos (ten examples of each deictic gesture) from American TV News. Both samples were collected from *The Distributed Little Red Hen Lab* (Turner and Steen 2019), a multimodal library composed of thousands of video-recorded TV News, talk shows and TV advertising data from all over the world. All our data was, therefore, recorded in non-controlled environments, since we did not manipulate the recording environment, and an *a posteriori* analysis was made, without the subject's knowledge.

To perform the gestural form and function analysis, we followed the annotation procedures proposed by the system: at first, in order not to be biased by the speech content, the sound of the video was turned off and the gesture stroke form was described; next, the sound was turned on, and, after the orthographic transcription, gesture modes of representation were categorized. Finally, gestures were analyzed along with the linguistic context they co-occurred with, and the gestural functions were identified. In the next section, these procedures will be presented.

3.2 The linguistic annotation system for gestures: gestural forms and functions

Bressem and collaborators (2013) propose a Linguistic Annotation System for Gestures (LASG) that allows the description and detection of a grammar of gestures, since the system proposes to describe the relation between gesture forms and functions. Furthermore, gestures can be analyzed from the perspective of multi-

3 Referential gestures depict concrete objects or abstract entities, ideas, relations, or actions. They will be illustrated in section 3.2.

modal grammar, as the system also allows the simultaneous description of gestures and speech. To narrow down the parameters of form, the authors base their proposition on four form parameters established for describing sign languages:

(1) Handshape, such as: open or closed hand, extended or bent index finger:

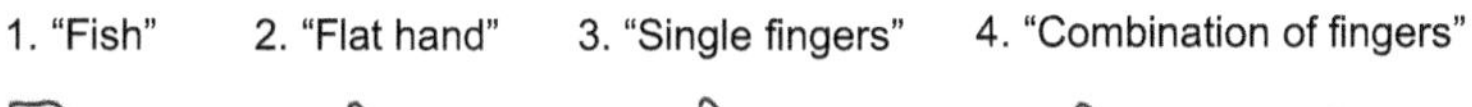

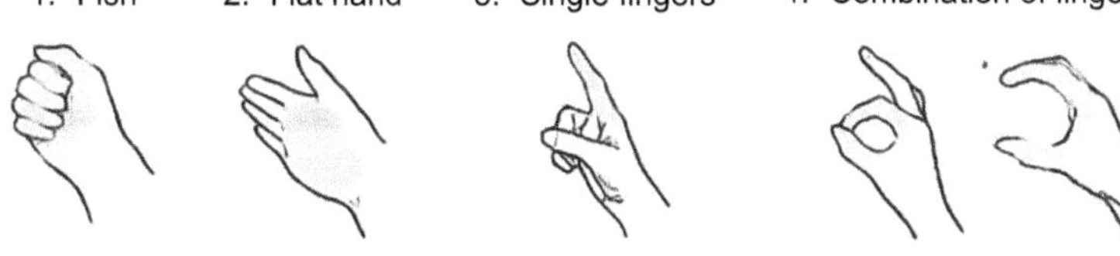

Figure 4: Hand orientation general parameters.[4]
Source: Bressem et al. (2013: 1087)

(2) Palm-orientation, such as pronated, supinated, horizontal, vertical, or diagonal;

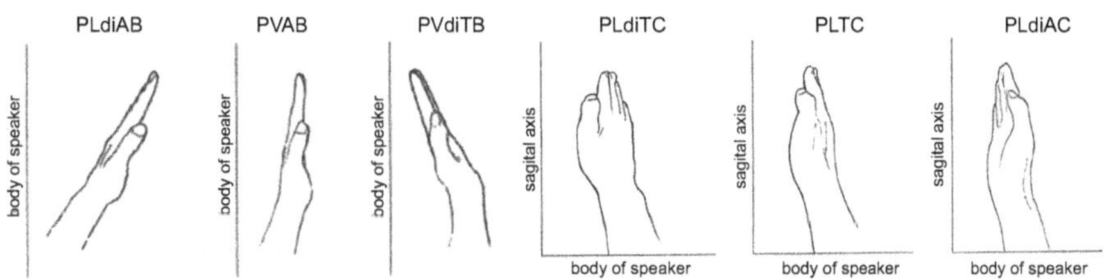

Figure 5: Palm-orientation general parameters.
PL: palm-lateral; di: diagonal; PV: palm-vertical; TC: towards the center AC: away from the center; AB: away from the body; TB: towards the body
Source: Bressem et al. (2013: 1087)

4 The permission to use the images was granted by the editors.

(3) Movement, such as up, down, to the right, to the left, towards and away from the body;

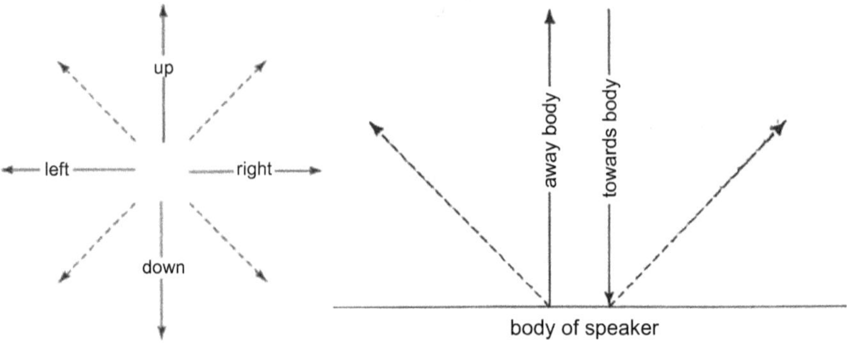

Figure 6: Movement general parameters
Source: Bressem et al. (2013: 1089–1090).

(4) Position in the space, such as self-gesture (away/towards the speaker's own body), proximal, medium, and distal.

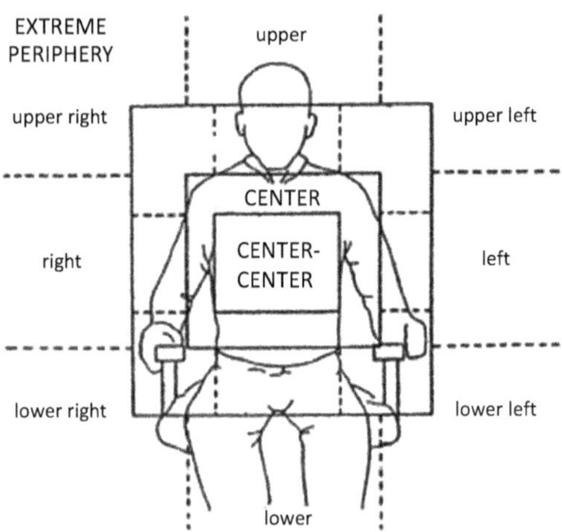

Figure 7: Position general parameters.
Source: Bressem et al. (2013: 1091)

According to Bressem and collaborators (2013), the system also allows for a description of the following gestures' modes of representation:

(1) Enacting, in which the hands move in such a way that they represent engagement in a functional act, often one involving the manipulation of something:

Figure 8: Speaker representing the act of writing.
Source: Müller (2014: 141).

(2) Embodying, in which the hand stands for the entity it represents by substituting it:

Figure 9: Speaker representing an object (a bow and arrow).
Source: Müller (2014: 141)

(3) Drawing, in which the hand or hands move, usually with the tip(s) of the extended finger(s) being the 'active zone', so as to leave an imagined trace of the form being depicted:

Figure 10: Speaker drawing an oval object.
Source: Müller (2014: 141)

(4) Holding/Molding, in which the hands shape a 3D object:

Figure 11: Speaker molding a 3D object.
Source: Müller (2014: 141)

(5) Pointing, in which the index finger or the open hand is used to point to something or somewhere, included in the repertoire of this particular study:

Figure 12: Pointing gestures.
Source: Kendon (2004: 209)

Regarding parameters of function, the LASG system (Bressem *et al.* 2013) proposes the following description:

(1) Referential gestures, which depict concrete objects or abstract entities, ideas, relations, or actions:

O ser humano é como **uma** (1, 2) **esponja** (1, 2) *[The human being is like a sponge (1, 2)]*

(1) right open hand, (2) right closed hand

Figure 13: Speaker depicting the referent "sponge".
Source: Brazilian House of Representatives' YouTube channel

(2) Pragmatic gestures, which enact a speech act or mark the speaker's attitude:

Vou fazer uma declaração profética [. . .] Todo tipo de lei que venha a destruir a família aqui nesta casa caia por terra. *[I'm going to make a prophetic declaration [. . .]* ***All (1) kinds (2) of laws (3) proposed (4) to destroy (5) the family (6)*** *in this House will fall to the ground]*
(1-6) Right index finger coming back and forth

Figure 14: Speaker making an alert to the interlocutor.
Source: Brazilian House of Representatives' YouTube channel

(3) Discursive gestures, which structure the accompanying verbal utterance, for example, by marking emphasis (Bressem *et al.* 2013; Cienki 2017):

Espero **que essa casa** (1) **aqui** (2), **os senhores** (3) **aqui** (4) *[I hope this house (1) here (2), the gentlemen (3) here (4)]*

Palm-down Index Finger (PDIF)

Figure 15: Speaker emphasizing a whole portion of his speech.
Source: Brazilian House of Representatives' YouTube channel

In the next section, results will be presented and discussed.

4 Results and discussion

4.1 Gesture forms: pointing and other gesture modes of representation

In this section, we will present results related to our first hypothesis, which states that pointing gestures are the most frequent gestures that go along with the uttered locative deictic in both languages. For the other gesture modes of representation, we maintained the quaternary distinction proposed by Bressem and collaborators (2013): Enacting, Embodying, Holding/Molding (3D), and Drawing (2D). Aiming at describing the gesture forms with pointing gestures, the following categorization with the index finger was used: Palm-down bent index finger (PDBIF); Palm-down extended index finger (PDEIF); Palm-away index finger (PAIF); Palm-vertical index finger (PVIF). Pointing gestures with the open hand were categorized in the following way: Palm-up open hand (PUOH); Palm-down open hand (PDOH); Palm-vertical open hand (PVOH). Gesture forms showed the following distribution in Brazilian Portuguese and American English:

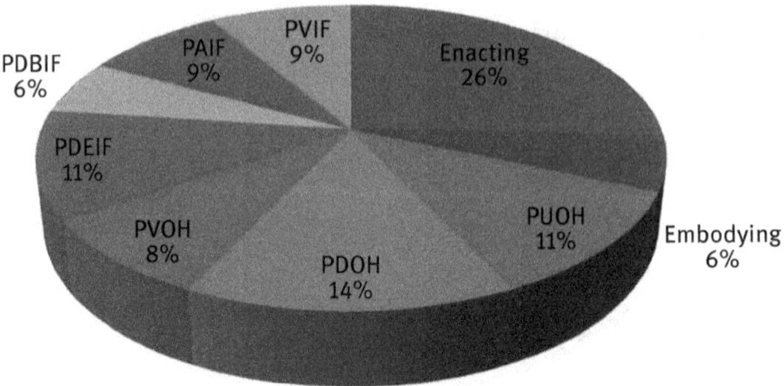

Figure 16: Gesture forms (Brazilian Portuguese).

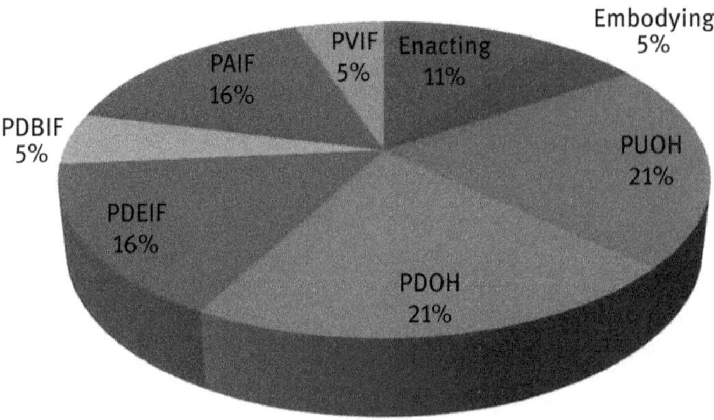

Figure 17: Gesture forms (American English).

As can be observed in Figures 16 and 17, Pointing gestures are, indeed, the predominant gesture form, corresponding to 68% and 84% of the overall forms in Brazilian Portuguese and in American English, respectively. As to the specific type of Pointing, Brazilian Portuguese shows a slight predominance of Pointing with the Index Finger, corresponding to 35% of the occurrences, followed by Pointing with the Open Hand, with 34%. As for American English, there is an equal prominence of 42% of the occurrences in both Pointing with the Open Hand (21%) and Pointing with the Index Finger (21%). In both cases, the gestures were performed with variable palm orientations.

It is worth mentioning that, from a multimodal perspective, Kendon (2004:208) observed that the combinations with the Index Finger are usually associated with deictic words – especially with spatial deictics –, while the combinations with the Open Hand are less frequently associated with deictic words, as this handshape is frequently indicating the conversational topic or something (usually the exemplary of a category or the location of an activity) related to that topic and, for that reason, should be regarded with attention.

As predicted by Kendon (2004: 207), Pointing with the Index Finger is used when speakers are locating a specific entity or object in the immediate visible scene, such as the physical location shown by the speakers in Figures 18a and 18b:

a) **Aqui embaixo** era um presidio.
[*Down here, there was a prison*]

Palm-down Bent Index Finger (PDBIF)

Figure 18a: Pointing with the Index Finger to a location in the immediate scene.
Source: Domingo Espetacular

b) He looks amazing **up there** on that billboard.

Palm-away Index Finger (PAIF)

Figure 18b: Pointing with the Index Finger to a billboard in the immediate scene.
Source: Entertainment Tonight

In both languages, Pointing with the Open Hand, as predicted by Kendon (2004: 207) as well, is used when speakers are presenting a specific entity or object. Nevertheless, the primary topic is not the object or entity itself but something linked to the topic. In Figure 19 below, the speaker metaphorically refers to the location of health problems in Brazil. In Figure 20, the speaker refers to the metaphorical location of some activity under discussion[5]. Both Figures are shown next:

Quando eles [os problemas de saúde do Brasil] estão **ali**, é porque todo o resto faltou.
When they [health problems in Brazil] are ***there****, that's because all the rest is missing*

Palm-down open hand (PDOH)

Figure 19: Pointing with the Open Hand (Proned palm).
Source: Programa Altas Horas (Late Hours TV show)

There's a compromise **right there** [with the people involved.]

Palm-up open hand (PUOH)

Figure 20: Pointing with the Open Hand (Presenting Palms).
Source: Late Show with David Letterman

Considering this study's first hypothesis, for both languages, pointing was shown to be the predominant gesture form in utterances with locative deictic terms in American English and Brazilian Portuguese. Regarding the datasets of both languages, our first hypothesis is completely supported by the Brazilian Portuguese and the American English data analysis, since there is a predominance of pointing gestures with the uttered locatives. Nevertheless, there is a slight qualitative difference regarding the type of pointing gestures that occur mostly in both languages: in Brazilian Portuguese, there is a slight predominance of Pointing with

5 As proposed by Conceptual Metaphor Theory (Lakoff & Johnson 1980), the metaphoric mapping in those cases refers to a concrete source domain – e.g., physical locations prototypically represented by locative deictics – that represents an abstract target domain – e.g., health problems and compromises.

the Index Finger, followed by Pointing with the Open Hand. In English, though, the proportion is the same for both types of Pointing gestures. This slight difference shows that while both languages depart from the same cognitive basis for relating pointing gestures to locative deictics, there may be cultural differences motivating the specific choice of handshape for pointing.

4.2 Gesture functions

This study's second hypothesis, in which we established that the predominant gestural function would be referential, is supported by our findings. The referential function corresponds to 87% of Brazilian Portuguese and 90% of American English data, shown in both graphs below:

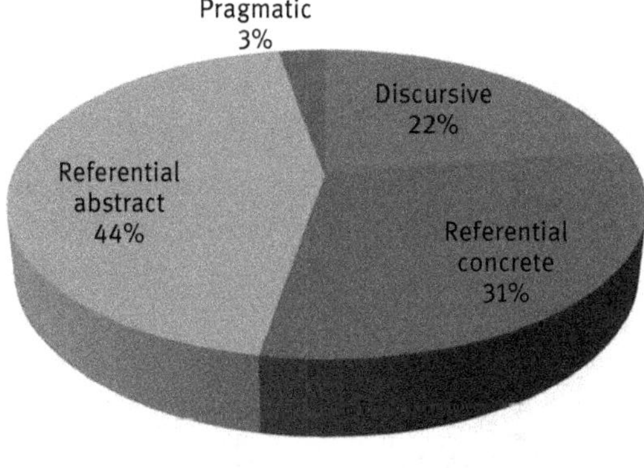

Figure 21: Gesture functions (Brazilian Portuguese).

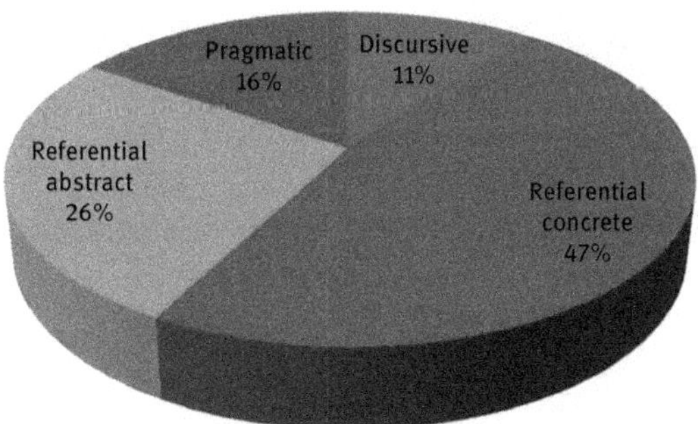

Figure 22: Gesture functions (American English).

Both graphs show that the referential gesture function is the predominant one, corresponding to 75% and 73% of the overall functions in Brazilian Portuguese and in American English, respectively. Nevertheless, when the referential function was divided into concrete and abstract, Brazilian Portuguese shows a predominance of abstract referential function (44%), whereas American English shows a predominance of concrete referential function (47%). In order to illustrate the difference between what was considered concrete and what was considered abstract referents, and to illustrate pragmatic and discursive functions, the following samples can be observed:

This lady **right here**

Palm-down Index Finger (PDIF)

Figure 23: Referential gestures (concrete referents).
Source: Ellen Show

The first type of referential gesture (Figure 23) illustrates cases structured by the ICM of Deixis: the speaker is the deictic center, and points to a concrete object or entity located in the immediate scene.

I haven't been over there [at the narrated place], but I have a friend that actually has. In fact, she used to work **over there**.

Palm-vertical index finger (PVIF)

Figure 24: Referential gesture (abstract referents).
Source: The Tonight Show starring Jimmy Fallon

The second type (Figure 24) of referential gesture illustrates a case of abstract deixis (McNeill, Cassell and Levy 1993), since the referent is not located in the immediate scene.

Pragmatic gestures (Figure 25a, b, c below) can be illustrated by iterative gestures (Bressem 2014):

a) E agora ele tá **aí** (1) **se expondo** (2), **fez rede social** (3), **Twitter** (4) [. . .]
And now he's ***there*** *(1)* ***exposing himself*** *(2),* ***logging into social media*** *(3),* ***Twitter*** *(4) [. . .]*

Cyclic gesture (Enacting)

b) **I actually heard** (1)

Palm-vertical index finger (PVIF)

c) **That you have drinks here** (2)

Palm-down bended index finger (PDBIF)

Figure 25: Pragmatic gestures.
Source a): Altas Horas (Late Night talk-show)
Source b) and c): The Late Show with Stephen Colbert

In the first case, Figure 25a, the repetition of cyclic gestures, marked in the description with numbers that represent the same stroke performed over and over, performs the pragmatic function of enumerating a list of actions carried out by a specific character in the guest's narrative[6]. In case 25b and c, repetition is marked by iterative gestures or the same stroke performed many times along the speech. This iteration can be linked to the speaker's attitude (Sperber and Wilson 1995) towards the fact that the interlocutor is having drinks on set, a procedure that normally would be forbidden and is highlighted as such by the speaker. In the first case, iteration is related to enumeration, and, in the second case, it is related to the disclosure of something by the speaker.

Discursive gestures can be related to the structure of the narrative itself, as in Figure 26 (a, b)

a) **E aí** (1) aconteceu algo inédito na madrugada *[And then something new happened at dawn.]*

Left closed hand (Embodying)

b) And **here's** what she did.

Palm-away index finger (PAIF)

Figure 26: Discursive gestures.
Source a): Zero1
Source b): Entertainment Tonight

In Figure 26a, the speaker marks an additional narrative sequence, using the deictic expression "e aí" ("and then", that doesn't have a locative expression in

6 As the gesture is not performing a prototypical referential function with the uttered deictic "there", this use is considered metaphoric, since it is related to the idea of TIME (the target domain), represented as SPACE (the source-domain).

English).[7] In Figure 26b, the speaker uses the deictic expression "and here's [what she did]". Although both expressions conserve traces of the prototypical locative, related to SPACE (the source-domain), they are used to demarcate TIME (the target-domain) unfolding. In both cases, the expressions constitute a metaphorized use of the locatives.

These results partially support the second hypothesis, which established that the referential function performed by the gestures would be the most common one, linked with referents located in the immediate scene. It is shown that the referential gesture function is the predominant one both in Brazilian Portuguese and in American English. Nevertheless, only American English shows a predominance of concrete referential function, as predicted. It may be the case, however, that the predominance of the abstract referential function in the Brazilian Portuguese corpus, which is mostly based on narratives made by talk-show hosts or participants, demonstrates the occurrence of more abstract topics in this kind of context, whereas American English data involve more locally situated references, as the hosts are presenting people physically present in the actual scenes.

4.3 Correlation between prototypicality and metaphoricity degree in spatial deictics

As explained by Ferrari (2014), radial categories do not objectively exist in outside reality.[8] Instead, together with the existence of polysemic chains, they provide evidence for a theory of cognitive models. Ferrari (2014) also states that the most prototypical member of a category is the one that perfectly fits the ICM. Based on our findings regarding both gestural form and function related to the deictic terms uttered in speech, we propose the following diagram for the verbo-gestural locative compounds:

7 English and Brazilian Portuguese differ on this matter. While English conventionally uses the temporal marker "then" to indicate consecutive events in narratives, Brazilian Portuguese metaphorically signals the unfolding of discourse in time as movement in space (TIME IS SPACE), by using the locative deictic "aí".

8 From a cognitive linguistics perspective, the so-called outside reality is a reference to our perception of the world around us. But it is important to bear in mind that this perception is structured by our cognitive endowment.

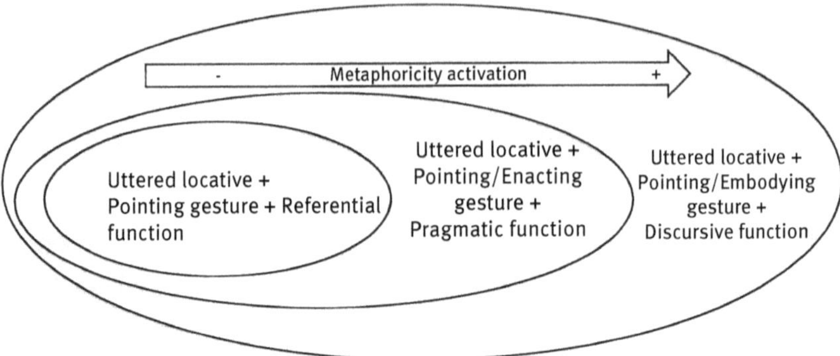

Figure 27: Prototypicality scale and metaphoricity gradience.

It can be observed that the radial categories proposed for the uses of verbo-gestural locative deictic terms present scalar properties. The prototypical central member can be related to concrete objects or entities present in the immediate scene and thus performs a referential function in the American English data samples. In the same way, even though the most conventionalized uses in the Brazilian Portuguese data samples can be related to abstract referents, the categorical center is not only determined by frequency, but by its adequacy to the ICM of Deixis. In cognitive terms, the gradience of metaphoricity activation depends on the proximity of the verbo-gestural compound to the prototypical center.

The nearer the verbo-gestural locative is to the deictic center, the less metaphoricity can be activated in the investigated online interactions. On the other hand, the farther the cognitive category is from the deictic center, the more metaphoricity can be activated in the investigated online interactions (cf. Figures 18a, 18b and 19 in section 4.1). In that sense, the peripheral cases are all metaphoric extensions of the prototypical center: they can be related to abstract ideas, objects or entities, and can also perform discursive and pragmatic functions through the gestures that co-occur with the uttered locatives. In short, metaphoricity can be low or highly activated in online interactive use and has proven to serve speakers' different purposes: to draw the interlocutor's attention to a person, to enumerate narrated actions, and to emphasize the speaker's attitude towards the hearer.

5 Concluding remarks

In this chapter, we investigated verbo-gestural data related to locative deictic elements in both Brazilian Portuguese and American English. Results showed that, for both languages, Pointing is the predominant gestural form co-occurring with the uttered locative. Therefore, results from both language data samples support the first research hypothesis, namely that, in both languages, the most frequent gestures that go along with the verbally uttered deictic term was the pointing gesture. It was also suggested, however, that there seem to be cultural differences in the performance of Pointing Gestures: Brazilian Portuguese speakers prefer Pointing with Index Finger and American English speakers mostly choose Pointing with Open Hand. As previously remarked, gestures performed with the Index Finger are usually associated with more prototypical deictic uses, which make reference to the spatial relations set up by the locative use, whereas Pointing with the Open Hand is more associated with abstract ideas related to the conversational topic.

Considering gesture functions, the second hypothesis is also supported, since pointing gestures were found to be mostly referential in both data samples, either locating entities or objects related to the immediate speech scene, but entities, ideas, objects or processes related to a narrated scene. Nevertheless, these findings point to differences related to context-specific locative uses: in the Brazilian Portuguese samples, speakers make more references to narrative scenes being reenacted, whereas in American English, the speakers make more reference to the guests and other people or objects located in the immediate scene. These findings point to the validity of the semi-institutional feature of the late-night talk show genre, as the hosts follow the protocol of presenting the guest, and, at the same time, guests feel free to tell stories and even make jokes with the host.

The results presented here reflect an initial multimodal analysis of locative deictics, contrasting two unrelated languages. Although not fully generalizable, these preliminary findings suggest new research paths, such as the need to investigate the relation between locative deictic uses and discourse genres, as well as the role of cultural motivations in gesture differences.

References

Austin, John. 1962. *How to do things with words*. Oxford: Oxford University Press.

Avelar, Maíra & Lilian Ferrari. 2017. Integração experiencial e dêixis locativa: o papel discursivo dos gestos. *Cadernos de Estudos Linguísticos* 59 (1). 73–89. https://periodicos.sbu.unicamp.br/ojs/index.php/cel/article/view/8648300 (accessed 14 May 2019).

Avelar, Maíra & Hayat Pinheiro. 2017. Uma análise cognitiva do dêitico "aqui" em dados orais e multimodais. *Signo* 42 (75). https://online.unisc.br/seer/index.php/signo/article/view/9815. (accessed 05/14/2019.

Avelar, Maíra & Hayat Pinheiro. In press. Análise do dêitico "aqui" em dados multimodais: dos usos prototípicos aos usos metafóricos. *NOVALing: Selected papers from the 13th Forum for Linguistics*. Centro de Linguística da Universidade NOVA de Lisboa.

Bressem, Jana, Silva Ladewig & Cornelia Müller. 2013. Linguistic annotation system for gestures. In Cornelia Müller, Alan Cienki, Ellen Fricke, Silva Ladewig, David McNeill & Sedinha Teßendorf (eds.), *Body – language – communication. An international handbook on multimodality in human interaction*. Volume 1, 1098–1124. Berlin: De Gruyter Mouton.

Bressem, Jana. 2014. Repetitions in gestures. In Cornelia Müller, Alan Cienki, Ellen Fricke, Silva Ladewig, David McNeill & Jana Bressem (eds.), *Body – language –communication. An international handbook on multimodality in human interaction*. Volume 2, 1641–1649 Berlin: De Gruyter Mouton.

Cienki, Alan. 2008. Why to study metaphor and gesture? In Alan Cienki & Cornelia Müller (eds.), *Metaphor and gesture*, 3–26. Amsterdam: John Benjamins.

Cienki, Alan. 2016. Cognitive linguistics, gesture studies3 and multimodal communication. *Cognitive Linguistics* 27 (4). 603–618.

Cienki, Alan. 2017. Analysing metaphor and gesture: a set of metaphor identification guidelines for gesture. In: Semino, Elena & Zsófia Demjén (eds.), *The Routledge handbook of metaphor and language*, 131–147. London, New York: Routledge.

Cienki, Alan, Maíra Avelar, Sally Donlon, Cacilda Vilela & Vera Pacheco. 2019. Spatial deixis in speech and gesture in Brazilian Portuguese: an experimental pilot-study. *Signo* 44 (79). https://online.unisc.br/seer/index.php/signo/article/view/12829. (accessed 14 May 2019).

Ferrari, Lilian. 2014. Blending, subjectivity and deixis: Evidence from English and Brazilian Portuguese. *Online Proceedings of UK-CLA Meetings – Selected Papers* 1: 102–116. https://lincufrj.wordpress.com/artigos/. (accessed 17 February 2020).

Janda, Laura. 2007. From cognitive linguistics to cultural linguistics. *Word & Sense* 8. 48–68. http://ansatte.uit.no/laura.janda/mypubs/slovo%20a%20smysl%20cultural%20ling.pdf. (accessed 28 April 2020).

Kendon, Adam. 2004. *Gesture: Visible action as utterance*. Cambridge: Cambridge University Press.

Johnson, Mark. 1999. *The body in the mind: the bodily basis of meaning, imagination and reason*. Chicago: Chicago University Press.

Johnson, Mark. 2007. *The meaning of the body: Aesthetics of human understanding*. Chicago: The Chicago University Press.

Lakoff, George & Mark Johnson 1980. *Metaphors we live by.* Chicago: Chicago University Press.

Lakoff, George. 1987. *Women, fire and dangerous things: what categories reveal about the mind.* Chicago: Chicago University Press.

Lakoff, George. 1990. The invariance hypothesis: is abstract reason based on image schemas? *Cognitive Linguistics* 1 (1). 39–74.

Langacker, Ronald. 2008. *Cognitive grammar: A basic introduction*. Oxford: Oxford University Press.

Lewandowska-Tomaszczyk, Barbara. 2007. Polysemy, prototypes and radial categories. In: Dirk Geeraerts & Hanne Cuyckens (eds.), *The Oxford handbook of cognitive linguistics*, 139–169. Oxford: Oxford University Press.

Marmaridou, Sophia. 2000. *Pragmatic meaning and cognition*. Amsterdam, Philadelphia: John Benjamins Publishing Company.

McNeill, David, Justine Cassell, & Elena T. Levy. 1993. Abstract deixis. *Semiotica* 95 (1). 5–19.

Molek-Kosakowska, Katarziyna. 2013. The late-night TV talk show as a strategic genre in American political campaigning. In: Piotr Cap & Urzula Okulska (eds.), *Analysing genres in political communication: Theory and practice*, 321–343. Amsterdam, John Benjamins.

Müller, Cornelia. 2008. What gestures reveal about the nature of metaphor. In Alan Cienki & Cornelia Müller (eds), *Metaphor and gesture*, 219–247. Amsterdam: John Benjamins.

Müller, Cornelia. 2014. Gesture as "deliberate expressive movement". In Mandana Seyfeddinipur & Marianne Gullberg (eds.), *From gesture in conversation to visible action as utterance: Essays in honor of Adam Kendon*, 127–152. Amsterdam: John Benjamins.

Rosch, Eleanor. 1973. On the internal structure of perceptual and semantic categories. In: Moore, Timothy (ed.), *Cognitive development and the acquisition of language*, 111–144. New York: Academic Press.

Rosch, Eleanor. 1978. Principles of categorization. In: Rosch, Eleanor & Barbara Lloyd (eds.) *Cognition and categorization*, 27–48. Hillsdale, NJ: Lawrence Erlbaum.

Sessão Solene em Honra à Família. *Câmara dos Deputados* (YouTube channel). https://www.youtube.com/watch?v=zSd3U2h1MWs. (accessed 15 May 2020).

Sperber, Dan & Deirdre Wilson. 1995. *Relevance: communication and cognition*. New York: Blackwell Publishing.

Turner, Mark. & Francis Steen. *The Distributed Little Red Hen Lab*. http://newsscape.library.ucla.edu/ (accessed 14 May 2019).

Wittgenstein, Ludwig. 1958. *Philosophical investigations*. Oxford: Blackwell.

Karsten Senkbeil, Nicola Hoppe

Of wars and vengeance goddesses: metaphorical conceptualizations of Sars-CoV-2

Abstract: This chapter examines the metaphorical conceptualizations of the coronavirus (Sars-CoV-2) by analyzing and comparing public discourse from the spring of 2020 in two languages, English and German.

Firstly, the chapter discusses pragmalinguistic knowledge from health communication research, which has demonstrated how metaphorical conceptualizations help patients make sense of illnesses. This illuminates how the appearance of Covid-19 in 2020 demanded new ways of speaking about the impact of illness on the individual but, in this case, also on a societal, even global scale. For a full understanding of the metaphorical construals of Sars-CoV-2 as a target domain, it proves helpful to recapitulate the history of INFECTION and CONTAGION as metaphoric source domains, mapped on various domains of practice in many cultural and societal spheres. The empirical part of this chapter then presents the results of a cognitive and pragmatic analysis of metaphors framing Sars-CoV-2 and its ensuing illness, Covid-19. This shows how, during the 'first wave' of 2020, fairly conventional metaphoric mappings of INFECTION and CONTAGION became the basis for new, ad hoc conceptualizations in both journalistic and political discourse, blurring the boundaries between, and sometimes reversing, source and target domains. Our analysis demonstrates how the meaning-making qualities of metaphors have helped journalists, politicians, and other social actors to make the ambiguous biological threat intelligible. Necessary social and political actions and reactions to the pandemic were often communicated to the public through metaphors, alluding to domains such as WAR, NATURAL DISASTERS, JOURNEYS, and RELIGION. On a final note, the chapter discusses how different metaphor choices (by different actors, in different sociocultural contexts) may reveal different ideological and philosophical perspectives on society, nature, and human agency.

Keywords: CMT, cognitive metaphors, Covid-19, virus metaphors, public health, pandemics, media, corona, health communication

Karsten Senkbeil, Nicola Hoppe, University of Hildesheim

https://doi.org/10.1515/9783110688306-010

1 Introduction

This chapter examines the metaphorical conceptualizations of the coronavirus (Sars-CoV-2) by analyzing and comparing a news corpus from spring 2020 (i.e. the so-called first wave of the pandemic) from three countries: the USA, the UK, and Germany. With a combined perspective of a cognitive linguistic, metaphor-theoretical, and a pragmatic, discourse-oriented viewpoint, it first discusses the status quo of sociolinguistic approaches to health communication (section 2). This research has shown that, to fully understand the impact of illness on our lives, we need to take into account the sociocultural context and discursive interpretations of what it means to suffer from a disease; both for the person affected, and for their social environment. Health discourse analyses have demonstrated how metaphorical conceptualizations can help affected individuals make sense of illnesses, which emerge in their lives as random and agentless events, and which demand new interpretations of a patient's identity and agency. We apply this knowledge to the outbreak of Covid-19 in early 2020, which produced discourse on health and illness both on the micro-level of individual patients and on the macro-level in terms of the societal reactions to a global problem.

Metaphorical conceptualizations are no 'one-way street'. Lakoff's 'Invariance Principle' (1993) has been extended by Fauconnier & Turner's Blending Theory (2003), which argues that source and target domains of common metaphorical mappings can blend into conventionalized tropes, exchanging and mixing characteristics. In public discourse, this leads to a blurring of boundaries between, and sometimes reversals of, source and target domains. This is true for discourse about viruses as well: section 3 of this chapter discusses how commonly used target domains of virus metaphors from before 2020 (for example in popular culture) became the first choice for metaphorical conceptualizations when Sars-CoV-2 threatened societies, i.e. when a literal virus became the target instead of the source domain of metaphorical mappings. It shows how INFECTION, VIRALITY, and CONTAGION have been common source domains for the cultural conceptualization of many abstract target domains (e.g., in popular culture) for a long while, before Sars-CoV-2 spread across the globe, and VIRALITY and CONTAGION became serious literal problems. We intend to show that the collective mindset of many societies was communicatively prepared by cultural tropes and conventional idioms revolving around CONTAGION when Sars-CoV-2 became the most eminent topic in public discourse.

Conceptual metaphor theory (CMT), augmented by an appreciation of the discourse-analytical perspective on the illocutionary forces of metaphors, provides helpful tools for understanding both the cognitive and the cultural dimensions of such metaphoric meaning-making. The empirical part of this chapter (section 4) therefore presents the results of a cognitive and pragmatic analysis of metaphors framing Sars-CoV-2, its ensuing illness Covid-19, and governmental and societal reactions to it in public discourse between March and June 2020. The analytic strength of CMT is thus augmented by a socio-cultural, interpretive type to discourse analysis, based on the Foucauldian approach to public discourse as the sphere in which political power is not only exerted but also negotiated and justified (Musolff & Zinken 2009, Charteris-Black 2004).

Our analysis will show that fairly conventional metaphoric mappings of INFECTION and CONTAGION became the basis for ad hoc conceptualizations by public actors, and how the meaning-making qualities of metaphors have helped politicians, medical professionals, and journalists to render the ambiguous biological threat intelligible and meaningful to the public during the first months of the pandemic. Alluding to domains such as WAR and RELIGION, these conceptualizations may also have had counterproductive sociocultural, political, and health-related consequences, as critical voices have discussed.

Metaphors are important carriers of socio-cultural ideologies, even philosophies, so finally, this chapter shows how different choices of metaphorical conceptualizations may arise from different communicative intents as well as ideological positions, and are thus, ultimately, cultural.

2 Health, illness, and (social) identity

Health and illness are sociocultural phenomena because on the one hand they are subjective, intimate experiences, and on the other hand they are nonetheless interpreted through the lens of how cultures view the body, the mind, and humans' physical and mental capabilities. As an individual experience, illness or ill-health are individual and elementary biological or psychological events. As a personal state of being, it is often associated not only with physical discomfort but also with feelings of fear, isolation, anxiety, and, potentially, shame (Semino 2008: 175f.). As such, serious illness inevitably changes the affected person's life and thus often translates into identity crises (Plunger 2013: 158) or even identity loss (Senkbeil and Hoppe 2016: 13; Charmaz 1983; Bury 2001). Researchers across the disciplines of medical sociology (Parsons 1970; Frank 2002, 2010, 2016), health communication (e.g., Harvey and Adolphs 2014), and narrative medicine (Lucius-Hoene 2008; Boothe 2011; Soff 2011) agree that illness can cause a breakdown of meaning on several levels. People who fall seriously ill are suddenly faced with new challenges that infringe upon every aspect of their daily lives. They have to reevaluate the control they can still exert over their bodies in social interaction

(Frank 2010), find new ways to manage emotional responses and interpersonal relationships (Plunger 2013), and renegotiate the meaning of their own physicality, possibly even mortality (Papathomas, Smith and Lavallee 2015; Hydén 1997: 52). Thus, severe and chronic illness is "an experience that disrupts the patient's everyday life and the forms of knowledge underpinning it" (Pierret 2003: 7). In order to visualize this, Kleinmann uses the metaphor of a sponge soaking up "personal and social significance from the world of the sick person" (1988: 31). Severe illness, he continues, "absorbs and intensifies life meanings while creating circumstances for which new interpretations are needed" (Kleinmann 1988: 32). Referring to Goffman's (1959, 1963) thoughts on stigma and the presentation of the self in everyday life, Frank (2010) summarizes that for both the individual and the social environment, the state of illness means learning to live with the fact that multiple sources of control within the realm of the ill person's life have been stripped from them (see also Sharf and Vanderford 2009: 19).

Note that Frank, Pierret, and the other health communication scholars quoted here commented on cases of individual illnesses of single patients. Concerning the topic of this chapter, we hold that their insights need to be transferred to the macrosocial sphere, when communication about an illness took place not on the individual, local level, but on the largest possible level of significance, during a pandemic affecting each and every one.

To summarize the prior paragraph: illnesses create circumstances that *limit agency and autonomy* and entail *loss of control*, at least temporarily, and they provoke the necessity to communicate about these circumstances. At the same time, 'being in control' is an ideological cornerstone of modern civilization; 'losing control' is stigmatized – individually (concerning the individual patient), but also politically. Facing Covid-19 in 2020, when there was no cure or vaccine yet, served as one of the strongest reminders of a) the limits of our individual control over our physical health, and b) the limited control of governments over truly momentous problems in a globalized world.

Elias noted in the early 20th century that the history of civilization as we know it is in fact the history of humanity's ever-growing control over bodily functions, including primitive drives and urges, which translated into steadily growing standards of hygiene, hiding necessary body functions from the public eye, and culminating in, for example, complicated dining etiquette (Elias 1978). In that vein, the loss of our full control over our body (through illness) is a form of temporary de-civilization of individuals, a taboo, which leads to all sorts of stigmatizing attitudes towards different illnesses. In the sense of Althusser's ([1969] 2020) theory of the state as carrier of social ideologies, a person suffering from a severe acute or chronic physical or mental condition is subconsciously categorized as a threat to the social system because affected individuals jeopardize the system's ability to reproduce itself. Ill people cannot participate in the economy and contribute their share, might not be able to participate in social life, to find a partner and be able to maintain interpersonal relationships, care for their families, and so forth. The idea of illnesses – in practice: ill people – as systemic threats was echoed during the corona crisis in particular; for example, discussions about which public services should remain functional during the lockdown led to different professions being sorted by their degree of 'systemic importance', echoing the perception that the situation was not just a threat to a growing number of individuals, but a threat to 'the system' itself.

During the coronavirus pandemic, the social uncertainty as outlined above, combined with the threat of our bodies being affected by a potentially lethal disease, gave rise to a number of complex, occasionally confusing and contradictory emotional and conceptual responses. Due to their ability to reduce the complexity of our lifeworld (Schmitt 2016: 11f.), metaphors turn out to be of immense communicative power when it comes to translating complex, subjective, embodied illness experiences into the realm of linguistic interpretations (Sontag 1979; Semino 2008; Semino et al. 2018; to name only a few).

3 Infection, contagion, and metaphors

"Through metaphor, body and mind are inextricably intertwined," Geary (2012: 93) notes, echoing a core idea of CMT first introduced by Lakoff and Johnson (1999), emphasizing that many conceptual metaphors have their experiential basis in the functioning of the human body. Later developments in CMT came to fundamentally reject the classic Western mind-body dichotomy and the notion that cognition is "purely internal, symbolic, computational, and disembodied" (Gibbs 2005: 9). Today, CMT stresses the fundamentally embodied nature of reason, meaning, and imagination, and, consequently, language that "provide[s] part of the fundamental grounding for language and thought" (Gibbs 2005: 9; see also Hampe and Grady 2005; Frank, Ziemke & Zlatev 2008). As humans across cultures share a very similar body, CMT further argues, metaphorical language that has bodily experiences as a source domain facilitates sense-making and meaning construction, and thus represents the perfect medium for sharing complicated experiences interpersonally, particularly abstract and/or emotional ones (compare Gibbs 2005; Lakoff and Johnson 1999; Senkbeil and Hoppe 2016). As discussed above, illness experience is inherently embodied (see Gjelsvik, Lovric and Williams 2018): the gravity of literal diseases and the immediate influence they have on our lives make them universally salient (with salience being defined as a combination of frequency, familiarity, and conventionality, see Giora 2003). Thus, they have long been potent resources for metaphoric meaning-making.

Despite the fact that the perception of illness is an individual, partly embodied process of interpretation, the metaphors used to conceptualize them can only be fully understood against their sociocultural background (Plunger 2013: 159). Frank (2002, 2010, 2016) emphasizes the distinction between the biological concept of a disease and the sociocultural concept of an illness and points out that the way members of a specific culture interpret and respond to a diseased body's breakdown in discourse "is one of the most fundamental ways that we humans organize ourselves as social" (Frank 2016: 9). The coronavirus pandemic made that painfully clear: Sars-CoV-2 does not only threaten single individuals, but puts in doubt "the collective myth of a taken-for-granted future as well as the personal belief in sustained health" (Charmaz 1999: 366). In its early phases, the pandemic appeared to threaten societies as a whole and thus did not only create the conceptual need for individual ILLNESS metaphors, but also called for a conceptual re-evaluation of how we perceive ourselves as currently healthy but potential future carriers of an unknown disease in a larger social system.

The individual embodied experience of illness, on the one hand, and the sociocultural dimension of illness as a social phenomenon, on the other hand, are also linked to the two-faced character of embodied metaphor in general (Senkbeil and Hoppe 2016: 6). The philosophy of the embodied mind proposes that human cognition operates on embodied frameworks of thought that are highly generic frames of reference shared by all human beings (Lakoff and Johnson 1999) – i.e. the macro-level of embodiment theory. These generic frames provide the materials for the metaphorization of highly subjective and view-pointed embodied experiences, i.e., the micro-level (see also Dancygier and Sweetser 2014). This is not to say, though, that all embodied experience is always interpersonally shared or shareable. This distinction is important when discussing illnesses and the metaphors for them: many illnesses – Covid-19 is one of them – are common topics in communication (the macro-societal level), but still only a small percentage of the population has actually suffered from them and may attempt to communicate what it subjectively feels like (the micro-subjective level). This discrepancy needs to be taken into account, when, for example, public figures conveyed during the pandemic that the whole society (often indicated by an inclusive deictic 'we') had 'fallen ill' with the coronavirus, which is only metonymically true, but not scientifically. With this perspective in mind, and based on the dual level of embodiment theory, we will, in the following chapter, approach the history of metaphors using INFECTIOUS DISEASES and CONTAGION as source domains, particularly in cultural (including ideological and sociopolitical) contexts.

3.1 The CONTAGION metaphor

The coronavirus pandemic did not come as a surprise. Both in science and in public discourse, the fear of a lethal infectious disease spreading across the globe had been topical for a while. Viruses, or rather mankind's knowledge about how they work, had become so common during the late 20th century that by 2019 VIRALITY was a common trope and conventional metaphor in many genres and for many target domains, ranging from harmful computer software to trending videos on social media. Academic disciplines have used CONTAGION as a source domain for theories that attempt to explain an unplanned and often unpredictable spread of ideas, views, or other abstract entities, e.g., "social contagion" in psychology (Braha 2012), or "financial contagion" in macroeconomics (Peckham 2013). In popular culture – and thus more accessible to the majority of people than academic theorizing – the pandemic apocalypse narrative became a popular subgenre of the science fiction / horror genre, often involving aliens, zombies, mad scientists, and the like. While Sars-CoV-2 in real-life involves none of these poetic ontological ingredients, it helps to shortly review the fictional take on INFECTION and CONTAGION narratives. As will become apparent in the empirical part of this chapter, commonly used target domains of virus metaphors from before 2020 (for example in popular culture) became the first choice for metaphorical conceptualizations when an actual virus, Sars-CoV-2, threatened societies, i.e., when a literal virus became the target instead of the source domain of metaphorical mappings.

An appreciation of the CONTAGION metaphor should look beyond a descriptive overview of which domains exactly have been its target: as mentioned, from technology, via social movements, to economic theory, the CONTAGION metaphor has been multivalent. Mitchell (2012) documents this in a comprehensive historical overview. Her key insight, however, is that the CONTAGION metaphor has been contagious itself: once the metaphorical mapping that an abstract entity (an idea) spreads like a disease among people had been accepted as sensible and an accurate description of societal processes, it spread into other academic and popular discourses. When, for example, the fear that spies and saboteurs would spread communist ideas among American citizens, this was closely related to other theories of behavioral contagion in the mid-20th century (e.g., Wheeler 1966). The fear of communist contagion (and the counter-strategy: containment) both within the U.S. and in Asia and Europe during the McCarthy era then contributed to the Golden Age of science fiction literature with the mentioned results in popular culture. This generated stable literary motifs, e.g., the alien impostor who willingly infects its victims, in lieu with anxiety of self-propulsing artificial intelligence, which, in turn, contributed to computer experts of the late 20th century labeling harmful software 'viruses'.

From a cognitive linguistic perspective, emphasizing that metaphorical mappings rely on universal skeletal conceptual structures, image schemas, based on the spatial and force-dynamic embeddedness of our minds and bodies in the world (cf. Cienki 1997; Hampe and Grady 2005), it is not surprising that all these instances of the CONTAGION metaphor are thus closely related. Image schemas can combine into complex, but still cognitively grounded compound schemas (Kimmel 2008, 2009; Senkbeil 2017), which may be highly conventional, but "neither linguistically signalled, nor tied to one specific [metaphorical] expression" (Kimmel 2009: 181). INFECTION is, as has been argued in Senkbeil (2017), one of these compounds. Specifically, it is a sub-case of the SHUTTLE schema, which has been identified as central in how people (classically) conceptualize COMMUNICATION (see for example Grady 1998, on the so-called CONDUIT metaphor), and the transfer of knowledge in general (cf. also Benczes 2006: 116). The SHUTTLE schema can be deconstructed into smaller, highly conventional metaphoric units: it consists of two ontological entities A ('the virus') and B ('the infected person'), the latter having the characteristics of a container, and thus a clearly defined inside/outside orientation. After the ontological element A has entered the container B in a place X, B moves and transports A along a path P (a linear movement in either space, or time, or both). During this phase, A reprograms B to some extent, which helps A grow and/or multiply. The container reaches a different space Y, where it releases A and its multitude of identical copies, enabling them to spread and have an effect in a theretofore clean and healthy environment.

In other words, CONTAGION is, both literally and metaphorically, a complex process with multiple steps, several ontological entities of different types, causal connections, and motion in terms of both space and time. The key to understanding its cultural and psychological potential in metaphorical communication, however, lies in the fact that all of these steps and elements rely on image schemas in the CMT-sense. This observation will become relevant when we discuss the (inter-)cultural dimensions of virus metaphors in section 4: for the mentioned reasons, compound schemas are not tied to one specific language or culture (as opposed to many other metaphors), and they thus represent potent resources for intercultural communication, despite their complexity (Musolff and MacArthur 2014; Senkbeil 2017b).

So historically, the CONTAGION metaphor has related to widely different target domains, but strikingly, the question of whether CONTAGION is a positive or a negative process would have to be answered differently in different metaphorical scenarios: when, for example, sleeper cell terrorists allegedly spread their 'sick' ideas among an oblivious population, this is defined as a highly undesirable process; but when social media content 'goes viral', usually both the creators and the 'infected' rejoice. Ideologically, the CONTAGION metaphor would seem to befit traditionalist, conservative values better than a left-progressivist one, as the fear of contagion presupposes a healthy, pure, untainted space to begin with, such as a homoethnic and homosocial group (e.g., a nation). And indeed, labelling outsiders as disease bringers is a strategy of conservative in- and out-grouping that may be as old as mankind itself. Then again, today's left-leaning thinkers use the metaphor as well, as for example Niemann (2020), who accuses neoliberalism of having spread like a virus into every sphere of our lives, and Huggins, who argues that "racism is an aggressive virus, which has been handed down from generation to generation for centuries" (Huggins quoted in Iken 2020, para. 2).

The one characteristic these diverse instances of the same compound schema have in common is, however, the centrality of the second ontological entity (apart from the virus), the container, or shuttle, for the process of spreading. To counteract further contagion – which is usually the communicative goal of those using the CONTAGION metaphor as part of a warning – it is thus necessary to stop the shuttle on its path (be it spatial or temporal), rather than neutralize the virus (idea, opinion) itself. As viruses and ideas are too small or too abstract to be visible, the fight against contagion usually addresses the shuttle, the carrier of the germ. Stopping and eliminating the shuttle before it bursts and spreads its matured germs thus becomes the most effective countermeasure. In popular culture, this usually leads to interesting plot drivers in spy thrillers and science fiction movies, i.e., when the hunt for an alien that pretends to be human, or a terrorist who pretends to be a good American, results in exciting action scenes. And it may also work when, to protect ourselves from a harmful email attachment, we delete the whole suspicious email. But when the metaphorical mapping is reversed, and CONTAGION metaphors are used in the opposite direction than in conventional popular culture, fighting the shuttle rather than the virus may have very undesirable side effects. In the case of Sars-CoV-2, the infected person should, first and foremost, be considered a patient who needs help and medical care, not blame, social shaming, or even hatred. The results of such metaphorical reversal may not only lead to discrimination, nationalist and racist sentiments, but even enable the further spread of the literal virus, as individuals might push off seeing a doctor and be diagnosed to avoid social stigma. In fact, those who contracted and unknowingly spread the coronavirus in its early phases reported that the psychological burden of having spread the potentially deadly virus in their community – a mixture of a feeling of guilt and real or perceived social ostracizing – adds to the burden of being physically unwell (Fritsch 2020).

This may have deeper cultural effects in the long run: Sloterdijk (quoted in Soboczinski 2020, para. 1) argues that "the symptomless virus carrier" will remain an archetypal figure (i.e., a conventional metaphor) after the coronavirus pandemic, and in fact, this trope has been used in literature before, as we will discuss in the following section.

3.2 Viruses as vengeance

During the Covid-19-induced lockdown in most societies, many turned to literature for interpretations of and possibly guidance through these times of crisis. Camus's *The Plague* of 1947 re-entered bestseller lists in many countries (see Flood 2020), a novel in which the title-giving epidemic serves as an existentialist metaphor (similar to the ones described in the prior section) rather than an actual illness. We are of the opinion that Philip Roth's *Nemesis* from 2010 represents an even more insightful pandemic narrative. Roth's novel is organized around the idea that the worst situation during a deadly virus epidemic (specifically: polio in New Jersey in the 1940s, which is a factual historical event) is not necessarily to fall ill oneself, but to learn in hindsight that one has brought the germ to those who one sought to protect. Roth's novel microscopically depicts how fear and hysteria among a homosocial community leads to overwrought hygiene measures first, then to social finger-pointing, and ultimately to cultural racism against other ethnicities, while the actual source of the disease, the polio virus, remains mysterious and obscure. *Nemesis* makes ample use of the INFECTION-BY-SHUTTLE compound schema as depicted above. In the tragic ending of the narrative, it introduces what we have called the "inadvertent infector compound schema" (Senkbeil 2017: 332), i.e., it negotiates the horror of ourselves being the shuttle in a chain of infection that results in our friends' and family members' death. This plot twist adds a second metaphor, which also explains the novel's title. Roth's protagonist interprets his role as the inadvertent infector of theretofore healthy, innocent children as god's wrath for his selfishness: the polio virus becomes the title-giving goddess of vengeance, Nemesis, i.e., god's – or fate's – way of punishing people for their carelessness. Here, Roth's literary ambition moves beyond the social dynamism of virus epidemics: his novel serves as a macro-metaphor for the philosophical question of teleology in times of crisis. It examines how those who believe that every event means something as the expression of the will of a higher power are able to cope with the random cruelties that befall our lives and communities from time to time, such as individual illness on a small scale, and epidemics on a larger one. For Roth's protagonist, the randomness and meaninglessness of polio, which kills and cripples blameless children, ultimately remains unacceptable. Instead, he comes to the conclusion that god must exist, and that he does not mean well (see Senkbeil 2017).

The philosophical and explanatory power of Roth's work goes beyond the purely poetic and literary, as we will show in the following empirical analysis. *Nemesis* in 2010 anticipated an explanatory motif that took hold in public discourse in 2020 as well: the idea that the virus Sars-CoV-2 is a form of vengeance for our (mankind's) wrongdoings.

4 Metaphors for Sars-CoV-2

The fact that target and source domains can be interchangeable, and mix and blend their characteristics, is a central idea of blending theory (Fauconnier and Turner 2002). It comes as no surprise then that after decades of using viruses as source domains for describing the target domain ASYMMETRIC WARFARE against in some way hidden enemy forces (war against jungle-based guerilla, against German or Japanese saboteurs in World War II, against communist agitators in the Cold War, against sleeper cell terrorists in the War on Terror), the reverse metaphor FIGHTING THE CORONAVIRUS IS WAR quickly became the first choice for communicating about the situation in March and April of 2020. An analysis of the usage of the WAR metaphor in its communicative context will hence be the first step in the following section, with sections 4.2 and 4.3 elaborating on alternative metaphorical mappings.

For such an analysis of metaphors for Sars-CoV-2 and Covid-19 in context, we compiled a news corpus of written texts with an eye on both representativeness (newspapers and websites with larger reach outweigh small blogs, etc.) and balance (roughly similar sizes for the three source cultures the UK, the USA, and Germany). With a, broadly speaking, discourse-oriented perspective, we analyzed each metaphor regarding its underlying conceptualizations in a CMT sense, and secondly examined the context for the communicative purpose behind its use. As will become evident below, different metaphoric expressions concerning the coronavirus are often founded in the same or very similar primary metaphors and image schemas – which is not unusual in CMT – and at the same time, rather different (conceptual) metaphors, used by different actors, can be applied for similar communicative intents. Our triangulated methodology helps understand these cases at the intersection of cognitive linguistics and pragmatics.

4.1 The WAR metaphor during the coronavirus pandemic

National crises are a time for the executive branch of government. People expect their heads of state to act quickly, take decisive measures, and communicate their reasoning for these measures. In the particular case of an analysis of discourse during the coronavirus crisis, it thus helps to take a top-down approach to metaphor usage, and pay attention to official statements by government officials first, which, for obvious reasons, have then been ventilated (and questioned and negotiated) by the press.

Two leading political figures, who are known to otherwise rarely agree, used the same metaphor early on. The French president Emmanuel Macron set the tone in his urgent address to the French people on March 16, 2020 (BBC.com 2020a), when he told the nation "nous sommes en guerre [we are at war]."[1] On the same day, U.S. president Donald Trump labeled Sars-CoV-2 "an invisible enemy" (quoted in Shafer 2020, para. 1), and later commented that he did indeed consider himself a "wartime president" (quoted in Smith 2020, para. 1). The British prime minister Boris Johnson followed suit and justified his actions by arguing that "we must act like any wartime government" (BBC.com 2020b).

It may not be a complete coincidence that those three nations have had mostly successful wars as central elements in their national collective memory, but also that they have had particularly serious incidents with terrorism in the years before the coronavirus crisis. The 'war on terror' in these countries can be considered prime examples of the type of asymmetric warfare, which invites CONTAGION, CONTAINMENT, and VIRUS metaphors (as discussed in chapter 3), for example, in that they feature invisible enemies, and dangerous ideas that spread among apparently harmless citizens without being noted by the authorities. In other words, the French, British, and U.S. American public is certainly at least vaguely aware of the perspective that the war on terror is comparable to fighting a virus, so that the direct reversal, FIGHTING THE CORONAVIRUS IS WAR, may appear all too logical and produce little cognitive friction.

It soon became noticeable though that, forty years after Lakoff and Johnson's seminal work (1980) on the power of metaphors to shape our worldview, the key insight of CMT is common knowledge not only among linguists, but also among quality press journalists. One immediate response to these presidential statements thus was a critique of the WAR metaphor on several levels and channels. From renowned metaphor researchers, such as Semino and Koller, who turned to Twitter and campaigned to #ReframeCovid (Semino et al. 2020), to international journalists (e.g., Rucker and Parker 2020, Löhndorf 2020), many criticized that the WAR metaphor was not an apt conceptualization for the current situation, as it emphasized (and demanded) pugnacity and grit, while turning away attention from important (but underfunded) healthcare logistics and from the much-needed societal solidarity with the sick, the elderly, and potentially dying patients.

Why then have leaders of governments in particular used this metaphor? Trump's usage of this hyperbolic conceptualization (THE CORONA PANDEMIC IS A WAR) may be accounted for by his lack of rhetorical finesse to frame the situation differently, and/or his tendency for self-aggrandizement: labeling himself a

---

1 Obviously, Macron spoke French in his address to the French people, while we aim at analyzing public discourse in German and English. Still, Macron's speech belongs in this chapter: it made headlines across Europe and the world, and is a precedent for later statements by (English- and German-speaking) politicians and other actors, as the rest of this section discusses.

'wartime president' puts him on equal footing with Lincoln and Roosevelt. Then again, Macron is not known for a careless use of rhetoric.

A pragmatic approach to metaphor usage helps clarify the communicative intent of the utterance, and at that, the three mentioned heads of state certainly followed similar agendas when choosing their metaphoric expressions: in times of war, presidents and prime ministers act as commanders in chief and orchestrate the power of not just the military, but the whole state. Historically, literal wartime presidents have enjoyed unusual amounts of executive power (through emergency legislation, for example) and simultaneously very high levels of popularity among their citizens, so the WAR metaphor aims at a consolidation of power of the politician using it.

On a second level, the WAR metaphor entails several illocutionary forces towards the listeners, i.e., the people, who, in a democracy, can be forced to behave in a certain manner only to a limited degree. War imagery demands discipline, the acceptance of unpopular but necessary restrictions to the normal lifestyle of peacetime, and unwavering support of those fighting on the front lines, in this case medical professionals and care workers. The WAR metaphor transforms average people from passive, fearful victims into courageous soldiers in a collective effort against a common enemy. The loss of control over our bodies that illness entails and that makes illness a systemic threat to civilization (see section 2) is mitigated by strengthening the feeling of agency and empowerment in a group of likeminded fighters.

Even critics of this metaphor have agreed that the second strand of communicative entailments may have helped clarify the gravity of the situation and emphasize the necessity of a whole society's collective effort (e.g., Meretoja 2020, Beschloss quoted in Rucker and Parker 2020), particularly during a period when the key aspect to stopping the further spread of Sars-CoV-2 was everyone's strict obedience to social distancing rules, even though they were new and naturally unpopular.

Conversely, the reasons why critical scholars and journalists problematized the WAR metaphor are similar to those discussed in section 2 of this chapter: WAR metaphors for illnesses may ultimately blame the victim, i.e., the deceased, for not battling hard enough; they imply outdated strategies about how crises can be overcome (such as grit and toughness) while backgrounding more humanistic aspects, such as kindness and empathy with patients and their families. They also belittle the horrors of real warfare (Hyde 2020). And in the particular case of an infectious disease like Covid-19, the war discourse may in fact harm those it apparently valorizes. As Meretoja (2020, para. 12) writes: "Wars inevitably have casualties. Wars require sacrifice. The narrative of war heroes is used to justify putting health workers at risk". Furthermore, particularly U.S. American President Trump received criticism for not only his lackluster response to the first wave in his country, but also the entailments of his metaphors. During the climax of his war-based rhetoric in mid-March, he used the attribute ‘invisible’ to describe the ‘enemy’ in his ‘war’ not once, but multiple times in different channels, which critics interpreted as an attempt to hide from responsibility. Shafer’s interpretation for *Politico.com* may serve as an example: “By calling the virus ‘invisible,’ Trump implies that he can’t be responsible for its wreckage because who can be expected to see an invisible thing coming? And once the unseeable thing has arrived, there are limits to what one can be expected to do about it!” (2020, para. 6).

The dominance of the WAR metaphor continued through March and April of 2020. We refrain from quoting further examples from broadcast and social media, though they are plentiful and occasionally involve colorful entailments and extensions. One might argue that its career ended on April 11th 2020, when another head of state, Frank-Walter Steinmeier of Germany in his Easter address to the German people explicitly contradicted its validity and stated: “No, this pandemic is not a war. [. . .] It is a trial of our humanity” (quoted in ZEIT.de 2020; this and all following translations from German by the authors of this chapter). There are certainly (inter-)cultural dimensions at work here, e.g., that German politicians per default shy away from WAR metaphors for obvious historical reasons. In fact, neither chancellor Merkel, nor president Steinmeier, nor any German state governor appropriated the WAR metaphor at any point (see section 4.3 for alternatives from Germany, especially from the domain of sports). But also, Steinmeier had the advantage of taking his time before addressing the people: his speech was recorded approximately three weeks after the mentioned public speeches by Macron, Trump, and Johnson, at a point in time when the immediate urgency of telling people to stay at home had somewhat receded. Like this, it seems fair to say that (like epidemics) metaphor usages come and recede in waves. The WAR metaphor was challenged and, at least to some degree, substituted by other metaphors, which will be the focus in the following sections.

4.2 The virus as a message

Let us remain with Steinmeier’s reframing of the pandemic for a moment and remark on the fact that, while rebuking the WAR metaphor, he still appropriates figurative language for a counter-narrative. In the German original statement, “eine Prüfung unserer Menschlichkeit”, the noun “Prüfung” translates to “trial”, but also to “examination” / “exam” (such as in school or university). In this metaphoric scenario, the examinees are rather clear, as indicated by the deictic “unserer” (”our”). But who might be the examiner in such an exam?

Steinmeier is known to be an active member of a protestant Christian church, so clearly, we are entering the realm of religion here, a particularly metaphor-rich sphere, one may add. Pope Francis – in a way a head of state as well – is known to be an outspoken ecologist, independently of the corona crisis. So it came as no surprise that he connected Sars-CoV-2 with ecological topics: he cited the corona pandemic in line with the wildfires in Australia and the melting arctic ice as examples of nature suffering from human mistakes, to then add "I don't know if these [crises] are the revenge of nature, but they are certainly nature's responses" (Pope Francis, cited in Gallagher 2020, para. 4). Responses are more vague and less threatening than revenge, but from a CMT perspective, the wording of both indicates that nature is perceived as an agent in the form of a classic personification metaphor (see, e.g., Dorst 2011). Personification, as the most obvious of ontological metaphors, is a cognitive mechanism used to ascribe human characteristics to seemingly agentless abstractions that allows us to perceive inexplicable, accidental, or otherwise disruptive events as "produced by an active, willful agent" (Kövecses 2010: 56). Viewing something as abstract and threatening as the coronavirus in human terms creates communicative and explanatory power (Lakoff and Johnson 1980: 43). It construes the virus as a message, a communicative act that must, in some way, make sense. Such a metaphoric framing of the virus as a message may lead to a psychological sigh of relief for people who have been utterly confused by the magnitude, on the one hand, and the meaninglessness, on the other hand, of the coronavirus pandemic in early 2020. Claiming that SARS-COV-2 IS A MESSAGE BY A HIGHER POWER also implies that we can ourselves respond to it, and that our future actions may appease the (currently angry and vengeful) agent.

While Steinmeier's examiner was left blank, Francis cites nature (note: not god himself) as the personified power behind the coronavirus. The catholic church has in common with most other major religions that it is based on an intrinsically teleological philosophy: god has a plan, and while human beings are generally free to counteract god's will, the genesis of a virus (or its sudden leap from bats to humans) would fall into the responsibility of the omnipotent. The idea that huge catastrophes are god's way of telling humans that they went wrong is as old as religion itself.

At the same time, these two permutations of the metaphor SARS-COV-2 IS A MESSAGE FROM AN ANGRY HIGHER POWER remain vague when it comes to who is the actual personified source of this anger. The influential German priest Pirmin Spiegel said in an interview that he too believed that there was a connection between the greed of global capitalism, ecological issues, and the coronavirus: "Earth is bleeding, and it is bleeding out. Multinational corporations have cut open the veins of our Mother Earth" (Spiegel and Berninger 2020, para. 6) – a remarkable mixed metaphor evoking the frame of severe injury induced by intentional violence, combined with MOTHERHOOD as a larger frame of reference, which certainly evokes not just religious, but also Freudian interpretations; note also the deictic "our" ("*unsere* Mutter Erde"). In a less drastic section of the same interview, Spiegel explains the logic behind his hybrid anti-capitalistic and Christian-ecological perspective: "Because rainforests are decimated, the space for fauna is decimated as well. Contacts between humans and wild animals increase, which also increases the risk of diseases and pandemics" (Spiegel and Berninger 2020, para. 2). All metaphoricity and teleology aside, he has a point with the latter statement: scientists without religious backgrounds have also argued that there is a causal connection between the destruction of natural ecosystems and a rising risk of zoonotic viruses in human communities (Vidal 2020).

We hold that the two metaphors discussed so far (the WAR metaphor and the MESSAGE metaphor) have been the prime contenders in terms of the question which metaphoric framing for the Sars-CoV-2 pandemic dominates public discourse. In fact, there is a structural reason for these metaphors to be alternative, or rather mutually exclusive, options. To develop this argument, let us quote a slightly longer example from a text from *The Guardian* (Clarke 2020) written by a British doctor recapitulating her experiences with patients with severe cases of Covid-19. She is aware and critical of the dominance of the WAR metaphor, particularly since prime minister Johnson needed to receive treatment at hospital in April 2020.

> The language of war has been rife during the pandemic [. . .]. Cabinet members assured us Boris Johnson would beat the disease because he's a fighter, as though survival is somehow a test of character, a matter primarily of valour. The reality, of course, is more banal. People do not die from this illness – or from any other – because they lack grit. Nor do they live by sheer pugnaciousness. I look down at the bedsheets, stained with sweat [. . .] It could not be plainer to anyone here that Winston [a 83 year-old, severely ill patient] is no participant in a battle. He is, instead, merely the battlefield. [. . .] Character has precisely nothing to do with it. It never does in the real world of the hospital where the good, the bad, the brave and the timid all kneel alike before cancers and microbes. (Clarke 2020, para. 12–13)

Dr Clarke's literary ambitions are clear (she is an author and journalist, besides being a MD), and she uses the metaphoric repertoire with argumentative clarity. She develops the standard WAR metaphor into a related one with a different focus: AN ILL BODY IS A BATTLEFIELD (of virus vs. immune system), which rejects the implication of soldierly valor or character as part of illness and recovery. This metaphoric shift detaches the person from their ill body (which is not unusual in health communication, see Frank 2002: 12). She then introduces an alternative metaphor by claiming that "all kneel alike" before the immediate threat of an illness such as Covid-19. Kneeling is a classic religious act, and in this metaphoric conceptualization, both "cancers and microbes" acquire the status of gods, or at least their worldly representation (e.g., an altar).

In the larger picture, Clarke's narrative negotiates the psychological burden of dealing with the feeling of powerlessness and helplessness when faced with a lethal infectious disease against which there is no medicine (yet) among all who are involved: patients, relatives, and medical staff. So her article echoes many of the observations outlined in section 2 about crises of agency and anxieties about losing control as sociocultural reactions to illness. The psychosocial and communicative-linguistic results of the coronavirus pandemic on health communication in hospitals, by and among healthcare professionals will be a highly relevant topic for further research, which cannot be addressed in more detail here. We have chosen to discuss this example in a bit more detail because, in terms of metaphors, Clarke's choice to deconstruct the aptitude of the WAR metaphor, to then end on a version of the MESSAGE FROM GOD metaphor may lead the way to understanding the central philosophical difference underlying the two.

The WAR metaphor, as discussed, attempts to emphasize human agency as a countermeasure to the suffering the pandemic has brought. The subtext of this empowerment may be problematic, as discussed above, but it reveals the firm belief that problems, even dramatic global ones, are solvable by human action (e.g., collective efforts, governmental decisions, soldierly discipline, etc.). The REVENGE metaphor derives from the philosophically opposite direction: fatalism. Those who generally believe in the limits of humanity may have found it easy to picture the Sars-CoV-2 as – yet another – sign for the fact that the universe is beyond human control.

Whether the revenge theme is emphasized or not (in Clarke's narrative, for example, revenge plays little or no role) is a secondary question to the key idea: humility. Mankind is humbled by the power of, in this case, a virus. The religious/ spiritual perspective emphasizes mankind's faults and a higher power's logical reaction to punish the sinners (e.g., Francis's and Spiegel's statements) or at least test their morals (e.g. Steinmeier's statement). A purely scientific perspective of course rejects the teleological view that this virus has a purpose, and that it is sending a message. Still, even doctors and scientists have used metaphors to frame the virus and what it vividly shows, mortality, in whose face "we all kneel alike", which is an ultimately fatalistic perspective as well (e.g., Clarke's statement).

4.3 Diversity and similarities

Our observation in the prior section, that the WAR metaphor and the MESSAGE metaphor have represented the main contenders to conceptualize Sars-CoV-2 metaphorically in the early phase of the pandemic, was made on the grounds that they are philosophically diametrically opposed. It should not stay unmentioned though that a plethora of other metaphorical conceptualizations have been published and certainly have influenced public discourse and perception. Collecting, mapping, describing, and potentially quantifying these metaphor usages, their common source domains, and the inner differentiations of the target domain is a task that will deserve central attention among CMT scholars in the near future. Metaphor researchers have used social media to lay the foundation for a concerted effort of scholars from various linguistic and cultural backgrounds (see Semino's and Koller's research and social media project #ReframeCovid).

Many results in Semino et al.'s collection intersect with our own research and corpus. As a preliminary conclusion, we found that the coronavirus crisis shows many family resemblances with other crises and large-scale problems when it comes to which semantic domains serve as metaphorical sources. The Sars-CoV-2 pandemic has, unsurprisingly, been described as a natural disaster (wildfire, tsunami, etc.), occasionally a "natural disaster in slow-motion" (Friebe 2020, para. 6); and it has been personified in more than one way, i.e., not just as an enemy soldier, but also as an "uninvited guest" (Stringer et al. 2020), or as a criminal (Shariatmadari 2020). A highly conventional domain for describing collective, strategic, goal-oriented effort – in this case: by governments and societies – is the domain of SPORTS. Unsurprisingly, the enduring efforts to cope with the crisis have been framed as a "marathon" (German chancellor Angela Merkel quoted in Welt.de 2020, para. 10), other forms of races (e.g., "a world-wide race for a vaccine", DW 2020), or competitive ball sports (football matches, e.g., the Bavarian prime minister Söder, see Lanz 2020). Many of these metaphoric scenarios are combinations of primary metaphors that, again, are neither unconventional nor unusual in this particular crisis as compared to other crises. For example, the JOURNEY metaphor intersects with the NATURAL DISASTER frame in the statement "we are not in the same boat, we are in the same storm" (Henry quoted in Porter 2020, para. 15). Then, also, a marathon is both a sports competition *and* a long journey; a widely different context, but still closely related to the JOURNEY metaphor.

We are of the opinion that the discourse analytic approach to CMT greatly expands the perspective beyond the descriptive towards a communicative-analytical perspective in the face of such metaphorical diversity. In other words, while the various and diverse forms of metaphorical conceptualizations may be interesting in and of themselves, to get to the bottom of the sociocultural values and ideologies in which they are embedded and which they purport, one must ask for the communicative intent of those using them in a concrete context. To name a simple example: a highly recurrent metaphoric motif in the spring of 2020 was the concept that NURSES ARE SUPERHEROES, most famously in Banksy's artwork in a British hospital (cited in Morris 2020), but also in many other media texts, such as editorial cartoons etc. It indirectly also metaphorically personifies the virus,

SARS-COV-2 IS A SUPERVILLAIN, but that seems to be besides the communicative point. Valorizing healthcare professionals in times of a medical crisis, in which their professional knowledge and dedication is essential, is more than a symbol of society's thankfulness (as which it was commonly interpreted). It also communicated to said healthcare workers that they ought to keep going, despite the fact that they were often overworked and underpaid, that hospitals were understaffed due to healthcare privatization, that security measures to protect their own health were occasionally sketchy – because that is what is expected of superheroes. They sacrifice, put themselves at risk, and, in common comic book logic, their existence is necessary because governments and their representatives fail to protect their people. In that manner, the SUPERHERO metaphor may have been eerily adequate in the British and American context. A closer analysis of its communicative context gives much less reason for optimism than a simple reading of the metaphoric conceptualization at face value would imply.

In a further step, mapping and comparing metaphoric blends on the abstract level – their "event structure" in Dancygier and Sweetser's sense (2014) – is necessary for a full understanding of family resemblances in metaphoric mappings in order to understand their ideological undercurrents. SPORTS metaphors, for example, are close relatives of the WAR metaphor on several levels, though here also, many have criticized and deconstructed the conventional metaphor of SPORT IS WAR (Senkbeil 2011, Butterworth 2012). Still, since it also emphasizes agency, the combination of willpower and strategy, as well as the possibility to ultimately win, the idea that THE CORONAVIRUS CRISIS AS A LONG DISTANCE RACE is related to the WAR metaphor concerning its basic event structure.

The NATURAL DISASTER metaphor, conversely, emphasizes the lack of control and limited power of humans in the face of nature's force, as mentioned earlier. It generally functions without personification and without pointing the blame at god or Mother Nature, but still is related to what has been discussed in chapter 4.2, in that the only logical reaction to a natural disaster that encompasses the whole world is humility. Human agency plays a much smaller role, so this second family of metaphors is generally less optimistic and less future-oriented than the SPORTS or WAR metaphor: simply put, one cannot win (against) a tsunami or a storm.

5 Conclusion

Viewing metaphors for Sars-CoV-2 and Covid-19 through the lens of CMT has proven useful in showing that viruses and epidemics are particularly prone for metaphoric construals that make them appear less alien and less mysterious.

Even though the coronavirus itself, as a biological entity, is concrete and ontological, it must be considered a highly abstract target domain in early 2020, not only because it is invisible to the human eye, but also because it was steeped in intellectual and emotional uncertainty, e.g., regarding how it spreads, whom it was going to befall, how it affected the human body and the social system. Our analysis has shown that two underlying event structures dominated the diverse metaphoric landscape in the public discourse of the three countries under examination here. Firstly, personification of the VIRUS AS AN OPPONENT founded in a rather generic EVENTS ARE ACTIONS frame helped people make sense of the apparent randomness of the disruptive events brought forth by an unknown illness of an unprecedented magnitude (at least for those living today). The CORONAVIRUS PANDEMIC IS A WAR and, logically, SARS-COV-2 IS AN ENEMY dominated the political discourse in the UK and the USA in the spring of 2020. SPORTS metaphors – such as those used by German government officials – tone down some of the entailments, but they generally relate to the same event structure.

The second recurrent metaphoric construal we found claims SARS-COV-2 IS A MESSAGE, which, interestingly, also uses EVENTS ARE ACTIONS as well as personification, but moves the personified entity one step further away from us (societies suffering from the virus). If Sars-CoV-2 is a message, then the sender of this message is its personified origin, and here, many different interpretations are possible: god, nature, death, and a teacher (testing us) were the ones we found in our corpus.

We have argued that the two main trends of giving the pandemic an event structure follow two general ideologically and philosophically opposed perspectives: fatalism versus an agency-based philosophy akin to liberal modernism. It also appears relevant to emphasize that these two trends in metaphorical construals of and around the coronavirus pandemic are decidedly *not* congruent with traditional political camps in other spheres of life. That is to say: not only conservative, right-leaning voices have framed the pandemic as a war effort, in which closed borders, a strong nation state, and punishment of socially deviant behavior was necessary. Even the most left-liberal governments closed their borders during the pandemic. Vice versa, not only left-liberal ecologists with standpoints critical of global capitalism and unimpeded exploitation of natural resources used the framing that SARS-COV-2 IS A MESSAGE (to learn humility and change our ways).

That is not to say that the metaphors we have analyzed are apolitical. In fact, our discourse analytical lens has shown how creative metaphors crafted from the skeletal structures we mentioned above help politicians to push agendas (e.g., preventing serious opposition against their executive orders) and to motivate the public to comply with restrictions protecting the population from contagion, while infringing on basic rights to freedom, which must logically lead to political uproar in pluralistic societies (such as the ones under examination in this chapter). Other metaphorical choices appear to have a long-term perspective as their underlying motivation: framing the coronavirus as a response to mankind's exploitation of nature aims at political change in the long run. When the acute coronavirus crisis will have been overcome, the ecological crises that surround us will still be in place, so even though there is good reason to criticize the teleological approach as to why the virus hit in 2020 (scientifically, viruses are not tools of Mother Nature's vengeance), its communicative intent is not without merit – and in some ways more humanistic than the WAR metaphor.

An international and bilingual data set such as ours also renders visible cultural differences regarding metaphoric constructions that are at work beneath the linguistic surface: all Western government officials that we quoted here framed Sars-CoV-2 as an OPPONENT in discourse in one way or another, but the basic personification is furnished with different characteristics regarding the opponent's level of vindictiveness, visibility, and violent intents in different cultural contexts. To name just one example of the (inter-)cultural elements we found: the metaphors used by German politicians such as a RACE or an EXAM (even if the examiner might be a deity) imply that we (mankind) can 'win' or 'pass', and that things will be fine in the end, which conveys a different kind of threat level than being a soldier in a war against an 'invisible enemy' (Trump) lurking in the shadows.

We have outlined in section 2 and 3 of this paper that embodiment is a central theoretical approach with which to understand illness communication and metaphors, including the ones mentioned above. The dual character of embodied knowledge in communication finds striking parallels in how the virus and the pandemic have been framed: as the literal virus enters literal bodies and makes them ill, this has led to metaphorical conceptualizations such as AN ILL BODY IS A BATTLEFIELD. Macroscopically, as the virus entered nation after nation and affected whole societies (though technically only few people had fallen ill yet), similar metaphors and compound schemas (such as the INFECTION-BY-SHUTTLE schema) were constructed from similar embodied set pieces. Public discourse about Covid-19 thus framed individual body and societal body in a metonymic relationship, just as embodiment theory predicts.

Naturally, we are aware that our data collection represents only a very small fraction of the extensive global coronavirus discourse, that our data is grounded in decidedly Western cultural perspectives, and that our analysis is probably biased by the choice of national contexts and languages. For a more comprehensive approach, metaphoric Covid-19 conceptualizations in non-Western discourses and in other languages should be included in the analysis, which might ultimately also help to understand how different cultures have responded communicatively to the breakdown of the body induced by the coronavirus, and the perceived temporary breakdown of society it induced as well.

References

Althusser, Louis. 2020 [1970]. *On ideology*. London: Verso books.

Boothe, Brigitte. 2011. Ein erzählanalytisches Programm für die psychodynamische Diagnostik. In: Gerd Jüttemann (ed.), *Biographische Diagnostik*, 196–204. Lengerich: Pabst Science Publications.

Benczes, Reka. 2006. *Creative compounding in English: The semantics of metaphorical and metonymical noun-noun combinations*. Amsterdam: John Benajmins.

Braha, Dan. 2012. Global civil unrest: Contagion, self-organization and prediction. (Ed.) Yamir Moreno. *PLoS ONE* 7(10). e48596. https://doi.org/10.1371/journal.pone.0048596.

Bury, Michael. 2001. Illness narratives: fact or fiction? *Sociology of Health and Illness* 23 (3). 263–285.

Butterworth, Michael L. 2012. Militarism and memorializing at the pro football hall of fame. *Communication and Critical/Cultural Studies* 9 (3). 241–258. https://doi.org/10.1080/14791420.2012.675438.

Charmaz, Kathy. 1983. Loss of self. A fundamental form of suffering in the chronically ill. *Sociology of Health and Illness* 5 (2). 168–195.

Charteris-Black, Jonathan. 2004. *Corpus approaches to critical metaphor analysis*. Houndmills, Basingstoke, Hampshire ; New York: Palgrave Macmillan.

Cienki, Alan. 1997. Some properties and groupings of image schemas. In Marjolijn Verspoor, Kee Dong Lee & Eve Sweetser (eds.), *Current issues in linguistic theory*, vol. 150, 3–16. Amsterdam: John Benjamins Publishing Company. https://benjamins.com/catalog/cilt.150.04cie (accessed 28 October 2015).

Clarke, Rachel. 2020. “This man knows he’s dying as surely as I do”: a doctor’s dispatches from the NHS frontline. *theguardian.com*. London. https://www.theguardian.com/books/2020/may/30/this-man-knows-hes-dying-as-surely-as-i-do-a-doctors-dispatches-from-intensive-care (accessed 23 June 2020).

Corrigan, Patrick W. & Anne C. Watson. 2002. Self-stigma & mental illness. *Clinical Psychology: Science and Practice* 9 (1). 34–53.

Dancygier, Barbara & Eve Sweetser. 2014. *Figurative language*. New York: Cambridge University Press.

Dorst, Aletta G. 2011. Personification in discourse: Linguistic forms, conceptual structures and communicative functions. *Language and Literature* 20 (2). 113–135. https://doi.org/10.1177/0963947010395522.

Elias, Norbert. 1978. The civilizing process. *Theory and Society* 5 (2). 219–228.

Fauconnier, Gilles & Mark Turner. 2003. *The way we think: conceptual blending and the mind’s hidden complexities*. New York, NY: Basic Books.

Flood, Alison. 2020. Publishers report sales boom in novels about fictional epidemics. *theguardian.com*. London. https://www.theguardian.com/books/2020/mar/05/publishers-report-sales-boom-in-novels-about-fictional-epidemics-camus-the-plague-dean-koontz (accessed 24 June 2020).

Frank, Arthur. 2016. From sick role to narrative subject: an analytic memoir. *Health* 20 (1). 9–21.

Frank, Arthur. 2010. The body’s problems with illness. In: Mary Kosut & Lisa J. Moore (eds.), *The body reader. Essential social and cultural readings*, 31–47. New York & London: New York University Press.

Frank, Arthur. 2002. *At the will of the body. Reflections in illness*. Boston & New York: Mariner Books.

Frank, Roslyn M., Tom Ziemke & Jordan Zlatev (eds). 2008. *Body, language and mind. Volume 1: Embodiment*. Berlin & New York: Mouton de Gruyter.

Friebe, Richard. 2020. Coronavirus als „Naturkatastrophe in Zeitlupe" – Deutschland hat das Virus erst viel zu spät ernst genommen [Coronavirus as 'natural disaster in slow motion' – Germany has taken the virus seriously much too late] *tagesspiegel.de*. Berlin. https://www.tagesspiegel.de/politik/coronavirus-als-naturkatastrophe-in-zeitlupe-deutschland-hat-das-virus-erst-viel-zu-spaet-ernst-genommen/25643008.html (accessed 23 June 2020).

Fritsch, Oliver. 2020. Ich hab's gehabt. [I had it.] *ZEIT.de*. Hamburg. https://www.zeit.de/zeit-magazin/leben/2020-04/covid-19-genesung-patient-pandemie-coronavirus/seite-1 (accessed 24 June 2020).

Gallagher, Delia. 2020. Pope says coronavirus pandemic could be nature's response to climate crisis. *cnn.com*. https://edition.cnn.com/2020/04/08/europe/pope-francis-coronavirus-nature-response-intl/index.html (accessed 23 June 2020).

Geary, James. 2012. *I is an other. The secret life of metaphor and how it shapes the way we see the world*. New York: Harper Perennial.

Gibbs, Raymond W. 2005. *Embodiment and cognitive science*. Cambridge: Cambridge University Press.

Giora, Rachel. 2003. *On our mind: salience, context, and figurative language*. New York: Oxford University Press. http://public.eblib.com/choice/publicfullrecord.aspx?p=281337 (accessed 3 May 2017).

Gjelsvik, Bergljot, Darko Lovric & J. Mark G. Williams. 2018. Embodied cognition and emotional disorders: Embodiment and abstraction in understanding depression. *Journal of Experimental Psychopathology*. July-September 2018. 1–41. https://doi.org/10.5127/pr.035714.

Goffman, Erving. 1963. Stigma. Notes on the management of spoiled identity. New York: Touchstone.

Goffman, Erving. 1959. The presentation of self in everyday life. New York: Anchor Books.

Grady, Joseph A. 1998. The "conduit metaphor" revisited: A reassessment of metaphors for communication. In Jean-Pierre Koenig (ed.), Discourse and cognition: bridging the gap, 205–218. Stanford, Calif: CSLI Publications.

Hampe, Beate & Joseph E. Grady (eds.). 2005. *From perception to meaning: image schemas in cognitive linguistics* (Cognitive Linguistics Research 29). Berlin & New York: Mouton de Gruyter.

Harvey, Kevin & Svenja Adolphs. 2014. Discourse and healthcare. In: James P. Gee & Michael Handford (eds.), *The Routledge handbook of discourse analysis*, 470–481. London & New York: Routledge

Hyde, Marina. 2020. The horror of coronavirus is all too real. Don't turn it into an imaginary war. *the guardian.com*. London. https://www.theguardian.com/commentisfree/2020/apr/07/horror-coronavirus-real-imaginary-war-britain (accessed 23 June 2020).

Hydén, Lars-Christer. 1997. Illness and narrative. Sociology of health and illness 19 (1). 48–69.

Iken, Katja. 2020. Rassismus ist ein aggressives Virus. *SPIEGEL.de*. Hamburg. https://www.spiegel.de/geschichte/black-panther-veteranin-ericka-huggins-rassismus-ist-ein-aggressives-virus (accessed 24 June 2020).

Johnson, Mark. 1987. *The body in the mind. The bodily basis of meaning, imagination and reason*. Chicago, London: University of Chicago Press.
Kimmel, Michael. 2008. Image schemas in narrative macrostructure: combining cognitive linguistic with psycholinguistic approaches. In Jan Auracher & Willie van Peer (eds.), *New beginnings in literary studies*, 158–184. Newcastle: Cambridge Scholars Pub.
Kimmel, Michael. 2009. Analyzing image schemas in literature. *Cognitive Semiotics* 9 (5). 159–188. https://doi.org/10.3726/81609_159.
Kleinmann, Arthur. 1988. *The illness narratives. Suffering, healing and the human condition*. New York: Basic Books.
Kövecses, Zoltan. 2010. *Metaphor. A practical introduction*. Oxford university press.
Kövecses, Zoltán. 2007. *Metaphor in culture: universality and variation*. 1st paperback ed. Cambridge: University Press.
Lakoff, George. 1993. The contemporary theory of metaphor. In Andrew Ortony (ed.), *Metaphor and Thought*, 202–251. 2nd edn. Cambridge University Press.
Lakoff, George & Mark Johnson. 1999. *Philosophy in the flesh. The embodied mind and its challenge to Western thought*. New York: Basic Books.
Lakoff, George & Mark Johnson. 1980. *Metaphors we live by*. Cambridge University Press.
Lakoff, George & Mark Johnson. 2003. *Metaphors we live by*. Chicago: University of Chicago Press.
Lanz, Markus. 2020. Talkshow. *Markus Lanz*. Hamburg: ZDF. https://www.youtube.com/watch?v=U7lC_cRHohY (accessed 24 June 2020).
Löhndorf, Marion. 2020. Mit Kanonen auf Viren schiessen: Kriegsmetaphern haben in Corona-Zeiten Konjunktur. *Neue Zürcher Zeitung*. Zürich. https://www.nzz.ch/feuilleton/corona-und-kriegsrhetorik-ld.1560145 (accessed 24 June 2020).
Lucius-Hoene, Gabriele. 2008. Krankheitserzählungen und die narrative Medizin. *Rehabilitation* 47 (2). 90–97.
Matthews, Steve, Robyn Dwyer & Anke Snoek. 2017. Stigma and self-stigma in addiction. *Journal of Bioethical Inquiry* 14 (2). 275–286. https://doi.org/10.1007/s11673-017-9784-y.
Meretoja, Hanna. 2020. Stop narrating the pandemic as a story of war. *openDemocracy*. https://www.opendemocracy.net/en/transformation/stop-narrating-pandemic-story-war/ (accessed 23 June 2020).
Morris, Steven. 2020. New Banksy piece celebrates superhero health workers. *theguardian.com*. London. https://www.theguardian.com/artanddesign/2020/may/06/banksy-artwork-superhero-nurse-nhs-coronavirus-covid-19-southampton-general-hospital (accessed 24 June 2020).
Musolff, Andreas, Fiona Macarthur & Giulio Pagani (eds.). 2014. *Metaphor and intercultural communication*. London & New York: Bloomsbury Academic.
Musolff, Andreas & Jörg Zinken (eds.). 2009. *Metaphor and discourse*. Basingstoke; New York: Palgrave Macmillan.
Mitchell, Peta. 2012. *Contagious metaphor*. London & New York: Continuum.
Niemann, Norbert. 2020. Das Virus des Neoliberalismus . *ZEIT.de*. Hamburg. https://www.zeit.de/kultur/literatur/freitext/neoliberalismus-virus-metapher-krankheit (accessed 24 June 2020).
Papathomas, Anthony, Brett Smith & David Lavellee. 2015. Family experiences of living with an eating disorder: A narrative analysis. *Journal of Health Psychology* 20 (3). 313–325.
Parsons, Talcott. 1970. Some theoretical considerations bearing on the field of medical sociology. In: Parsons, Talcott (ed.), *Social structure and personality*, 325–358. New York: Free Press.

Peckham, Robert. 2013. Economies of contagion: financial crisis and pandemic. *Economy and Society* 42 (2). 226–248. https://doi.org/10.1080/03085147.2012.718626.

Pierret, Janine. (2013). The illness experience: state of knowledge and perspectives for research. *Sociology of Health & Illness* 25. Silver Anniversary Issue. 4–22.

Plunger, Petra. 2013. *Heilsames Erzählen. Krankheitsnarrative am Beispiel der homöopathischen Behandlung und Betreuung*. Wiesbaden: Springer.

Porter, Catherine. 2020. The Top Doctor Who Aced the Coronavirus Test. *New York Times*. New York, NY. https://www.nytimes.com/2020/06/05/world/canada/bonnie-henry-british-columbia-coronavirus.html (accessed 24 June 2020).

Roth, Philip. 2010. *Nemesis*. London: Cape.

Rucker, Philip & Ashley Parker. 2020. Seven days as a 'wartime president': Trump's up-and-down command of a pandemic. *washingtonpost.com*. Washington D.C. https://www.washingtonpost.com/politics/seven-days-as-a-wartime-president-trumps-up-and-down-command-of-a-pandemic/2020/03/20/0dac3610-6ad6-11ea-9923-57073adce27c_story.html (accessed 23 June 2020).

Schmitt, Rudolf. 2016. *Systematische Metaphernanalyse als Methode der qualitativen Sozialforschung [Systematic metaphor analysis as a method of qualitative sociology]*. Wiesbaden: Springer.

Semino, Elena. 2020. #ReframeCovid. Twitter.com. (accessed 23 June 2020).

Semino, Elena. 2008. *Metaphor in discourse*. Cambridge: Cambridge University Press.

Semino, Elena, Zsofia Demjen, Andrew Hardie, Sheila A. Payne & Paul Rayson. 2018. *Metaphor, cancer and the end of life: A corpus-based study*. London: Routledge.

Senkbeil, Karsten & Nicola Hoppe. 2016. "The sickness stands at your shoulder . . .": Embodiment and cognitive metaphor in Hornbacher's Wasted: A Memoir of Anorexia and Bulimia. *Language and Literature* 25 (1). 3–17. https://doi.org/10.1177/0963947015608084.

Senkbeil, Karsten. 2011. *Ideology in American sports: a corpus-assisted discourse study*. Heidelberg: Winter.

Senkbeil, Karsten. 2017a. Image schemas across modes and across cultures: communicating horror in Philip Roth's Nemesis and Ridley Scott's Alien. *Language and Literature* 26 (4). 323–339. https://doi.org/s://doi.org/10.1177/0963947017739741.

Senkbeil, Karsten. 2017b. Figurative language in intercultural communication – a case study of German-Southern African international academic discourse. *Intercultural Pragmatics* 14 (4). 465–491. https://doi.org/10.1515/ip-2017-0022.

Shafer, Jack. 2020. Behind Trump's strange 'invisible enemy' rhetoric. *Politico.com*. https://www.politico.com/news/magazine/2020/04/09/trump-coronavirus-invisible-enemy-177894 (accessed 23 June 2020).

Sharf, Barbara F. & Marsha L. Vanderford. 2009. Illness narratives and the social construction of health. In: Teresa Thompson, Alicia Dorsey, Roxanne Parrot & Katherine Miller (eds.), *Handbook of health communication*, 9–34. New York, Abingdon: Routledge.

Shariatmadari, David. 2020. "Invisible mugger": how Boris Johnson's language hints at his thinking. *theguardian.com*. London. https://www.theguardian.com/politics/2020/apr/27/muggers-and-invisible-enemies-how-boris-johnsons-metaphors-reveals-his-thinking (accessed 23 June 2020).

Smith, David. 2020. Trump talks himself up as "wartime president" to lead America through a crisis. *theguardian.com*. London. https://www.theguardian.com/us-news/2020/mar/22/trump-coronavirus-election-november-2020 (accessed 23 June 2020).

Soboczinski, Adam. 2020. Peter Sloterdijk "Für Übertreibungen ist kein Platz mehr." *ZEIT*. Hamburg, 16/2020 edition. https://www.zeit.de/2020/16/peter-sloterdijk-corona-krise-gesundheitspolitik (accessed 24 June 2020).

Soff, Marianne. 2011. Biographische Diagnostik im Tagebuch. In: Gerd Jüttemann (ed.), *Biographische Diagnostik*, 205–213. Lengerich: Pabst Science Publications.

Sontag, Susan. 1978. *Illness as metaphor*. New York: Farrar, Straus & Giroux Macmillan.

Spiegel, Pirmin & Matthias Berninger. 2020. Bayer versus Misereor: "Die Multi-Konzerne haben die Adern von Mutter Erde aufgeschnitten." Interview by Ileana Grabitz & Marlies Uken. ZEIT.de. https://www.zeit.de/wirtschaft/2020-05/bayer-monsanto-misereor.

Stringer, Kathleen A., Michael A. Puskarich, Michael T. Kenes & Robert P. Dickson. 2020. COVID-19: The uninvited guest in the intensive care unit – Implications for pharmacotherapy. *Pharmacotherapy: The Journal of Human Pharmacology and Drug Therapy* 40 (5). 382–386. https://doi.org/10.1002/phar.2394.

Vidal, John. 2020. "Tip of the iceberg": is our destruction of nature responsible for Covid-19? *theguardian.com*. London. https://www.theguardian.com/environment/2020/mar/18/tip-of-the-iceberg-is-our-destruction-of-nature-responsible-for-covid-19-aoe (accessed 23 June 2020).

Wheeler, Ladd. 1966. Toward a theory of behavioral contagion. *Psychological Review* 73 (2). 179–192. https://doi.org/10.1037/h0023023.

2020a. Coronavirus: "We are at war" – Macron. *BBC.com*. London. https://www.bbc.com/news/av/51917380/coronavirus-we-are-at-war-macron (accessed 23 June 2020).

2020b. Coronavirus: "We must act like any wartime government." *BBC.com*. London. https://www.bbc.com/news/av/uk-51936760/coronavirus-we-must-act-like-any-wartime-government (accessed 23 June 2020).

2020c. Frank-Walter Steinmeier ruft zu Solidarität in Europa auf. [Frank-Walter Steinmeier calls for solidarity within Europe]. *ZEIT.de*. Hamburg. https://www.zeit.de/politik/deutschland/2020-04/frank-walter-steinmeier-bundespraesident-corona-krise-solidaritaet (accessed 23 June 2020).

2020d. Weltweites Rennen um Corona-Impfstoff. [Worldwide race for corona vaccine] *DW.com*. https://www.dw.com/de/weltweites-rennen-um-corona-impfstoff/av-53190498 (accessed 24 June 2020).

2020e. „Unsere Richtwerte waren richtig" – Merkel verteidigt Corona-Kommunikation und gibt ein Ziel aus. ["Our guidelines were right" – Merkel defends corona communication and defines a target]. *WELT.de*. Berlin. https://www.welt.de/politik/article207641467/Coronakrise-Merkel-verteidigt-Corona-Kommunikation-und-gibt-Ziel-aus.html (accessed 23 June 2020).

Section IV: Intercultural metaphorical conceptualizations

Adriana Fernandes Barbosa

Conceptual fluency and meaning negotiation in the German as a Foreign Language classroom: a multimodal analysis of teacher-student interactions

Abstract: This chapter aims at debating the relevance of conceptual fluency for the research on German as a Foreign Language. In order to do so, it demonstrates how cognitive structures such as image schemas as well as conceptual metaphors are displayed in gestures produced by native teachers of German and their Brazilian learners while discussing the meanings of particle and prefixed verbs. The lessons were videotaped, transcribed, and annotated according to the Linguistic Annotation System for Gestures (LASG). The multimodal analysis of teacher-student interactions provides empirical evidence of embodied conceptual thinking, since the gestures found in these interactions portray image schemas and metaphorical mappings underneath the meanings of particle and prefixed verbs. Such mappings indicate that these structures are cognitively activated for interlocutors during the conversation. Moreover, the analysis of gestures sheds some light on the importance of a comprehensive inclusion of cognitive linguistics in the second language learning and teaching agenda. The results show that language and embodiment can be explored in the classroom and help students develop their conceptual fluency in the target language.

Keywords: German as a Foreign Language, particle and prefixed verbs, conceptual fluency, metaphorical competence, gestures in classroom interaction

Note: This work is part of my doctoral research, which was partly funded by CAPES - Coordination for the Improvement of Higher Education Personnel (*Coordenação de Aperfeiçoamento de Pessoal de Nível Superior*). It is also part of the project "(Inter)cultural key concepts at the interface between interaction, cognition and variation", which was developed within the research group *Intercultural Communication in Multimodal Interactions* - ICMI with the support of the Alexander von Humboldt Foundation and the Minas Gerais State Research Foundation - FAPEMIG.

I would like to thank Ulrike Schröder for reviewing my speech transcriptions.

Adriana Fernandes Barbosa, State University of Southwestern Bahia

https://doi.org/10.1515/9783110688306-011

1 Introduction

Second language acquisition theories have made considerable advances concerning the issue of how we learn other languages. Consequently, different methods and approaches, especially regarding foreign language learning and teaching, have been put forward so far. The oldest but most predominant one is Vygotskian sociocultural theory. Moeller and Catalano (2015: 238) explain that, according to sociocultural theory, "participation in culturally organized activities is essential for learning to occur. Active engagement in social dialogue is important. Learning is regarded as intentional, goal-directed, and meaningful and is not a passive or incidental process but is always conscious and intentional." It is in the light of Vygotskian sociocultural theory and mostly based on cognitive linguistics that Danesi (2017) proposes his conceptual fluency theory, which has been developed since the mid-1980s upon the concepts of conceptual fluency and metaphorical competence. The author claims that being fluent in a language involves more than just developing linguistic or communicative competences. In order to be fully fluent in a language, learners must develop metaphorical competence.

Concerning the field of German as a Foreign Language [*Deutsch als Fremdsprache*, henceforth DaF], some researchers like Bellavia (2007, 2014) and Strietz and Kopchuk (2009) investigated the teaching of conceptual metaphors to DaF-learners and showed that it is possible to teach the motivation of linguistic metaphors by explaining their image source as well as by comparing the conceptualizations of L1 and L2. Likewise, Roche and Scheller (2004), Scheller (2008), and Grass (2013) developed experiments based on cognitive principles to explain grammatical structures, such as *Wechselpräpositionen*,[1] to advanced DaF-learners. They demonstrated how this cognitive approach not only facilitated but also improved the learning of these structures. Similarly, Barbosa (2015) observed how teachers explained the preposition *über* during DaF-lessons at a Brazilian university. She pointed out that the use of image schemas motivated teachers to perform gestures and draw pictures that illustrated the different meanings of this preposition.

As gesture studies have shown, cognitive processes such as metonymical and metaphorical mapping can be empirically observed through the gestures produced by the participants during face-to-face interaction (e.g., Müller 2008; Müller and Cienki 2009; Cienki 2010, 2013). Also, gestures may reflect the development of L2-learners' skills and competences (e.g., Stam 2006, 2014, 2017; Gullberg 2009). Nevertheless, the bulk of studies on the relationship between gestures and

1 A group of nine prepositions, namely *an, auf, hinter, in, neben, unter, über, vor*, and *zwischen*, may take either the dative or the accusative case, depending on the context.

L2 acquisition have focused on the production of gestures by L2-learners/speakers during pre-designed experiments, and only few studies have paid attention to the analysis of gesture production by teachers within classroom interaction, which may help to shed some light on the role of gestures in L2 teaching.

Therefore, this chapter intends to explore how conceptual knowledge regarding the meaning of particle and prefixed verbs in German can be revealed through the gestures produced by teachers and learners during DaF-lessons. Additionally, it will be observed how much conceptual and metaphorical competence varies between native and non-native speakers. Firstly, I will present the conceptual fluency theory as defined by Danesi (1995, 2017). Secondly, I will explain, from a cognitive-semantic perspective, the use and meaning of *unter* in particles as well as in prefixed verbs. Then, I will discuss how gestures reveal conceptualizations and help in foregrounding metaphorical thinking during interactions. Next, I will explain the methodology I used to analyze the gestures performed by teachers and students while discussing the meanings of the particle and prefixed forms of the verb *unterstellen*. Finally, I will present the analysis and discuss how the gestures revealed the conceptual fluency of the native speaker teacher and the different levels of metaphorical competence of two Brazilian learners of German.

2 Conceptual fluency theory

Although many linguists have been discussing the interface between cognitive and applied linguistics, Marcel Danesi was the first to mention the term *conceptual fluency* in 1986. Since then, his work has generated much research that validates conceptual fluency as a viable theoretical pedagogical framework for L2 teaching and learning. The basic premise of conceptual fluency theory (henceforth CFT) is that "knowledge of conceptual systems plays a much larger role in guiding the formulation and use of speech acts than pure pragmatic knowledge and, as corollary, that the achievement of L2 proficiency requires knowledge of these systems" (Danesi 2017: 24). In other words, to be conceptually fluent in L2, learners must build up their conceptual competence so that they can accurately associate language structure and conceptual knowledge, or vice versa.

Before defining conceptual competence, I will review some crucial points related to the concepts of linguistic and communicative competences. Building upon the Saussurian concepts of *langue* and *parole*, Chomsky first brought up the notion of linguistic competence in 1965, which he described as the tacit, implicit knowledge a native speaker has of the grammar and lexicon of their language. Fernández and Cairns (2010: 60) explain that this tacit knowledge "means that people do not have conscious access to the principles and rules that govern the combination of sounds, words, and sentences; however, they do recognize when those rules and principles have been violated". They also state that understanding language as a distinct system is an important premise for Chomskyan linguists since our linguistic system functions independently from other related activities such as speech, thought, and communication (Fernández and Cairns 2010: 3). The notion of communicative competence, in turn, was first put forth by Dell Hymes, who advocated that linguistic competence could not work without language use. Therefore, a communicatively competent speaker knows how to use the language for specific purposes of communication "based on a specific system of implicit rules of usage and locutionary adaptation that it entails" (Danesi 2017: 16-17).

Although the research on linguistic and communicative competence has resulted in a variety of pedagogical methods and approaches, Danesi (1995) noted that autonomous student discourse still might lack the conceptual richness that characterizes native speaker discourse. For the author, it is the notion of conceptual metaphor that could give us "a probable explanation as to why student discourse is often so unnatural, no matter what methodological orientation is used to impart knowledge of the L2" (Danesi 1995: 4). In other words, what students lack is conceptual fluency based on the development of metaphorical competence.

Based on the cognitive principle of classification, CFT acknowledges conceptual knowledge as the basis for organizing and storing mental lexicon and even grammatical rules. This idea was first suggested by Franz Boas (1940 cited in Danesi 2017: 21) in his linguistic-anthropological work with American indigenous languages. Boas observed that some languages provided speakers with specific verbal structures that are related to their environmental and social realities. The work of Boas inspired linguists as Edward Sapir and Benjamin Lee Whorf to develop similar research culminating in the Sapir-Whorf hypothesis, which claims that "language categories predispose speakers to attend certain concepts as being necessary. They do so because they are used to classify the world in specific (specialized) ways" (Danesi 2017: 23). The Whorfian hypothesis is pivotal to CFT since the conceptual system, which is manifested in specific language structures, emerges from culturally-based classificatory needs. Consequently, conceptual knowledge is crucial for both language usage and use.

CFT thus defines conceptual fluency as the ability to accurately formulate structures in order to convey appropriate literal and figurative meaning in the L2. Conceptual fluency depends on the development of conceptual competence, which, according to Danesi (2017: 39), includes linguistic, communicative, and metaphorical competences working together to produce appropriate and comprehensible speech acts, ranging from information exchanges (literal meaning) to highly interpretative ones (figurative meaning). That is the most relevant contribution of conceptual fluency theory: introducing conceptual and metaphorical competence as new paradigms in SLA. Danesi (2017: 74) defines metaphorical competence as the learners' ability to appropriately comprehend and produce conceptual metaphors and conceptual metonymies in the L2.

Furthermore, lack of conceptual fluency might lead to conceptual calquing, that is, leaners *speak* with the formal structures of the L2, but they *think* in terms of their native conceptual system (C1). In other words, they use L2 words and structures as *carriers* of their own L1 concepts. For this reason, CFT advocates that learners must have systematic and progressive access (explicit instruction) to the L2 conceptual system in order to develop conceptual fluency. It is important to remember that a conceptual system also includes grammar since language, as an integral part of our cognitive system, is based on the speaker's conceptualizations of the world. In the next section, I will explain how particle and prefixed verbs in German are an example of how spatial conceptualization impacts the grammar as well as motivates metaphorical meanings.

3 Particle and prefixed verbs in German

Multi-word verbs in German are divided into particle verbs and prefixed verbs. They are also known in language course books and grammars as separable (particle) and inseparable (prefixed) verbs (*trennbare und untrennbare Verben*). In many cases, the particles as well as prefixes derive from prepositions. I will show in this section how the meaning of these verbs is cognitively motivated by perspectival modes and image schemas. Knowledge of such cognitive processes and structures is not only essential for developing conceptual competence in German as a Foreign Language (DaF) but also helps analysts to observe these phenomena in gestures produced by DaF-teachers and learners.

According to Dewell (1996: 109), the most common prepositions that constitute verbal particles and prefixes are *durch* ('through'), *über* ('over' / 'above'), *unter* ('under'), and *um* ('around')[2], building verbs that can be separable and inseparable at the same time. The (in)separability of the particles and prefixes impacts not only the syntactic but also the prosodic structure of the verb. In separable verb constructions, the particle must be detached from its base verb, for instance, when we conjugate the verb in the present tense or when we form its past participle. In this case, the word stress falls on the particle. By contrast, inseparable

2 These translations are based on the spatial meaning of these prepositions. Their translations may vary in different contexts of use.

prefixes are never detached from their base verbs and the word stress is placed on the base verb, usually on the first syllable.

Language course books and grammars usually focus only on these structural differences when teaching separable and inseparable verbs. At the most advanced levels, however, some semantic differences between particle and prefixed verbs may be discussed in some textbooks. They usually highlight the tendency for separable verbs to have concrete (spatial) meanings while their correlative inseparable forms assume abstract (nonspatial) meanings. In this process, named by Talmy (2000) as *fictive motion*, the image schema[3] that structures the spatial meaning is partially transferred to the nonspatial meaning, which maintains the schema but does not imply a physical movement.

Nevertheless, as Dewell (2011: 9-10) explains, there are many occurrences of prefixed verbs with concrete meanings as well as particle verbs with abstract meanings. For the author, the (in)separability of verbal prefixes are not necessarily motivated by its metaphoricity but rather by other cognitive aspects such as synoptical and sequential perspectival modes (Talmy 2000):

> Particle verb constructions consistently prompt us to concentrate our focal attention on particular parts of a path, most typically on a moving figure or a salient part of a moving figure, and they thus portray the path as a temporal sequence of particular locations (such as the beginning and end). They call for an interpretation in sequential perspectival mode. Prefixed verb constructions consistently prompt us to distribute focal attention more evenly over the whole scene and the whole path. They call for an interpretation in synoptic perspectival mode. (Dewell 2011: 16-17)

Consequently, Dewell (2011) first establishes the prototypical image schema that underlies the prepositions *durch*, *über*, *um*, and *unter*, and then describes how these schemas remain as the core meaning in different particle and prefixed verbs composed by these prepositions.

---

3 Johnson (1987: xiv, xvi) first defined image schema as "a recurring dynamic pattern of our perceptual interactions and motor programs that gives coherence and structure to our experience." Lakoff (1987: 458) also explains that paths are examples of imagistic-schematic reasoning because "[i]f a trajector is at a given point on a path, it follows that it has been on all previous points on the path." Langacker (2008: 70-71), in his turn, highlights the profiling aspect of the relationship between a trajector and a landmark: "When a relationship is profiled, varying degrees of prominence are conferred on its participants. The most prominent participant, called the trajector (TR), is the entity construed as being located, evaluated, or described. Impressionistically, it can be characterized as the primary focus within the profiled relationship. Often some other participant is made prominent as a secondary focus. If so, this is called a landmark (LM). Expressions can have the same content, and profile the same relationship, but differ in meaning because they make different choices of trajector and landmark."

Considering that the upcoming analyses will focus on the particle verb *UNTERstellen* as well as on the prefixed verb *unterstellen*,[4] I present a prototypical image schema for *unter* 'under' in Figure 1, where the trajector (TR) path is represented by an arrow while the rectangle is the landmark (LM).

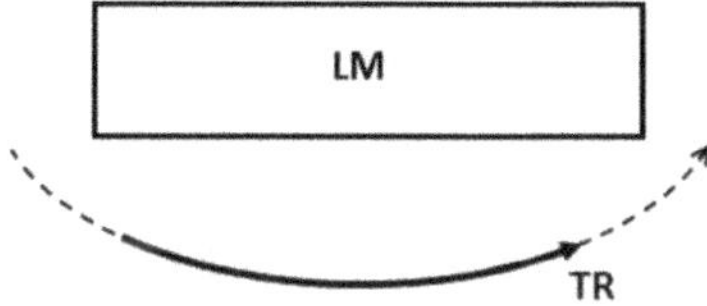

Figure 1: Prototypical route-path schema for *unter* 'under' as verbal particle/prefix.
Source: Adapted from Dewell (2011: 25)

This route-path schema[5] can be described as the movement of a TR[6] that passes through a point below a LM, or at least on its bottom surface, so that the path undergone by TR is profiled in relation to the position of the LM.

Nevertheless, Dewell (2011: 23) shows that, although route-path schemas prototypically represent verbal particles and prefixes in German, *unter* has only a peripheral meaning when compared to other particles and prefixes.

> The preposition *unter* usually describes a location rather than a route, and the route-path meaning is often avoided because of potential confusion with a goal path. That is, a phrase such as *unter die Brücke* would probably describe a path that ends at a destination underneath the bridge, and speakers usually prefer constructions such as *unter der Brücke durch* to make it clear that the path in question is a route path that passes through that location and continues on. (Dewell 2011: 25)

In other words, when *unter* is employed to denote direction, it tends to describe goal paths as in *Marion geht unter die Brücke* (Marion goes under the-ACC[7] bridge), as Figure 2 illustrates. Conversely, to make it clear that the TR goes all the way through the LM, as in Figure 1 (route-path schema), speakers tend to use the adverb *durch* 'through' as in *Marion fährt unter der Brücke durch* (Marion drives under the-DAT bridge through*).

---

4 Following Dewell (2011), I will use capital letters to emphasize the separability of the particle, as in *UNTERstellen*, in which UNTER 'under' is the separable particle and *stellen* 'to place' is the base verb. Similarly, I will use small letters to refer to the inseparable verbs, as in *unterstellen*.

5 According to Dewell (2011: 24), a route path "is defined in relation to a location that is intermediate between the start of the path [. . .] and the end of the path." He contrasts route-path schemas to goal-path schemas, following the taxonomy of paths proposed in Jackendoff (1983).

6 Dewell (2011) uses Leonard Talmy's nomenclature, which names the prominent entity figure (FG) instead of trajectory (TR).

7 Like all the dual case prepositions (*Wechselpräpositionen*), *unter* must be used with the accusative case when it denotes direction. Conversely, when it denotes location, it must be used with the dative case.

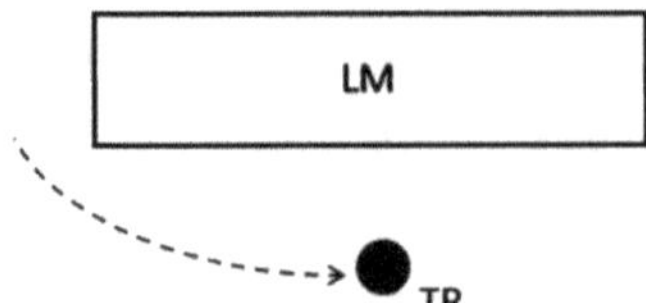

Figure 2: Goal-path schema for *unter.*
Source: Elaborated based on Dewell (2011:25)

This characteristic can be observed in the verbs *UNTERstellen* and *unterstellen*. The particle verb *UNTERstellen* means *sich zum Schutz vor Regen oder Unwetter unter ein schützendes Dach stellen* (to go stand under a protective roof in order to protect oneself against rain or bad weather) but also *etwas zur Aufbewahrung vorläufig unterbringen* (to keep something temporarily for safekeeping) or simply *etwas unter etwas stellen* (to place something under something else).[8] Therefore, the separable particle *UNTER* plus the base verb *stellen* 'to place' can be illustrated by the goal-path schema in Figure 2, which describes a TR that is placed under a LM. The question is not *how* the TR is moving (sequential mode), but *where* it is moving (synoptical mode) or even *why* it is moving (that is, to find shelter under the LM).

On the other hand, the inseparable verb *unterstellen* usually describes either a subordinating action, such as *er wurde dem Direktor direkt unterstellt* (he was directly subordinate to the director), or the act of maliciously attributing words or deeds to someone through unfair allegations or insinuations. There is also another less frequent meaning, which is the act of "hypothetically presuming something for the sake of discussion" (Dewell 2011: 223). I will concentrate here only on the context of unfair allegation, since it is the case that will be analyzed later. This use of *unterstellen* suggests a more abstract TR "such as a motive or an opinion that does not so clearly exist independent of the person it is being attributed to, and so is not so clearly being transferred in a sequential change from one particular focal location to another" (Dewell 2011: 75). As Dewell describes, *unter* in this case means that the act is deceptive or underhanded. To some extent, this meaning can be related to the local preposition *unter*, 'under', which can also be the destination of the goal-path schema, as described above. In the next session, I will discuss how cognitive structures, such as image schemas and metaphors, can be observed in gesture production and how verbo-gestural metaphor theories are helpful for demonstrating conceptual competence and fluency in native and non-native speakers of German.

8 "*unterstellen*", In: DWDS - Digitales Wörterbuch der deutschen Sprache. https://www.dwds.de/wb/unterstellen (accessed on 08 Mar. 2020).

4 Detecting conceptual fluency and competence through gestures

Gesture studies have shown that cognitive processes can be observed empirically through the gestures produced by participants in face-to-face interaction. Based on Lakoff and Johnson's (2003, [1980]) concept of *embodied mind*, we know that our mind is anchored in our body in that our knowledge as well as our language are structured via cognitive processes associated with our motor and perceptual systems. The cognitive view of gesture was first put forth by David McNeill (1992), who claimed that the analysis of involuntary gestures would be a way for us to access the speaker's mind as well as their conceptualizations of the world. Moreover, McNeill's theory maintains that gesture and speech are part of the same system. He points out that "gestures are an integral part of language as much as are words, phrases, and sentences – gesture and language are one system" (McNeill 1992: 2).

Mittelberg (2018) claims that gestures, as a true phenomenon of human communicative behavior, may be more or less consciously produced at different moments of the interaction. According to the author, it is precisely the less conscious aspects of gestures that make them a valuable source of insights into the functioning of cognition and language, enabling us "to empirically study the origins and nature of the deeply embodied aspects of the human mind to which image schemas (and metaphor) clearly belong" (Mittelberg 2018: 2). Cienki (2005: 436), for instance, explains that PATH image schemas "can be indicated with one's forearm and hand outstretched, or by moving one's hand in a line and tracing a path". Williams (2008) also demonstrates how the PATH schema is revealed by the circular manual gestures performed by a teacher around the face of a clock while teaching students how to tell the time. In addition, Mittelberg (2018) shows how an American English speaker conceptualized the metaphor TIME IS SPACE when describing for how long she has been watching a sitcom. While uttering the segment "*from the point of where I was till like the end of the season*", the speaker "designates the point of departure with her left, almost vertically held, open hand and the end point with her open right hand, which is likewise held vertically, thus reinforcing the idea of a bounded space" (Mittelberg 2018: 4). Thus, her gesture and speech simultaneously profiles the three parts of the PATH schema (which is the imagistic source of the metaphor TIME IS SPACE): the SOURCE, by saying "from where I was", the PATH through time, by saying "till like", and the GOAL, by saying "the end of the season".

Müller and Tag (2010: 94) points out that gestures may activate the metaphoricity of a given verbal expression by foregrounding some semantic elements of the metaphor's source domain, such as image schemas. To put it differently, gestures can be an empirical evidence of the metaphorical mapping (Cienki and Müller 2008: 493). This is one of the tenets within Cornelia Müller's (2008) dynamic view of metaphor. Among other modalities, the author considers gesture as an indicator of activated metaphoricity in discourse (Müller 2008: 198). While the linguistic theory of metaphor proposes a static division into novel and *dead* (conventionalized) metaphors – as the semantic source domain becomes inaccessible to speakers through the process of conventionalization –, Müller (2008) maintains that the accessibility to the source domain is not a matter of conventionalization but rather of opacity and transparency within conventionalized metaphors. On the one hand, there are the conventionalized metaphors that are opaque (dead) to contemporary speakers; that is, the origin of the metaphor remains further back in language history and can only be accessed through an etymological analysis of the lexical item. On the other hand, there are the entrenched metaphors which are conventionalized but still transparent to speakers since their source domain can be retrieved when needed. An example of an entrenched metaphor is the idiom *to fall in love*. Although this idiom is highly conventionalized in English, speakers still have access to the concrete meaning of the verb *fall*. Therefore, they can perceive *Anna fell in love with Richard* as metaphorical when comparing this sentence with *Anna fell off the stairs*. This differentiation between opaque and transparent metaphors is essential to the dynamic view of metaphor because only transparent metaphors can vary in their degree of metaphoricity; that is, they can be minimally or highly active for speakers during interaction (Müller 2008: 200).

Regarding the gestural production in face-to-face interactions, when metaphoric concepts are expressed in only one mode, either speech or gesture, they are considered monomodal or *sleeping* metaphors for they are minimally active for speakers during interaction. Nevertheless, when a metaphor is simultaneously expressed by two different modalities, like verbal-gestural metaphors, they become highly active for participants during interaction. These active metaphors are the *waking* metaphors. Therefore, different elements help to activate metaphoricity of multimodal metaphors, such as semantic correspondence of gesture form and lexical item (such as correspondence between gesture form and image schemas), the co-occurrence of gesture stroke and focal accent, speaker's gaze at their own gesture (focus of attention), realization of the gesture in the center of the gesture space, among others.

Giving that image schemas motivate the meanings of some separable and inseparable verbs in German, and that these verbs may vary in their degree of metaphoricity, I utilized the dynamic view of metaphor and its cognitive perspective on gestures to analyze the gestural production of both teachers and learners of German within classroom interaction while they discussed the possible meanings of the verbs *UNTERstellen* and *unterstellen* (as discussed in section 3). Their gestural production was used then to assess their levels of conceptual fluency and/or metaphorical competence regarding the use of these verbs. Next, I will present the methodological approach for annotating and analyzing speech and gesture.

5 Methodology for gesture analysis

The analyses presented in this chapter are part of my doctoral dissertation (Barbosa 2020), whose data basis comprises over 9 hours of videotaped DaF-lessons.[9] The two examples analyzed in the next section were taken from two different lessons. The first lesson was filmed in 2014 and was part of the course German 4 (level B1) offered within the German Undergraduate Program at a Brazilian university. The participants are five Brazilian undergraduates and a native-speaker professor who is also fluent in Brazilian Portuguese. The second lesson was filmed in 2018 at a private language school in Brazil. The participants are two advanced learners of German and their instructor, a German-Portuguese balanced bilingual. The participants consented to the use of their images for research purposes.

For the annotation and analysis of gestures, I use the Linguistic Annotation System for Gestures (LASG) since its analytical steps allow the identification of different levels of conceptual (metaphorical) competence in teachers and students during classroom interaction. This annotation system encompasses the first three blocks of MGA,[10] namely: "1) form, 2) sequential structure of gestures in relation to speech and other gestures, 3) local context of use, i.e. gestures' relation to syntactic, semantic, and pragmatic aspects of speech" (Bressen, Ladewig, and Müller 2013: 1100). The foundation of the LASG is the notion that through gestures "we see and experience the embodied basis of verbal meaning while speaking" (Bressem, Ladewig, and Müller 2013: 1104). Therefore, a crucial step of this annotation system is to identify the gesture's meaning by comparing the form and movement of the hands to motor patterns, image schemas, or action schemas whilst considering the four modes of gestural representation proposed

9 The data basis is part of the ICMI corpus which is available on <http://www.letras.ufmg.br/icmi/>
10 This acronym stands for 'Methods of Gesture Analysis' and describes a set of methods divided into four blocks of analysis that systematically reconstructs the meaning of a gesture.

by Müller (2010): *shaping, drawing, representing,* or *acting as if*. LASG is thus a bottom up approach to gesture analysis that starts by describing the gesture's form and structure and then determining its semantic, syntactic, and/or pragmatic functions.

Following LASG, I began the analysis by establishing the limits of the gesture unit and then dividing it into distinct phases. The annotation of a gesture unit begins by indicating the initial position, or resting position, of the speaker's hands. Next comes the preparation phase, when hands and arms position themselves to perform the gesture that will follow. After the preparation phase, the speaker produces the stroke of the gesture, which is the nucleus of the gesture unit and, therefore, carries the meaning of the gesture. The stroke is followed by the retraction phase, when the hands return to the initial resting position, ending the gesture unit or they reconfigure themselves to perform another stroke, initiating another gesture unit. A hold phase may happen right after the stroke, when the speaker retains the gesture's configuration for a while. The hold phase may evolve to another stroke, initiating a new gesture unit, or move straight to a retraction phase (Bressem, Ladewig, and Müller 2013: 1102). After defining the gesture unit, I annotated the shape of the hands, the palm orientation, and the position of the gesture in relation to the speaker's body (gesture space). The description of gesture form follows some parameters proposed by Bressem (2013), namely hand shape, palm orientation, and types of movement. Table 1 shows the acronyms I used during gesture annotation:

Table 1: Hand shape and palm orientation.

Description	Short form
Left hand	LH
Right hand	RH
Both hands	BH
Palm down	PD
Palm up	PU
Palm towards body	PTB
Palm away from body	PAB

Source: Adapted from Bressem (2013)

Moving on to the second block of analysis in LASG, I annotated the temporal relation between gesture and speech, that is, I determined whether the gesture stroke co-occurred with a co-expressive speech segment, which in this case are the separable and inseparable verbs discussed during the lesson. After that, in the third and final block of analysis, it was possible to determine the gesture's semantic functions based on three types of semantic relations: *redundant*, when the gesture's form matches the image schema underneath the verbal prefix, emphasizing its meaning; *complementary* or *supplementary* relation, when the gesture's form does not match the image schema but still contributes to the meaning of the verb in general; and *replacing*, when the gesture occurred in the absence of speech, substituting the verb or verb phrase[11] (Bressem, Ladewig, and Müller 2013: 1111).

LASG recommends the use of GAT 2[12] conventions (Couper-Kuhlen and Barth-Weingarten 2011) to annotate the speech. These conventions allow the analyst to divide the speech into turns or intonation units as well as to annotate prosodic elements, such as final pitch movements and focal accents. The transcriptions presented in this chapter are divided into intonation units, since the data is part of the ICMI Corpus,[13] whose transcription standards follow this pattern.

The gestures were annotated using the software ELAN and the text outputs were exported to an Excel spreadsheet so I could better edit the annotation tables. I also transcribed the speech using EXMARaLDA since this software automatically generates a more reader-friendly output[14] for speech transcriptions following GAT 2 conventions. This output will be presented separately from the annotation tables for it facilitates the analysis of the interactional aspects in gesture's production.

---

11 LASG also considers the contrary semantic relation, which occurs when gesture and speech have contrary semantic features; however, this relation was not found in the data.

12 GAT 2 (*GesprächsAnalytisches Transkriptionssystem*) is the second version of a unified transcription system developed "for notating, first and foremost, the wording and prosody of natural everyday talk-in-interaction" (Couper-Kuhlen and Barth-Weingarten 2011: 2). It has three annotation levels: minimal, basic, and fine. The minimum level notates only few verbal aspects such as intonation phrases and pauses and is considered, therefore, only as a working tool that precedes more detailed linguistic analysis. The basic and fine levels allow us to insert prosodic and visual elements for more detailed linguistic analysis. LASG recommend the basic level, which I also use here, since it is important to notate final pitch movements and focal accents within intonation units in order to determine some gestural functions.

13 The ICMI corpus (former: NUCOI corpus) is currently comprised of about 2,496 minutes of videotaped interactions and their transcriptions with a total of 56,164 intonation units. The recordings are based on elicited, institutional, and natural interactions among participants from different cultures, as well as among participants with the same linguistic and cultural background. The corpus can be accessed at: http://www.letras.ufmg.br/icmi/

14 The running transcript is subdivided into segments that correspond to each intonation unit. Each segment is numbered, and each number is followed by the speaker ID. Under each segment line, I inserted the translation in English.

6 Data analysis

This section looks at two excerpts of classroom interaction where teachers and learners are discussing the meanings of the separable verb *UNTERstellen* and the inseparable form *unterstellen*. The first excerpt is an example of how conceptual fluency can be detected through the gestures of a native speaker of German. In the second excerpt, I demonstrate how gestures may reveal different levels of conceptual (metaphorical) competence in DaF-learners. For each example, I first show an extended transcription of the speech in order to provide a broader context for the gesture production. Then I present the annotation tables for the gestures, followed by a detailed description of the gesture form, temporal, and semantic relation as well as semantic function. The discussion concerning the relevance of the gestures regarding conceptual fluency as well as possible pedagogical repercussions will be presented in a separate section.

6.1 Example 1

This first excerpt was taken from a German language course taught to undergraduate students. In the transcript below the native speaker professor is comparing the separable verb *UNTERstellen* with the inseparable *unterstellen*. He gives an example with a spatial context to explain the separable form, whereas the inseparable verb is explained through a highly metaphorical example, as shown in (1) and (2):

(1) *Es regne-t und wir müss-en uns unter ein Dach*
It rain-3.SG and we must-2.PL ourselves under a-ACC.N roof
unter-stell-en.
unter-PAR-place-INF
'It's raining and we have to shelter under a roof.'

(2) *Das ist eine Unter-stellung*
That is an-NOM.F unter-PAR-placement
'That's an unfair allegation'

His full explanation follows in the transcript below:

2014BHAula01-parte03 ((17:46-19:33))

001 P: ah:m rapidamente um OUtro exEmplo,
quickly another example

002 ah:m (-) que eu jÁ dei uma OUtra vez,
that I've already given before

003 ah:m UNterstellen,
to shelter

004 (1.7) ja zum BEIspiel,
yeah for example

005 es (---) REgnet,
it's raining

006 (1.8) und wir mÜssen uns (---)<<highlighting the tonic accent on the board> ↑UNterstellen,>
and we have to shelter

007 <<pointing to the board> quer dizEr também num sentido conCREto (-) né;>
I mean in a concrete sense right

008 wir mÜssen uns (-) UNterstellen,
we have to shelter

009 unter ei::n unter ein DACH (.) ne,
under a under a roof right

010 (---) und das PERfekt ist <<pointing to the whiteboard> Also,>
and the participle form will be then

011 wir HAben uns,
we have

012 (3.2)

013 S2: UNtergestEllt;
sheltered

014 P: UNtergestEllt (-) ne;
sheltered right.

015 ((writes on the whiteboard for approx. 3.3))
<<writing the verb on the board> gE (1.9) STELLT (1.4) ne;>

016 (--) und (-) na wenn es UNterstellen gibt,
and if there is *UNTERstellen*

017 <<writing on the board> dann (.) gibts natürlich AUCH unter↑stEllen;>
then there's also *unterstellen*

018 ((writes the verb on the board for approx. 6.3)) unterSTELlen;

019 (1.8) es ist (-) auch was dass es absTRAKT ist;
it's also something that is abstract

020 das-
this

021 (1.8) hhh° (1.3) <<acc> etwas (xxx) man> das ist zum BEIspiel,
something one this is for example

022 eine diffaMIErung,
a defamation

023 (--) äh: (-) jemand (-) SAGT,
someone says

024 <<pointing to S5> S5 (.) du hAst> <<pointing to the computer in the room> äh:::> einen comPUter (-) gestOhlen;
S5 you stole the computer

025 S5: [((laughs))]

026 P: [((laughs))] você rouBOU (--) o computAdor;
you stole the computer

027 (1.3) ne,
right

028 (-) das heißt es ist eine beHAUPtung,
I mean that's a statement

029 uma afirmação SEM (.) fundamEnto,
an unfounded claim

030 sem PROva,
with no evidence

031 das ist eine unter↑STELlung
it is an (unfair) allegation

032 (---) não sei qual seria o TERmo-
I don't know what the word would be

033 (2.8) mais adeQUAdo,
the most appropriate one

034 mas a idEia é DE (.) ser uma:-
but the idea is that it is

035 uma uma caLÚnia,
a a slander

036 uma difamaÇÃO,
a defamation

037 (1.3) alguma cOiIsa nesse (-) senTIdo;
something in this regard

From lines 004 to 015, the professor explains the separable verb *UNTERstellen*. First, in line 005, he gives the context of the action by saying *it's raining*. Next, in line 006, he introduces the verb in the sentence *und wir mÜssen uns ↑UNterstellen* (and we have to shelter) and emphasizes the separable particle with a small pitch upstep to make clear that the separable verbs have their stress syllable always on the particle: ↑*UNterstellen*. At the same time, he writes the accent mark on the first syllable of the verb on the board. In the next segment, he draws students' attention to the fact that the separable form is being used with a concrete meaning. Then he repeats his example in lines 008 and adds the prepositional phrase *unter ei::n unter ein DACH* (under a roof) in line 009, while performing a gesture, as shown in Annotation Table 01.

The professor repeatedly moves the open right hand, with the palm facing down, back and forth over his head. This gesture form suggests that the teacher is molding a flat surface over his head that can be used as protection from the rain. The stroke phase begins at the end of the intonation unit in line 008 and lasts until the beginning of the next unit, co-occurring with the speech segment *UNters-tellen, unter ei::n*, which also has a primary focal accent. It is interesting to note that he prolongs the pronunciation of the indefinite article *ein* by about 0.7 seconds while repeating the stroke, and then retracts the gesture while saying *unter ein DACH;*. Based on the gesture-speech temporal correlation, I claim that his gesture is a metonymical representation of the goal-path schema underlying *UNTERstellen*, as shown in Figure 03, rather than only an iconic representation of a place where people can hide from the rain.

Annotation Table 01: Gesture for *UNTERstellen*.

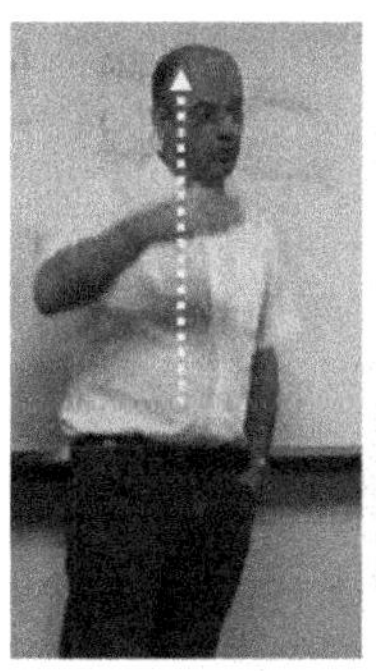

preparation stroke

T-Speech:	wir mÜssen uns|	(-)	|**UNterstellen,**	**unter ei::n**|	unter ein DACH
T-translation:	and we must |	...	|**shelter**	**under a**	| under a roof right
T-phase:		|prep.|		**stroke**	| retraction
T-Gesture:	Open LH-PD moves repeatedly forwards and backwards over the head in a straight-line path.				

Figure 3: Image schema for *sich unter ein Dach unterstellen* (to shelter under a roof).

As the transcript shows, the teacher added a pleonastic directional prepositional phrase (pleonastic PP)[15] *unter ein Dach* after saying the main verb *unterstellen.*[16] According to Dewell (2011: 42), "pleonastic PPs typically specify a particular LM in the spatial context" that is usually implicit in constructions with particle verbs. Therefore, the teacher not only models the shape of the LM, but also uses his own body (his head) to represent the destination of the TR under the LM, that is, the whole configuration of hands and body foregrounds the goal-path schema of *UNTERstellen.*

Continuing his explanation in line 017, the professor introduces the inseparable verb *unterstellen* with small pitch upstep before the secondary focus accent `unter↑stEllen;` once again to make clear that the word stress in prefixed verbs is on the base verb. He then states that this verb has an abstract meaning and compares it to the word *Diffamierung*, 'defamation', perhaps because of its phonological approximation to the Portuguese word *difamação*. Then, in line 024, he gives a more specific example by saying that someone could accuse a student of stealing a computer: he points to a student and then to the computer in the classroom and says *du hast den Computer gestohlen* (you stole the computer). He repeats the example sentence in Portuguese and then explains in lines 029 and 030 that such accusation is "an unfounded claim, with no evidence".

In the next segment, he finally mentions the nominalized form of the verb *unterstellen*, performing a gesture simultaneously, as Annotation Table 02 shows:

---

15 According to Olsen (1996: 311-312), the *pleonastiche Direktionale* are PPs whose preposition has the same form as in the particle verb. She argues that particle verbs in German do not inherit the original *P-Relatum*, that is, the object of the original PP is suppressed in particle-verb constructions. Thus, in order to restore the original P-Relatum, the speaker has two strategies: the addition of a dative object or a pleonastic directional PP.

16 In sentences with modal verbs in German, the canonical position of the main verb is at the end of the sentence.

Annotation Table 02: Gesture for *Unterstellung.*

preparation

stroke

T-Speech:	das ist |	**eine unter↑STELlung;**	|
T-translation:	it is |	**an [unfair] allegation**	|
T-phase:	preparation |	**stroke**	| retraction
T-Gesture:	Curved RH-PTB moves diagonally downwards until the palm is completely opened		

The teacher moves his right hand diagonally downwards, with the palm towards his body. The stroke occurs simultaneously to the speech segment *eine unter↑STELlung;* 'an [unfair] allegation', which also carries the primary accent within the intonation unit. At the beginning of the stroke phase, the palm is bent, but the teacher opens his hand slowly during the movement, finishing the gesture with a flat palm. Since the downward movement matches the prototypical image schema of *unter* (Dewell 2011: 40), I consider that the teacher performed a verbal-gestural metaphor. The lexicalized meaning of *unterstellen* in this context expresses an unfair and false allegation that can be associated with the idea of a deceptive or underhanded act (Dewell 2011: 223). To put it in other words, one can argue that the *unter*-schema, which represents the action of putting (hiding) something under something, motivates the metaphorical meaning of *unterstellen*, since a false allegation is not only unfair but also hides the really guilty person. In the following segment, the teacher confirms this interpretation:

032 (---) não sei qual seria o TERmo-
I don't know what the word would be
033 (2.8) mais adeQUAdo,
the most appropriate one
034 mas a idEia é DE (.) ser uma:-
but the idea is that it is
035 uma uma caLÚnia,
a a slander
036 uma difamaÇÃO,
a defamation
037 (1.3) alguma cOisa nesse (-) senTIdo;
something in this regard

In lines 032 to 036 he says he is not sure what the best translation for *unterstellen* in Portuguese would be, but he suggests it can be related to the idea of *calúnia* 'slander' or *difamação* 'defamation'. Therefore, the teacher's gesture, alongside the use of verbal elaborations of the metaphor such as the different translations into Portuguese, activates the metaphoricity (Müller 2008) of *Unterstellung*, the nominalized form of the verb *unterstellen*.

6.2 Example 2

The second example was extracted from a DaF-lesson in a private language school. The learners were doing a grammatical exercise in which they should write sentences using the correct form of separable and inseparable verbs in the present perfect tense (*Perfekt*). The excerpt transcribed below shows teacher and students discussing the meaning of the participle form of *UNTERstellen* in the following sentence:

(3) *Während der Reise hat er sein-e Pflanz-en bei*
During the-GEN.F trip AUX.3.SG he his-ACC.F plants-PL with
ein-em Freund unter-gestellt
a-DAT.M friend under-PAR-place-PTCP
'While he was away on a trip, he left his plants with a friend'.

As we observe in lines 009 and 010 of the transcript below, student S2 did not understand the meaning of the verb. Then her classmate S1 suggests in line 011 that it means "to water plants."

```
2018BHAula02-parte02 ((19:33 - 20:19))
                                      [...]
009 S2:  (1.8) ah was ist dies unter UNterges;=
               what does unterges(tellt) mean
010      =was eh verSTEhe ich nicht;
          what I don't understand
011 S1:  é joGAR água assim;
         it's to throw water like this
012 T:   ↑UNtergestellt?
013      (---) so also so so tipo (.) abriGAR;
               so (it's) like sheltering
014 S2:  ah:m UNterges-
015      [UNter (-) stEllen;]
          under      place
016 T:   [   ((nods))       ][<<nodding> jA;>]
                                            yes
017 S2:                      [<<pp> ah BOM;> ]
                                    ah ok
018 S1:  imaginei que era joGAR água;
         I thought it was like to throw water
019 S2:  [aHAM;               ]
020 S1:  [fui pelo conCREto;]
          I went for the concrete (meaning)
021 S2:  (1.2) ah::;
022      [((laughs))]
023 S1:  [((laughs))]
```

S1's suggestion in line 011 is accompanied by a gesture that is described in Annotation Table 03 below. While saying `é joGAR água assim` (it's to throw water like this), the student produces a gesture whose hand shape and movement simulates the action of watering a plant: she makes a fist with her left hand and slightly bends the wrist as if she were holding a thin object, such as the handle of a watering can. Then she moves the hand in a spiral path to the left, emulating the action of watering plants with a can. Since the stroke of the gesture co-occurs with the speech segment `joGAR água assim;` one could argue that the gesture-speech relation is redundant in that the gesture's form matches the action schema of throwing water. Nevertheless, such action could be performed in several ways, like using a glass, a kettle, a bucket, etc. Thus, even if S1 never explicitly uttered the Portuguese expression *aguar plantas*, 'to water plants', I claim that her gesture corresponds to the action schema of this verb. Since she uses the demonstrative *assim*, ´like this', she is clearly making a reference to her own gesture and, consequently, specifying how and why someone is throwing the water. In other words, by complementing her speech with her own gesture, S1 is also modifying the semantic content of this speech segment.

Annotation Table 03: Gesture for *jogar água assim* (to throw water like this).

S1-speech:	| é |	**joGAR água assim;** |
S1-translation	| it's |	**to throw water like this** |
S1-phase:	| preparation |	**stroke** |
S1-Gesture:	Closed LH in fist with bending wrist moves to the right in a spiral path movement as if holding an object	

T-speech:	| ↑UNtergestellt? |	**(---) so also so so tipo (.) abriGAR;** |	
T-translation	|	**so [it's] like sheltering** |	
S2-speech:		|	aha:m
S1-phase:	stroke |	**hold** |	

Annotation Table 03 (continued)

S1-Gesture:	S1 holds the gesture position while looking at S2 and until the teacher finishes her explanation

Another interesting aspect of this gesture is the length of the hold phase, which lasts for approximately 3.4 seconds and overlaps with the teacher's speech segment in 013. It is during this segment that the teacher provides her interpretation of the verb *UNTERstellen* by saying *so also so so tipo (.) AbriGAR;*[17] (it's like sheltering). Moreover, we also notice that during the hold phase student S2 looks and frowns at S1 as if considering her classmate's explanation very strange. S1 retracts her gesture only after the teacher's explanation. This phase overlaps with S2's speech segment ah:m in line 014, which indicates she understood the teacher.

In the next segment, in line 015, S2 performs two gestures that corroborate her understanding of the separable verb *UNTERstellen*, as shown in Annotation Table 04. In the first gesture, she moves both open hands with palms down in a straight path downwards. The stroke co-occurs with the particle *unter,* which also carries the focal accent within the intonation unit. The gesture's downward-movement partially matches the goal-path schema of *unter,* which indicates that the schema is active for S2 during the interaction.

Following the first stroke, S2 retracts her hands and then initiates a second stroke that co-occurs with the verb base *stellen* 'to place'. This gesture has a shorter extension: she moves both curved hands, palms towards center, in a straight path downwards, as if she were placing an object in front of her. Both the shape and the movement of the hands are consistent with the semantic features of the verb *stellen.* Moreover, S2 performs both gestures by looking at the teacher, who nods her head in agreement. During the retraction phase, S2 also expresses understanding by nodding and saying ah BOM; (ah, ok!).

17 The German-Portuguese balanced bilingual teacher often code-switches during the lesson. Nonetheless, this aspect is not considered in this analysis since the code-switches are not directed related to the student's gesture.

Annotation Table 04: Student's gesture for *UNTERstellen.*

preparation stroke

<table>
<tr><td>S2-speech:</td><td>(-) | UNter | (-)</td></tr>
<tr><td>S2-translation:</td><td>| under |</td></tr>
<tr><td>S2-phase:</td><td>preparation| stroke | retraction</td></tr>
<tr><td>S2-Gesture:</td><td>Open curved BH-PD move downwards in a straight path</td></tr>
</table>

preparation stroke

<table>
<tr><td>S2-speech:</td><td>|stEllen;| <<pp> ah B|OM;></td></tr>
<tr><td>S2-translation:</td><td>| place |</td></tr>
<tr><td>S2-phase:</td><td>| stroke | retraction</td></tr>
<tr><td>S2-Gesture:</td><td>Open curved BH-PTC move downwards as if placing an object in front of her</td></tr>
</table>

In the next section, I will discuss how this gesture and the others reveal the levels of conceptual fluency as well as metaphorical competence of both teachers and students.

7 Discussion

Both gestures performed by the native-speaker teacher in example 1 are empirical evidence of his conceptual fluency in German, for these gestures represent the image schemas that motivate the conceptualizations of the particle verb *UNTERstellen* as well as the prefixed verb *unterstellen*. I demonstrated how the teacher was capable to explain not only the structural but also the conceptual differences between the separable (particle) and inseparable (prefixed) forms. By using a strictly spatial context, the professor performed a gesture that made the meaning of the particle verb more visual for students. As Hotze (2018: 313) points out, the visual aids provided by gestures facilitate the understanding of lexical items and relieves the cognitive burden on learners. Nevertheless, I explained how the teacher applied different metaphoricity indicators while explaining the inseparable verb *unterstellen*. He not only executes a gesture that foregrounds the image schema of *unter*, but also elaborates the metaphor verbally by giving a contextualized example of the verb as well as by repeating different synonyms for *Unterstellung* in German and in Portuguese. Both gestural and verbal elaborations of the metaphor helped to activate the metaphoricity of this lexical item.

In Example 2, I showed how gestures may reveal different levels of conceptual (metaphorical) competence in non-native speakers. Although the example sentence (3) *Während der Reise hat er seine Pflanzen bei einem Freund untergestellt* implies that the plants were actually moved from one place to another (spatial meaning), it still holds some degree of metaphoricity since the original meaning of protection conveyed by *UNTERstellen* was extended to the idea of 'taking care of'. To interpret this metaphorical extension, one needs firstly to understand the metonymical mapping underneath the collocation *etwas bei einem Freund UNTERstellen*, that is, "to place something under the roof of a friend's place" means 'to store something at a friend's place'. As a result, a conceptually fluent speaker of German can easily conclude that *er hat seine Pflanzen bei einem Freund untergestellt* means metonymically and metaphorically that he left his plants in his friend's care. Thus, S2's gestures, which represent the movement of "placing something under" (Annotation Table 04), reveal that she somehow understood the underlying conceptualization of the verb *UNTERstellen*. In other words, the student demonstrated an appropriate level of metaphorical competence in that she was able to figure out the degree of metaphoricity the sentence has (which is not very high). Moreover, the use of gestures helps the student to memorize a new lexical item. Hupp und Gingras (2016 cited in Hotze 2018: 313) have shown how iconic gestures promotes the learning of vocabulary. Consequently, the use of multimodal utterances is not only necessary for the teacher, but also for the learner, since the regular use of gestures semantically identical to speech increases learning and retention of vocabulary.

Furthermore, Gullberg (2006) explains that gestures, in the form in which they are produced in an L2, can provide valuable information about language acquisition processes, such as the influence of the L1 on the L2 and other interlanguage phenomena, as well as reveal the behavior of learners with regard to difficulties in expressing and understanding the L2. Therefore, the difficulties that both students had in understanding the meaning of *UNTERstellen* may be associated with the degree of abstraction necessary to interpret this verb in that specific context of use. As we discussed above, student S1 understood the verb as 'watering plants', which her gestures visually demonstrated (Annotation Table 03). This is not an erroneous assumption to make, since the use of the temporal adverbial phrase *während der Reise*, "during the trip", as well as the words *Pflanzen*, "plants" and *Freund*, "friend", draws the association to a typical Brazilian habit of asking a friend to water one's plants while one is away on a trip (instead of bringing the plants over to a friend's place). In other words, the sentence evokes a cultural frame that allows S1 to make such a statement (see Kövecses, this volume). What she probably missed was the metaphorical competence to construe the whole sentence scenario. Therefore, the low level of metaphorical competence in German made S1 transfer her L1 conceptual system to L2, leading her to such an inaccurate interpretation. The student justifies her interpretation some turns later by saying "I thought it was to throw water" and "I went for the concrete [meaning]", which confirms that she knew the verb was used with a concrete meaning, however she did not understand it properly.

8 Concluding remarks

The analyses presented in this chapter compared the gestures performed by native and non-native speakers of German, showing that conceptual fluency as well as metaphorical competence can be accessed through gestures. The results corroborate the dynamic view of metaphor, as teachers and students multimodally co-construct the meanings of particles and prefixed verbs based on the local context of use. Moreover, the multimodal analyses of teacher-student interactions gave us empirical evidence of embodied conceptual thinking since the gestures foregrounded image schemas as well as metonymical/metaphorical mappings, indicating that these cognitive structures were active for the participants during interaction. Therefore, I claim that gestures can be an important didactic resource in classroom interaction, working not only as a visual aid for meaning clarification but also as an essential linguistic input for L2-learning since gesture is an integral part of speech (McNeill 1992). Nevertheless, I point out the need for more studies that investigate the relationship between gesture and speech production in L2 from a cognitive-linguistic perspective so that we can better understand how the conceptual systems can influence language learning/acquisition.

In addition, the results made evident the need for a more comprehensive inclusion of cognitive linguistics in the design of L2 coursebooks and grammars as well as teacher-training curricula. Based on conceptual fluency theory, I maintain that the development of metaphorical competence must go beyond the teaching of idioms or any other figurative expressions that might sooner or later appear during L2 lessons. As I demonstrated above, the appropriate understanding of particle and prefixed verbs in German depends on identifying their different degrees of metaphoricity as well as knowing how to use these verbs based on rules and patterns that are motivated by the German conceptual system. Finally, this work has shed light on how the development of metaphorical competence goes far beyond understanding figurative expressions. As Danesi (2017) points out, being conceptually fluent means understanding how language relates form and meaning on a conceptual level since metaphorical thinking is what characterizes proficient speakers of both L1 and L2.

References

Barbosa, Adriana Fernandes. 2015. *O papel da linguística cognitiva na formação do professor de alemão como língua estrangeira: um estudo sobre o ensino da preposição über com base em esquemas imagéticos e metáforas conceptuais.*[The role of cognitive linguistics in the training of DaF-teachers: a case study on the teaching of the preposition *über* based on image schemes and conceptual metaphors]. Belo Horizonte: Federal Univeristy of Minas Gerais MA Thesis.

Barbosa, Adriana Fernandes. 2020. *Cognição em (inter)ação: uma análise multimodal do ensino de verbos separáveis e inseparáveis em aulas de alemão como língua estrangeira* [Cognition in (inter)action: a multimodal analysis of separable and inseparable verbs in German as a foreign language classroom]. Belo Horizonte: Federal Univeristy of Minas Gerais dissertation.

Bellavia, Elena. 2007. *Erfahrung, Imagination und Sprache: die Bedeutung der Metaphern der Alltagssprache für das Fremdsprachenlernen am Beispiel der deutschen Präpositionen.* Giessener Beiträge zur Fremdsprachendidaktik. Tübingen: Gunter Narr.

Bellavia, Elena. 2014. The role of metaphors in the teaching of German as a foreign language. *Lingue e Linguaggi* 11. 7–28.

Boas, Franz. 1940. *Race, language, and culture.* New York: Free Press.

Bressem, Jana. 2013. A linguistic perspective on the notation of form features in gestures. In Cornelia Müller, Alan Cienki, Ellen Fricke, Silva H. Ladewig, David McNeill & Sedinha

Teßendorf (eds.), *Body – language – communication. An international handbook on multimodality in human interaction*, 1098–1124. Berlin & Boston: De Gruyter Mouton

Bressem, Jana, Silva H. Ladewig & Cornelia Müller. 2013. A linguistic annotation system for gesture. In Cornelia Müller, Alan Cienki, Ellen Fricke, Silva H. Ladewig, David McNeill & Sedinha Teßendorf (eds.), *Body – language – communication. An international handbook on multimodality in human interaction*, 1079–1098. Berlin & Boston: De Gruyter Mouton.

Cienki, Alan 2005. Image schemas and gesture. In B. Hampe (ed.), From perception to meaning: Image schemas in cognitive linguistics, 421–441. Berlin: Mouton de Gruyter.

Cienki, Alan & Cornelia Müller. 2008. Metaphor, gesture and thought. In Raymond W. Gibbs (ed.), The Cambridge handbook of metaphor and thought, 483–501. New York: Cambridge University Press.

Cienki, Alan. 2010. Multimodal metaphor analysis. In Lynne Cameron & Robert Maslen (eds.), *Metaphor analysis*, 195–214. London: Equinox.

Cienki, Alan. 2013. Cognitive linguistics: Spoken language and gesture as expressions of conceptualization. In Cornelia Müller, Alan Cienki, Ellen Fricke, Silva H. Ladewig, David McNeill & Sedinha Teßendorf (eds.), *Body – language – communication. An international handbook on multimodality in human interaction*, 182–201. Berlin, Boston: De Gruyter Mouton.

Couper-Kuhlen, Elizabeth & Dagmar Barth-Weingarten. 2011. A system for transcribing talk-in-interaction: GAT 2. *Gesprächsforschung – Online-Zeitschrift zur verbalen Interaktion* 12. 1–51. http://www.gespraechsforschung-ozs.de/fileadmin/dateien/heft2011/px-gat2-englisch.pdf. (accessed 14 March 2020).

Danesi, Marcel. 1995. Learning and teaching languages: the role of "conceptual fluency". *International Journal of Applied Linguistics* 5 (1). 3–20.

Danesi, Marcel. 2017. *Conceptual fluency theory and the teaching of foreign languages.* New York: Nova Science Publishers.

Dewell, Robert. 1996. The separability of German *über-*: a cognitive approach. In Martin Pütz & René Dirven (eds.), *The construal of space in language and thought [Cognitive Linguistics Research 8]*, 109–133. Berlin: Mouton de Gruyter.

Dewell, Robert. 2011. *The meaning of particle / prefix constructions in German* (Human Cognitive Processing v. 34). Amsterdam & Philadelphia: John Benjamins. (accessed 14 March 2020)

DWDS – Digitales Wörterbuch der deutschen Sprache, Berlin-Brandenburgischen Akademie der Wissenschaften. https://www.dwds.de/d/wb-dwdswb. (accessed 08 March 2020).

Fernández, Eva M. & Helen Smith Cairns. 2010. *Fundamentals of psycholinguistics.* West Sussex: Wiley-Blackwell.

Grass, Anja. 2013. Zur Veränderung mentaler Modelle beim Lernen mit Grammatikanimationen: Ziele, Methoden und Ergebnisse einer Pilotstudie. *Zeitschrift für interkulturellen Fremdsprachenunterricht* 18 (1). 99–109. https://tujournals.ulb.tu-darmstadt.de/index.php/zif/article/view/68 (accessed 07 August 2020).

Gullberg, Marianne. 2006. Some reasons for studying gesture and second language acquisition (Hommage à Adam Kendon). *IRAL - International Review of Applied Linguistics in Language Teaching* 44 (2). 103–124.

Gullberg, Marianne. 2009. Gestures and the development of semantic representations in first and second language acquisition. *Acquisition et interaction en langue étrangère* [Online], Aile. . . Lia 1. 117–139. http://journals.openedition.org/aile/4514 (accessed 07 August 2020).

Hotze, Lena. 2018. Gesten im Fremdsprachunterricht: Verstehen, Memorieren, Problemlösen. In Moiken Jessen, Johan Blomberg & Jörg Roche (eds.), *Kognitve Linguistik*, 308–316. Tübingen: Narr Francke Attempto Verlag.

Hupp, Julie M. & Mary C. Gingras. 2016. The role of gesture meaningfulness in word learning. *Gesture* 15 (3). 340–356.

Jackendoff, Ray. 1983. *Semantics and cognition*. Cambridge, Massachusetts: MIT Press.

Johnson, Mark. 1987. *The body in the mind: the bodily basis of meaning, imagination, and reason*. Chicago: The University of Chicago Press.

Kövecses, Zoltán. this volume. Extended conceptual metaphor theory: the cognition-context interface. In Schröder, Ulrike; Milene Mendes de Oliveira & Adriana Maria Tenuta (eds.). *(Inter)cultural perspectives on metaphorical conceptualizations*. Berlin, New York: De Gruyter.

Lakoff, George. 1987. *Women, fire, and dangerous things*. University of Chicago Press.

Lakoff, George & Mark Johnson. 2003. *Metaphors we live by*. Chicago: The University of Chicago Press.

Langacker, Ronald W. 2008. *Grammar: A basic introduction*. Oxford University Press.

McNeill, David. 1992. *Hand and mind: What gestures reveal about thought*. Chicago: University of Chicago Press.

Mittelberg, Irene. (2018). Gestures as image schemas and force gestalts: A dynamic systems approach augmented with motion-capture data analyses. *Cognitive Semiotics*, 11(1). https://doi.org/10.1515/cogsem-2018-0002. (accessed 03 April 2021).

Moeller, Aleidine Kramer & Theresa Catalano. 2015. Foreign language teaching and learning. In James D. Wright (ed.), *International encyclopedia for social and behavioral sciences*, 2nd edn. vol. 9., 327–332. Oxford: Pergamon Press. https://doi.org/10.1016/B978-0-08-097086-8.92082-8 (accessed 14 March 2020).

Müller, Cornelia. 2008. *Metaphors dead and alive, sleeping and waking: A dynamic view*. London & Chicago: University of Chicago Press.

Müller, Cornelia. 2010. Wie Gesten bedeuten. Eine kognitiv-linguistische und sequenzanalytische Perspektive. *Sprache und Literatur* 41. 37–68

Müller, Cornelia & Alan Cienki. 2009. Words, gestures, and beyond: forms of multimodal metaphor in the use of spoken language. In: Charles Forceville & Eduardo Urios-Aparisi. (eds.), *Multimodal metaphor*, 297–328. Berlin & New York: Mouton de Gruyter.

Müller, Cornelia & Susanne Tag. 2010. The dynamics of metaphor: Foregrounding and activating metaphoricity in conversational interaction. *Cognitive Semiotics* 10. 85–120.

Olsen, Susan. 1996. Pleonastische Direktionale. In: Gisela Harras & Manfred Bierwisch (eds.), *Wenn die Semantik arbeitet*, 303–327. Tübingen: Max Niemeyer Verlag.

Roche, Jörg & Julija Scheller. 2014. Zur Effizienz von Grammatikanimationen beim Spracherwerb: ein empirischer Beitrag zu einer kognitiven Theorie des multimedialen Fremdsprachenerwerbs. *Zeitschrift für Interkulturellen Fremdsprachenunterricht* 9 (1). 1–14. https://tujournals.ulb.tu-darmstadt.de/index.php/zif/article/view/464 (accessed 10 August 2020).

Scheller, Julija. 2008. *Animationen in der Grammatikvermittlung: multimedialer Spracherwerb am Beispiel von Wechselpräpositionen*. Berlin: LIT.

Stam, Gale. 2006. Thinking for speaking about motion: L1 and L2 speech and gesture. *International Review of Applies Linguistics* 44 (2). 143–169.

Stam, Gale. 2014. Further changes in L2 thinking for speaking? In: Cornelia Müller, Alan Cienki, Ellen Fricke, Silva H. Ladewig, David McNeill & Jana Bressem (eds.), *Body – language –*

communication. An international handbook on multimodality in human interaction 2, 1875–1886. Berlin & Boston: De Gruyter Mouton.

Stam, Gale. 2017. Verb-framed, satellite-framed or in between? A L2 learner's thinking for speaking in her L1 and L2 over 14 years. In Iraide Ibarretxe-Antuñano (ed.), *Motion and space across languages*, 329–366. Amsterdam: John Benjamins Publishing.

Strietz, Monika & Ljubov Kopchuk. 2009. Metaphern in Deutsch als Fremdsprache. In: Evgenia Goncharova (ed.), *Arbeitspapiere GIP Herzen – Humboldt. Themenheft 1. Tempus – Metaphern – Text*, 82–102. St. Petersburg: Izdatel'stvo SPbGPU.

Talmy, Leonard. 2000. *Toward a cognitive semantics I: Concept structuring systems*. Cambridge & London: MIT Press.

Williams, Robert F. 2008. Gesture as a conceptual mapping tool. In Alan Cienki & Cornelia Müller (eds.), *Metaphor and gesture*, 55–92. Amsterdam & Philadelphia: John Benjamins.

Ulrike Schröder

How interculture is built on the common ground of alterity experience: a cognitive-multimodal approach to talk-in-interaction

Abstract: Despite the meanwhile widespread concept of 'interculture' (Koole and Thije 2001; Kecskes 2014), there is still little research regarding the conceptual level of intercultural encounters. Schröder (2017, 2018) has shown that metacommunication might be a point of access for focusing on this issue since 'standing between the cultures' frequently favors a meta-reflexive attitude through questioning and objectifying both 'worldviews' from a more distant angle. Koole and Thije (2001) propose the concept of 'discursive interculture' that may emerge in interaction as an intermediate space sharing both properties of home and host culture, additionally comprising those discourse elements and structures that result from culture contact (Koole and Thije 2001). Kecskes (2014) also points to meaning in intercultural encounters as co-constructed *ad hoc* and *in situ*; however, he admits that those emergent and co-constructed phenomena concurrently rely on cultural norms and models, and proposes, therefore, a dialectical relationship in his socio-cognitive approach to intercultural pragmatics.

Based on three sequences that stem from the corpus of the research group *(Inter)Cultural Communication in Interaction*, I take these frameworks as a starting point to show how verbal, corporal-gestural, and prosodic means contribute to co-constructing intercultures in talk-in-interaction. We will see how the experience of 'being a stranger' and the metaphorical conceptualization of CULTURE as CONTAINER (Lakoff and Johnson 1999; Marschak 2005; Schröder 2015), as well as the oscillation between Character and Observer Viewpoints (McNeill 1992), serve to build an intercultural space and to reflect on it. Additionally, I will reveal how strategies such as 'perspectivizing' (Thije 2005) and 'multiple viewpoint con-

Acknowledgement: First of all, I would like to thank the sponsorship for the institutional partnership between the UFMG and the University of Potsdam by the Research Group Linkage Programme, due to the Alexander von Humboldt-Foundation, Germany. Additionally, I would also like to thank CAPES, the Coordination for the Improvement of Higher Education Personnel (*Coordenação de Aperfeiçoamento de Pessoal de Nível Superior*), for their fellowship Capes-PrInt programme which enabled my postdoctoral research year at the University of Texas at Austin, USA, and the University Duisburg-Essen, Germany.

Ulrike Schröder, Federal University of Minas Gerais

https://doi.org/10.1515/9783110688306-012

struction' (Mittelberg 2017) are used to build incrementally personal common ground between the co-participants, and how emotional involvement and affiliation tokens are displayed by ironic as well as emotional viewpoints (Sweetser 2013) and exaggerated speech styles (Selting 1994).

Keywords: interculture; gesture; metaphor; viewpoint

1 Introduction

Intercultural communication has been discussed in innumerable conceivable manners by multidisciplinary approaches over many decades and in strong dependence on the particular spirit of the current dominating academic discourse. After having focused on differences for over more than two decades from a more macro-analytic approach adopted especially in anthropological and psychological intercultural communication studies, the elaboration of dichotomous categories – and even the concept of 'culture' as such – has fallen into disrepute primarily in the field of the subsequently following cultural studies. Here, research has increasingly been dealing with the dissolution of cultural and social boundaries, and the essentialist view of culture has been replaced by a post-structuralist hybrid concept of transculturalism (Schröder 2015). From a more micro-analytic view, in linguistics, ten Thije (2006), Rehbein (2006), as well as Ehlich and ten Thije (2010), have suggested abandoning the mere problem-oriented approach to intercultural communication by pointing to the specific strategies that are applied in successful intercultural encounters despite different cultural backgrounds, which perhaps do not play such an important role as supposed before.

Proposing a socio-cognitive approach that overcomes the gap between a mere cultural *and* a mere functional or, to put it differently, a mere semantic *and* a mere pragmatic perspective, Kecskes (2014) focuses on the creative and dynamic aspect of 'interculture' – without ignoring the stock of knowledge that individuals bring into a discourse situation from their cultural background – by defining 'intercultures' as "*situationally emergent and co-constructed phenomena that rely both on relatively definable cultural norms and models as well as situationally evolving features*. Intercultures are usually ad hoc creations" (Kecskes 2014: 15). Starting from concrete sequences of interactions, Kecskes illustrates how such intercultures are created *ad hoc* and *in situ* by analyzing short sequences in which lexemes and their meanings in English as a lingua franca are created which do not exist in native English but work perfectly to co-coordinate the communicative behavior of the interlocutors involved in the intercultural encounter. Another instructive empirical study is conducted by Senkbeil (2017), who shows the impact of metaphorical thinking and speaking when researchers with different cultural and linguistic backgrounds talk about a common project. They do not just smoothly co-construct the project in terms of entrenched conceptual metaphors, but also seem to be able to create and elaborate innovative metaphors, so that one may conclude that the use of metaphors could be seen as an essential means for successful intercultural communication.

Beside the abovementioned studies, as far as I am aware, there are almost no studies about the interplay of intercultural communication and cultural conceptualizations. So, it would be interesting to know (a) in which way an intercultural experience itself could not only activate but also modify entrenched cultural conceptualizations regarding culture and viewpoints; and (b) to what extent those highlighted and modified or created (inter)cultural conceptualizations could themselves serve as an 'intercultural space' with respect to their function as 'common ground builder' for interactants with different linguistic and cultural backgrounds.

Below, at first, I will describe how 'intercultural communication' should be understood for our purposes and delineate the concept of 'interculture' from an 'intercultural pragmatics' perspective. Then, I will show how such intercultures and cultural conceptualizations involved can be analyzed from a cognitive and interactional perspective by focusing on the multimodal resources participants use. This includes a fine-grained analysis of vocal, corporal-visual, and prosodic means by which interlocutors co-construct meanings *in situ*. Afterwards, I will present three sequences from the ICMI corpus recorded by the research group *Intercultural Communication in Multimodal Interaction*[1] and show how interculture is built in an interaction between two German and two Brazilian students with and based on their intercultural experiences as a common ground builder.

2 Theoretical and methodological framework

2.1 Intercultural communication and the concept of 'interculture'

How can we delineate intercultural communication as opposed to other forms of interpersonal communication? In order to answer that question, it would be interesting to take a look at the communication theory as proposed by Gerold

1 ICMI = *Intercultural Communication in Multimodal Interactions*; access in Portuguese and English at the following website: www.letras.ufmg.br/icmi

Ungeheuer (1987a). For Ungeheuer, the non-decomposable unit of speaker and hearer represents the starting point for the establishment of the communication process as an objective of analysis in its own right. The pivotal question lies in the structure of interaction as social action dominated by the persuasive force of language for reciprocal coordination (Loenhoff and Schmitz 2012).[2] However, Ungeheuer ([1983] 2010: 9) emphasizes that people realize internal actions, which are exclusively experienced by the acting individual him- or herself, alongside external actions, which are also accessible to other individuals through perception. Starting from this postulate, he endorses that the linguistic signs displayed by the speaker are conceived as mere instructions for the hearer to realize certain internal experiential acts but cannot be seen as 'messages'. Additionally, we have to consider that, due to the social, cultural, historical, and personal conditions and presuppositions, every interlocutor has his or her own "individual world theory" (*individuelle Welttheorie*). On the one hand, this individual world theory represents one's stock of systematized experiences and explanations, and, on the other hand, it channels and guides all further presuppositions and experiences. As a consequence, understanding always occurs within the scope of construction processes which the particular individual realizes in line with his or her world theory. Due to the context meanings' dependency, it always remains approximate, fallible, and fragile (Ungeheuer 1987b: 58). Nevertheless, this does not unavoidably mean that we are condemned to solipsistic existences, since the individual's world theory also has an intersubjective character for sharing a certain stock of knowledge with the others, with whom he or she starts to build life experiences from a common linguistic and cultural location. However, against this reasoning, we can easily imagine that, if successful communication is already a fragile matter in intracultural communication, its improbability increases even more in case of intercultural encounter caused by the contingencies arising significantly (Loenhoff 1992: 190–192): the interlocutors have to deal with disparate patterns of interpretation, disparate systems of relevance and background structures, different communication styles and inferential process habits, as well as varying face work strategies. Concurrently, due to the lack of linguistic competence, the metacommunicative space is limited. As a consequence, the possibilities of success control are frequently directed to the prosodic and corporal levels of communication, in order to compensate the shortcomings on the verbal plane. To sum up, the differences we listed clearly point to a discrepancy between interpersonal and intercultural communication as a matter of degree rather than a question of essence.

2 Note that Ungeheuer particularly resorts to the cognitive, pragmatic, and functional approaches to language as suggested by Bühler ([1934] 1982) as well as by Wegener ([1885] 1991).

Starting from this understanding of 'intercultural communication', the idea of 'interculture' should rather be conceived in terms of a dynamic concept that emerges in the communication process between interlocutors from different cultures, and in which this aspect plays a crucial role in the creation of the manner a given sequence is co-constructed and can be labeled as 'intercultural'. I am leaning on previous attempts as proposed by Koole and ten Thije (1994, 2001), Rehbein (2006), as well as Kecskes (2014).

Koole and ten Thije (2001) choose a strict situational approach to intercultural communication and assume an 'intercultural discourse' to be an interaction in which participants from different cultures enact and construct practices as a here-and-now accomplishment by which a 'discursive interculture' might emerge. It refers to an intermediate culture sharing both properties of home as well as host culture. But, additionally and more importantly, the authors include in their concept also "those discourse elements and structures that result from the culture contact, but which cannot be traced back to one of the cultures in contact." (Koole and ten Thije 2001: 575). It is this emergence of something new that is crucial for the analysis which follows.

Rehbein (2006) describes how such an interculture could emerge in conversational terms. People normally tend to interpret their conversational routines according to their particular cultural patterns. Now, by activating a 'cultural apparatus', those standardized forms of acting and speaking are reconstructed and entangle the interactants in aporetic ways of communication. Thereby they construct means of understanding, such as making recourse to a higher level of mediation, generating productive and receptive new forms on the part of the interlocutors and giving rise to innovative forms of communication that might bring them to a synthesis (Rehbein 2006: 44). For ten Thije (2006) and Koole and ten Thije (1994), 'perspectivizing' is seen as a crucial tool activated by the cultural apparatus, and described as the "indication of the linguistic means that make the hearers interpret the report from a certain point of view" (Koole and ten Thije 1994: 105), such as co-referential nouns, verbs, and adjectives. By applying the 'cultural apparatus', interlocutors start to go beyond their routines and improve their hermeneutic abilities in everyday situations (Ehlich and ten Thije 2010: 266).

As briefly pointed out in the introduction, Kecskes (2014, 2015) tries to overcome the dualism between macro and micro approaches through his proposal of a socio-cognitive approach. 'Interculture' is indeed seen as co-constructed in the actual situational context, but communication "may contain elements from the participants' existing cultural background and ad hoc created elements as well" (Kecskes 2014: 5). One key element for Kecskes in the building of *ad hoc* interculture is common ground. As we have seen, it is a core trait of intercultural communication that common ground appears to be missing or to be limited and has to be co-constructed by shifting from the communal to the individual. However, Kecskes likewise warns against overgeneralizations at this point: common ground certainly exists to a smaller degree in intercultural communication, although people bring in their existing cultural models and norms. His recommendation is that a careful inductive analysis of interaction be conducted that allows for the identification of preexisting images and conceptions.

In a similar vein, building on a synthesis of cognitive and anthropological linguistics, current studies in cultural linguistics advocate a dynamic view of cultural models. Sharifian (2015: 474–476) develops a theoretical framework for his key notion of 'cultural conceptualizations' (i) by building on the notion of meaning from the perspective of 'distributed knowledge and cognition', which states that not all members of a cultural group share the same concepts, such as metaphor, metonymies, prototypes, schemas, models, etc., and (ii) by emphasizing that cultural cognition embraces the cultural knowledge that emerges from the interactions between members of a cultural group across time and space. Therefore it has to be seen as constantly being negotiated and renegotiated. By adding this dynamic aspect to previously mere static concepts, Sharifian highlights a crucial point: conceptualizations may be those that underlie our first language, but there also may be others that we have had access to as a result of living in a particular cultural environment, or even could have emerged or developed from interacting with people from other cultures. As we will see, there can even be an intercultural space that favors the creation or elaboration of specific conceptualizations related to the intercultural experience of being located 'between the cultures'.

2.2 Cognition in interaction

Over the last ten years, one has been able to observe increasing overlaps between different linguistic research areas that had previously been more or less strictly separated from each other. This is valid especially for approximations of cognitive linguistics, on the one hand, and interactional linguistics, on the other. If one takes a look at cognitive linguistics, a growing tendency in turning away from mere introspective matters is observable. Empirical studies have arisen over the last decades; firstly, those that are oriented towards corpus linguistics,[3] and

3 For an overview, see Semino (2017), and for a critical discussion regarding corpus linguistics, cognitive linguistics and their applicability to cultural conceptualizations, see Polzenhagen (this volume).

secondly, those that are directed towards multimodality as well as contextually and culturally anchored interaction. Zima and Brône (2015) point to the fact that cognitive linguistics has indeed always represented a 'usage-based' approach, however, over a long period of time it has not taken into account the most basic form of human communication, that is, face-to-face interaction. This scenario is currently changing. Apart from 'interactional construction grammar' (Zima and Brône 2015: 486), it is especially in the field of metaphor and cognition where one can find a growing number of studies that are dedicated to the multimodal aspects of metaphor use in real interaction.

One crucial contribution comes from the area of gesture studies[4] and is directed toward the processuality of metaphor based on interactions that are recorded and transcribed. These studies show in detail how gestures, whose metaphoricity is not any longer perceived on the verbal level, are reactivated. The reactivation is evidenced in that the speaker, for instance, executes a hand movement that corresponds to the lexical item, directs his gaze on it and marks it prosodically (Cienki and Müller 2008). Gestures highlight certain elements and aspects of a linguistic expression, contextualize them, and contribute therefore to the figure-ground organization. By doing so, gestures are used as information management in face-to-face interaction and guide the attention of the interlocutors: "activation of metaphoricity critically depends upon the dynamic flow of the speaker's focal attention" (Müller 2008: 219). Müller and Cienki (2009) distinguish between monomodal and multimodal metaphors, the former being those that only occur in one mode (verbal or nonverbal) and the latter those that occur co-expressively in both modes. Müller (2013) does not only stress the conceptual function of metaphor but also shows how the expressive, appealing, performative, and pragmatic functions become visible in gestural metaphors, which can be seen as a further approach of cognitive semantics towards pragmatic topics. Müller (2008: 224; Bressem and Müller 2014) and Streeck (2008a, 2008b) show how interlocutors mark certain arguments as obvious by an open hand, or as less plausible by signaling the throwing or brushing away of an object, or how interlocutors mark allocation of turns.

McNeill (1992: 118–119) was one of the first to attend to viewpoint in gesture. In his psychological-cognitive approach to gesture, he distinguishes between two ways of how gestures could convey viewpoints of actions that are being described: either by the 'character's viewpoint' (C-VPT), by which the narrator in discourse adopts the perspective from the inside of the story and, e.g., moves his arms up and down, as if climbing a ladder. In opposition to that, he could also make the hand form the character as a whole and cause it to rise upward,

4 Cf. for an overview Müller et al. (2013, 2014).

not being part of the scene and incorporating an 'observer viewpoint' (O-VPT), keeping distance from the story itself. That is, an O-VPT gesture excludes the speaker's body from the gesture space, while the C-VPT is participative. Narrators occasionally combine O-VPT and C-VPT gestures simultaneously, creating 'dual viewpoint' gestures (McNeill 1992; Parrill 2012).

Applying viewpoint to gesture in discourse in order to advocate an embodied and multimodal understanding of language, cognition, and interaction, is a current tendency in research gaining more and more attention. Mittelberg (2017) follows McNeill's and Parrill's insights on dual viewpoint and illustrates how multiple viewpoint construction is realized in experiential immersion when people describe spacial experiences, e.g., regarding their childhood memories about their living space. The author shows how an architecture student describes how she went down the staircases every day to get to kindergarten, from a 'mixed viewpoint': the speaker's body, head, and eye gaze show someone observing a scene from above, but, at the same time, her index finger portrays her own action from the observer's viewpoint while she is verbally describing it in detail using the first-person singular.

Beside metaphor, metonymy plays a crucial role in real interaction: according to Mittelberg and Waugh (2014), gestures are *per se* inherently metonymic. In interaction with concurrent speech, evanescent hand shapes and movements tend to abstract salient characteristics from or allude to persons, objects, events, scenarios, actions and contexts, by foregrounding specific aspects of them. Thereby, gestures trigger an ensuing associative chain of a larger semantic network and evoke frames through picking out certain aspects of basic scenes of experience that structure complex frames (Mittelberg 2019). Mittelberg and Waugh (2009) also illustrate how the transition from literal to metaphorical understanding proceeds in the case of the hand gesture 'drawing a frame', though the frame is never drawn as a whole, i.e., mostly only the edges. Thus, the traces in the air have to be interpreted as meaning a frame of some sort. This is the first metonymic step of meaning construction. Then, in a second metaphoric step, this frame might be interpreted, e.g., as the frame of a story instead of the frame of a picture (Mittelberg and Waugh 2009: 337).

As we have seen so far, studies on metaphor and metonymy in interaction mainly focus on the speaker's perspective rather than on the interaction from a more holistic angle that includes the dyad of speaker and hearer as a unit. A more dynamic and reciprocal view is elaborated in phenomenological, conversational, and ethnographic approaches even though, to date, studies are still limited to particular research questions. Thus, it is especially in the realm of facial gestures, pragmatic gestures, and turn taking activities that the interlocutor has come to the fore. Kendon (1967) first directed his attention to conversational interaction as a unit in its own right when he analyzed the variations in the amount of gaze of speakers towards their hearers and vice versa, its duration, its role in turn-taking and mutual gaze. Among other things he found out that speakers frequently redirected their gaze at the listener as they approach the end of their utterance. They also held their gaze on the listener after ending their utterance. Additionally, he could show that mutual monitoring and display of attention are naturally accomplished by mutual gaze. Building on these findings, Streeck (2014: 48) shows that mutual gaze can frequently be understood as a form of meta-communication: it expresses mutual commitment to the conversational course of action in progress. However, apart from work on gaze and nodding as a token of affiliation rather than a sign of alignment (Stivers 2008), there is almost no work on the co-construction of manual gestures. An exception is Kendon's (2004) work on so-called 'speech handling' gestures which are also composed of both speaker and hearer gestures. When shrugging, e.g., our bodies withdraw and retract from possible engagements and display distancing and disengagement. Likewise, the VP (vertical palm) gesture can be performed as both action or reaction. Here, the palm is facing away from the performer and can be projected onto many discourse domains generally conveying rejection, repulsion, stopping, refusal, objection, and negation, carrying the core idea that the current line of action should be halted.

In contrast to the extensive work in the field of gestural metaphor, there is still little work in the field of prosody and cognition. Perlman and Gibbs (2013: 524) map the dynamic and scalar model of gestural metaphors that might be "more or less frozen or defrosted, more or less awake or asleep" (Cienki 2008: 10) onto the iconic relation of the semantic and phonological poles: "When active, these iconic relations become accentuated and take form as vocal gesture" (Perlman and Gibbs 2013: 524). They illustrate this by means of the elongated pronunciation of the word *slooowly*. Müller and Cienki (2009: 299) call this phenomenon 'oral/aural modality', in correspondence to 'spatial/visual modality'. For instance, when intonation rises and falls afterwards, subjects in an experiment interpret this procedure schematically as a circle, whereas a rising intonation is interpreted as a path (Müller and Cienki 2009: 299). However, there is almost no work in the field of real interaction.

This is where interactional linguistics makes an indispensible complementary contribution. Especially the detailed work on prosody in interaction (Couper-Kuhlen and Selting 2018; Selting and Couper-Kuhlen 2001; Couper-Kuhlen and Selting 1996) takes up Gumperz' (1982) insight that we have to conceive prosodic cues as contextual signs of specific communicative situations. Günthner (1999) shows how past dialogues are reenacted in activities of accusations and how polyphonic stylization is used to mark these as morally correct or reprehensible.

Such evaluations are frequently carried out by means of prosodic, lexical, and rhetoric arrangement of the reported speech. Selting (1994) also touches cognitive matters when she highlights as a special case of rhythmic and intonational stylization the emphatic speech style marked by extensive prosody and large pitch jumps that emerge in narratives, and focuses on so called "peaks of involvement" (Selting 1994: 404). In a similar vein, Goodwin (2015) relies on Goffman's (1981) deconstructions of the narrator in 'sounding box', as well as 'animator', and the protagonist in 'author', 'principal', as well as 'figure'. Thereby he shows in what complex ways the narrative has to be understood as a "field of action built collaboratively by structurally different actors using a variety of semiotic resources within face-to-face interaction" (Goodwin 2015: 204). Shifts of footing – that is, shifts regarding this participation framework – go along with shifts of stances, which frequently co-occur with prosodic cuing, interjections, and discourse, as well as deictic markers. Self-quotations are also often used and the speaker's body becomes that of the figure being enacted; that is, speakers can report private, internal thoughts that need not to have been externalized at all. For example, a quotative construction such as "I thought" can be introduced as a direct report through the use of "well", which functions as a turn-initial discourse marker signaling the beginning of silent speech as a report of one's thoughts (Couper-Kuhlen and Selting 2018: Online-Chapter C: 58). Despite these developments, a deeper theoretical-methodological discussion around the elaboration of cognition in talk is still missing, as Deppermann (2012) states. He underpins that it is especially in conversation analysis where semantic matters are still abandoned as a research issue in its own right.

3 The ICMI corpus and the selected sequences

The empirical data shown in this chapter originates from the ICMI corpus of the research group *Intercultural Communication in Multimodal Interactions*. This group initiated its activities at the University of Minas Gerais (UFMG) in Brazil in 2012.[5] Primarily, the project aims to videotape interactions between participants with different nationalities as well as between participants from the same cultural background, for comparative purposes. Every member of the research group develops his or her own research questions, but the corpus is created (filmed and transcribed) in teamwork. Until today, we have primarily filmed arranged elicited conversations between exchange students with conversation tasks (Kasper 2008: 287–288; Senft

5 The project's website can be visited at <http://www.letras.ufmg.br/icmi>

1995: 579–580), as well as institutional settings, such as foreign language classroom teaching. Lately, the group has been working on the collection of so-called natural conversations as the third communicative genre of the ICMI corpus. In the case of the elicited conversations, in order to gain insights into culture- and language-related reflexive processes displayed by the participants *in situ* and to make these visible on the (meta)communicative level, cultural and intercultural topics serve as stimuli for eliciting discussions. The studies conducted so far by the group take a theoretical framework as a starting point which seeks to integrate three principal areas of research: (a) conversation analysis and interactional linguistics; (b) cognitive and cultural linguistics; and (c) intercultural pragmatics. After the recording, the videotapes are transcribed in the software program EXMARaLDA (Schmidt and Wörner 2009)[6] following the conventions of GAT 2 (Selting et al. 2011).[7] At the present moment, the corpus is comprised of about 2,496 minutes of videotaped interactions with a total of 56,164 intonation units.

The following two sequences are from an elicited conversation between two Brazilian students and two German exchange students in Brazil who are discussing the topic of 'homeland' (*Heimat*).[8] They are all students of the Humanities and speak Portuguese or German as a foreign language. In Table 1, information is given on the participants in the interaction.

Table 1: Participants in the interaction (Silva 2015).

	Initials	Age	Stay in Brazil/ Germany	Course/Profession
Brazilians	B1	28	1 year	Bachelor: Literature and Linguistics/Teacher
	B2	29	2 years	Master: International Relations/Teacher
Germans	G1	23	6 months	Master: Anthropology
	G2	28	10 months	Master: European Studies/Teacher

Since the two Brazilians had studied German and spent one and, respectively, two years in Germany, while the two Germans had arrived in Brazil more recently, the conversation was mostly conducted in German. The recorded interaction lasted

6 <www.exmaralda.org>, last accessed on March 26, 2019.

7 The transcription conventions can be found in the appendix.

8 This main objective of the conversation is not related to the present article but was the aim of the master's thesis of Diogo Henrique Alves da Silva (2015) entitled "A construção do conceito Heimat (Alemanha) / Pátria (Brasil) no âmbito intercultural" (*The construction of the concept Heimat (Germany) / Pátria (Brazil) in intercultural interaction*).

70 minutes, of which 52 were transcribed. Cue cards asked about the key concept *Heimat* and served to initiate and maintain the discussion between the interactants about this special topic. What is relevant for our concerns here is the common ground of intercultural experience all co-participants share since they all have already lived abroad for a longer period of time, which has improved their ability to reflect upon their experience on alterity. The video footage described below aimed at revealing how the participants co-construct and negotiate these topics:

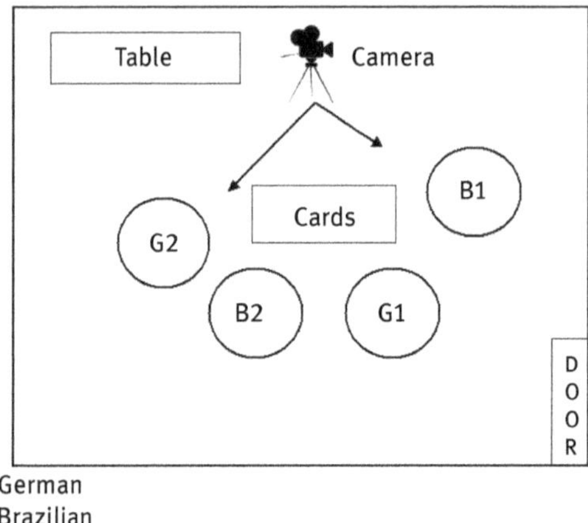

Figure 1: Film shooting of the interaction *Heimat*; modified version from Silva (2015).

Consequently, the interaction type we find here, which also applies to most of the interactions within the NUCOI corpus, is an elicited conversation that can be classified as (1) non-public, (2) discursive and non-practical, (3) naturally arranged, (4) face-to-face interaction (5) in a small group (6) with unprepared participants mostly unknown to one another (7) who are in a symmetrical relationship (Henne and Rehbock 2001: 26–27).

After the recording, the videotapes were transcribed in the software program EXMARaLDA[9] (Schmidt and Wörner 2009) following the conventions of GAT 2 (Selting et al. 2011).[10] The decision for EXMARaLDA and GAT 2 was based on the fact that both tools permit the integration of prosodic as well as corporal-gestural means of communication to a high degree of precision.[11]

9 www.exmaralda.org

10 In the present case, the video was transcribed by Diogo Henrique Alves and revised by the author of this article.

11 The conventions used here can be found in section 6.

4 Analysis

4.1 I'm like the German foreigner

In the first sequence, G2 is talking about the experience of being labeled as a 'foreigner' by natives once one lives in a foreign country:

```
Sequence 2015BHAlBrHe01 ((18:59-19:16))[12]

01 G2:  =oder ich bin ganz schnell im ´AUSland?
          or I'm quite quickly abroad
02      is man schnell der <<len> `!AUS!länder.>
        you're immediately the foreigner
03      [oder der (.) oder DIE-]
          or the or the
04 B2:  [ja toTAL.            ]
          yeah totally
05 G2:  [<<all> hier halt die> DEUTsche;=ne,>]
                  here rather the German right
06 B1:  [((laughs))                          ]
07 G2:  <<moves left hand on to her chest> also ist ja egAl ob_ich
        ri↑CARda bin;>
        well it doesn't matter if I'm ricarda
08      oder ob ich hier <<laughing, all> was ich hier ↑MACHe;>-
        or if I'm here what I'm doing here
09      =so NE,=
          so right
10      =ich bin SO;
          I'm like
11 B1:  ((smiles and nods))
12 G2:  [<<smiling and moving the left hand to the left with open
        palm facing downwards> ah JA;]
                                 ah yeah
13 B2:  [ja.                         ]
          yes
14 G2:  die `!DEUT!sche.>
        the German
```

12 The video can be accessed at the following link: https://youtu.be/rSxP1Gu51jo

```
15        [<<turning the left hand palm up> ah ja die AUS>]
                                             ah the for
16   B1:  [((laughs))                                      ]
17   B2:  [((smiles))                                      ]
18   G1:  [((smiles))                                      ]
     G2:  <<laughing> länderin;=ne,>
                       eigner right
19        [oder (-) in INdien            ] ganz [stark halt auch die ]
           or in india also absolutely the
20   B2:  [<<smiling> ↑!JA!ja:: toTA:L.>]
                       yeah yeah totally
21   B1:                                        [die GRINga.         ]
                                                 the gringa
     G2:  WEI[ße;]
          white
22   B2:     [ja.]
              yeah
23   G2:  [<<looking at B1 with wide open eyes> die GRINga.>]
                                                 the gringa
24   B1:  [((laughs loudly))                               ]
```

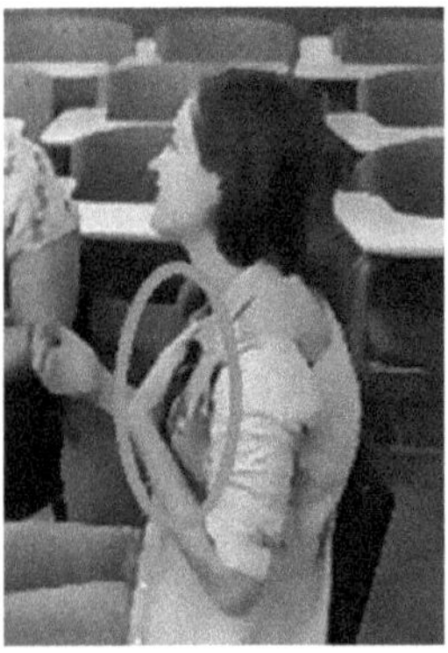

Figure 2a: <<moves left hand on to her chest> **also ist ja egAl ob_ich ri↑CARda bin;**> (L07)
well it doesn't matter if I'm ricarda

Figure 2b: <<smiling and pointing left hand index to the left with open palm facing downwards> **ah JA; die `!DEUT!sche.**> (L12-14)
ah yeah the German

Figure 2: C-VPT and O-VPT by conceptualizing the self-positioning as a foreigner.

The issue broached in this sequence is the 'in-between-perspective', typical for the metareflexive angle of someone who, as the pioneer of intercultural studies Alfred Schütz (1944: 507) describes it, "remains a 'marginal man,' a cultural hybrid on the verge of two different patterns of group life, not knowing to which of them he belongs". This topic is strongly reflected in the linguistic-gestural display of G2 and ratified by the co-participants.

First, G2 gives special emphasis to the key term `` `!AUS!länder `` (*foreigner*) in L02 through an extra strong accent, falling pitch movement and slow tempo, while shortly afterwards (L07) moving her left hand on to her chest. This represents a deictic gesture from a 'character viewpoint' (C-VPT, McNeill 1992; Parrill 2012) because it shows her experiencing the observation of the other directed towards her as 'the foreigner' (Figure 2a). Interestingly, immediately after this turn, she continues to talk about herself, but now from a distant angle, since she is pointing the left hand index to the left as if she were next to herself, which indicates an O-VPT (McNeill 1992; Parrill 2012), and using third-person singular: `` die `!DEUT!sche `` (*the German*, L12). At the same time, this pointing gesture incorporates the pragmatic gesture of "moving something aside" (Streeck 2008a: 259) or "throwing something away" (Bressem and Müller 2014: 1581), which marks a negative stance inherent to the labelling of the foreigner as 'the German' (Figure 2b).[13]

The narrated event represents an experience shared by the co-participants, which is reflected by the response tokens given by them, since they do not only express alignment but high affiliation (Stivers 2008, 2013), such as the repetitive reactive expressions[14] `ja toTAL` (*yes totally*, L04), `↑!JΛ!ja:: toTA:L` (*yes yes totally*, L20) given by B2, additionally highlighted by extra strong accent, pitch jump upstep, and lengthening. On a corporal level, there are smiles and nods as affiliative back-channel responses (Duncan and Fiske 1985: 58–59) given by all co-participants (L06, 11, 16, 17, 18, 20, 24). In L19-21, we can observe what Duncan and Fiske (1985: 58–59) call 'sentence completion', meaning that the co-participant completes the speaker's sentence:

```
19  G2: [oder (-) in Indien          ] ganz [stark halt auch die]
         or in India also absolutely the
20  B2: [<<smiling> ↑!JΛ!ja:: toTA:L.>]
                         yeah yeah totally
```

13 All interactants who are recorded receive and sign a consent form declaring that they agree with the scientific use of the data for analysis, as well as the disclosure of the videos and transcriptions for academic purposes. This also includes the use of images in academic articles.

14 These lexical items were classified as non-floor-taking positive assessments by Clancy et al. (1996, *apud* Xudong 2009: 114).

21 B1: [die GRINga.]
the gringa
G2: WEI[ße;]
white

The participants allude to common ground partly shared by a common stock of knowledge at hand and partly co-constructed incrementally by the key term *gringa*, which can be seen as a syncretically blended, more or less fully entrenched concept,[15] since it originates in Spanish.[16] The term is used frequently to pejoratively refer to a white foreigner to whom exaggerate characteristics are frequently attributed, such as squeamishness, over correctness, brutality, sobriety, etc.[17]

The sequence continues thirteen seconds later when G2 again returns to the topic of being seen as a foreigner:

2015BHAlBrHe01 ((19:29-19:41))[18]

01 G2: =(aber) es gibt so situationen wo man <<all, drawing a semicircle with palms vertical away from body> SCHNELL so;>
but there are situations where you quickly like
02 <<calibrating with palms vertical away from body> (-) ja so die AUßensEiterin;
yeah like the outsider
03 <<all, h, drawing a semicircle with palms towards body> oder die die nicht daZUgehörige;>=
or that of not belonging to them
04 =<<all, putting her hands together drawing a circle with palms lateral towards body> naja also es sind dann brasi↑LIAner,>=
well then these are Brazilians
05 =<<all, repeating the movement> oder die die ↑INder,>=
or the Indians

15 See Schmid et al. (2008) for a description of such blended concepts that are stored in long-term memory, as opposed to the blended concepts as constructed on the fly, according to blending theory.
16 According to the etymological dictionary *Diccionario Etimológico de la Lengua Castellana* by Joan Coromines, the origin of *gringo* comes from the Spanish *griego* and is related to the idea of an incomprehensible language ("It's all Greek to me"). Starting from the eighteenth century, the lexeme was used to refer to speakers of foreign languages, especially to English speakers who didn't speak Spanish before it was expanded to refer to white people in general. There are also folk-etymological sources stating that the term was used in the war between Mexico and the United States (1846–1848) by the Mexicans, to designate the US soldiers' green uniform and results either from the phrase "Green, go!" or "green coat". However, there is no secure source regarding this hypothesis.
17 See for example the discourse analysis of language school advertising using the term *gringo* by Marques (2014).
18 The video can be accessed at the following link: https://youtu.be/IF4gkKuPnx4

06 `=<<all> oder die keine Ahnung wo_auch `IMmer;>`
or i don't know the wherever

07 `und (.) man ist so (-) jemand ANderes so:.`
and you're someone else somehow

08 `nich:t <<f> zu der gruppe> <<dim> zugehÖrig.>`
not belonging to the group

Figure 3a: =(aber) es gibt so situationen wo man <<all, drawing a semicircle with palms vertical away from body> **SCHNELL so;**> <<calibrating with palms vertical away from body> (-) **ja so die AUßensEiterin;**
but there are situations where you quickly like yeah like the outsider (L01-02)

Figure 3b: <<all, h, drawing a semicircle with palms towards body> **oder die die nicht daZUgehörige;**>=
or that of not belonging to them (L03)

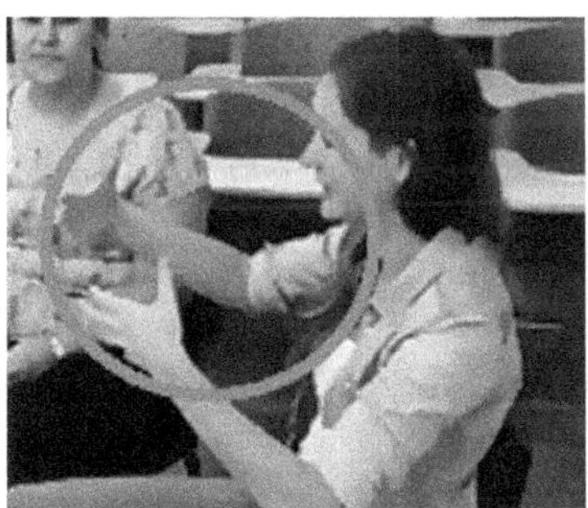

Figure 3c: =<<all, putting her hands together drawing a circle with palms lateral towards body> **naja also es sind dann brasi↑LIAner,**>=
well then these are Brazilians (L05)

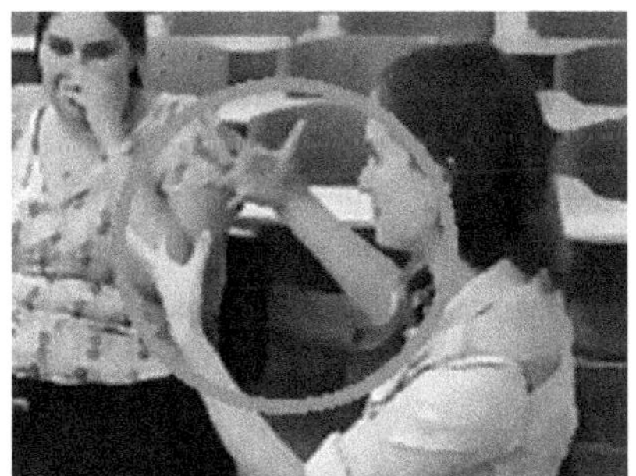

Figure 3d: =<<all, repeating the movement> **oder die die ↑INder,**>=
or the Indians (L05)

Figure 3: Mixed viewpoint by expressing THE CULTURE IS A CONTAINER metaphor.

G2 is now deepening her description of not belonging to the target community and how it was to be seen as a foreigner during her stay abroad, an experience shared by the others and now already built as a common ground in the first part of the sequence, as we have seen. In doing so, she incorporates the capacity of switching the reflexive perspective, which is shown by the gestural switch in L01-02. While saying: `(aber) es gibt so situationen wo man SCHNELL so; (-) ja so die AUßensEiterin;` (*but there are situations where you quickly like yeah like the outsider*), she is drawing a semicircle with her palms vertical away from her body as if she were observing the situation with herself being outside the container, the container being the target culture (Figure 3a). In this sense, the gesture represents a monomodal metaphoric gesture (McNeill 1992; Cienki and Müller 2008), meaning that it occurs only on the gestural level, and the viewpoint can be described as "dual or "mixed" (McNeill 1992; Mittelberg 2017), that is, as O-VPT and C-VPT at the same time, according to the reflexivity of G2: she is looking into the container while concurrently reporting what it is like being in the container but not feeling as though you in fact belonged to it. Then she switches the viewpoint to the eyes of the natives, which is indicated by the gestural switch in L03-05. She continues to explain this situation by now drawing a semicircle with her palms towards her body and simultaneously stating `oder die die nicht daZUgehörige` (*or that of not belonging to them*), which also expresses this change in perspective with regard to the chosen pronoun (Figure 3b). Again, it is not clear whether her outsider position belongs to the described scenario (C-VPT) or whether she describes the scenario from an O-VPT. This can be seen as a consequence of the in-between perspective, since the intercultural point of view naturally corresponds to an observative standpoint.

Subsequently, she explicitly refers to cultural groups as units being labeled as such when she puts her hands together and again draws a circle with her palms lateral towards her body, saying `naja also es sind dann brasi↑LIAner,` (*well then these are Brazilians*; Figure 3c). Immediately afterwards, she repeats this movement now referring to the Indians (L05; Figure 3d). The whole sequence reflects the classical conceptual metaphor CULTURE IS A CONTAINER (Marschak 2005: 321; Schröder 2015; Schröder and Carneiro Mendes 2015), which can be traced back to the image schema or primary metaphor of CONTAINER (Lakoff and Johnson ([1980] 2003, 1999; Johnson 1987) but is explicitly elaborated and deepened here as problematic. Thus, she refers to herself as being labeled as 'the German' instead of being referred to by her name. And by her verbo-gestural depiction of the container as reflecting a particular nation-based cultural group, she points to the problematic homogeneity of 'Indians' or 'Brazilians' that puts herself in the position of an 'outsider'. Since all co-participants have lived in another country for a longer period and are therefore familiar with this kind of experience, we can observe an active realization and elaboration of a cultural conceptualization in an intercultural space, a schema shared by all co-participants.

4.2 Here in Brazil everyone hugs everyone

The second sequence shows how presuppositions and cross-cultural background knowledge in conjunction with multimodal affiliation and reciprocal empathy tokens co-built interculture as a space for sharing personal intercultural experience. In cognitive terms, the centre of the sequence is where cultural conceptualization (Sharifian 2011, 2015) of COLD and WARM PEOPLE related to the German and Brazilian culture unfolds and is intertwined with the concept of BRAZILIAN CORDIALITY. These two cultural dimensions can frequently be found in the ICMI corpus (Schröder 2017; forthcoming). The topic of discussion is how homeland coins people's worldview and behavior:

2015BHAlBrHe01 ((35:06-36:05))

01 G1: es geht_auch durch die (-) durch die HEImat;=
it also has to do with one's homeland
02 =halt auch irgendwie gePRÄGT;=
it also somehow has shaped you
03 =und zum BEIspiel mit;
and for example with
04 (--) hier in brasilien <<stretching her left arm with curved open hand> um`ARmen sich alle wAahnsinnig viel;>
here in Brazil everybody hugs everyone incredibly much
05 <<touching B1's arm with her right hand> und das ist wAhnsinnig VIEL;>
and that's quite a lot
06 [<<stroking the air with her right hand> da fassen sich alle AN;>]
everybody touches everyone
07 B1: [((laughs))]
08 G2: [((laughs))]
09 G1: <<laughing, looking at B1, h> ja das ist bei uns halt einfach ERST> also;
yeah there that's just at first well
10 <<looking at B1> das war wahrscheinlich für Euch auch am Anfang> <<looking at B2> [total] ↑SCHWIErig;
probably for you that was quite difficult at first
11 B1: [ja.]
yes
12 G1: dass sich irgendwie LEUte vielleicht nich so:;
that somehow people perhaps don't somehow

13 B2: hm_HM.
14 [ja (-) SCHWIErig;]
yeah difficult
15 G1: <<moving torso, shoulder, arm and open right hand palm up forward> einfach nicht so HERZ>] ja.
just not so hearty yes
16 G2: ((laughs))
17 B2: <<pointing to the cards on the table> und sagen wir die schwIerigkeit von diese:r (.) ersten FRAge;>
and let's say the problem with this first question
18 <<pointing with the forefinger to her head> dann habe ich mich grade (-) erINnert,
then I just remembered
19 (--) vo:n dieser situaTION;>=
this situation
20 =weil (.) meine gastMUTter (-) ist eine ´deutsche (-) `frau.=
cause my host mother is a German woman
21 G1: ja.
yes
22 B2: =ne,
right
23 G1: ((laughs))
24 B2: U:ND_äh;
and ah
25 Also eine deutsche FRAU,
well a German woman
26 sie: (---) ((clicks her tongue)) ALso;
she well
27 [sie war <<h> ein BISschen ahm:;>]
she was a little bit ahm
28 G1: [((laughs))]
29 B2: °°h
30 G2: MERKwürdig.
weird
31 G1: ((laughs))
32 G1: [((laughs))]
33 B2: [ja.]
yeah
34 G1: ((laughs))
35 [((laughs))]
36 B2: [<<smiling> und sie sie und>]
and she she and

```
37        <<smiling> ich DACHte sie (-) mochte mich !NICHT!;>
                     I thought she didn't like me
38  G1:   [`hm::.]
39  G2:   [oh::, ]
40  B2:   WEIL sie w_w-
          cause she c_c
41        <<opening her arms and hands sideward to the torso> ich
          !DACH!te sie war so kalt;>
           I thought she was so cold
42  G1:   <<strong nodding, h> hm::_>[HM::;>]
43                                   [ALso:;]
                                      well
44  G2:                              [hm_HM.]
45  B2:   (--) aber <<h> dAnn habe ich geMERKT;>
               but then I noticed
46        ↑nein das ist ´NUR;
           no it's only
47  G1:   ja.
          yes
48  B2:   <<h> wie sie IST;>
               the way she is
49        [und DANN ich bin]
           and then I am
50        [((laughs))      ] (.) jetzt auch ein bissche:n [ahm   ]
                                 now I'm also a little bit ahm
51  G2:                                                   [kalt.]
                                                           cold
52  B2:   [kalt.      ]
           cold
53  G2:   [((laughs))]
54  B2:   [oder      ]
           or
55  G1:   [((laughs))]
56  G2:   [((laughs))]
57  B2:   [SO;=      ]
           like that
58  B1:   [((laughs))]
59  G2:   [((laughs))]
60  B2:   =(kalt) JA:.
            cold yes
```

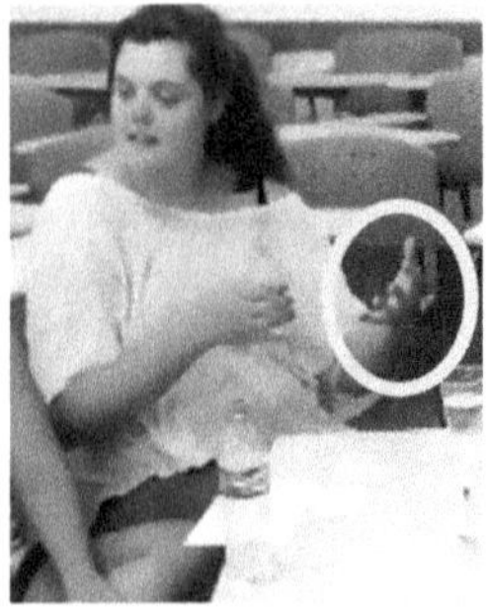

Figure 4a: `(--) hier in brasilien <<stretching her left arm with curved open hand>` **`um`ARmen sich alle wAahnsinnig viel;`**`>`
here in Brazil everybody hugs everyone incredibly much (L04)

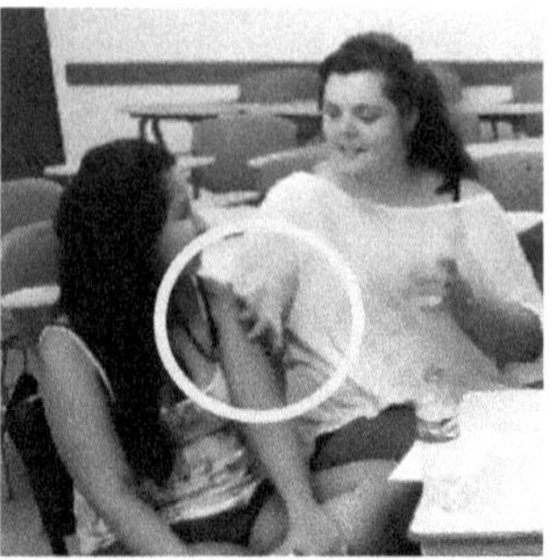

Figure 4b: `<<touching B1's arm with her right hand>` **`und das ist wAhnsinnig VIEL;`**`>`
and that's quite a lot (L05)

Figure 4c: `<<stroking the air with her right hand>` **`da fassen sich alle AN;`**`>`
everybody touches everyone (L06)

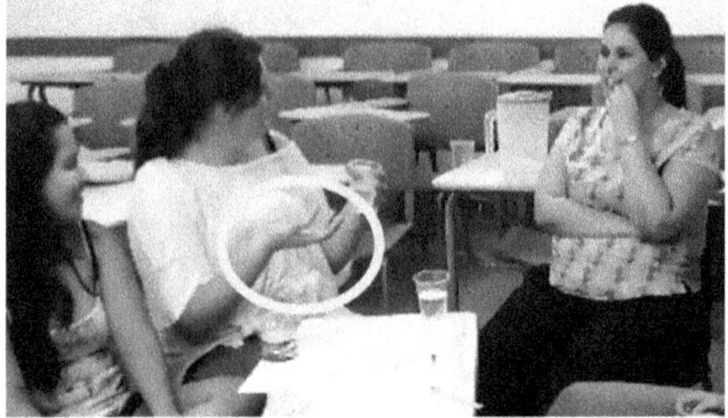

Figure 4d: `<<moving torso, shoulder, arm and open right hand palm up forward>` **`einfach nicht so HERZ`**`> ja.`
just not so heartfelt yes (L15)

Figure 4: Frame metonymy and cultural metaphor related to Brazilian cordiality.

G1 initiates her turn by introducing a comment about how the homeland shapes one's character, and gives as an example the Brazilian way of interacting with one another, concurrently incorporating the German perspective by highlighting this difference in an exaggerated manner: `hier in brasilien um`ARmen sich alle wAahnsinnig viel; und das ist wAhnsin-`

nig VIEL; da fassen sich alle AN; (*here in Brazil everybody hugs everyone incredibly much and that's quite a lot everybody touches everyone*, L04-06). The exaggeration is displayed through the use of 'extreme case formulations' (Pomerantz 1986) such as the indefinite pronoun *everybody* and corporal means such as touching B1. At the same time, the complex frame of the cultural conceptualization of Brazilian cordiality is unfolded metonymically by basic scenes of action frames constituting the complex cultural frame (Mittelberg 2019): (a) (--) hier in brasilien um`ARmen sich alle wAahnsinnig viel; (*here in Brazil everybody hugs everyone incredibly much*, L04) is uttered while G2 concurrently stretches her left arm with a curved opened hand, alluding on the gestural level metonymically to the act of embracing someone (Figure 4a); (b) G1 continues her turn by saying und das ist wAhnsinnig VIEL;> (*and that's quite a lot*, L05), while touching B1's arm with her right hand repeatedly, thus illustrating how Brazilians touch each other (Figure 4b); and (c) by then asserting da fassen sich alle AN; (*everybody touches everyone*, L06), she strokes the air with her right hand as if she were was touching someone in front of her (Figure 4c). She gains laughter from B1 (L07), responds to it with her own laughter (L09), and continues by now referring to the viewpoint of the Brazilians experiencing the German way of interacting: <<looking at B1> das war wahrscheinlich für Euch auch am Anfang> <<looking at B2> [total] ↑SCHWIErig; dass sich irgendwie LEUte vielleicht nich so:; (*probably for you that was quite difficult at first that somehow people perhaps don't somehow*; L10-12).

We can apply Koole and Ten Thije's (1994; ten Thije 2006) concept of 'perspectivizing' here, which is considered as an outcome of the communicative apparatus in the above delineated sense from Rehbein (2006): discourse procedures are applied by participants who anticipate cultural differences or show high intercultural competence in order to ensure intercultural understanding. By doing so, 'perspectivizing' represents a strategy of the cultural apparatus by which the propositional content in the actual communicative situation is located in such a manner that the cultural standards of the co-participants are taken into account, and, subsequently, attain an appropriate interpretation of the discourse going on. How exactly is this achieved here?

G1 builds incrementally on a change of perspective and creates an atmosphere of reciprocal empathy: after her turn has being ratified by the others through verbalized back-channel responses (Duncan and Fiske 1985: 58–59), such as those given by B1 in L11 ja. (*yes*) and B2 in L13-14 hm_HM. ja (-) SCHWIErig; (*yeah difficult*), she adds that Germans are simply less affectionate towards each other: einfach nicht so HERZ ja. (*just not so hearty yes*; L15), concurrently moving torso, shoulder, arm and her open right hand palm up forward. That represents, on the one hand, an assertive gesture that traces back to the conduit metaphor, whereby she offers her interlocutor the information through the 'Palm Up Open Hand' gesture (Müller 2008: 224). With the introduction of the CONDUIT metaphor, Reddy ([1979] 1993) reveals the transport model of communication. In this model, speaker and hearer are conceptualized as containers for objectified thoughts and emotions, whereby linguistic expressions are symbolized by containers for objects of meaning that are sent by a speaker to a hearer. Müller (2008: 224) and Streeck (2008a: 259) show how pragmatic gestures reflect this metaphor by visualizing certain arguments as obvious – through an open hand – or as less plausible – through brushing aside – as well as through 'handing over' the conversation. At the same time, on the other hand, this gesture metaphorically incorporates the idea of handing something over to someone and gives emphasis to G1's implicit statement about Brazilian cordiality (Figure 4d).

By doing so, G1 creates a common ground of reciprocal intercultural experience of alterity, which is reinforced by a considerable use of modal particles such as *irgendwie* (*somehow*, L02, 12), *halt* (*just*, L09) and *einfach* (*simply*, L09), whose function it is "to connect the current utterance to a pragmatic pretext, to a proposition 'at hand', which is part of the non-verbal argumentative context" (Fischer 2007: 51). This context is formed by a 'personal common ground'[19] being the stock of knowledge each participant has regarding the customs and values of the other culture presupposed by the intercultural experience they have. Thus, the modal particles displayed in our sequence serve as "evidential markers" (Schoonjans 2018: 45).

In fact, against this pre-established common ground, B2 now initiates a 'small story' (König 2010) or anecdote about her host mother, whom she at first perceived to be a cold person: `ich !DACH!te sie war so kalt;>` (*I thought she was so cold*; L41). On the semantic level, we can already observe the same as before; there is reference to a deeper entrenched metaphor understood and known by all participants since the description of 'warm' and 'cold' people points to the 'primary metaphor' (Lakoff and Johnson 1999), 'attribution metaphor' (Baldauf 1997) or 'generic-level metaphor' INTENSITY OF EMOTION IS HEAT (Kövecses 2003: 41). It is frequently related to cultural groups, more specifically also to the difference between Brazilians and Germans (Schröder 2017) and refers back to the already introduced CORDIALITY concept. The whole story is narrated in an exaggerated manner, marked by strong emotional effects, which come to the fore as "peaks of involvement" (Selting 1994: 404) that are visible especially on the prosodic level when B2 gives extra

---

19 In opposition to a "communal common ground" Clark 1996: 100–112) which would include the shared knowledge of a whole social or cultural group.

strong accent on lexical items such as `!NICHT!` (*not*, L37), `!DACH!te` (*thought*, L41) as well as emphasis on items that are not accentuated in German, such as the conjunctions `U:ND` (L24), `ALso` (*well*, L26), `WEIL` (*because*, L40) and `DANN` (*then*, L48). Although it may be seen as a typical marker of someone who speaks German as a foreign language to stress these lexemes, the density and intensity in this context allude to a high emphatic speech style (Selting 1994). Another hint is the number of pauses longer than 0.5 seconds inserted into her story (L19, 26, 27, 41) as well as the use of a higher pitch register that sounds mannered (L27, 45, 48). The co-participants ratify the small story by positioning themselves unequivocally and totally in line with each other, which is indicated through "emotional stance markers" (Deppermann 2015: 380) such as laughter (L23, 28, 31, 32, 34, 35, 46, 49, 51, 52, 54, 55), sentence completion (L30), and strong nodding (L38). Notably, G1 underpins her affiliation by two mannered and quite exaggerated verbalized back-channel responses (Duncan and Fiske 1985: 58–59), which are markedly lengthened, displaying a very strong form of emotional stance, which resembles mother-child talk: `` `hm::. `` (L38) and `oh::,` (L39).

5 Concluding remarks

The two sequences under analysis brought to light how intercultures are co-constructed in talk-in-interaction between two Brazilian and two German students who chose German as the medium of conversation. We have seen that the intercultural experience of alterity itself, as well as the experience of being perceived as a stranger, can set up an interculture which serves as a common ground for the creation of a discourse space. The first sequence showed that the co-participants rely on conceptualizations that are part of their cultural stock of knowledge at hand and also pertain to a collection of entrenched conceptual metaphors and schemas shared by both groups as an occidental "community of shared images" (*Bildgemeinschaft*), as Harald Weinrich (1976: 287) put it. This refers especially to the conceptual metaphor CULTURE IS A CONTAINER. However, in the intercultural space, and based on the common ground of intercultural experience, this entrenched, conventional metaphor is reactivated, elaborated, expanded, observed, and scrutinized because it is part of the (self)reflexive experience itself. This was revealed especially through another metaphor, active only implicitly but also part of our entrenched schemas: the viewpoint represented here on gestural levels and incorporating the location of the foreigner as not belonging to the container but as being an individual located 'in-between'.

Based on this fundamental experience, the second sequence cast some light on the way in which interculture is built incrementally based on personal common ground and by means of strategies which imply 'perspectivizing'. We have seen that knowing behavior patterns of the other culture and adopting the perspective of the other to contrast it with own patterns of behavior can promote common ground for intercultural discourse. Moreover, this common ground may also lead to emotional involvement and reciprocal empathy since the co-participants can grasp the idea that the individual 'from the other culture who lives as a foreigner in my own culture of origin' passes through similar intercultural experiences. Finally, here, again, the emotional involvement was supported on the cognitive-semantic level by the entrenched metaphor of COLD AND WARM PEOPLE related to the stereotype of Germans and Brazilians, although introduced here from a reflexive and ironic viewpoint, expressed by the mannered and exaggerated speech style.

6 Appendix: Transcription conventions GAT 2

Short, adapted version of GAT 2 according to Selting et al. (2011).

[ ] [ ]	overlap and simultaneous talk
=	fast, immediate continuation with a new turn or segment (latching)
and_uh	cliticizations within units
hm_hm	bi-syllabic tokens
(.)	micro pause, up to 0.2 sec.
(-)	short pause of 0.2-0.5 sec.
(--)	intermediary pause of 0.5-0.8 sec.
(2.0)	measured pause of 2.0 sec.
:, ::, :::	lengthening (0.2-0.5 sec.; 0.5-0.8 sec.; 0.8-1.0 sec.)
((laughs))	non-verbal vocal actions and events
<<laughing> >	para-verbal and non-verbal action as accompanying speech with indication of scope
<<acc>	accelerando
(may i)	assumed wording
(i say/let's say)	possible alternatives
°hh hh°	in- and outbreaths
(xxx)	one unintelligible syllable
acCENT	focus accent
accEnt	secondary accent
ac!CENT!	extra strong accent

?	rising to high final pitch movement of intonation unit
,	rising to mid final pitch movement of intonation unit
-	level final pitch movement of intonation unit; falling to mid final pitch movement of intonation unit
.	falling to low final pitch movement of intonation unit
ˆSO	rising-falling accent pitch movement
ˇSO	falling-rising accent pitch movement
´SO	rising accent pitch movement
\`SO	falling accent pitch movement
↑	pitch upstep
↓	pitch downstep

References

Baldauf, Christa. 1997. *Metapher und Kognition. Grundlagen einer neuen Theorie der Alltagsmetapher.* Frankfurt am Main: Peter Lang.

Bühler, Karl. [1934] 1982. *Sprachtheorie: die Darstellungsfunktion der Sprache*. Stuttgart: Fischer.

Cienki, Alan. 2008. Why study metaphor and gesture? In Alan Cienki & Cornelia Müller (eds.), *Metaphor and gesture*, 5–25. Amsterdam, Philadelhpia: John Benjamins.

Cienki, Alan & Cornelia Müller. 2008. Metaphor, gesture, and thought. In Raymond W. Jr. Gibbs (ed.), *The Cambridge handbook of metaphor and thought*, 483–501. Cambridge: Cambridge University Press.

Clancy, Patricia M., Sandra A. Thompson, Ryoko Suzuki & Hongyin Tao. 1996. The conversational use of reactive tokens in English, Japanese, and Mandarin. *Journal of Pragmatics* 26. 355–387.

Couper-Kuhlen, Elizabeth & Margret Selting (eds.). 1996. *Prosody in conversation*. Cambridge: Cambridge University Press.

Couper-Kuhlen, Elizabeth & Margret Selting. 2018. *Interacional linguistics: Studying language in social interaction*. Cambridge: Cambridge University Press.

Deppermann, Arnulf. 2012. How does 'cognition' matter to the analysis of talk-in-interaction? *Language Sciences* 34. 746–767.

Deppermann, Arnulf. 2015 Positioning. In Anna de Fina & Alexandra Georgakopoulou (eds.), 369–387. *The handbook of narrative analysis*. Malden, Oxford: Wiley Blackwell.

Duncan, Starkey & Donald Fiske. 1985. *Interaction structure and strategy*. Cambridge: Cambridge University Press.

Ehlich, Konrad & Jan D. ten Thije. 2010. Linguistisch begründete Verfahren der Analyse interkultureller Kommunikation. In: Arne Weidemann, Jürgen Straub & Steffi Nothnagel (eds.), *Wie lehrt man interkulturelle Kompetenz. Theorien, Methoden und Praxis in der Hochschulausbildung. Ein Handbuch*, 265–285. Bielefeld: transcript.

Fischer, Kerstin. 2007. Grounding and common ground: Modal particles and their translation equivalents. In Anita Fetzer & Kerstin Fischer (eds.), *Lexical markers of common grounds. Studies in pragmatics*, 47–66. Amsterdam: Elsevier.

Goffman, Erving. 1981. *Forms of talk*. Philadelphia: University of Pennsylvania Press.
Goodwin, Charles. 1981. Restarts, pauses, and the achievement of a state of mutual gaze at turn-beginnings. *Sociological Inquiry* 50(3–4). 272–302.
Goodwin, Charles. 2015. Narrative as talk-in-interaction. In Anna Fina & Alexandra Georgakopoulou (eds.), *The handbook of narrative analysis*, 197–218. Malden, Oxford: Wiley Blackwell.
Gumperz, John. 1982. *Discourse strategies*. Cambridge: Cambridge University Press.
Günthner, Susanne. 1999. Polyphony and the 'layering of voices' in reported dialogues: an analysis of the use of prosodic devices in everyday reported speech. *Journal of Pragmatics* 31. 685–708.
Henne, Helmut & Helmut Rehbock. 2001. *Einführung in die Gesprächsanalyse*. Berlin, New York: Walter de Gruyter.
Johnson, Mark. 1987. *The body in the mind: The bodily basis of meaning, imagination, and reason*. Chicago: University of Chicago Press.
Kasper, Gabriele. 2008. Data collection in pragmatics research. In Helen Spencer-Oatey (ed.), *Culturally speaking. Culture, communication and politeness theory*, 279–303. London: Continuum.
Kecskes, Istvan. 2014. *Intercultural pragmatics*. New York, Oxford: Oxford University Press.
Kecskes, Istvan. 2015. Language, culture, and context. In Farzad Sharifian (ed.), *The Routledge handbook of language and culture*, 113–128. Oxford & New York: Routledge.
Kendon, Adam. 1967. Some functions of gaze direction in two-person conversation. *Acta Psychologica* 26. 22–63.
Kendon, Adam. 2004. *Gesture: Visible action as utterance*. Cambridge: Cambridge UniversityPress.
König, Katharina. 2010. Sprachliche Kategorisierungsverfahren und subjektive Theorien über Sprache in narrativen Interviews. *Zeitschrift für Angewandte Linguistik* 53. 31–57.
Koole, Tom & Jan D. ten Thije. 1994. *The construction of intercultural discourse. Team discussions of educational advisers*. Amsterdam & Atlanta: RODOPI.
Koole, Tom & Jan D. ten Thije. 2001. The reconstruction of intercultural discourse: Methodological considerations. *Journal of Pragmatics* 33. 571–587.
Kövecses, Zoltán. 2003. *Metaphor and emotion. Language, culture, and body in human feeling*. Cambridge: Cambridge University Press.
Lakoff, George & Mark Johnson. [1980] 2003. *Metaphors we live by*. Chicago: The University of Chicago Press.
Lakoff, George & Mark Johnson. 1999. *Philosophy in the flesh. The embodied mind and its challenge to western thought*. New York: Basic Books.
Loenhoff, Jens. 1992. *Interkulturelle Verständigung. Zum Problem grenzüberschreitender Kommunikation*. Opladen: Leske & Budrich.
Loenhoff, Jens & H. Walter Schmitz. 2012. Kommunikative und extrakommunikative Betrachtungsweisen. Folgen für Theoriebildung und empirische Forschung in der Kommunikationswissenschaft. In Dirk Hartmann, Amir Mohseni, Erhard Reckwitz, Tim Rojek & Ulrich Steckmann (eds.), *Methoden der Geisteswissenschaften. Eine Selbstverständigung*, 35–59. Weilerswist: Velbrück Wissenschaft, 2012.
Marques, Welisson. 2014. *Análise do discurso publicitário de cursos de idiomas: Verdades atinentes a sujeitos aprendizes e aprendizagem de língua inglesa* [Discourse analysis of English course advertising: realities related to learners and learning of English]. Uberlândia: Federal University of Uberlândia, PhD thesis. https://repositorio.ufu.br/bitstream/123456789/15302/1/AnaliseDiscursoPublicitario.pdf (accessed 29 January 2020).

Marschark, Marc. 2005. Metaphors in sign language and sign language users: A window into relations of language and thought. In Herbert L. Colston & Albert N. Katz (eds.), *Figurative language comprehension: Social and cultural influences*, 209–334. Mahwah, NJ: Lawrence Erlbaum Associates.

McNeill, David. 1992. *Hand and mind: What gestures reveal about thought.* Chicago: University of Chicago Press.

Mittelberg, Irene. 2017. Experiencing and construing spatial artifacts from within: Simulated artifact immersion as a multimodal viewpoint strategy. *Cognitive Linguistics* 28 (3), 381–415.

Mittelberg, Irene. 2019. Visuo-kinetic signs are inherently metonymic: How embodied metonymy motivates forms, functions, and schematic patterns in gesture. *Frontiers in Psychology* 10. 1–18. https://www.frontiersin.org/articles/10.3389/fpsyg.2019.00254/full (accessed 27 January 2020).

Mittelberg, Irene & Linda R. Waugh. 2009. Metonymy first, metaphor second: A cognitive-semiotic approach to multimodal figures of thought in co-speech gesture. In Charles J. Forceville & Eduardo Urios-Aparisi (eds.), *Multimodal Metaphor*, 329–355. Berlin, New York: Mouton de Gruyter.

Mittelberg, Irene & Linda R. Waugh. 2014. Gestures and metonymy. In Cornelia Müller, Alan Cienki, Ellen Fricke, Silva H. Ladewig, David McNeill & Jana Bressem (eds.), *Body – language – communication. An international handbook on multimodality in human interaction. Volume 2*, 1747–1766. Berlin, Boston: De Gruyter Mouton.

Müller, Cornelia. 2008. What gestures reveal about the nature of metaphor. In Alan Cienki & Cornelia Müller (eds.), *Metaphor and gesture*, 219–245. Amsterdam, Philadelphia: John Benjamins.

Müller, Cornelia. 2013. Gestures as a medium of expression: The linguistic potential of gestures. In Cornelia Müller, Alan Cienki, Ellen Fricke, Silva H. Ladewig, David McNeill & Jana Bressem (eds.), *Body – language – communication. An international handbook on multimodality in human interaction. Volume 1*, 202–217. Berlin, Boston: De Gruyter Mouton.

Müller, Cornelia & Alan Cienki. 2009. Words, gestures, and beyond: Forms of multimodal metaphor in the use of spoken language. In Charles Forceville & Eduardo Urios-Aparisi (eds.), Multimodal metaphor, 297–328. Berlin, New York: Mouton de Gruyter.

Müller, Cornelia, Alan Cienki, Ellen Fricke, Silva H. Ladewig, David McNeill & Jana Bressem (eds.). 2013. *Body – language – communication. An international handbook on multimodality in human interaction. Volume 1.* Berlin, Boston: De Gruyter Mouton.

Müller, Cornelia, Alan Cienki, Ellen Fricke, Silva H. Ladewig, David McNeill & Jana Bressem (eds.). 2014. *Body – language – communication. An international handbook on multimodality in human interaction. Volume 2.* Berlin, Boston: De Gruyter Mouton.

Parrill, Fey. 2012. Interactions between discourse status and viewpoint in co-speech gesture. In Barbara Dancygier & Eve Sweetser (eds.), *Viewpoint in language: A multimodal perspective*, 97–112. Cambridge: Cambridge University Press.

Perlman, Marcus & Raymond W. Jr. Gibbs. 2013. Sensorimotor simulation in speaking, gesturing, and understanding. In Cornelia Müller, Alan Cienki, Ellen Fricke, Silva H. Ladewig, David McNeill & Jana Bressem (eds.), *Body – language – communication. An international handbook on multimodality in human interaction. Volume 1*, 512– 533. Berlin, Boston: De Gruyter Mouton.

Polzenhagen, Frank. Forthcoming. Critical reflections on the use of corpora for cross-varietal metaphor research. In Ulrike Schröder, Milene Mendes de Oliveira & Adriana Maria Tenuta (eds.), *(Inter)cultural perspectives on metaphorical conceptualizations*. Berlin, New York: De Gruyter.

Pomerantz, Anita. 1986. Extreme case formulations. A way of legitimizing claims. *Human Studies* 9 (2). 219–229.

Reddy, Michael J. [1979] 1993. The conduit metaphor: A case of frame conflict in our language about language. In Andrew Ortony (ed.), *Metaphor and thought*, 164–201. Cambridge: Cambridge University Press.

Rehbein, Jochen. 2006. The cultural apparatus. Thoughts on the relationship between language, culture, and society. In Kristin Bührig & Jan D. ten Thije (eds.), *Beyond misunderstanding. The linguistic reconstruction of intercultural discourse*, 43–96. Amsterdam: John Benjamins.

Schmid, Hans-Jörg, Dymitr Ibriszimos, Karina Kopatsch & Peter Gottschligg. 2008. Conceptual blending in language, cognition, and culture. Towards a methodology for the lingustic study of syncretic concepts. In Afe Adogame, Magnus Echtler & Ulf Vierke (eds.), *Unpacking the new: Critical perspectives on cultural syncretization in Africa and beyond*, 93–124. Zürich, Berlin: LIT Verlag.

Schmidt, Thomas & Kai Wörner. 2009. EXMARaLDA – Creating, analysing and sharing spoken language corpora for pragmatic research. *Pragmatics* 19. 565–582.

Schoonjans, Steven. 2018. *Modalpartikeln als multimodale Konstruktionen. Eine korpusbasierte Kookkurrenzanalyse von Modalpartikeln und Gestik im Deutschen*. Berlin, Boston: De Gruyter.

Schröder, Ulrike. 2015. Society and culture as container: (Re-)drawing borders and their metaphorical foundation from a communicative and extracommunicative point of view. *International Journal of Language and Culture* 2. 38–61.

Schröder, Ulrike. 2017. Multimodal metaphors as cognitive pivots for the construction of cultural otherness in talk. *Intercultural Pragmatics* 14 (4). 493–524.

Schröder, Ulrike. 2021. *Jeitinho* as a cultural conceptualisation in Brazilian Portuguese: a cultural linguistics' approach to talk-in-interaction. In Neele Mundt & Arne Peters (eds.), *Applied cultural linguistics*. Trends, directions and implications, 31–59. Berlin: Peter Lang.

Schröder, Ulrike & Mariana Carneiro Mendes. 2015. A utilização da metáfora cultura é um contêiner e sua contextualização multimodal em uma interação intercultural: uma análise a partir das perspectivas comunicativas e extracomunicativas [The use of the metaphor culture is a container and its multimodal contextualization in an intercultural interaction: an analysis from communicative and extracommunicative perspectives]. *Antares* 7 (14). 107–128.

Schütz, Alfred. 1944. The stranger. An essay in social psychology. *The American Journal of Sociology* XLIX (6). 499–507.

Selting, Margret. 1994. Emphatic speech style – with special focus on the prosodic signalling of heightened emotive involvement in conversation. *Journal of Pragmatics* 22. 375–408.

Selting, Margret & Elisabeth Couper-Kuhlen (eds.). 2001. *Studies in interactional linguistics*. Amsterdam, Philadelphia: Benjamins.

Selting, Margret, Peter Auer, Dagmar Barth-Weingarten, Jörg Bergmann, Pia Bergmann, Karin Birkner, Elizabeth Couper-Kuhlen, Arnulf Deppermann, Peter Gilles, Susanne Günthner, Martin Hartung, Friederike Kern, Christine Mertzlufft, Christian Meyer, Miriam Morek, Frank Oberzaucher, Jörg Peters, Uta Quasthoff, Wilfried Schütte, Anja Stukenbrock &

Susanne Uhmann. 2011. A system for transcribing talk-in-interaction: GAT 2; translated and adapted for English by Elizabeth Couper-Kuhlen and DagmarBarth-Weingarten. *Gesprächsforschung – Online-Zeitschrift zur verbalen Interaktion* 12. 1–51. http://www.gespraechsforschung-ozs.de/fileadmin/dateien/heft2011/px-gat2-englisch.pdf. (accessed 16 January 2015).

Semino, Elena. 2017. Corpus linguistics and metaphor. In Barbara Dancygier (ed.), *The Cambrige handbook of cognitive linguistics*, 463–476. Cambridge: Cambridge University Press.

Senft, Gunter. 1995. Elicitation. In Jef Verschueren, Jan-Ola Östman & Jan Blommaert (eds.), *Handbook of pragmatics: Manual*, 577–581. Amsterdam: John Benjamins.

Senkbeil, Karsten. 2017. Figurative language in intercultural communication – a case study of German-Southern African international academic discourse. *Intercultural Pragmatics* 14 (4). 465–491.

Sharifian, Farzad. 2011. *Cultural conceptualisations and language: Theoretical framework and applications*. Amsterdam: John Benjamins.

Sharifian, Farzad. 2015. Cultural linguistics. In Farzad Sharifian (ed.), *The Routledge handbook of language and culture*, 473–492. London & New York: Routledge.

Silva, Diogo H. A. 2015. *A construção do conceito de 'Heimat' (Alemanha) / 'Pátria' (Brasil) em âmbito intercultural* [The construction of the concept of 'Heimat' (Germany / 'Pátria' (Brazil) in the intercultural domain]. Belo Horizonte: Federal University of Minas Gerais MA thesis.

Stivers, Tanya. 2008. When nodding is a token of affiliation. *Research on Language & Social Interaction* 41 (1). 31–57.

Stivers, Tanya. 2013. Sequence organization. In Jack Sidnell & Tanya Stivers (eds.), *The handbook of conversation analysis*, 191–209. Malden, Oxford, Chichester: Wiley-Blackwell.

Streeck, Jürgen. 2008a. Metaphor and gesture: A view from the microanalysis of interaction. In Alan Cienki & Cornelia Müller (eds.), *Metaphor and gesture*, 259–264. Amsterdam, Philadelphia: John Benjamins.

Streeck, Jürgen. 2008b. *Gesturecraft. The manu-facture of meaning*. Amsterdam, Philadelphia: John Benjamins.

Streeck, Jürgen. 2014. Mutual gaze and recognition. Revisiting Kendon's "Gaze direction in two-person conversation". In Mandana Seyfeddinipur & Marianne Gullberg (eds.), *From gesture in conversation to visible action as utterance*, 35–55. Amsterdam & Philadelphia: John Benjamins.

Thije, Jan D. ten. 2006. Notions of perspective and perspectivising in intercultural communication research. In Kristin Bührig & Jan D. ten Thije (eds.), Beyond misunderstanding. Linguistic analyses of intercultural communication, 97–151. Amsterdam & Philadelphia: John Benjamins.

Ungeheuer, Gerold. [1983] 2010. *Einführung in die Kommunikationstheorie*. Edited by Karin Kolb, Jens Loenhoff und H. Walter Schmitz. Münster: Nodus Publikationen.

Ungeheuer, Gerold. 1987a. Vor-Urteile über Sprechen, Mitteilen, Verstehen. In: Gerold Ungeheuer. *Kommunikationstheoretische Schriften I: Sprechen, Mitteilen, Verstehen*, Edited by Johann G. Juchem, 290–338. Aachen: Rader Publikationen, 1987a.

Ungeheuer, Gerold. 1987b. Was heißt ‚Verständigung durch Sprechen'?. In: Ungeheuer, Gerold. *Kommunikationstheoretische Schriften I: Sprechen, Mitteilen, Verstehen*. Edited by Johann G. Juchem, 34–69. Aachen: Rader Publikationen.

Wegener, Philipp. [1885] 1991. *Untersuchungen über die Grundfragen des Sprachlebens.* Re-edited by Konrad Koerner. Amsterdam: John Benjamins.
Weinrich, Harald. 1976. *Sprache in Texten.* Stuttgart: Ernst Klett.
Xudong, Deng. 2009. Listener response. In Sigurd D'hondt, Jan-Ola Östman & Jef Verschueren (eds.). *The pragmatics of interaction*, 104–124. Amsterdam, Philadelhpa: John Benjamins.
Zima Elisabeth & Geert Brône. 2015. Cognitive linguistics and interactional discourse: time to enter into dialogue. *Language and Cognition* 7. 485–498.

Index

https://doi.org/10.1515/9783110688306-013

www.ingramcontent.com/pod-product-compliance
Lightning Source LLC
LaVergne TN
LVHW010852110826
845149LV00005B/1390

* 9 7 8 3 1 1 1 3 5 3 4 7 0 *